THE HARD OF HEARING CHILD

THE HARD OF HEARING CHILD

Clinical and Educational Management

Edited by
FREDERICK S. BERG

Specialist in Educational Audiology
Utah State University

SAMUEL G. FLETCHER

Director
Laboratory for Biocommunication Studies
University of New Mexico

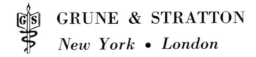 **GRUNE & STRATTON**
New York • London

Grune & Stratton, Inc.
757 Third Avenue
New York, New York 10017

Library of Congress Catalog Card Number: 70-110449
International Standard Book Number: 0-8089-0642-9

Printed in the United States of America (PC-B)

Contents

Preface

In 1967 the United States Office of Education sponsored an institute entitled "Characteristics and Needs of the Hard of Hearing Child." This institute revealed a critical need for the availability of materials which would organize current information on the hard of hearing child as well as provide guidelines for future programming. The present volume is a response to the urgent need for a pooling of data from knowledgeable specialists faced with the dilemma of helping hard of hearing children to adjust optimally to their environment and to learn at their potential despite their hearing deficiency.

This volume is for the many persons interested in the welfare and education of the hard of hearing child. It is designed particularly for those who will provide leadership in initiating, implementing, and evaluating clinical and educational programs which seek to alleviate disability arising from auditory disorders. Designed as a tool for action, the book also has important reference value for clinical centers, school systems, and specialists and parents faced with the challenge of such programs. The many references cited in the book will also enable the serious student in speech pathology, audiology, language pathology, psychology, and deaf education to pursue areas of individual interest in his own major field.

The book is organized into three major sections. Following Chapter 1, which presents an introduction to and overview of the work to follow, Chapters 2 and 3 define the hard of hearing child, describe his prevalence in our population, and trace the locus of his past and current educational programs. Eight chapters make up the second section. Three of these deal with information emerging from five major disciplines: speech and hearing science, psychology, sociology, linguistics, and professional education. The information is fundamental to an understanding of the hard of hearing child himself and of the evolving technology being placed at the fingertips of the specialists who have responsibility for his care. The final eight chapters deal with specific planning and programming for the hard of hearing child. While the material is presented in a practical vein, the points of view and suggestions are supported throughout by explicit theory and research. In fact, the contributors have specifically sought to summarize and crystallize the current status of knowledge in the topics considered and identify and isolate trends which should be fostered in future programming for the hard of hearing child from infancy to adulthood.

The following publishers and copyright holders have kindly given permission to use quoted materials: Acta Oto-Laryngologia, Alexander Graham Bell

vii

Association for the Deaf, American Annals of the Deaf, Cleft Palate Journal, the Institute of Electrical and Electronics Engineers, Inc., Journal of Acoustical Society of America, Journal of Experimental Psychology, Journal of Speech and Hearing Disorders, Stanwix House, Inc., University of Minnesota Press, and W. B. Saunders Co.

Finally, we wish to recognize the support and sacrifices of the wives, the families, and the secretaries of the authors.

F.S.B.

S.G.F.

Contributing Authors

Frederick S. Berg, Ph.D. *Specialist in Educational Audiology, Utah State University, Logan*

Thomas C. Clark, M.A. *Assistant Professor, Audiology-Speech Pathology, Utah State University, Logan*

Marvin F. Daley, Ph.D. *Deputy Director of Research and Development, Upper Midwest Regional Educational Laboratories, Minneapolis*

David M. Feldman, Ph.D. *Chairman, Department of Linguistics, California State College, Fullerton*

Samuel G. Fletcher, Ph.D. *Director, Laboratory for Biocommunication Studies, University of New Mexico, Albuquerque*

Carl W. Fuller, Ph.D. *Professor of Audiology, University of Indiana Medical School, Indianapolis*

Barry Griffing, M.A. *Consultant in Education for the Deaf and Hard of Hearing, California State Department of Education, Los Angeles*

Miriam B. Kapfer, Ph.D. *Research Consultant, Clark County School District, Las Vegas*

Clifford J. Lawrence, Ed.D. *Associate Superintendent—Instruction, Clark County School District, Las Vegas*

Robert E. Stepp, Ph.D. *Director, Midwest Regional Media Center for the Deaf, The University of Nebraska, Lincoln*

McCay Vernon, Ph.D. *Editor, American Annals of the Deaf, Gallaudet College, Washington, D.C. and Professor of Psychology, Western Maryland College, Westminster*

Erik Wedenberg, D.D.S., M.D. *Karolinska Sjukhuset, Stockholm, Sweden*

Marta Wedenberg, D.D.S. *Stockholm, Sweden*

Peter C. Wolff, Ph.D. *Professor of Psychology, State University College at Potsdam, New York*

Wayne E. Wright, Ed.D. *American Institutes for Research, Pittsburgh and Professor of Psychology, Head of Counseling and Guidance, Utah State University, Logan*

ix

PART I

BACKGROUND

Chapter 1

Introduction

SAMUEL G. FLETCHER, Ph.D.

Alice in Wonderland was wandering through the forest when she was startled by the sudden appearance of the Cheshire Cat sitting on the bough of a tree. She was concerned about being lost so she said, "Would you tell me, please, which way I ought to go from here?"

"That depends a good deal on where you want to get to," said the Cat.

"I don't much care where _____," said Alice.

"Then it doesn't matter which way you go," said the Cat.

"_____ so long as I get somewhere," Alice added as an explanation.

"Oh, you're sure to do that," said the Cat, "if you only walk long enough."

In a similar vein it was observed that Milo in *The Phantom Tollbooth* always hurried along for "while he was never anxious to be where he was going, he liked to get there as quickly as possible."

In some ways the present plight of the hard of hearing child seems to reflect a joining of forces between the Alices and the Milos. It really hasn't mattered much which way educators and others who have hard of hearing children in their groups have travelled—or where they started from—since the destination was not known. Certain urgency has been evident to get them somewhere but just where that somewhere is has been uncertain.

For true progress, it makes a great deal of difference, however, to have both a destination and a place to start. These vantage points allow a continual view and review of the results.

As we view the starting place for work with the hard of hearing child, an initial question comes to mind: Why at this time are the educational problems of the hearing impaired child seeming to come into focus? Perhaps it is because of increased recognition of the relationship between socioeconomic level and intellectual development; perhaps it stems from awareness of the rights of minorities; perhaps it arises from increased efficiency in use of the educational processes which now makes the hard of hearing child stand out as different.

By definition, a child is handicapped only so far as he differs from a comparison group; therefore, the concept of working with a handicapped child must consider the relative efficiency of the nonhandicapped child. The typical person seems to acquire information at 50 percent to 60 percent of his potential rate of learning. This leaves 40 percent to 50 percent of his potential un-

3

tapped. To compete favorably with his more richly endowed associates the child with a disability must excel in his rate of learning. In other words, if the child with an impairment achieves closer to his efficiency potential he may close the educational gap between him and his more favorably endowed peers.

During the past few decades an increasing focus of national concern and money has been given to education. This attention is reaping success; the educational performance of the normal child has improved. This very improvement, however, has had a backwash of problems for children with imbalances in their learning capabilities. Certain individuals who have heretofore competed favorably are finding more and more difficulty in maintaining the pace without special programs and assistance.

Historically, special educational programs have been available only to children who were dramatically different from other school age children and were so handicapped that they have been unable to function in their home communities. These groups include the deaf, the blind, the severely emotionally disturbed, and the severely mentally retarded. Efforts to serve these groups have been admittedly uneven in quality, still the basic recognition of unique problems has existed. School programs for less dramatically impaired students have developed only during the last few decades.

The particular concern of this book is the hearing impaired child who has sufficient hearing to use the auditory system as the primary avenue for learning but whose efficiency in using this system reduces his effectiveness in a regular school environment.

Special programs for the hard of hearing child who is similar to his peers in a great many ways have been especially slow to develop. The hearing impaired child has the same physical appearance as his friends who have normal hearing; he also behaves essentially as they do. Even his disabilities may be easily misunderstood as merely negative variations of normal behavior. For example, when the teacher of a child with a hearing defect speaks to him one time, he may be watching her and—with what he receives from hearing reinforced by what he receives from sight—responds correctly. Another time when she speaks, the background noise may cover too much of what she says for him to decode the message correctly, or he may miss some of the essential cues from her face if it is turned away from him. This time he misunderstands and responds erroneously. His behavior is thus erratic depending upon such factors as the auditory characteristics of his hearing and of the background noises, manner with which the teacher speaks, and her position relative to his view, in addition to the random variations found in any child. But then, the child with normal hearing is often inattentive or distracted by other events and, therefore, is erratic in his responses to spoken language. For this reason the teacher is likely to interpret the intermittency in performance of the hard of hearing child to lack of self-discipline. When he does "pay attention" he seems to "get along fine."

The hard of hearing child is difficult to isolate from other children by his behavior, and he is also difficult to identify by his scholastic performance. By the time he arrives at the seventh to ninth grade, the typical hard of hearing child has a one- to two-year deficit in educational achievement. Other than the fact that this deficit centers around language, the achievement pattern is again highly erratic. It depends upon such variables as the types of teachers he has had, how much help he has received at home, where he happens to have been seated in his classrooms, the type and severity of his hearing loss, how well he has learned to use his residual hearing, what type of amplification he has, how much confidence he has in his scholastic ability, and many others. Adequate programming is highly important.

The goal in educational and clinical programming for the hearing impaired child is to close the efficiency gap between him and his peers with normal hearing. This means (1) detailed knowledge of his current and potential abilities to receive and use a linguistic code; (2) removal of all possible impairments to the organs used for speaking and hearing and assistance to achieve the highest possible efficiency in use of the sensory system he has; and (3) an environment which, as far as possible, maximizes his potential for achievement and satisfaction in his social and educational experiences. These goals encompass a starting point and a destination and suggest a route to follow to close the gap.

The current century has seen a gradual accumulation of knowledge concerning the structures, processes, and behavior underlying communication. This has come from such diverse sources as engineers concerned with the technical aspects of acoustic transmission and reception of speech and other coded material; physiologists, physicians, and others concerned with the biological functions and integrity of structures used to generate and receive messages; speech and hearing scientists seeking to determine the physiologic and acoustical characteristics of the basic building blocks of spoken language as it emerges from seemingly random vocal behavior; linguists attempting to describe and predict patterns of communication used by particular groups of individuals and societies; and speech pathologists and audiologists seeking principles and procedures by which to identify and alter communicative behavior which is found to be inefficient and ineffective.

The convergence of interest in communication from a variety of specialties has resulted in an impressive body of knowledge which is potentially beneficial to the hearing impaired child. The very diversity of this interest has been a major hurdle to use of the information. Each specialization has described communication with a different set of words and interpreted their findings from highly divergent viewpoints. The ultimate result is that use of this information is fraught with difficulty, and errors of interpretation are common. Consequently, the educator or clinician whose primary responsibility has been to serve the handicapped child has built a patchwork quilt from bits of information he could accumulate and then by trial and error arrived at a system which seems to work. With the rapid evolution of general education this inefficient approach was, and is, doomed to failure.

The goals of this book are to pull together information from the many disciplines concerned with communication, education, and hearing impairment and to present a rather concise summary of the present technology available to assist in education and management of the hard of hearing child. An attempt has been made to display these materials in a meaningful way, to highlight the basic principles that govern the processes of communication, and to point out to the reader ways in which these principles can be meaningfully used to assist the hearing impaired child.

The first major section of the book is devoted to the basic sciences whereby the communication process itself may be understood and manipulated. The principal function of this section is to provide a pool of basic principles upon which the later chapters can draw. Throughout the book an attempt has been made to emphasize those principles which have universal application and to describe those parts of the technology which seem to be evolving and are likely to be of particular importance in the future. Practices that are of historical interest only or that are inconsistent with known principles governing the communication process are referred to only incidentally. As noted, the primary focus of the book is to provide a basis for future action.

The absence of a large body of past tradition in working with the hard of hearing child has certain advantages. This allows us to readily apply the scientific principle of "parsimony," i.e., to recognize the simplest explanation which is most likely to be correct. Complex "traditional" approaches barring the way to innovation and to application of evolving technology are essentially non-existent. The creation of programs to meet the explicit needs of hearing handicapped children thus poses a unique challenge.

In this volume many principles which are known to govern communication behavior are presented in such a way as to make them available for use by any profession which needs them. We are a long way from reducing all of the differences of the hard of hearing child to their simplest form, because many different facets of the basic and clinical sciences must still be uncovered and clarified. We urge the reader to examine the various materials carefully, both from a theoretic and practical standpoint, to test it in his own situation, and to share observations and experiences which seem to be particularly significant. Recognition, mastery, and application of the principles from the firm foundation of acoustical, physiological, and behavioral science now at our fingertips to the special communication needs of the hearing impaired child, represents both a challenge and an obligation to enable this child to reach a rewarding, meaningful destination of living successfully in the modern world.

Chapter 2

Definition and Incidence

FREDERICK S. BERG, Ph.D.

Considerable confusion justifiably exists among both specialists and laymen concerning the definition and prevalence of hard of hearing children. The many parameters of hearing impairment including degree, type, age of onset, and auditory experience complicate the determination of definition and incidence. In the context of this book, the hard of hearing child may be best identified by comparison with the deaf child and the normal hearing child.

The *hard of hearing* child is a hearing impaired individual who can identify through hearing and without visual receptive communication enough of the distinguishing features of speech to permit at least partial recognition of the spoken language. With the addition of visual receptive communication such as speech reading, he may understand even more language provided the vocabulary and syntax are a part of his linguistic code.

The *deaf* child is a hearing impaired person who can identify through hearing at best only a few of the prosodic and phonetic features of speech and then not enough to permit auditory recognition of sound or word combinations. He relies mainly or entirely upon speechreading or some other form of visual receptive communication for the perception of the spoken or manual form of language. Provided the communicative content is within his linguistic code, he understands language in many instances. His linguistic code typically is less developed than that of a hard of hearing child.

The *normal hearing* child, in contrast to either a hard of hearing or deaf child, can recognize all the distinguishing features of speech under good listening conditions and without the aid of speechreading or some other visual form of receptive communication. His linguistic code characteristically is more developed than that of the hard of hearing child and especially of that of the deaf child.

The hearing impaired child referred to as hard of hearing above is the individual who has been labeled as hard of hearing by the Committee on Nomenclature of the Conference of Executives of American Schools for the Deaf (1938), partially hearing by the Amended School Health Service and Handicapped Pupils Regulations of 1962 (Watson, 1967), and hard of hearing and partially hearing as suggested by the Secretary of Health, Education, and Welfare's Advisory Committee on the Education of the Deaf (1965).

7

Conference of Executives

The hard of hearing—"those in whom the sense of hearing, although defective, is functional with or without a hearing aid."

The deaf—"those in whom the sense of hearing is nonfunctional for the ordinary purposes of life."

English Regulations of 1962

The partially hearing—"pupils with impaired hearing whose development of speech and language, even if retarded, is following a normal pattern, who require for their education special arrangements or facilities though not necessarily all the educational methods used for deaf pupils."

The deaf—"those with impaired hearing who require education by methods suitable for pupils with little or no naturally acquired speech or language" (Watson, 1967).

HEW Advisory Committee

The hard of hearing—"those children with moderate hearing losses, who are still able to understand readily fluent speech through hearing whether or not amplification is used. Educationally speaking, these are the children who, with some assistance, are able to attend classes with normally hearing children."

The partially hearing—"those children whose loss of hearing is so severe as to require a special educational curriculum and program of training that involves full-time auditory training along with vision for developing language and communication skills; children, who because of the severity of their loss of hearing, need the full-time services of a special teacher for their education. These are children, who, as a result of early identification of hearing loss and early auditory training, are able to progress academically at a somewhat more rapid rate than those classified as deaf by virtue of more efficient use of their residual hearing."

The deaf—"those children whose principal source for learning language and communication skills is mainly visual and whose loss of hearing, with or without amplification, is so great that it is of little or no practical value in learning to understand verbal communication auditorially, and whose loss of hearing was acquired prelingually."

In the United States and elsewhere, considerable numbers of hard of hearing children exist. Table 1 provides a preliminary estimate of the number of hard of hearing children with potentially educationally significant acoustic impairment.

The data appearing in Table 1 is based upon the Pittsburgh study of incidence of hearing impairment among public school children (Eagles et al., 1963) and upon our estimates of the number of hard of hearing children in schools and classes for the deaf. It can serve as a starting point for further study into the prevalence of hard of hearing children within each state. Ten guidelines

Table 1. Estimated Number of Hard of Hearing Individuals Less than 18 Years of Age in Each of the 50 States of the United States Based on the 1967 Preliminary Census Figures

State	Faint Speech 26–40 db	Difficulty with Normal Speech 41–55 db	Loud Speech 56–70 db	Severely Hard of Hearing 71–90 db	Total
Alabama	11,907	6,615	2,646	265	21,433
Alaska	1,062	590	236	24	1,912
Arizona	5,814	3,230	1,292	129	10,465
Arkansas	6,390	3,550	1,420	142	11,502
California	60,921	33,845	13,538	1,354	109,658
Colorado	6,543	3,635	1,454	145	11,777
Connecticut	9,081	5,045	2,018	202	16,346
Delaware	1,782	990	396	40	3,208
Florida	18,459	10,255	4,102	410	33,226
Georgia	15,318	8,510	3,404	340	27,572
Hawaii	2,592	1,440	576	58	4,666
Idaho	2,394	1,330	532	53	4,309
Illinois	34,524	19,180	7,672	767	62,143
Indiana	16,497	9,165	3,666	367	29,695
Iowa	8,802	4,890	1,956	196	15,844
Kansas	7,227	4,015	1,606	161	13,009
Kentucky	10,368	5,760	2,304	230	18,662
Louisiana	13,140	7,300	2,920	292	23,652
Maine	3,150	1,750	700	70	5,670
Maryland	12,204	6,780	2,712	271	21,967
Massachusetts	16,677	9,265	3,706	371	30,019
Michigan	29,070	16,150	6,460	646	52,326
Minnesota	12,141	6,745	2,698	270	21,854
Mississippi	8,406	4,670	1,868	187	15,131
Missouri	14,166	7,870	3,148	315	25,499
Montana	2,394	1,330	532	53	4,309
Nebraska	4,653	2,585	1,034	103	8,375
Nevada	1,521	845	338	34	2,738
New Hampshire	2,169	1,205	482	48	3,904
New Jersey	21,321	11,845	4,738	473	37,951
New Mexico	3,915	2,175	870	87	7,047
New York	54,333	30,185	12,074	1,207	97,799
North Caolina	16,578	9,210	3,684	368	29,840
North Dakota	2,205	1,225	490	49	3,969
Ohio	34,182	18,990	7,596	760	61,528
Oklahoma	7,578	4,210	1,684	168	13,640
Oregon	6,156	3,420	1,368	137	11,081
Pennsylvania	35,037	19,465	7,786	779	63,067
Rhode Island	2,700	1,500	600	60	4,860
South Carolina	9,108	5,060	2,024	202	16,394

Table 1—Continued

State	Faint Speech 26–40 db	Difficulty with Normal Speech 41–55 db	Loud Speech 56–70 db	Severely Hard of Hearing 71–90 db	Total
South Dakota	2,313	1,285	514	51	4,163
Tennessee	12,366	6,870	2,748	275	22,259
Texas	36,909	20,505	8,202	820	66,436
Utah	3,879	2,155	862	86	6,982
Vermont	1,359	755	302	30	2,446
Virginia	14,715	8,175	3,270	327	26,487
Washington	9,774	5,430	2,172	217	17,593
West Virginia	5,589	3,105	1,242	124	10,060
Wisconsin	13,977	7,765	3,106	311	25,159
Wyoming	1,071	595	238	24	1,928
Washington, D.C.	2,529	1,405	562	56	4,552
United States	636,975	353,875	141,550	14,155	1,146,555

SOURCE: Dept. of Commerce, Bureau of the Census; *Current Population Reports,* Series P-25, No. 384.

for more detailed investigation are advanced on the basis of this data and additional information.

1. The db values given in this chapter and elsewhere in the book relate to the 1964 ISO standard. In many instances, db notations have been converted from the 1951 ASA standard to the ISO reference.

2. The educational and psychological impact of the hearing impairment upon the child will depend upon educational parameters as well as upon audiological parameters. Whereas Goetzinger (1962) suggested that small perceptive hearing losses of 40 to 45 db in the speech frequencies induce a speech and language retardation of about one year, a great many hard of hearing children having an even greater impairment may not be educationally retarded provided they have strong educational and audiological support.

3. The incidence of hard of hearing children decreases as severity of auditory impairment increases. According to Eagles et al., it is 0.9 percent for children with 26 to 40 db losses, 0.5 percent for those with 41 to 55 db impairments, 0.2 percent for those with 56 to 70 db losses, and 0.05 percent for hearing impaired children with losses 71 db and greater. We have used a figure of 0.02 percent for the 71 to 91 db category; the other 0.03 percent would apply to deaf children in the public schools.

4. Some 15,000 hard of hearing children are enrolled in schools and classes where they are educated alongside of deaf children. Most of these hard of hearing children have severe losses, many moderate, and some marginal; corresponding to 71 to 91 db, 56 to 70 db, and 41 to 55 db, respectively.

5. The other 1 million plus hard of hearing children, particularly those with less severe hearing impairment, are mingled among hearing children.

6. As many as 150,000 hard of hearing children are potentially in need of considerable language, communication, academic, and counseling assistance. These are the individuals with moderate to severe hearing impairment of a bilateral nature.

7. Another 950,000 hard of hearing children, having mild and marginal hearing impairment corresponding to 26 to 55 db losses, typically require assistance of a less extensive nature. This help includes one or more of speechreading training, preferential seating, hearing aid fitting and counseling, speech and auditory training, vocabulary enrichment, general counseling, and study support.

8. As many as 500,000 hard of hearing children, particularly those with greater hearing impairment of a perceptive type, will exhibit defective speech.

9. Various investigations reveal that improved prenatal and postnatal medical care is indirectly resulting in a higher percentage of hearing impaired children (Frisina, 1959). The lives of children may be saved while hearing impairments remain.

10. Occasionally epidemics cause temporary surges in prevalence of hearing impairment. For example, 10,000 American children approaching school age may be hearing impaired because of the recent rubella outbreak. Many of these children also are multiply handicapped (Hardy, 1968). This population is not included in Table 1.

Often officials of local school districts are unaware that considerable numbers of troubled hard of hearing children are located in their localities. One director of special education in Illinois, for example, searched the school files and located 121 children with hearing impairments in excess of 40 db. He had their teachers rate their performance on a questionnaire. The results should shake what Kodman (1963) refers to as "a general apathy on the part of the public schools and a failure to grapple realistically with the special educational needs of the hard of hearing school-age child." Only 11 of the 121 children were rated as normally participating class members. Of the other 110, 28 had failed one or more grades, 43 were underachievers, 28 were socially introverted, and 17 were considered social problems (Bothwell, 1968).

References

Bothwell, H. 1968. Supervision of programs at state and local levels. Final Report of the National Research Conference on Day Programs for Hearing Impaired Children. Washington, D.C.: The Volta Bureau. Pp. 77–89.

Committee on Nomenclature, Conference of Executives, American Schools for the Deaf. 1938. American Annals of the Deaf 83:1–3.

Dept. of Commerce, Bureau of the Census. Current Population Reports. Series P-25, No. 384.

Eagles, E. L., S. M. Wishik, and L. G. Doerfler. 1963. Hearing sensitivity and related factors in children. Monograph. St. Louis: The Laryngoscope.

Education of the Deaf: A Report to the Secretary of Health, Education, and Welfare. 1965. Washington, D.C.: U.S. Department of Health, Education, and Welfare.

Frisina, D. R. 1959. Statistical information concerning the deaf and the hard of hearing in the United States. American Annals of the Deaf 104:265–270.

Goetzinger, C. P. 1962. Effects of small perceptive losses on language and on speech discrimination. Volta Review 64:408–414.

Hardy, J. B. 1968. Early identification of hearing impaired children. Final Report of the National Research Conference on Day Programs for Hearing Impaired Children. Washington, D.C.: The Volta Bureau. Pp. 101–111.

Kodman, F. 1963. Educational status of hard-of-hearing children in the classroom. Journal of Speech and Hearing Disorders 28:297–299.

Watson, T. J. 1962. The Education of Hearing-Handicapped Children. Springfield, Ill.: Charles C Thomas.

Chapter 3

The Locus of the Education of the Hard of Hearing Child

FREDERICK S. BERG, Ph.D.

The Misplaced Child

In the United States, the hard of hearing child typically is not obtaining an adequate education to compete in society. Whether in a regular school or in a school for the deaf, he seldom has the advantage of an educational program designed to meet his unique needs (Berg and Fletcher, 1967). Instead, he is treated as a hearing person or as a deaf individual (Ross and Calvert, 1967).

In the regular school, the hard of hearing child tends to be a maladjusted individual. As compared to his normal hearing peers, he more frequently misunderstands the teacher, demonstrates poorer study habits, exhibits less desirable attitudes toward school, and reveals greater emotional variability (O'Neill, 1964; Goetzinger, Harrison, and Baer, 1964).

The combination of communication deficiency and psychological maladjustment is devastating to the educational achievement of the hard of hearing child. This may be exemplified in the instance of one 18-year-old hard of hearing girl who would neither wear a hearing aid she could benefit from nor be singled out for special assistance. Her word could not be trusted whenever she felt that her hearing loss might be exposed. This young lady graduated from high school but was unusually academically retarded. Toward the end of her high school career she scored 123 on the performance battery of the Weschler Adult Intelligence Scale but only 77 on the verbal battery.

Referred to a school for the deaf, the hard of hearing child is inappropriately educated alongside of children who misunderstand oral communication more often than he does. Necessarily, the pace of instruction is slowed down (Brill, 1956) or reliance is placed on the use of the sign language and fingerspelling. Understandably, the hard of hearing child in this environment often performs at a relatively low educational level. Miller (1958) noted a tendency for the hard of hearing child in a school for the deaf to achieve academically as if he were deaf. If this is so, and evidence seems to substantiate it, an unusually high percentage of older hard of hearing youngsters are

13

functionally illiterate (Boatner, 1965; Furth, 1966; McClure, 1966; Moores, 1967). Also, upon social promotion from high school, the hard of hearing youngster is not ready for post-secondary study.

The Past 150 Years

Most historical information on the education of the hard of hearing child must be gleaned from narratives on the schooling of the deaf. In 1817, the first American school for the deaf was established (Myklebust, 1964). During the next 50 years as additional schools for the deaf were opened in this country, the language of signs and fingerspelling prevailed in preference to the use of oral communication (Quigley, 1969).

The hard of hearing child, like the deaf child, found in this manual method of communication a facile media for conversation if not for instruction. However, the manual language had its disadvantages. It was a language limited in vocabulary, syntax, and morphology. But even more so, it was only learned through extensive practice and, therefore, not applicable with people outside the school environment. In addition, utilization of this manual language system was not accompanied by training in oral communication. Thus, the hard of hearing child tended to find his social life restricted to the deaf society.

By 1867, oral schools and classes for deaf and hard of hearing children began to be established (O'Connor, 1967; Waite, 1967). These special educational institutions were committed to the oral philosophy introduced from Germany. This philosophy was that speech should be taught and an environment should be set up within which oral communication could be fostered (Silverman, 1957). Oralism thrived in the few schools for the deaf where class size was small, teachers were orally trained and experienced, administrative commitment existed, and children had oral aptitude. The success of oralism led administrators of most other schools for the deaf to provide speech training to all young deaf and hard of hearing children. However, an oral atmosphere was seldom provided in these other schools, particularly for the benefit of the older students, so that speech could be utilized extensively.

Where the oral star rose in the United States, the hard of hearing child tended to benefit more so than did the deaf. He was well represented among the hearing impaired children referred to as "oral successes." Particularly in an oral environment, he developed intelligible speech as well as skill in understanding the speech of others. Obviously, his chances of acquiring oral facility were greater than those of the deaf child because of the contribution of his residual hearing to speech comprehension.

In 1878, the simultaneous use of speech and fingerspelling was originated by Westervelt at the newly established Rochester School for the Deaf (1963). This method displaced the use of signs both in and out of the classrooms at all age levels. As a system for facilitating verbal and academic growth, it was particularly effective with the hard of hearing child because he could perceive varying amounts of the prosodic features of speech not identifiable from the lips or the fingers of the speaker. Scouten (1957) stated that its application at the Rochester School resulted in a general upward shift in verbal and academic competencies among hearing impaired children. Currently, however, few schools for the deaf are utilizing the speech-fingerspelling approach at all educational levels. Many more schools for the deaf are employing it at the intermediate and the advanced academic levels (Quigley, 1969).

Another communicative system which has made an impact upon the education of the hearing impaired child is that of "Cued Speech." Developed by Cornett (1967) to satisfy both oral and manual philosophical criteria, it is being used experimentally in many educational settings throughout the country. Under this communicative system the deaf child can recognize phonetic or articulatory aspects of speech by noting the visible cues from the lips in combination with 12 hand formation cues. According to design, the deaf child must rely upon lipreading to understand speech; he cannot rely upon the hand formations only. With "Cued Speech" the hard of hearing child fares even better because he can identify additional features of speech through audition, also.

In 1914 Max Goldstein introduced the Acoustic Method at the newly established Central Institute for the Deaf (Goldstein, 1939). Developed by Urbantschitsch of Vienna, this method was most effective with hard of hearing children who were enrolled at CID.

Interest in the utilization of residual hearing among educators of the deaf developed rapidly after the development of electronic amplification systems. By 1950 Hudgins had demonstrated that sound amplification might improve speech perception and speech production of even profoundly hearing impaired children (Hudgins, 1953). In 1951 Erik Wedenberg described a longitudinal experiment in auditory training (Wedenberg, 1954). His own functionally deaf son Staffan became a hard of hearing child after many months of day by day auditory stimulation. Staffan went on to receive his education in the regular schools of Sweden. Further data on the Wedenberg investigation is described in two later chapters.

The success of Staffan Wedenberg was duplicated elsewhere. In every instance hearing loss was identified at an early age, appropriate sound amplification was provided, and intensive assistance from parents was supplied. Children with very severe hearing impairment became hard of hearing individuals whereas they had been deaf before. Erik Wedenberg (1967b) estimated that 80 percent of children currently enrolled in schools for the deaf were at least potentially hard of hearing.

The Infant Years

During the past 25 years, the home has become the ideal site for the beginning education of the hard of hearing child. It is during the first two years of life that a "listening attitude" can often be developed in a severely hearing impaired child (Wedenberg, 1967a). Unfortunately, appropriate materials and instructions have not been made generally available to parents of young hard of hearing children. Information that has been distributed, such as the John Tracy Correspondence materials (1961), have presented guidelines for the early education of the deaf child rather than the hard of hearing child. It should be emphasized that the procedures for the special teaching of these two types of hearing impaired children are only similar in some respects. A waste of human potential may result from indiscriminately using a guide for the deaf in the education of the hard of hearing child.

A successful home program for a hard of hearing child depends in large part upon the counsel and guidance given to the parents (Downs, 1967). At present such parental support is provided through the speech and hearing centers of universities, hospitals, clinics, and special schools. Appropriate explanation and demonstration ideally can be provided parents at or from these centers. Again, separate training programs must be established to meet both the needs of the hard of hearing child and of the deaf child.

The kitchen seems to be the best location in the house for the education of the young hearing impaired child (Simmons, 1967). The many activities associated with meals and snacks provide numerous opportunities for parent-child communication. By contrast, one of the worst sites in the house might be the TV room where action and conversation are limited to the picture tube. Currently, many speech and hearing centers as well as special schools are developing laboratory house programs for the hearing impaired (McConnell, 1968).

The key to the early language development of the hard of hearing child is frequently repeated association of experience and speech stimulation. The parent is close to the child and describes the action. Staffan Wedenberg's mother, for example, spent hour after hour in work and play with him. As the events of Staffan's day occurred, his mother continually commented on them. Staffan heard her because she was right next to him. His father played the same role as his mother did during evenings and weekends.

The home will become an even more effective language learning laboratory for the hard of hearing child as electronic amplification systems are perfected. Even now it is electronically feasible to produce a miniaturized but high quality "walkie-talkie" system which enables the parent to stimulate the child with speech from a distance. For example, the hard of hearing toddler who falls down would be able to hear his mother across the room say, "Oh, you fell *down!* But now you are getting *up.*" Many other instances of *down* and *up* could be coupled with language, also. On the other hand, the hard of hearing child using the typical hearing aid of today would not hear his mother's voice from a distance in many instances. Normally hearing children in the house could also be equipped with miniaturized microphone-transmitter units so that they could also serve as language stimulation agents.

Preschool Program

In the United States, nearly half of all 3–5 year old hearing impaired children are enrolled in preschool nursery programs for the deaf. A study by

Craig (1964) raised real questions about the efficacy of such programs. He found that a group of hearing impaired children who had not received preschool training performed as well academically and verbally as those who had been enrolled in special nursery training. Interestingly enough, Lane (1942) had made a similar comparison at Central Institute for the Deaf many years before. She noted that children who had attended nursery school at CID completed the eighth grade earlier and attended high school much more often than those who had not begun school until after 5 years of age.

The difference in the findings of these two studies may be attributed primarily to the higher level of education received by hearing impaired children attending CID as opposed to the public residential schools for the deaf where Craig's subjects were selected. The intelligence-achievement gap of children graduating from CID is much less than it is at the typical school for the deaf. The additional time that a hearing impaired child spends at CID in the preschool program often enables him to attain functional literacy!

The hard of hearing child also usually benefits from nursery school training. Like other children he typically grows and adjusts socially through such activities as directed play, sharing, and following routine. Also, he has unique language and communication needs which can be alleviated further during the nursery-age years. However, his particular needs again are best met in an educational setting where the laborious task of educating deaf children does not exist. He might learn best in a nursery class managed by a combination of a child specialist and a teacher of the hearing impaired. Such units are established in the state of Illinois (Bothwell, 1967).

Elementary and Secondary Education

Relatively few educational programs exclusively for hard of hearing children are currently established in the schools for the deaf of the United States. At one time the Illinois School for the Deaf included a special department for hard of hearing children (Johnson, 1948). Unfortunately, this unit called the Acoustic Department, no longer exists at the Illinois School in deference to grouping children on the basis of academic achievement rather than oral communication competence (Scott, 1968). The other residential schools for the deaf throughout the United States, enrolling about 50 percent of all severely hearing impaired children and youth, typically also group children for instruction on an academic achievement basis only.

Recognizing the benefit of separate grouping, Kopp reorganized the Detroit Day School for the Deaf to include separate classes for the hard of hearing. As a result, many hard of hearing children have been able to be integrated with hearing children at an earlier age than would have occurred otherwise. Similar programs exist in some other cities of the United States. For example, the Seattle school district of Washington features an exclusively hard of hearing classroom program (Thomas, 1964).

In contrast, separate educational programs for hard of hearing children are commonplace in Europe and in the Soviet Union (Hoag, 1965; Johnson,

1967; Mikaelyan, 1968). In such educational settings oral communication is emphasized, and the pace of instruction is faster than would be typical of a class enrolling deaf children. Pratt (1965) noted that children in such schools were taught more like hearing children than like deaf children. He recognized, however, that the hard of hearing also had special communication and language training needs.

Four unique educational models for deaf children also offer particular promise for hard of hearing children. One is established in Wyoming and, therefore, has particular relevance for rural areas (Anderson, 1964). According to the Wyoming plan, all young hearing impaired children of the state are educated orally in an elementary school at Casper. The children whose parents do not live in the Casper area are housed in foster homes. Educational costs are relatively low as compared to those in a residential school, even though class size is kept to as few as 4 to 6 children in many instances. The classrooms are acoustically treated, including use of nonparallel walls. Graduates of the school enroll in regular junior high schools of their home localities. A continuing contact is made with them by the director of the Wyoming school.

A second relevant educational model has been established in New Zealand (Dale, 1967). This model consists of a specially designed classroom in an elementary school. A regular teacher and a special teacher are both assigned to this classroom. The hearing impaired children are grouped in a small wing of the room for special instruction during part of the day. During the remainder of school hours, they are taught alongside of normally hearing children. The overall reactions of children, parents, and teachers have been favorable enough to lead to a plan for the organization of similar educational units in New Zealand.

A third unique model is established in Sweden where many hard of hearing children are educated alongside of normally hearing children during the entire school day. The regular teacher can give special assistance to them because each class enrollment is limited to 16 pupils. A team of specialists including an otologist, an audiologist, an electronic specialist, and a teacher of the hearing impaired provide supportive assistance. Such educational units are located throughout Sweden in addition to special preschool units for the hard of hearing. The impetus for this unique country-wide plan has come from Erik Wedenberg (Wedenberg, 1967b).

Another model for the education of hard of hearing children have been developing between two school districts of rural northern Utah since 1963. An educational audiologist provides supportive instruction to approximately eight hard of hearing children of varying age and hearing levels. Only a minimum of grouping in special instruction can be utilized because the children vary considerably in academic achievement. Those children who are 5 years and older also spend part of the day in regular classes.

Streng (1960) and Kopp (1968) have raised opposition against the development of small programs for hearing impaired children. They reason that the teacher of such a unit is seldom well enough trained or supervised to meet the unique problems arising from the representation of several academic and age levels. In short, the small unit tends to be a return to the one-room country schoolhouse concept. Their criticism is not as applicable to hard of hearing children, however, as it is to deaf children.

The success of the Utah model may depend considerably upon such innovations as self-instructional materials, teacher and parent aids, and educational adjustments in the regular classroom. If successful, the model may have widespread educational implications and may decrease the cost of educating hard of hearing children. Currently, the annual cost per pupil is as high as $6000 in a school for the deaf.

Since 1884 an ever-growing trend has existed in the United States to educate hearing impaired children in day rather than residential programs (Mulholland, 1968). By 1967 more than 60 percent of all American children receiving special academic instruction were attending day schools for the deaf, entered as day pupils in residential schools, or attending special classes for the deaf and hard of hearing in regular schools. Mulholland (1968) summarized the educational facilities for hearing impaired children then available in the United States.

Type Facility	Number*
Public residential schools	66
Private residential schools	14
Public day schools	15
Private day schools	11
Public day classes	352
Private day classes	53
Public classes for the multiply handicapped	15
Private classes for the multiply handicapped	2

* Reprinted by permission of the Alexander Graham Bell Association for the Deaf (conference supported by Grant #OEG 1-7-002540-2006) awarded by the U.S. Office of Education.

Notwithstanding the variety of educational plans at the elementary school level, the criterion for effective class placement for the hard of hearing child is a setting where spoken and written language skills can be developed optimally. The language barrier must be broken before the child can become functionally literate. The severely hard of hearing child usually needs a great deal of intensive special instruction over many years. The moderately hard of hearing child typically also needs long-range special assistance but not as much of it. A child with a marginal or even a mild hearing loss should be given special assistance as necessary, also.

Special facilitative programming for the secondary age hard of hearing child is an extension of the services provided at the elementary level. The usual plan is for an itinerant specialist to travel from school to school where hard of hearing children are enrolled for regular classwork. Tutoring, communication training, and consultation with regular school personnel and with parents are optimally provided. Such facilitative programs are established in a number of large school districts such as in Portland, Detroit, and New York City. However, a great many more programs of this type are needed in the United States.

The task of providing special assistance to the hard of hearing teenager is characteristically very difficult. At this age particularly the child does not want to be singled out as being different from anyone else. In the regular school, the hard of hearing teenager tends to discard his hearing aid, sit in the back of the classroom, and miss remedial sessions. In the school for the deaf, he also may discontinue using his hearing aid and may lose motivation to improve speech competence if the language of signs can be relied upon. During the secondary years, he may fall further behind his normal hearing peers in study habits and academic performance.

The College Years

The hard of hearing youngster going on to college presents an unusual problem to an institution of higher learning (Berg, 1969a). He may manage to qualify for college but score low on an entrance examination. Permitted to enroll in post-secondary study programs, he poses communication, language, and academic deficiencies that place him at a severe disadvantage in competing for grades with his normal hearing peers. Because study demands in the university are rigorous, he usually becomes discouraged at this time, loses his motivation to remain in college, and terminates his formal education.

Until recently, the hard of hearing youngster who desired a college education could pursue either of two main routes. The first route led to Gallaudet College, or the like, where classroom instruction was accompanied by use of the language of signs and fingerspelling and where special tutoring services were provided. The second route led to enrollment in the typical university or college where special educational adjustments were either absent or sporadically applied. Only the exceptional person with a severe hearing imparment could succeed by following the latter route, whereas an acoustically handicapped individual with high motivation could complete a college education by attending a special school such as Gallaudet. Typically, however, the hard of hearing person who could complete a post-secondary study program in a regular university, where emphasis was given to oral communication, experienced greater career opportunities and job advancement (Crammate, 1968).

At least eight post-secondary institutions featuring manualism may be attended by a hard of hearing youngster. Gallaudet College, in existence for more than 100 years, is a special institution for the deaf. Classroom instruction is conducted by use of the simultaneous method incorporating the language of signs, fingerspelling, and oral and written means. A current enrollment of 1000 is expected to rise to 1800 by 1975.

The National Technical Institute for the Deaf is developing as a special college of the Rochester Institute of Technology (Frisina, 1968, 1969). It offers wider career potential than that of Gallaudet College. It features regular administrative and faculty support, institute-wide operation, computerized tutoring, notetakers and manual interpreters, and a strong research arm.

A third post-secondary program featuring manualism is that of San Fernando Valley State College (Jones, 1969). Developed as an extension of the Leadership Training Program for the Deaf, San Fernando currently enrolls 20 hearing impaired students alongside of the regular student population there. The facilitative design incorporates supportive services, special orientation and skills classes, block-scheduling of students to make the most efficient use of note takers and interpreters, wide selection of courses, and counseling and placement services.

A fourth program for deaf and hard of hearing students with technical training is that of Northern Illinois University. Alpiner and Walker (1964) and Austin (1969) described the program in 3 phases: a screening evaluation, a 6-week summer diagnostic and evaluative session, and a 9-month training and work program. However, only a small percentage of these students are college material. Many are graduates or dropouts from regular schools. The low academic level of these students is a severe denunciation of the lack of appropriate special programming for the hearing impaired in elementary and secondary schools.

Currently, four similar technical programs are also established at the junior college level. The first of these programs for the hearing impaired is located at Riverside City College in California. Brill (1962) described that deaf students there received academic instruction in a special class or through a special instructor of the deaf going to a regular class to act as an interpreter.

The next three technical programs have been developed in community colleges of Seattle, St. Paul, and New Orleans with the assistance of Craig (1969). These regional programs provide facilitative services at a lower level of training than that of the National Technical Institute for the Deaf. They are designed to meet the vocational needs of students who are not college material.

Quigley, Jenni, and Phillips (1968) completed a major survey of the extent to which deaf and hard of hearing persons are attending, or have attended, colleges and universities in the United States, and how successful they have been in this endeavor. They stated that it was reasonable to expect that greater numbers of hearing impaired persons could achieve in post-secondary study with provision of some special services. They also recommended that greater attention be given to the educational needs of moderately hard of hearing students.

A post-secondary facilitative program for the hard of hearing has been established at Utah State University recently (Berg, 1969). A unique feature of this new program is the reliance placed on the use of oral rather than manual communication. Other special features include a wide variety of educational adjustments. Also, a preparatory-year program exists for hearing impaired students who are somewhat retarded in language and academic skills.

The USU hypothesis is that an effective facilitative program for hard of hearing college students can exist without reliance upon manual forms of communication. Enrollment at USU includes primarily hard of hearing but some oral deaf students. A current focus is being played on a limited number of appropriate specializations. The USU program may serve as a model which can be duplicated in other states and regions of the United States.

National and State Planning

Currently, a growing awareness exists in the United States that the special needs of hard of hearing children and youth are largely unmet. In 1965, the Secretary of Health, Education, and Welfare's National Advisory Committee on the Education of the Deaf noted that the American people had experienced only limited success in educating hearing impaired children and preparing them for society. In 1967 a follow-up conference of the NACD resulted in an array of recommendations for improving educational programs for hearing impaired children of all age levels. The same year participants of the National Research Conference on Day Programs for Hearing Impaired Children agreed that few states had recognized the problems of educating deaf and hard of hearing children beyond narrow limits, and that even fewer had developed comprehensive state plans (1968).

One of the few states to develop a comprehensive state plan for the education of severely hearing impaired children is that of California (Hayes and Griffing, 1967). Standards have been recommended to the legislature for class size, number of classes per program, teacher and supervisor qualification, teacher-supervisor ratio, auxiliary services, method of communication, development and coordination of curriculum, physical facilities, guidance and counseling, size of geographic area served by a special program, age of enrollment, home teachers, time limit for meeting program standards, residential school responsibilities, and financial support. If made law, substantial improvements in educational achievement among hearing impaired children in California should be realized, particularly in day school programs where services tend to be substandard.

The California plan does not specifically indicate that programming for deaf and hard of hearing children should be separated. However, it does not recommend that such children necessarily be grouped together, either. Currently, many separate programs for hard of hearing children do exist in California. Griffing, a state consultant, describes program needs for hard of hearing children in a separate chapter of this book. Brill (1956), the superintendent of the Southern California School for the Deaf, has voiced strong opposition against educating deaf and hard of hearing children together.

Another one of the few states developing a comprehensive state plan for the education of hearing impaired children is Illinois (Bothwell, 1967). Recognizing in 1960 that only 19 of 102 counties had educational programs for the hearing impaired, educational leaders from Illinois met and committed themselves to vigorous and cooperative action. They sought to develop a plan that would enable most hearing impaired children to be educated within the mainstream of the home community rather than at the state public residential school for the deaf. The Illinois State Department of Public Instruction initiated a three-pronged program to (1) develop a workable legislative and administrative framework in special education, (2) alleviate the critical shortage of professional specialists, and (3) promote and coordinate interagency services such as education, health, and rehabilitation.

An Illinois Committee on Hearing Impairment was established in 1966 with the charge of promoting the development of statewide services for deaf and hard of hearing children. This committee met on numerous occasions and decided to set up two pilot projects which would provide guidelines for future planning. One project was the establishment of a diagnostic and learning center for hearing impaired children of a highly populated area. The other was the development of a similar center in a rural area of Illinois. One of the important features of the rural project was the establishment of language and communication programs for hard of hearing children attending schools in their home communities. Again this development reveals that special programming for hard of hearing children is only in its infancy.

Dyer (1969) recently completed a survey of educational programs for hearing impaired children in 60 large school districts throughout the United States. The survey reveals two findings pertinent to educational programming for hard of hearing children. One is that special classroom services for the severely hearing impaired generally are not provided at the upper elementary and secondary levels. The other is that itinerant and resource services for hearing impaired children in general are deficient at all educational levels.

A New Specialization

Any state, regional, or national plan for the education of hearing impaired children will succeed only if a sufficient number of highly qualified specialists are available. Currently, a critical shortage of teachers of the hearing impaired exists throughout the country. Bothwell (1966), for example, indicated that more than 100 specialists were needed to work with hard of hearing children, exclusive of schools and classes for the deaf in Illinois. She estimated that only 1537 out of 6629 educationally hard of hearing children in Illinois were enrolled in some type of special educational program (Bothwell, 1967).

The task of meeting this critical need is more than the matter of the preparation of a great many more teachers of the deaf, speech pathologists, and audiologists. Programs for the deaf in this country have existed for 150 years, and it has been presumed by some that the deaf educator is trained to meet the unique needs of the hard of hearing child because of his special preparation in the teaching of language skills (Berg and Fletcher, 1967). It has also been presumed by others that both the clinical audiologist and the speech pathologist are trained to meet these special needs, A great loss in human potential can result from this thinking, for none of these specialists is able to encompass the unique educational needs of the hard of hearing child.

Teachers of the deaf generally have not been vitally concerned with the utilization of residual hearing, notwithstanding the widespread use of hearing aids in schools for the hearing impaired. Clinical audiologists typically have focused their energies and talents on audiological evaluation with little emphasis on communication training and even less on language and academic development. Speech pathologists generally have been actively engaged in facilitating speech development and, to a lesser extent, language proficiency, with little emphasis on academic progress.

A new specialization called educational audiology has emerged to isolate the parameters of hearing impairment, to identify the educational and psychological deficiencies rising from hearing disability, to assess these deficiencies as they relate to the unique problems of particular persons, and to develop educational programs which will foster effective functioning in a hearing world (Berg and Fletcher, 1967). It seeks to spearhead the alleviation of the educational retardation characteristic of so many hard of hearing children and youth, particularly those with moderate to severe hearing impairment.

Support for the educational audiology specialization as a three-year prototype program in the area of the hard of hearing has been received from the Bureau of the Education for Handicapped of the United States Office of Education (Berg, 1969b). By 1972 an evaluation of the effectiveness of the educational audiologist for establishing and managing educational programs for hard of hearing children may be available. This evaluation may encompass both the hard of hearing child in the regular schools as well as the hard of hearing child in a special school for the hearing impaired.

References

Alpiner, J. G. and R. A. Walker. 1964. A residential vocational rehabilitation program for young adults with severely impaired hearing. The Volta Review 66:118–121, 163.

Anderson, N. 1964. Wyoming's unique program for the hearing impaired. The Volta Review 66:537–539.

Austin, G. F. 1969. Division of Vocational Rehabilitation Program. DeKalb: Northern Illinois University.

Berg F. and S. Fletcher. 1967. The hard of hearing child and educational audiology. Proceedings of International Conference on Oral Education of the Deaf: The Alexander Graham Bell Association for the Deaf 874–885.

Berg, F. 1969a. University facilitative program for young hard of hearing adults. Social Rehabilitation Service: Unpublished Progress Report, RD-2766-SH.

Berg, F. 1969b. Educational Audiology, Hard of Hearing, Special Project #6, Bureau of Education for the Handicapped. Washington, D.C.: Office of Education.

Boatner, E. B. 1965. The need of a realistic approach to the education of the deaf. Paper given to the joint convention of the California Association of Parents of Deaf and Hard of Hearing Children, California Association of Teachers of the Deaf and Hard of Hearing, and the California Association of the Deaf, November 6, 1965.

Bothwell, H. 1966. Personal communication.

Bothwell, H. 1967. Developing a comprehensive program for hearing impaired children on a statewide basis. Proceedings of Office of Education Sponsored Institute on Characteristics and Needs of the Hard of Hearing Child. Unpublished material, Utah State University.

Brill, R. G. 1956. Education of the deaf and the hard of hearing. Exceptional Children 23:194–198.

Brill, R. G. 1962. Junior college program at Riverside. The Silent Worker: 3–4.

Cornett, R. O. 1967. Cued speech. American Annals of the Deaf 112:3–13.

Craig, W. 1964. Effects of preschool training on the development of reading and lipreading skills of deaf children. American Annals of the Deaf 109:280–296.

Craig, W. 1969. Personal communication.

Crammate, A. B. 1968. Deaf Persons in Professional Employment. Springfield, Ill.: Charles C Thomas.

Dale, D. 1967. Recent developments in educating children with defective hearing in New Zealand. Proceedings of International Conference on Oral Education of the Deaf. Washington, D.C.: The Alexander Graham Bell Association for the Deaf. Pp. 399–405.

Downs, M. 1967. Early identification and principles of management. Proceedings of International Conference on Oral Education of the Deaf. Washington, D.C.: The Alexander Graham Bell Association for the Deaf. Pp. 746–757.

Dyer, D. G. 1969. Program development guidelines for hard of hearing children in the Tulsa Public Schools. Unpublished M.S. Thesis, Utah State University.

Education for the Deaf. 1965. A report to the Secretary of Health, Education, and Welfare by his Advisory committee on the education of the deaf. Washington, D.C.: U.S. Department of Health, Education, and Welfare.

Education of the Deaf. 1967. The challenge and the charge. A Report of the National Conference on Education of the Deaf. Washington, D.C.: U.S. Department of Health, Education, and Welfare.

Frisina, D. R. 1968. National Technical Institute for the Deaf. Report of first year ending December 20, 1967. Rochester, New York.

Frisina, D. R. 1969. National Technical Institute for the Deaf. Report of the second year ending December 31, 1968. Rochester, New York.

Furth, H. G. 1966. A comparison of reading test norms of deaf and hearing children. American Annals of the Deaf 111:461–462.

Goetzinger, C., C. Harrison, and C. Baer. 1964. Small perceptive hearing loss: its effect in school-age children. The Volta Review 66:124–131.

Goldstein, M. 1939. The acoustic method for the training of the deaf and hard of hearing child. Laryngoscope. St. Louis.

Hayes, G. M. and B. L. Griffing. 1967. A proposed plan for the improvement of the education of the deaf and severely hard of hearing in California. Sacramento: California State Department of Education.

Hoag, R. 1965. Observations of programs for the education of hearing impaired children in five countries in Europe. Education of the Deaf. Washington, D.C.: U.S. Department of Health, Education, and Welfare. Appendix C, 1–11.

Hudgins, C. 1953. The response of profoundly deaf children to auditory training. Journal of Speech and Hearing Disorders 18:273–288.

John Tracy Clinic. 1961. John Tracy Clinic Correspondence Course for Parents of Little Deaf Children. Los Angeles: John Tracy Clinic.

Johnson, E. 1948. The ability of pupils in a school for the deaf to understand various methods of communication. American Annals of the Deaf 93:258–314.

Johnson, E. M. 1967. Educational provision for children with impaired hearing in England. Proceedings of International Conference on Oral Education of the Deaf. Washington, D.C.: Alexander Graham Bell Association for the Deaf. Pp. 293–300.

Jones, R. 1969. Personal communication.

Kopp, H. 1968. Summary Report: National Research Conference on Day Programs for Hearing Impaired Children. Washington, D.C.: The Volta Bureau. Pp. 27–34.

Lane, H. 1942. Influence of nursery school education on school achievement. The Volta Review 44:677–681.

McClure, W. J. 1966. Current problems and trends in the the education of the deaf. Deaf American:8–14. (Jan. issue.)

McConnell, F. 1968. Proceedings of the Conference on Current Practices in the Management of Deaf Infants, Supported by U.S. Office of Education. Nashville: The Bill Wilkerson Hearing and Speech Center.

Mikaelyan, K. 1968. From the experience of work in the utilization and development of auditory perception in a school for hard of hearing children. Russian Translations on Speech and Hearing, ASHA Reports Number 3. Washington, D.C.: American Speech and Hearing Association. Pp. 177–185.

Miller, J. 1958. Academic achievement. Volta Review 60:302–304.

Moores, D. F. 1967. Applications of "Cloze" procedures to the assessment of psycholinguistic abilities of the deaf. Unpublished Doctoral Dissertation, University of Illinois.

Mulholland, A. 1968. The day program movement in the education of the hearing impaired. National Research Conference on Day Programs for Hearing Impaired Children. Washington, D.C.: Alexander Graham Bell Association for the Deaf. Pp. 49–57.

Myklebust, H. 1964. Chapter 1. The Psychology of Deafness. New York: Grune & Stratton.

National Research Conference on Day Programs for Hearing Impaired Children. 1968. Washington, D.C.: The Volta Bureau.

O'Connor, C. 1967. Lexington school's first century of oral education of the deaf. The Volta Review 69:128–136.

O'Neill, J. 1964. The Hard of Hearing. Englewood Cliffs, N.J.: Prentice-Hall.

Pratt, G. 1965. Personal correspondence.

Quigley, S. P., W. C. Jenni, and S. B. Phillips. 1968. Deaf students in colleges and universities. Washington, D.C.: Alexander Graham Bell Association for the Deaf.

Quigley, S. P. 1969. The influence of fingerspelling on the development of language, communication, and educational achievement in deaf children, report of research grant RD 1299s. Washington, D.C.: Rehabilitation Services Administration, Dept. of Health, Education, and Welfare.

Rochester School for the Deaf. 1963. The Rochester Method of Instructing the Deaf. New York: Rochester School for the Deaf.

Ross, M. and D. Calvert. 1967. The semantics of deafness. The Volta Review 69:644–649.

Scott, E. 1968. Personal communication.

Scouten, E. 1957. Personal communication.

Silverman, S. R. 1957. Clinical and educational procedures for the deaf, in L. Travis (Ed.) Handbook of Speech Pathology. New York: Appleton-Century-Crofts.

Simmons, A. 1967. Home language stimulation for hearing impaired children. U.S. Office of Education supported Institute on Characteristics and Needs of Hard of Hearing Children. Unpublished Proceedings, Utah State University.

Streng, A. 1960. Children with impaired hearing. Council for Exceptional Children. Washington, D.C.: National Education Association.

Thomas, D. 1964. Separate Programming for the Deaf and Hard of Hearing. The Volta Review 66:436–438.

Waite, H. 1967. 100 years of conquest of silence. The Volta Review 69:118–126.

Wedenberg, E. 1951. Auditory training of deaf and hard of hearing children. Acta Otolaryngologica, supplementum 94:1–129.

Wedenberg, E. 1954. Auditory training of severely hard of hearing preschool children. Acta Otolaryngologica, supplementum 110.

Wedenberg, E. 1967a. Experience from 30 years, auditory training. The Volta Review 69:588–594.

Wedenberg, E. 1967b. The status of hard of hearing students in Sweden. U.S. Office of Education supported Institute on the Characteristics and Needs of Hard of Hearing Children. Unpublished Proceedings, Utah State University.

PART II

BASIC CONSIDERATIONS

Chapter 4

The Hearing Mechanism

SAMUEL G. FLETCHER, Ph.D.

Considerable insight into behavior of the hearing impaired person may be obtained from a study of the acoustical system. The ear is a masterpiece of biological engineering. The structural and functional efficiency of this complex organ buried within the hardest bone of the body continues to challenge the most astute observers. Occupying a space of only about $1\frac{1}{2}$ inches in diameter the auditory system is capable of focusing sound energy surrounding the head, transmitting it with essentially no loss of energy through a series of variable air, bone, and fluid channels, and transforming it into a code of nerve impulses which can be interpreted by the brain. Naturally, within the limits of a single chapter of a book, one can present only a framework which a reader may use to open the door to the anatomical and physiological information which has been and is still rapidly accumulating about the ear.

The chapter is arranged in the order sound follows as it enters and passes through the auditory channels to the brain. At the end of each of the first three major divisions of the auditory system, a short discussion of embryonic development is given. This type of information is increasingly useful in understanding problems in audition arising from congenital disturbances.

The auditory system is most easily visualized as four components which differ from almost their first moment of formation. These are: (1) the external ear that receives and conducts sound and helps isolate the direction of the vibratory field; (2) the middle ear which changes the signals into mechanical energy and amplifies the vibrations; (3) the inner ear which analyzes the sound waves, transduces the vibrations into electrochemical energy, and initiates nerve signals; and, finally, (4) the sensory pathways that relay the nerve signals to the brain and other processing centers for final assessment of the acoustical incident.

The External Ear

The *auricle* or *pinna* identifies the outer portion of the ear. It is in the form of a shell attached to the side of the head at about a 30° angle, and consists of an external fold, the *helix*, which circles the auricle to the *tragus* projecting over the canal.

29

The *antihelix* is also a concentric ridge. It parallels the helix and encircles the deepest depression called the *concha* or shell. The concha lies in the center of the auricle. The lower extremity of the auricle is the *lobule* which lacks cartilaginous support.

The auricle is attached to the skull by three muscles, vestigial in man but which give animals extremely good control of the pinna for localizing sound. This attachment is further strengthened by anterior and posterior ligaments.

The auricle funnels into the *external auditory meatus* or ear canal. The outer ear space has a cartilaginous skeleton while the skeleton of the inner third is bony. The total length of the passage plus the concha is about 35 mm. and the diameter shows individual variation from 4–10 mm. The diameter gradually decreases to reach its narrowest dimension at an isthmus not far from where it terminates blindly at the *tympanic membrane* or eardrum. A tube of this length that is closed at one end would have a resonance frequency of about 2300 Hz if it were of constant dimension. A resonator shaped like a horn has somewhat higher resonant frequencies (Fant, 1960, chapter 14). This means that the outer ear is "tuned" to receive most efficiently the soft, higher frequency consonant sounds and thus enhance speech perception. The inner surface of the meatus is lined with skin and the cartilaginous part is covered with glands that secrete a yellowish-brown *cerumen* or wax. This protects the skin from drying out. It also has laterally directed hairs and sebaceous glands to prevent intrusion of insects and other foreign bodies. The soft surface and hairs also assist in absorbing extraneous sound not in the resonance frequency bands.

Innervation of the External Ear

Sensation is provided to the superior and posterior surface of the ear canal and the superior $\frac{2}{3}$ of the ear drum by the auriculo-temporal branch of the trigeminal nerve. A branch of the vagus nerve serves sensation to the anterior and inferior surfaces of the ear canal and to the inferior $\frac{1}{3}$ of the eardrum. The vagus nerve also serves sensation in the pharynx and larynx. For this reason when the ear canal is touched, as during an otological examination, the person may feel tickling in his throat and cough.

Embryology of the External Ear

The auricle develops from six embryonic mounds or hillocks formed below and behind the lower jaw. This is called the hyoid arch. The hillocks are seen first in the sixth week embryo and are well-developed by the third month of fetal life. No external canal is present at the earlier time, however. All parts of the auricle except the tragus develop from these hillocks. The tragus comes from the mandibular arch. Because of this difference in embryonic origin, the point at which the tragus and other structures meet is the site of occasional preauricular fistulas.

During the second month of fetal life, a solid core of outer body tissue is formed and pushes inward from the auricle. A shallow middle ear is also beginning to be formed as an extension of the pharynx. The inner end of the epithelial core from outside is destined to become the outer layer of the tympanic membrane. During the sixth month the delicate core begins to break down and by the middle of the seventh month an open canal is present. It may be seen that developmental arrest could cause absence of the auricle before the third fetal month, absence of the ear canal before the sixth month, or atresia of the canal with a normal auricle if something stops the outer ear development later in fetal life.

The Middle Ear

The middle ear consists essentially of an intermittently ventilated pocket of air cavities containing the *ossicles—the malleus, incus,* and *stapes—*and their muscles. The principal cavity of the middle ear is the *tympanic cavity* or *tympanum.* It is separated from the ear canal by the thin, three-layered tympanic membrane. Recently, studies have shown that with the exception of the tympanic membrane and part of the posterior wall and roof of the tympanum, the entire tympanic cavity and the *eustachian tube* (which connects the middle ear with the pharynx) is ciliated and lined with mucous glands (Sade, 1966). These cilia are arranged so that their motion can sweep mucus and other debris from the cavity through the eustachian tube to the nasopharynx. This action is needed because the eustachian tube leaves the cavity from its superior, inside wall and slopes downward only after it passes an isthmus about one-third of the distance to the pharynx. Thus, passive clearance is not fostered by the anatomical orientation of the tube.

The Tympanic Membrane

The tympanic membrane is a thin, transparent, elastic sheet of tissue which upon inspection has the appearance of a smooth, glistening, pinkish pearl curtain slanted inward at the deepest point of the external auditory meatus. The membrane is tightly stretched on a bony frame. In its upper section is a less tense area called the *pars flaccida* or *Shrappnel's membrane.* This area is bounded anteriorly and posteriorly by thickened borders called the *malleolar folds.* The remainder of the membrane is termed the *pars tensa.* The outside surface of the tympanic membrane is concave. The deepest part of the concavity, termed the *umbo,* corresponds with the flattened tip of the handle (manubrium) of the malleus imbedded in the membrane.

Although it has a thickness of only $\frac{1}{10}$ mm., the tympanic membrane is composed of three layers: an outer cutaneous layer of skin that is continuous with the lining of the external canal, an intermediate layer of connective tissue fibers, and an inner mucous layer which is, for the most part, a single layer of cells continuous with the mucous membrane lining the tympanic cavity.

For hearing the middle layer is the most important since its fibers maintain the tension of the membrane during vibration (Kirikae, 1963). This layer has an outer sheet of thin, straight, radial fibers stretched like spokes in a wheel between the umbo and the fibrous *annular tympanius* which attaches the membrane to the temporal bone. The inner sheet consists of circular and parabolic fibers especially prominent around the periphery and in a strip between the periphery and the umbo.

The vibration mode of the tympanic membrane varies with the frequency of the sounds received. At low frequencies such as 250 and 500 Hz the tympanic membrane vibrates as a unit. In middle frequencies it vibrates in two. Above 2400 Hz it shifts to a three-segment pattern with the intermediate section between the umbo and the outer attachment showing greatest amplitude.

Ossicles of the Middle Ear

As noted, the tympanic membrane is attached to the most external of the three middle ear ossicles. Consequently, movements of the ossicles reflect those of the membrane itself. The length of the malleus is about 8 mm.

The head of the *malleus* rests in an upper compartment of the tympanic cavity called the *epitympanic recess*. Above the malleus is the *tegmen* or roof of the cavity. The head of the malleus is attached to the tegmen by a thin ligament, the *superior malleolar ligament*. A lateral and an anterior ligament also attaches the malleus to surrounding bone to provide fixed point stability.

The *incus*, shaped something like a premolar tooth with very divergent roots, articulates with the malleus at the *incudomalleolar joint*. The short process of the incus is directed almost horizontally toward the posterior end of the epitympanic recess where it is fastened by ligaments to the wall. The long process of the incus extends downward and inward nearly parallel with the handle of the malleus. On its lower extremity (which is bent medially) is a minute spherical bone, the *lenticularis*, for articulation with the head of the stapes. The lenticular process is the smallest bone in the body.

The stapes consists of a head, a slightly constricted neck, and the two legs which diverge around the *obturator foremen* and attach to a footplate. The footplate is framed in the oval window of the vestibule of the inner ear which it seals hermetically by means of the *annular ligament*.

The ossicular joints are different from other joints in the body in that they do not have overlying muscles to hold them in contact with each other. They depend entirely on an elastic capsule to keep the joint surfaces together (Harty, 1964).

Muscles of the Middle Ear

Movements of the ossicles may be modified by two muscles: the *tensor tympani* and the *stapedius*. The tensor tympani is lodged in a small compartment immediately above the eustachian tube. A bony and fibrous partition separates it from the eustachian tube.

The tensor tympani muscle arises from the upper part of the eustachian tube and the inside surface of its own canal. The muscle then tapers into a small round tendon which turns at a right angle as it leaves its canal, passes across the tympanic cavity, and attaches to the upper end of the malleolar handle. Contraction of this muscle pulls the handle medially and thereby reduces sensitivity to loud sounds. Ingelstedt and Jonson (1967) have shown that it also contributes to ventilation of the middle ear by pulling the tympanic membrane inward and producing an "overpressure." This can aid in separating the mucous membranes lining the eustachian tube. The muscle is supplied by a motor branch from the trigeminal cranial nerve (V).

The stapedius muscle is the smallest one in the body. It is completely encased in a small pyramid of bone jutting out on the back wall of the tympanic cavity. A delicate tendon of the stapedius enters the tympanum through a tiny aperture on the summit of the pyramid and is attached to the posterior surface of the neck of the stapes. Contraction of this muscle inhibits the rocking motion of the stapes in the oval window and also reduces sensitivity of the ear to sound pressures (Hilding, 1961). The muscle is supplied by a branch of the facial nerve (VII).

The combined attenuation from the tensor tympani and stapedial muscle to loud sound is about 20 db (Neergaard et al., 1954). The muscles have a latency of about 20 msec. between onset of sound and movement of the ossicles to which they are attached. Therefore, they are less effective in protecting the ear against sudden loud noises such as a gunshot than they are to sustained sound. These latencies diminish with increasing sound intensity. Fisch and Schulthess (1963) found that stapedial latencies were reduced to as small as 10 msec. to sound above 100 db in intensity.

The dimensions of the tympanic membrane is approximately 21 times that of the stapedial footplate (Wever and Laurence, 1954). The effective ratio is about 14 to 1 so that pressure at the stapes is increased by about 23 db. An additional 2–3 db is obtained from the lever action of the ossicles. Thus, a disruption in the ossicular chain would cause a loss in hearing of 25–26 db.

The eustachian or auditory tube extends from the middle ear to the pharynx.

At its isthmus it measures only 1–2 mm. in diameter. The remainder of its wall, 24–25 mm., is supported by cartilage. The part supported by cartilage is typically closed except during certain physiological activities such as swallowing or yawning.

Dilation of the auditory tube to equalize pressure on each side of the tympanic cavity is accomplished by contraction of the *dilator tubae* division of the *tensor veli palatini muscle* with some assistance from the *levator veli palatini muscle*.

As the eustachian tube opens into the pharynx, its orifice on the upper lateral wall is encircled by the *torus tubarius* cartilage. In the human adult the medial part of the tube has an upward angulation which facilitates drainage somewhat, although the outer third angles downward to the middle ear cavity (Sade, 1966). In the infant an upward angulation from the pharynx has not yet matured, thus drainage of the middle ear is more difficult (Graves and Edwards, 1944). If the eustachian tube is not functioning properly, the gases in the middle ear are gradually absorbed and auditory problems result. The daily ventilation for normal ear pressure is only 1–2 ml. according to Ingelstedt and Jonson (1967).

Several other structures of the middle ear are worthy of mention. These are the air-filled *mastoid antrum* and the *mastoid air cells* which communicate posteriorly from the epitympanic recess, the *facial nerve,* imbedded in the posterior wall of the tympanum, the *iter chordae nerve* which crosses from the canal of the seventh nerve through the tympanic cavity to join the fifth cranial nerve and serve taste sensation in the tongue, and the *round window* (fenestra rotunda) or secondary tympanum on the medial wall.

Embryonic Development of the Middle Ear

The embryonic primordia of the middle ear cavity is an outpouching of the pharynx (foregut) toward the body wall in the third week of development. The flattened end of this pouch forms a primitive tympanic cavity.

During the second month the ossicles begin to take shape in connective tissues above and lateral to the developing middle ear cavity. By the fourth month the ossicles are formed but not until the seventh month are they enclosed within the cavity. The malleus and incus are from Mechel's cartilage in the first branchial arch. The mandible also develops from this. The common origin of the malleus and incus and the mandible explains associated developmental disturbances involving both the mandible and the ossicles, as in the Treacher-Collins syndrome. The stapes arises later from the second arch and is not fully formed until after the fourth month. Elliott and Elliott (1964) note that in spite of rather gross congenital anomaly of the auditory ossicles "at least a remnant of the malleus handle can usually be found."

Pneumatization of the tympanic cavity is not completed until after the seventh month. Pneumatization of the tympanic antrum and the rest of the mastoid bone is not begun until after the fifth month and is apparently not completed until childhood.

The Inner Ear

The oval and round windows of the middle ear open into the inner ear. Because of its complicated channels and passages the inner ear is also called the *labyrinth.* In actuality the labyrinth consists of two sets of cavities, one inside the other. The outer cavity is a series of bony canals within the petrous part of the temporal bone. This is called the *osseus* labyrinth. The other set of cavities is a series of communicating sacs and ducts called the *membranous labyrinth.* It is filled with a fluid called *endolymph.* The space in the osseus labyrinth not occupied by the membranous labyrinth is filled with a fluid called *perilymph*. The membranous labyrinth is attached to the osseus labyrinth by numerous threads of connective tissue.

Divisions of the Inner Ear

The labyrinth is separated into two parts with a 3 × 5 mm. *vestibule* and a very narrow membranous canal, the *ductus reuniens*, communicating between them.

The posterior division of the labyrinth is devoted to sensations of movements of the head and orientation of the body in space. It is made up of three *semicircular canals*, and two larger cavities, the *utriculus* and the *sacculus*. The five openings of the semicircular canals (two of the canals fuse at one extremity) enter into the utriculus. Near their entrance the canals have enlargements, the *ampulae*, in which the sensory termination of the vestibular nerve, the *ampullae cupula*, is found.

The utriculus is connected to the sacculus by the utriculo-saccular, endolymphatic duct which is in turn connected to the cochlear endolymphatic duct by the ductus reuniens. Thus, the vestibular divisions of the labyrinth contain part of the total volume of fluid to which sound is delivered. In some cases of abnormality they must be taken into consideration. They need not be considered further here, however.

The anterior division of the labyrinth is coiled like a snail shell and for this reason is called the cochlea. The auditory function is delegated to this organ.

The Cochlea

The cochlea has a central bony pedestal called the *modiolus* which acts as an inner wall for the coiled tube which wraps about $2\frac{3}{4}$ turns around it. Projecting from and spiraling around the modiolus is a thin shelf of bone, the *spiral lamina*. From this shelf a tough membrane, the *basilar membrane*, stretches across the tube and attaches to the outer wall of the cochlea at the *spiral ligament*. The basilar membrane separates the tube into two passages for its full length except for a small opening at the apex, known as the helicotrema. In this free space at the summit the two passages join. The upper canal of the cochlea, the *scala vestibuli*, begins in the vestibule near the oval window, and spirals upward to the helicotrema. The *scala tympani*, begins at the helicotrema and spirals downward to the round window on the inner wall of the tympanic cavity. The round window is covered by a thin membrane separating this passage from the middle ear cavity.

Near the round window is the *cochlear aqueduct*, a small 6–7 mm. straight channel from the scala tympani to the fluid-filled subarachnoid space surrounding the brain. The cochlear aqueduct may serve to equalize pressures between the inner ear and the subarachnoid space; however, its small diameter of .09–.1 mm. would restrict such activity to a very slow rate (Ritter and Lawrence, 1965).

A second duct, the *vestibular aqueduct*, serves to balance pressure in the endolymphatic system. This duct exits from the sacculus and passes through the petrous pyramid. Upon emerging, it dilates to form a blind *endolymphatic sac* in the posterior cranial fossa under cover of the dura mater. Thus, the endolymphatic sac could release pressure in the endolymphatic system only by expanding like a balloon and thereby accepting additional fluid. Again, its small dimension would restrict this function to a very slow rate.

The cochlea is an extremely small organ. It measures only about 5 mm. from base to summit and has a breadth of about 8 mm. across the base. The spiral tube is about 35 mm. long. The basilar membrane within the spiral tube is about 32 mm. long and tapers in width from about $\frac{1}{2}$ mm. at the apex to about $\frac{1}{20}$ mm. at the basal turn. It is made up of about 24,000 individual fibers (strings arranged in parallel with each other and at right angles to the length of the membrane.

Extending diagonally from the spiral lamina to the outer wall of the cochlea is *Reisner's membrane*. It has a thickness of just one or two somewhat flattened cells. Reisner's membrane extends along the whole passage of the cochlea to join the basilar membrane at the helicotrama and form a completely sealed sac between it and the basilar membrane. This sac is endolymph filled. The *cochlear duct* or *scala media* communicates with the sacculus via the ductus reuniens. The other two passages, the scala vestibuli and scala media, contain perilymph. The outer wall of the scala media is covered by the *stria vascularis* (e.g., vascular strip) which has a dense layer of capillaries and specialized cells believed to secrete the endolymph (Bush and Jorgensen, 1964; Katasuki et al., 1966). Chemical contrast between the two fluids is shown in the list below (adapted from Ormerod, 1961).

Endolymph	*Perilymph*
High potassium content	Low potassium content
Low sodium content	Relatively high sodium content
Low protein content	Relatively high protein content compared with endolymph or cerebrospinal fluid
High positive electric potential	Negative electric potential, compared with endolymph
Mucopolysaccharids that vary with animal species.	Mucopolysaccharids that vary with species.

The sensory organ that transforms hydraulic sound waves into neural impulses is the *organ of Corti*. It is situated on the vestibular surface of the basilar membrane in the scala media.

The organ of Corti has two kinds of elements. One element is purely supportive and provides the framework of the structure. The other consists of hair cells embedded in the supportive cells. These are the specific sensory structures with nerve fibers. The cells of the organ of Corti are nurtured by the endolymph, and perhaps by cortilymph, and have no blood vessels which could introduce additional noise into the endolymphatic channel.

The substantial part of the supporting network of elements in the organ of Corti, are the *inner* and *outer rods* (pillars) *of corti*. These rods form a triangular tunnel with part of the basilar membrane between them. They are thick, stiff bodies, broad at their base, that divide the organ into the inner and outer portions. On the inner side of the tunnel of Corti is a single row of hair cells, the *inner hair cells,* supported by a row of *inner phalangeal cells,* or "fingerlike" cells, and other smaller supporting Cells of Held. On the outer side of the tunnel rods are three and sometimes four rows of smaller *outer hair cells* supported by phalangeal Cells of Deiters and with prominent intracellular spaces between them.

Engström (1960) has called attention to the difference in the fluids in the tunnel of Corti and in the intracellular spaces around the outer hair cells. He emphasized that although the general ionic content of this flud is similar to perilymph, considerably more macromolecular elements, possibly protein, were present. Spoendlin (1962) speculated that these elements were nutritional in nature for the base part of the external hair cells. With this uniqueness in mind, Engstrom suggested that the fluid contained in the tunnel of Corti be termed *cortilymph*. Thus, each outer hair cell is in direct relation with two different fluids. The endolymph bathes the top of the cell and the cortilymph the major part of the cell from contact with cortilymph in the intracellular spaces. Each of these fluids is rich in potential nutrient content.

The upper edges of the phalangeal cells supporting both the inner and outer hair cells contact each other to form a compact network. This network of cells is called the *reticular* membrane. The cilia or hairs penetrate the reticular membrane and are imbedded in the gelatinous *tectorial membrane* (Hilding, 1952) which winds in spiral fashion along the whole length of the organ of Corti.

Extending outward from the outer hair cells and their phalangeal supportive cells (Cells of Deiters) are the Cells of Hensen which are large supporting cells with fat globules. They form an integral part of the organ of Corti and form a series almost equal in width to the rest of the organ. They are of unequal height and built closely to the Cells of Deiters. A line of cuboidal shaped *Cells of Claudius* completes the lining of the vestibular surface of the basilar membrane to the spiral ligament.

About 3500 cells of approximately 12 M. in diameter are contained in the inner row of hair cells and about 20,000 cells of approximately 8 M. in diameter are in the outer row. The jug-shaped inner hair cells each have from 30 to 60 hairs on their surface which are 3–4 M. in length and 0.32 M. in diameter.

When sound waves pass through Reisner's membrane and move the tectorial membrane, distortional forces develop on the hair cells. These movements generate a cochlear response called *cochlear microphonics*. The microphonics are found to be a faithful reproduction of the sound wave form of the stimulus up to moderate intensities of sound stimulation. At the present time the microphonics are generally believed to arise in the nerve bearing end of the hair cells as the result of an ionic current flow through the cells (Katasuki et al., 1966). The precise way in which the mechanical motion of the sound wave is registered at different points along the cochlea and exactly how the hair cells are stimulated are still matters of considerable conjecture (Bekesy, 1966; Mygind, 1966; Naftalin, 1965).

The outer cells are cylindrical in shape with a round base. They lie with their bases in special hollows formed by the Cells of Deiters and incline parallel to the outer rods. The number of hairs on the hair cells varies to about 75 but may reach as many as 100. The auditory hairs are more prominent on the outer hair cells than on the inner but are only about 0.15 M. in diameter. Davis (1957) found the outer cells are more easily damaged by sound than the inner drugs. Many investigators have shown them more sensitive to drugs.

Iurato (1962) summarized the biological zones of the hair cells as follows:

> The apical zone, composed of the cuticle and the auditory hairs, is the device that receives the mechanical impulses generated by the hairs touching the tectorial membrane. . . . The underlying part, called the intermediate zone, well supplied with endoplasmic organoids, is the zone supplying the necessary energy to convert and amplify the mechanical stimulus. The perinuclear zone appears to handle conduction, while at the levels of the receptoneural junction the impulse passes to the nerve fibers.

Embryonic Development of the Inner Ear

The primordium of the membranous labyrinth is the first part of the ear to appear in the embryo. This may be first identified in the third week of development when a vaguely marked thickening of the ectoderm is found on either side of the primitive brain in the area subsequently to become the medulla. By the end of the third week this thickening has taken shape as a sharply differentiated plate called the *auditory placode*. The placode invaginates to form the *auditory pit* during the fourth week. As the pit deepens, its opening to the surface gradually closes and an epithelial sac, now known as the *auditory vesicle,* is formed.

In the ensuing days the auditory vesicle enlarges and changes from spheroidal to an elongate oval shape with a more expanded dorsal portion. This dorsal portion will develop into the vestibular part of the membranous labyrinth while the more slender anterior part will become the cochlea.

By the end of the sixth week of development conspicuous shelves push out from the vestibular portion of the main vesicle. As they do so, their central portions thin out and finally undergo resorption so that the original semilunate flanges are converted into looplike ducts to form the semicircular canals.

While the semicircular canals take shape, the main vestibular portion of the vesicle becomes subdivided by a progressively deepening constriction into a more dorsal utricular and a more ventral saccular portion. The semicircular canals then open off the utriculus. Near one of the two points of communication with the utriculus, each canal forms a local enlargement known as an *ampulla* within which develops the sensory area, the *crista*. Specialized areas called *maculae* develop later in the sacculus and utriculus.

The cochlear part of the membranous labyrinth elongates rapidly in the sixth week and develops a sharp bend at its extremity. The elongation and curling continues at an accelerated rate during the seventh and eighth weeks and the initial bend develops into the $2\frac{3}{4}$ spirals of the cochlea duct. As the cochlear duct is lengthened its original broad connection with the vestibular portion of the membranous labyrinth becomes narrowed to the slender ductus reuniens.

The cochlear division of the eighth nerve follows the cochlear duct as it grows in length, and its fibers fan out all along the duct. The *spiral ganglia* of the nerve appear on the fibers along the cochlear duct. The nerve becomes twisted as the cochlea curls into its mature form.

By the close of the third month the membranous labyrinth has achieved almost its adult configuration. During this time the mesenchyme surrounding the membranous labyrinth has become increasingly concentrated to form a cartilaginous shell with delicate strands of connective tissue developed to suspend the membranous labyrinth. The cartilage then is ossified to form the osseus labyrinth.

The first primordium of the organ of Corti becomes apparent in the third month of development as a localized thickening of the epithelium on the floor of the cochlear duct. The process of differentiation begins in the basal part and spreads gradually to the apex. McGrady and his co-workers (1938) found that differentiation of the basal parts of the cochlea coincides with onset of its function. For instance, in one species of opossum sound frequencies from 500 to 6000 Hz were perceived in the lower turn from the 2nd to the 59th day of fetal life in the pouch. As the middle and upper turns were developed after the 59th day, the fetus responded to sound frequencies from 300 to 10,000 Hz, and on the 60th day from 200 to 20,000 Hz.

From the third to the fifth month the entire cochlear duct undergoes considerable expansion. The tectorial membrane, formed over the epithelial thickening becomes more extensive and the developing organ of Corti beneath it begins to show marked specialization with formation of the hair cells. During the sixth month, some resorption occurs within the organ of Corti itself to form the tunnel of Corti which will later be supported by the developing supporting elements designated as the rods. The tunnel of Corti seems to develop later than the fluid spaces around the outer and inner hair cells (Engström, Ades, and Hawkins, 1965). The inner ear has practically its adult size at birth.

The Sensory Pathways

At this point a summary of the route of the acoustic signal through the mechanical pathways to its sensory conversion in the middle ear may be helpful. We will then consider the central neurological relays which enable the message to reach the brain and other processing centers for interpretation and reaction to the acoustic stimulus.

The process of audition begins when longitudinal sound waves, transmitted through air, are funneled by the auricle into the external auditory meatus and come in contact with the tympanic membrane at the end of the blind tunnel. The tympanic membrane moves in response to this compression-rarefaction collision. Energy thus imposed on the tympanic membrane is transferred to the ossicular chain system of the middle ear which amplifies the pressure by a lever and "hydraulic press" type of action. The movement of the stapes in the oval window of the labyrinth vestibule transmits the sound waves to the fluid of the scala vestibuli. A high degree of impedance matching by the ossicular chain between the air and fluid phase enables this transfer of sound energy without significant loss.

The acoustic vibrations then continue as hydraulic energy in the perilymphatic fluid through Reisner's membrane to the endolymphatic fluid. In the endolymph the vibrations press upon the tectorial membrane in such a fashion that the hair processes in the organ of Corti between the tectorial membrane and the basilar membrane are distorted. The force of this distortion is the stimulus which triggers hair cell activity which, in turn, generates nerve impulses. By some manner not presently agreed upon high tones are registered near the base of the cochlea and low tones at the apex. Energy travels around the helicotrema as well as through the basilar membrane to be absorbed by the round window.

Sound may also reach the inner ear by other routes although the above route is the most important. Two such alternative routes are: (1) directly across the middle ear to the round window membrane by air waves instead of through the ossicles, and (2) by transmission of sound to the inner ear through the bony structures of the skull. Inherent in both of these alternative routes of sound transmission is a great loss in acoustical energy to activate the inner ear. Therefore, under normal conditions these routes are relatively noncontributory to listening to other speakers. Bone conduction is an important source for the speaker to monitor his own voice.

The auditory sensory pathways begin at the inner and outer hair cells which differ from each other morphologically and also have a different pattern of innervation.

The nerve fibers to the cochlear hair cells pierce the basilar membrane at the *habenula perforata*. As they exit from the spiral lamina and enter the basilar membrane, they lose their myelin sheaths which insulate them from each other. From there to their terminations on the hair cells they course as naked nerve fibers, entirely unsheathed (Smith and Dempsay, 1957). Some of the fibers take a short, radial course primarily to the inner hair cells. These are, therefore, called *radial fibers*. Many of the fibers terminate just beneath the hair cell while others ascend the sides and may achieve considerably more length before terminating (Smith, 1961). Each inner cell is associated with one or two such radial fibers. Galombos (1954) noted that this nerve-to-cell arrangement would afford a clear basis for an hypothesis of a one-to-one relation between place on the basilar membrane and place in the central nervous system to extract frequency of a sound signal.

Fibers destined for the external hair cells cross the tunnel of Corti and for the most part spiral along the organ of Corti for 2 or 3 mm. before terminating at the hair cells. These are, therefore, called *spiral fibers*. They tend also to supply many different hair cells by numerous branches before ending. The nerve endings to the external hair cells are in contact only with the base of the cell. Galombos suggested that this nerve-to-cell arrangement could afford the basis for the "diffuse relationship" interpretation of sound frequency analysis.

A third type of nerve fiber is also present in the cochlea. This is a fiber with nerve endings containing numerous vesicles. Under the electron microscope these endings appear "much granulated" compared with the knoblike endings of the other nerves. On the basis of similarity between these "much granulated" nerve endings and other nerve endings in other parts of the body, Engström (1958) postulated that they were efferent fibers whereas the others were afferent. Ishii et al., 1967, found biochemical evidence that "all plexises within the organ of Corti contain fibers [that have] . . . both efferent and afferent components." Ishii and Balogh (1968) found that such efferent endings were only present in fibers serving the medium to high frequency range. The finer efferent fibers wind among the other two and are in extensive synaptic contact with the dendrites from both outer and inner hair cells (Iurato, 1962; Nomura and Kirikae, 1967). Although they are more concentrated in the outer row they belong to the descending auditory tract which likely inhibits activity of the cochlear nerves.

The afferent nerve fibers, which are bipolar neurons, leave the hair cells of the cochlea, pass by their cell bodies in the *spiral ganglion* of Corti, and join other such axons in the modiolus to form the cochlear nerve. The *cochlear nerve* leaves the auditory capsule in the petrous bone; it is joined by the *vestibular nerve* from the sensory organs in the semicircular canals, the sacculus and the utriculus. The two nerve bundles together are therafter referred to as the *acoustic nerve* (VIII). The acoustic nerve is met by the facial nerve (VII) and they pass to the brain stem together through the internal auditory meatus in the petrous pyramid of the temporal bone.

The bundle of fibers from the cochlea retain their frequency representation as they pass through the acoustic nerve (Linden et al., 1964). That is, the fibers in the middle of the high frequency range run straight through the axis of the nerve. The other fibers are twisted spirally around these in rope-like fashion. Those from the apex of the cochlea spiral one way, and the ones from the base in the opposite direction. This arrangement is likely a reflection of the twisting which occurred in the embryonic cochlea as it was coiled into its final spiral form.

The auditory nerve has been called a "bottle neck" of auditory sensation because all of the afferent and efferent impulses to and from the brain must pass through this single bundle of approximately 30,000 nerve fibers. The nerves are not scattered anatomically like those serving cutaneous or proprioceptive sensation. This anatomical arrangement makes the sensations liable to total disruption or impairment. On the other hand, this compactness suggests the possibility of direct stimulation of the nerve to circumvent a non-functioning cochlea (Simmons, et al., 1964).

When the acoustic nerve emerges from the internal auditory meatus, it enters the medulla and the cochlear and vestibular divisions are again separated. The cochlear nerve synapses at the ventral and dorsal cochlear nuclei. This is one of the main switching centers in the auditory system. Lorente de No (1933) differentiated 13 different subdivisions of the cochlear nuclei on the basis of the differences in the way the cells are arranged and the way incoming fibers terminate upon them.

Galambos (1954) observed that all afferent fibers from the cochlea make synapses in each of these 13 distinct subdivisions of the cochlear nucleus complex. Thus, each fiber terminates upon a great many cells. Again, the frequency characteristics of the cochlea are maintained. The conclusion is that in some if not all of its 13 subdivisions the geographical (spatial) arrangement for frequency established in the cochlea is repeated in this first central nucleus of the auditory system. In other words, "the cochlea is 'unrolled' at the cochlea nucleus, not just once, but repeatedly" (Galombos, 1954). Furthermore, frequencies which are not near the "best frequency" for the particular auditory area are apparently inhibited or suppressed (Gernandt and Ades, 1964). Similar frequency projections are retained in higher nuclei and on the brain itself where the high tones terminate deep within the auditory cortex while the low tones end in the outer folds near the surface.

From the dorsal and ventral cochlear nuclei complex interconnections establish several paths to the cortex and to other important relay centers in subcortical areas.

Classical studies of the auditory tracts have emphasized a four-neuron path (Rasmussen, 1935). The first neuron was depicted as traveling from the cochlea to the synapse at the dorsal and ventral cochlea nuclei. The second order neuron was supposed to travel from these nuclei to synapse in the superior olive, the accessory superior olive, the nucleus of the trapezoid body, and the nucleus of the inferior colliculus. The third order neuron then passed by way of the lateral lemniscus to synapse at the medial geniculate body and, finally, the fourth order neuron traversed the auditory radiations to the superior temporal girus of the cerebral cortex. The anatomical features of each of these major relay stations are discussed in detail in Golombos' excellent review (1954).

Tasaki (1957) summarized some interesting data from a variety of studies related to time required for arrival of nerve impulses at these various stations along the classical auditory route:

> The first sign of arrival of nerve impulses from the ear appears in the cortex (of a cat) approximately 10 mm. sec. after the start of the microphonics in the cochlea. Recent macro- and microelectrode studies indicate the latencies of responses to a strong click stimulus at various nuclei along the main auditory pathway are: Cochlear nuclei, 1.5 to 2 msec.; superior olivary complex approximately 4 msec.; inferior colliculus, 6 to 9 msec.; medial geniculate body, 7 to 10 msec.; and auditory cortex 8 to 12 msec.

The four-neuron schema of the auditory relay has been challenged by Galombos (1966) as a vast oversimplification of now known facts. Among new developments suggesting much greater complexity of the auditory and other sensory-motor systems is the highly significant work of Magoun and his co-workers at the UCLA Brain Research Institute. Their investigations have revealed the presence of a parallel pathway in the reticular formation of the brain. Incoming fibers send off shoots at all levels into these and other more medial regions of the brain and to the cerebellum. Gernandt and Ades (1964) also demonstrated the existence of "a diffusely projecting spinal system" which seemed to link descending tracts in the spinal cord with reticular formation connections.

Various synaptic relays through the alternate routes allow messages to be delivered to the cortex and other neural centers. Magoun (1963) notes that "in its ascending and descending relations with the cerebral cortex, the reticular system is intimately bound up with, and contributes to most categories of higher nervous activity . . . in most of the central integrative processes of the brain." The classical auditory avenues have been sectioned in animals leaving only the alternate lines intact (Galombos, 1966). Such animals are highly disabled in auditory activities for the first few weeks after such an operation. After several months they seem to regain the ability to perform well in auditory situations.

The descending auditory tracts have received less investigative attention than the ascending tracts. In 1946 Rasmussen first clearly identified and described an efferent bundle which consisted of nerves originating in the superior olive region of the medula. The fibers from one side of the medulla and thence peripherally to a spiral bundle next to the ganglion cells of the cochlea. Later (1953) he traced these fibers to the organ of Corti and concluded that they terminated on the hair cells. A variety of studies since that time have confirmed the presence of this efferent system and have also suggested additional routes at essentially all levels of potential auditory interaction (Kiangetal, 1965; Ishii et al., 1967). Additional clarification of the efferent systems may be expected.

Summary

From the welter of details in the discussion of the anatomy and physiology of the auditory system, certain main facts or principles of organization emerge. The central fact is the old but clearly confirmed observation that a remarkable orderliness exists at all levels of the auditory system. The system is so delicately arranged and balanced that almost infinitesimally small forces in the acoustic signal can be faithfully received, transduced a number of times, and relayed to higher centers with remarkable integrity. This relay system incorporates mechanical, hydraulic, and electrical transducers and amplifiers which seem to operate so efficiently that a tremendous amount of information is transmitted to the brain while relatively little additional noise is injected into the transmission channel.

The ear also has a built-in system to protect its biological integrity from unwanted or undesirable stimuli. This system extends from the noise reducing muscles of the middle ear through the inhibitory efferent nerve endings on the hair cells of the cochlea and apparently in inhibitory endings throughout all of the major relay centers of the brain.

Many gaps remain in our knowledge of the auditory system. Some of the information cited is based on experiments on animals far removed from man, and, therefore, is open to question in its application to man. This is especially so concerning studies of the sensory pathways. Nevertheless, a meaningful body of information is available upon which new knowledge of basic structure and function as well as understanding of the hearing impaired person may be built.

We can only conclude that the ear does indeed represent truly a masterpiece of engineering which will challenge and excite us as scientists, clinicians, and educators for many years to come.

References

Anson, B. J., J. A. Donaldson, R. L. Warpeka, and T. R. Winch. 1964. A critical appraisal of the anatomy of the perilymphatic system in man. Transactions of the American Otological, Rhinological, and Laryngological Society. Pp. 488–509.

Bekesy, G. von. 1966. Pressure and shearing forces as stimuli of labyrinthine epithelium. Archives of Otolaryngology 84:122–130.

Buch, N. H. and M. B. Jorgensen. 1964. Eustachian tube and middle ear. Embryology and Pathology. Archives of Otolaryngology 79:472–480.

Citron, L., D. Exley, and C. S. Hallpike. 1956. Formation, circulation and chemical properties of labyrinthine fluids. British Medical Journal 12: 101–104.

Davis, H. 1957. Biophysics and physiology of the inner ear. Physiological Review 37:1–49.

Elliott, G. B. and K. S. Elliott. 1964. Some pathological, radiological and clinical implications of the precocious development of the human ear. Laryngoscope 74:1160–1171.

Engström, H. 1958. On the double innervation of the sensory epithelia of the inner ear. Acta Otolaryngologica 49:109–118.

Engström, H. 1960. The cortilymph, the third lymph of the inner ear. Acta Morphologica Neerlando-Scandinavia.

Engström, H., H. W. Ades and J. E. Hawkins, Jr. 1965. Cellular pattern, nerve structures, and fluid spaces of the organ of Corti. Contributions to Sensory Physiology.

Fant, G. 1960. Acoustic Theory of Speech Production. Gravenhage: Mouton & Co.

Fisch, U. and G. U. Schulthess. 1963. Electromyographic studies on the human stapedial muscle. Acta Otolaryngologica 56:287–297.

Galombos, R. 1954. Neural mechanisms of audition. Physiological Review 34:497–528.

Galombos, R. 1956. Suppression of auditory nerve activity by stimulation of different fibers to the cochlea. Journal of Neurophysiology 19:424–437.

Galombos, R. 1966. Neuroanatomy and Physiology of the Auditory System. Short Course, 42nd Annual Convention, American Speech and Hearing Association.

Gernandt, B. E. and H. W. Ades. 1964. Spinal motor responses to acoustic stimulation. Experimental Neurology 10:52–66.

Graves, G. O. and L. F. Edwards. 1944. The eustachian tube: a review of its descriptive, microscopic, topographic and clinical anatomy. Archives of Otolaryngology 39:359–397.

Greenwood, D. D. and N. Maruyama. 1965. Excitatory and inhibitory response areas of auditory neurons in the cochlear nucleus. Journal of Neurophysiology 28:863–892.

Harty, M. 1964. The joints of the middle ear. Zeitschrift für Mikroskopisch-Anatomishe Forschung 71:24–31.

Hilding, A. C. 1952. Studies on the otic labyrinth: (1) On the origin and insertation of the tectorial membrane. Annals of Otology, Rhinology, and Laryngology 61:354–370.

Hilding, D. A. 1961. The protective value of the stapedius reflex: an experimental study. Transactions of the American Academy of Ophthalmology and Otolaryngology 65:297–307.

Ingelstedt, S. and B. Jonson. 1967. Mechanisms of the gas exchange in the normal human middle ear. Acta Otolaryngologica Supplement 224:452–461.

Ishii, D. and K. Balogh, Jr. 1968. Distribution of efferent nerve endings in the organ of Corti. Acta Otolaryngologica 66:282–288.

Ishii, T., Y. Murakami, and J. Balogh, Jr. 1967. Actylcholinesterase activity in the efferent nerve fibers of the human inner ear. Annals of Otology, Rhinology and Laryngology 76:69–82.

Iurato, S. 1962. Efferent fibers to the sensory cells of Corti's organ. Experimental Cell Research 27:162–164.

Iurato, S. 1962. The sensory cells of the membranous labyrinth. Archives of Otolaryngology 75:312–328.

Katasuki, Y., K. Yanagisawa and J. Kanzaki. 1966. Tetrathylammonium and Tetradotoxin: effects on cochlear potentials. Science 151:1544–1545.

Kiang, N. Y. S., R. R. Pfeiffer, W. B. Warr, and A. S. N. Backus. 1964. Stimulus coding in the cochlear nucleus. Transaction of the American Otological Society 53:35–58.

Kirikae, I. 1963. Physiology of the middle ear. Archives of Otolaryngology 78:317–328.

Linden, G., Band Nordlund, and J. D. Hawking, Jr. 1964. Significance of the stapedius reflex for the understanding of speech. Acta Otolaryngologica Supplement 188:275–279.

Lorento de No, R. 1933. Anatomy of the eighth nerve: the central projection of the nerve endings of the internal ear. Laryngoscope 43:1–38.

Magoun, H. W. 1963. The Waking Brain. Springfield, Ill.: Charles C Thomas.

McCrady, E., Jr. 1938. The embryology of the opossum. American Anatomical Memoir 16. Philadelphia: Wistor Institute of Anatomy and Biology.

Mygind, S. H. 1965, 1965, 1966. Functional Mechanism of the Labyrinthine Epithelium. Archives of Otolaryngology (I) 82:452–461, 1965; 82:587–590, 1965; (III) 83:3–9, 1966.

Naftalin, L. 1965. Some new proposals regarding acoustic transmission and transduction. Cold Spring Harbor Symposia on Quantitative Biology 30:169–180.

Neergaard, E. B., H. D. Anderson, C. C. Hansen, and O. Jepsen. 1954. Experimental studies on sound transmission in the human ear. III: Influence of the stapedius and tensor typanic muscles. Acta Otolaryngologica Supplement 188:280–286.

Nomura, Y. and I. Kirikae. 1967. Innervation of the human cochlea. Annals of Otology, Rhinology, and Laryngology 76:57–68.

Ormerod, F. C. 1961. The metabolism of the cochlear and vestibular end-organs. Journal of Laryngology and Otology 75:562–573.

Patten, B. M. 1953. Human Embryology. New York: Blakiston.

Rasmussen, A. T. 1935. The Principal Nervous Pathway. New York: Macmillan Co.

Rasmussen, G. L. 1946. The olivary peduncle and other fiber projections of the superior olivary complex. Journal of Comparative Neurology 84:141–219.

Ritter, F. N. and M. Lawrence. 1965. A histological and experimental study of cochlea aqueduct pathway in the dull human. Laryngoscope 75:1224–1233.

Sade, J. 1966. Middle ear mucosa. Archives of Otolaryngology 84:137–143.

Scheer, A. A. 1967. Correction of congenital middle ear deformities. Archives of Otolaryngology 85:269–277.

Simmons, F. B., C. J. Mongeon, W. R. Lewis, and D. A. Huntington. 1964. Electrical stimulation of acoustical nerve and inferior colliculus. Archives of Otolaryngology 70:559–567.

Smith, C. A. 1961. Innervation pattern of the cochlea: the internal hair cell. Annals of Otology, Rhinology, and Laryngology 70:504–527.

Smith, C. A. and E. W. Dempsey. 1957. Electron microscopy of the organ of Corti. American Journal of Anatomy 100:337–368.

Spoendlin, H. H. 1962. Ultrastructural features of the organ of Corti. Transactions of the American Otological Society 50:61–82.

Stevens, S. S. and H. Davis. 1938. Hearing. New York: John Wiley.

Tasaki, I. 1957. Hearing. Annual Review of Physiology 19:417–438.

Wever, E. G. and M. Lawrence. 1954. Physiological Acoustics. Princeton, N.J.: Princeton University Press.

Chapter 5

Levels of Communication

SAMUEL G. FLETCHER, Ph.D.

Constant bombardment by a variety of stimuli typifies man's world. His task is to sort this stimuli, classify it as to relevancy, and make selective decisions which will enable him to maintain equilibrium in the surrounding environment. In a general sense, we can say that information concerning the current state of his environment, including results of his own activity, contributes to the ongoing process by which his behavior is organized.

Certain stimuli in the environment arise from other members of the same or closely related species. In this instance new possibilities emerge. The possibility now exists for the individual to have his goals modified by actions of the other and by inducing changes in the other individual's behavior. The process whereby the "matrix of conditional probabilities" is altered when certain information is transmitted between two or more individuals is classified as the communication process. Clearly, communication introduces possibilities of large numbers of interactions which makes it logically impossible to dissociate the various parties in the communication art. They constitute for certain purposes a single goal-directed system. It is within this matrix of communication that the essence of human behavior is imbedded. In practice, communication links persons to persons and, scientifically speaking, this interrelatedness is understood best in terms of communication systems.

The total communication process includes such considerations as cognitive maps reflecting past experience of the communicators, selection of the message to be sent and transmission medium through which the signal will be sent, predictive distortion in the sending and receiving of the particular message pattern and interpretation and reaction to the message. Thus, the entire process of communication becomes inordinately complex. During the past several years interest and information concerning this topic has increased geometrically in the biological, behavioral, and physical sciences and valid theoretical formulations have appeared.

The goal of this chapter is to examine sensory systems in communication, to stratify this information on a maturational scale, and to examine the resultant product as it relates to partial deprivation in the auditory process of a child. By this means the hope is to highlight compensatory avenues which are available to use with hearing impaired individuals.

To establish a point of departure and to permit an orderly set of inferences about the communication phenomena with which we are concerned, the following postulates are suggested:

(1) Individuals will use all sensory systems with which they are endowed for purposes of communication.

In the processes of communicative behavior an individual must respond to a wide variety of stimuli which have differential intensity, frequency, temporal relationships, and behavioral significance (see Table 2.) And all of these

Table 2. Classification and Fundamental Qualities of Sensations

Sensory Categories	Fundamental Qualities
Audition	Sensations of pitch. About 4500 distinguishable *tonalities* may be reduced to a fundamental and a community of harmonics.
Vision	Sensations of hue and brightness. About 100 different shades are distinguishable which seem to be reducible to red, green, and blue.
Kinesthesia-general	Sensations of movements of body parts. These are reducible to *position* and movements of the joints, *strength* of muscle contraction, and *resistance* or tension on the tendons.
Kinesthesia-vestibular	Sensations of body position in space. These are reducible to static positions with respect to gravity and to translation or rotation bodily movements: forward-backward, right-left, above-below.
Tactility-mechanical	Sensations of touch, reducible to contact, pressure, and cutaneous displacement.
Tactility-thermal	Sensations of temperature, reducible to warmth and coldness.
Olfaction	Ill-defined sensations of smell. These seem to be reducible to four to eight fundamental odors.
Gustation	Sensations of taste, reducible to sweet, sour, bitter, and salty.

parameters are constantly shifting in their physical characteristics and their behavioral meaning. In the hierarchies of behavior certain avenues of perception may be expected to take precedence for receiving certain types of stimulus. And certain types of stimuli will take precedence as the focus of attention during any particular communication interchange. A natural concomitant of this diversity is the necessity for simultaneously monitoring different forms and elements of the signals among different sensory avenues. The focus of attention is, therefore, not fixed; rather it must be viewed as a fluctuating or oscillating phenomenon in which quick samples are taken rapidly of different stimuli and of various levels of the stimuli.

(2) Certain sensory avenues have differential communicative significance among different persons and within the same person at particular times.

Communication is an extremely dynamic phenomenon with a rapid rate of change of stimulus levels and of functions which range from transmission, conduction, and reception to evaluation. Those species of animals which are lowest on the phylogenetic scale have, in general, least specialization in their sensory systems. Therefore, they must rely on certain characteristics of the signals which are most critical for the *survival* and *progression* of the species. Higher animals such as man have the capability to process vast amounts of information from many sensory avenues, but still must rank this information as to relative significance to their survival and progression. Therefore, they must allocate central prominence to the one or two sensory avenues which dictate the immediate monitor need. Other avenues may then be used as subsystems which can be monitored periodically.

Communicative behavior of an individual is a reflection of his total physiological integration. Those sensory and motor channels most highly developed may be expected to be those which carry the main load for generating and receiving communicative information. Accordingly, the characteristics and comparative prominence of the sensory organs is an important consideration in the communication process.

(3) The nature of the communication information will determine to a large extent the sensory channel of reception.

The lowest forms of life are apparently capable of sensing only environmental signals generated in near proximity to the organism. Detection of chemicals is particularly important to them in mating, reproduction, nutrition, and many other significant aspects of their lives. Specialized receptors with great chemical sensitivity develop very early in the evolution of animals (Beidler, 1961). Their responses to immediate environmental signals tend to be stereotyped and narrow in scope, however (Case, 1966, p. 1).

As the phylogenetic scale is ascended, increasing potential for monitoring distant events becomes possible. This ability to sense distance phenomena permits greater variety in selective tuning to specific types of signals and greatly influences adaptive responses to the information received. For example, chemoreceptors such as the nose can be used by a person to maintain awareness of local events (i.e., the perfumed fragrance of a partner) while he is at the same time attending to a verbal message received through other modalities at a distance. If a proximity message becomes of increased importance, the central focus of attention can shift to it, scan its contents, and act accordingly. A principal thesis of the present model is that early organization of communication will tend to develop from proximal somasthetic sensations (i.e., cutaneous, proprioceptive, and visceral sensation) and chemoreception and gradually extend to sensing events at a distance. The lower systems are thus postulated to form the foundation for later responses to information received through the distance modalities of sight and hearing. This order of maturation is consistent with the orienting behavior of many vertebrates in other maturation patterns such as in perceptual development.

Despite recognition of a variety of sensory modalities used in communication, fundamental consideration of the communication act, especially in the human, has tended to ignore all avenues except vision and audition. This is likely because of the preeminence of these functions in adult communicative behavior of man. The present discussion will diverge in a fundamental way from this orientation. The model presented has special relevancy to residual forms of human communication which can be tapped for work with persons having sensory deprivation and seems to have powerful application in integrating our understanding of the total communication process in that the unique contribution of each sensory system is given appropriate recognition.

Figure 1 depicts an integrated model of communication which incorporates the various sensory avenues and suggests a pattern of maturation within the sensory systems. The scientific principle of parsimony decrees that one should explain as much of a model or concept as possible by the employment of as few terms, symbols, concepts, or formulas as possible. (Lastrucci, 1963, p. 14). With this in mind the following definitions of the terms of the model are offered.

Haptic communication.   Communication by means of signals generated during direct contact or immediate proximity of organisms. The sensory modalities through which haptic signals are received are touch, pressure, smell and perhaps taste.

Iterative communication.   Communication by means of signals characterized by vibratory strings of impulses which have a stable oscillation pattern. Any kinesthetic sensor may be used to receive iterative signals as long as it is able to detect the stable rhythm pattern among the impulses of an oscillation sequence.

Kinesic communication.   Communication by means of signals generated by movement and received through vision. These movements may be either in isolation or in a sequential activity. If they are in a sequential activity, they must be more than a mere oscillation of essentially the same movement.

Paralanguage communication.   Communication by means of unitary, noncoalescent sound signals generated from the nonarticulated vocal tract and

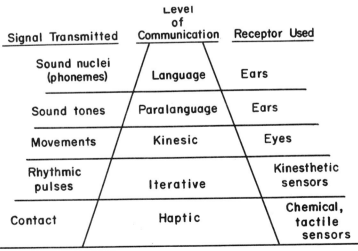

FIG. 1.   Systems of communication arranged in a maturational order. Haptic communication represents the lowest level.

received through audition. "Non-coalescent" means that the individual acoustic units or chunks of sounds are not combinable to modify or multiply meaning in the basic units. Within certain limits a paralanguage signal maintains symbolic meaning, irrespective of its immediate contextual environment.

Language communication. Communication by means of sounds generated by the articulated vocal tract and arranged in ordered, conventional sequences to form morphemes and words. These signals are received through audition. The articulatory movements impinging upon the phonic stream produces sets of phonetic units which by their distinctive features can be arranged into phonemic groups of perceptually equivalent sounds. These sounds are then sequentially combined in certain permitted sequences or acoustic strings to generate an infinite variety of meanings. Thus language and only language is released from the physical event, communication event linkage, which tends to characterize all other levels of communication.

These preliminary definitions now allow us to explore characteristic patterns of development and functional significance of these five systems of communication in greater depth.

A fundamental axiom of our discussion of the communication system used at any moment is that it will be determined first by the specific receptor systems which are available to be brought into action by the stimuli, and second by the relative maturation of the organism.

The most rudimentary system is seen to be that used for haptic communication. The mechanical receptors to sense, touch, and pressure and the chemical receptors to sense, odors, and tastes are well developed in essentially all species since they represent the final protection of an organism in a hostile environment. They also relay information as to sources of gratification of the bodily needs.

Haptic Communication

The lowest forms of animal life begin and end their experience on the haptic level of communication. This level also seems to form a fundamental stratum for communication of higher animals including man.

Spitz (1965, pp. 45–52) notes that by the eighth day of life an infant will turn his head to any person lifting him, but recognizes the cue of foods only when he is hungry. This cue must be tactile. In other words the stimulus must be placed in his mouth. Toward the beginning of the second month, movement of an adult toward the baby will cause him to "become quiet, open his mouth, or make sucking movements" if he is hungry. Two or three weeks later when the infant perceives a human face he follows its movements with concentrated attention and he "listens" intently to human sounds. The human face and voice have thus become associated with relief from displeasure and experience of pleasure. It may be seen that rudimentary haptic communications established through contact and close proximity have assumed symbolic significance and have begun to open the door to higher systems of communication.

Similar significance of haptic communication may be shown in other species. Some animals have tactile receptors of exquisite sensitivity. Receptors in the legs of honey bees are so sensitive that they could almost detect movements of particles in the insect's blood. Male moths can detect the odor of females with their antennae at distances up to 5 miles (Frings and Frings, 1964). Scent seems to be the major channel for identification of the species in nearly all animals. Tastes are not used as much in communication.

The importance of contact to the infant is evident in many ways. The close cuddling during feeding, the tendency to place things at the nose and in the mouth for tactile perception and exploration, the closeness of the young child to its mother in any condition of threat are all examples.

As a person matures, reliance on haptic communication is decreased, but still maintained in certain communication acts. For example, part of an initial greeting in the American culture is the handshake. And the pattern of the handshake itself is prescribed. It must include a firm squeeze. If such pressure is not present an interpretation of aloofness or coldness is given. The continuing desire for haptic communication is also shown by young children hanging onto their teacher's hand or pressing close to her desk as she urges them to "stand back." Dr. James Bosma, a very observant experimental pediatrician, once observed to the writer that if a child were unwilling to be taken by the hand and led to the examination room, chances of good rapport during the examination are markedly reduced.

Forms and patterns of haptic communication are rather well documented in other cultures. Even parts of the body involved in such communication is seen as significant. For example, in dances of India, the fingertips which represent the far extremity of the body are equivocated to intellectual functions whereas the palm is "emotional." The intensity of emotional content is accentuated as contact increasingly approaches the body from the palmar side of the hand. The validity of such interpretation is suggested by the fact that if one person wishes to get the attention of another but is uncertain as to the response of the other, he will tap the person lightly with his fingertips. If the status of communication is more congenial, the palm of the hand, or even an arm around the shoulder, will be used. It may be seen that considerable information is told about a person by the way he uses haptic communication. The back-slapping, hand-shaking politician certainly seems to sense the power of this communication system!

Iterative Communication

The system of communication which seems to emerge next is iterative. This system relies on a set, constant rate, rhythm pattern. Again it is observed in adult-child behavior from early infancy in such activities as patting the child during attempts to soothe it, rocking motions, high repetitiveness of the vocalizations. In all of these acts the overriding characteristic is a set oscillation pattern. Similar oscillations are evident in the child's early behavior which is highly repetitive and stereotyped. Essentially all signals used by insects and the lowest forms of animal life are endowed with this oscillatory characteristic. Alexander (1957) observed that the chief structural variation in insect sounds is the rhythm and rate of pulsation. The sudden cry of an animal when in mortal conflict does not have this rhythm content and is universally interpreted by other members of the species, and often other species as well, as acutely threatening.

Residuums of iterative communication may also be found in adult human communication efforts. Again, the initial greeting may be used to exemplify this behavior. Not only do people take each other's hands and squeeze, but they also accompany this with a rhythmic pumping pattern. The tendency of children to make certain movements over and over, to rhythmically shake their head as a gesture of refusal, to babble long strings of the same sounds, to play with rhyming words are all seen to be stratifications of the basic iterative communication which seems to underpin each new form of communication in its early stage of development.

Kinesic Communication

Kinesic communication is linked with movement which has greater variety than that described in iterative communication and is now linked with a special telereceptive sense, namely, vision. In reporting his findings on infant development Spitz (1965, pp. 65-69) places great emphasis on the fact that during nursing the infant stares at the mother's face. In this process, contact perception blends with distance perception and with its link to the feeding act mother's facial gestures assume high potential for reward. Gesell and Ilg (1937) note the infant predisposition to follow movements of the human face and explain that this happens because the human face is linked with numerous situations of expectancy. Spitz and Wolf (1946) made a detailed study of the infant smiling response. They noted that in the third month of life an infant begins gestures beyond the facial region. Very early he begins to arch his back and later learns to reach toward his mother's hands when they are extended. He also develops increasing skill in his own use of body gesture signals. A visual form of sign language is observed in all children as a stage in maturation of the kinesic system of communication. These movements are later molded into the highly sophisticated adult system of gestures in which a mere suggestion of the earlier movement is present. These are shown by such gestures as a slight depression of the corner of the mouth, a small shrug of the shoulder, and a slight outward push of the hand all of which rather subtlety represent rejection. The "wave 'bye 'bye" becomes a slight upward or outward gesture of an upraised hand.

Paralanguage Communication

Paralanguage is the first form of vocal communication to be considered. The principal characteristic of this system is that the vocal units tend to carry one and only one meaning. The total system can be rather restricted and crude as in the case of the Uinta ground squirrel which has only five acoustical signals to alert other members of its clan, or they can be extensive and remarkably precise as in the 29 acoustic signals of the vervat monkey that are used to communicate at least 20 different messages (Struhsaker, 1967). Tembrock (1963) observes that species which live in the open fields tend to use optical signals predominantly whereas inhabitants of the woods emphasize acoustical contact. He notes furthermore that sounds which are used for social communication seem to form four main groups: (1) alarm calls, (2) voice contact calls which keep the family unit or social group together, (3) group sounds with collective utterances within a society such as the "howling in unison" of the canids, and (4) sounds expressing a special mood. This last group of sounds tends to be found especially in highly differential societies with a rich, well-developed range of sound forms. The expressions of mood are highly variable and show many shades of mood. For example, the sounds of the primate, *Pan*, can be divided into four groups by mood: (1) Aggressive sounds (barking), (2) Sounds of ease and comfort (soft, nearly soundless barking), (3) Sounds of fear and pain (howling), and Sounds of excitement (very variable with oo-oo sound.)

The paralanguage sounds are typified by unity of meaning. That is, they cannot be placed in any sequence which markedly alters the basic meaning. For example, the snarling of the dog which means defensive threatening is not added to a bark which means aggressiveness to arrive at a more complex message.

Many paralanguage signals are found in human communication. Before a child has reached his first birthday he can receive and generate sounds in all four of the main paralanguage categories. That is, he cries out to signal alarm, he "calls" to other members of the family not in his view, he "enters" the social units around him by babbling in the same melody patterns as speakers in a group, and he expresses an increasing number of moods through his vocal patterning. As he matures the use of these forms of communication continue to be refined so that small nuances of feeling can be portrayed in the tonal qualities of his vocalizations.

Language Communication

It is interesting to note that all four of the lower communication systems discussed—haptic, iterative, kinesic, and paralanguage—tend to be rather universal in their function. That is, they are essentially independent of the particular race or culture in which the individual is raised. This characteristic is, of course, not present in language.

Language is the highest level of communication and one which only man has achieved. Three significant differences exist between language and the lower systems of communication as a group: First, a set of sound complexes, termed *phonemes*, exists in language as perceptually unique acoustic building blocks employed in any and all language acts. Second, a series of rules exists which dictate how the phonemes may be combined into words and phrases. Third, precise meanings are attached to the words and phrases according to the way they are ordered with respect to each other. In other words, language is an integrated nuclei system which provides high flexibility and unique power to transmit subtle nuances of meaning, but this is at the expense of a rather imposing set of rules which only man has been able to master. The language level of communication is considered in detail in other chapters of this book.

Application of the foregoing material concerning the five levels of communication to the hearing impaired person must be done somewhat cautiously. First we must recognize that auditory impairment itself poses problems of sensory deprivation. The work of Hebb and his associates investigating early sensory deprivation in animals has shown that an impoverished sensory environment with a reduced set of opportunities for manipulation and discrimination, tends to produce an adult with reduced ability to discriminate among sensory stimuli, stunted strategies for coping with problems, less desire for exploratory behavior, and a notably reduced tendency to draw inferences that organize the disparate events of the environment. Furthermore, unless some forms of stimulation take place before a certain time in life, the ability to make full use of sensory information seems to be intractably changed. The role of communication in relieving these effects of deprivation has not been investigated.

Another consideration in application of concepts concerning levels of communication is that maturation seems to progress across the categories of stratification. For example, a child's negative responses to food offered him seems to progress as follows: When the young infant does not want to eat something offered him, he avoids ingestion by tight closure of his lips. Thus, rejection is made to contact. This is a form of haptic communication. Later, he learns to turn his head from the food to avoid contact with his mouth. This is higher symbolically but is still haptic level. He then learns sequentially to flail rather repetitively in the general direction of the unwanted offering (iterative), to knock the food away with a rather precise movement (kinesic), to combine this gesture with a nondiscriminate but meaningful vocalization of dislike (paralanguage), and finally to say "no" or even to specify his degree of rejection in a sentence (language). If any of these interactions between the person offering the food and the child are unsuccessful in removing the threat, the child will tend to revert gradually toward lower and lower forms of communication until his goal is achieved or until he acquieses. Thus, the lower systems of communication seem to serve an important function as the substructure upon which each succeeding communication system is built.

Finally, communication seems to mature within as well as among communication categories. The limits of such maturation would be predictably lower for such categories as haptic or iterative communication than for the higher categories because they are cruder systems. Nevertheless, the hearing impaired child may profitably be observed closely to note the relative sophistication of his communication efforts within each of the sublanguage levels. The relative maturation as the integration of these different levels may provide considerable insight as to the potential for acquisition of useable language. It may even be that the relative enrichment of these lower symbolic systems will dictate to some extent the proficiency with which communication on the highest symbolic level is developed and mastered. Such a possibility would be of critical significance to linguistic development where hearing impairment is a factor. Whether these lower systems are viewed as supportive to general communication efficiency or as essential to ultimate performance in language certainly deserves serious attention in the total program of the hard of hearing child.

References

Alexander, R. D. 1957. Sound production and associated behavior in insects. Ohio J. Sci. 57:101–113.

Beidler, L. M. 1961. Biophysical approaches to taste. American Scientist 49:421–431.

Case, J. 1966. Sensory Mechanisms. New York: Macmillan.

Frings, H. and M. Frings. 1964. Animal Communication. New York: Blaisdell.

Gesell, A. and F. L. Ilg. 1937. Feeding Behavior of Insects: A Pediatric Approach to the Mental Hygiene of Early Life. Philadelphia: Lippincott.

Lastrucci, C. L. 1963. The Scientific Approach. Cambridge: Schenkman.

Spitz, R. A. 1965. The First Year of Life. New York: Int. Univ. Press.

Spitz, R. A. and K. M. Wolf. 1946. The smiling response. Genet. Psych. Monogr. 34:57–125.

Struhsaker, T. T. 1967. Auditory communication among Vervet monkeys (Carcopithecus aethiops). In S. A. Altmann (Ed.) Social Communication Among Primates. Chicago: Univ. of Chicago Press. Pp. 281–324.

Tembrock, G. 1963. Acoustic behavior of mammals. In R. G. Busnel (Ed.) Acoustic Behavior of Animals. New York: Elsevier. Pp. 751–786.

Chapter 6

Acoustic Phonetics

SAMUEL G. FLETCHER, Ph.D.

Most acoustic phenomena in nature, such as speech and music, are of momentary duration. They occur in a medium which is typically already in motion; therefore, they must compete amidst many vibrations with varying amounts of pattern similarity. The space boundaries into which such vibrations are introduced are usually highly irregular so that the sounds themselves are modified even as they are directed toward a listener. The relative intensities of the sounds are also fluctuating dramatically because of the many sources of sound in the environment. These and many other factors serve to make the task of listening a demanding one.

An acoustic event can be described completely if the following three parameters of the total event are known: frequency of the sound vibrations, intensity of the vibrations, and the duration of the event. In actuality, the product of these three parameters determines our ability to perceive the sound. If any of them is zero, according to the particular listener's ability to sense it, sound is zero.

Each listener has a finite set of ranges in frequency, intensity, and duration of sound which that listener can sense. For example, a dog can, in general, detect higher frequencies than can a man, bats can respond to sounds not perceptible to dogs. In this sense hearing impairment is seen to be a relative term. Hearing efficiency must ultimately be couched in terms of a person's capability to accomplish his own purposes in life.

By definition, the hard of hearing person is unable to detect certain sound waves that others are able to hear. Thus, he receives a different acoustic image than do his more richly endowed colleagues. When this deficiency is imposed on the already difficult task described above, it is little wonder that the hearing impaired person is frequently less than successful in unraveling his acoustical world when he is left to do so with little more than being "wired for sound."

The purpose of this chapter is to review some of the basic acoustic principles that must be known to study any auditory event and to tie this information to the phonetic system used by man to receive, decode, encode, and transmit spoken messages. We will be uniquely concerned with the physics of sound in a biologic environment and with the acoustics of sound in a verbal environment.

Bioacoustic Fundamentals

The production of speech involves a series of physiological operations each of which leaves its residual imprint on the final acoustic signal. This process may be viewed as a combination of transductions and modulations of the breath stream as it flows through the vocal tract. "Transductions" refers to basic changes in the flow patterns and resultant acoustic characteristics of the stream as it moves along the channel. "Modulations" reflect the secondary shifts within and among the frequency, intensity, and time parameters of sound as a result of the transductions and unique transmission characteristics within different parts of the tract.

As we trace the air stream through the channels of the vocal tract, four major energy transductions and one principal source of modulation are revealed. These may be classified as production of soundless hiatuses, periodic sounds, impulse noises, frictional noises, and modulation through cavity resonances. Each of these categories is worthy of careful consideration.

One of our most important means of studying the acoustic structure of the speech wave is through use of the sound spectrograph (Potter et al., 1947; Fant, 1966; Cooper, 1965). This instrument uses a variable filter tuned across a frequency range much as a radio is tuned to progressive frequency bands to find out what is available on the different stations. Either a narrow band (45 Hz) or a wide band (300 Hz) filter may be used. Figure 2 is a wide band sonagram of a person saying "Many are called, but few are chosen." Frequency is on the vertical axis and time is along the horizontal axis. Intensity is shown by the shade of darkness of the markings. The various acoustic characteristics enumerated are identified on the picture.

The Soundless Hiatus

A soundless hiatus (H) is a space inserted into the acoustic chain of speech by momentarily stopping the breath stream or by reducing breath pressure to the point where sound becomes, for all practical purposes, inaudible.

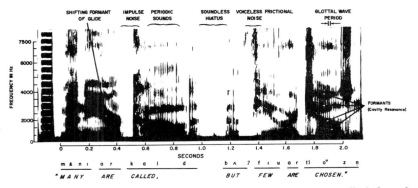

FIG. 2. Sound spectrogram of the sentence "Many are called but few are chosen" using wide band (300 Hz) analyzing filters.

Periodic Sound

Periodic sound (*P*) arises from vibratory motion patterns in the audible range that are repeated in equal intervals of time. The "period" itself is the time required to complete one full oscillation from an equilibrium position through positive pressure, past equilibrium through negative pressure, and back to equilibrium again. The number of oscillations per second is recorded in Hertz (Hz).

In the human voice periodicity is generated when the air stream is forced through a flutter valve, the larynx, and thereby segmented into quasiperiodic pulses. For a given speaker at a particular moment in time a principal focus of attention in laryngeal efficiency is the dynamics of laryngeal tension. The extra effort given by hearing impaired persons to speak intelligibly is often reflected in general tension throughout the vocal tract. At the laryngeal level such tension may be reflected in elevated pitch levels during their speaking efforts.

Movements of the human vocal folds are much more intricate than those of a simple mechanical oscillator such as a tuning fork. In actuality a series of submovements are superimposed upon the basic oscillation of the folds. This superimposition of partial movements upon the fundamental motion has the characteristic that all of the smaller motions are even multiples or harmonics of the fundamental; therefore, the total pattern is called *complex harmonic motion* or simply a *harmonic series*.

The acoustic manifestation of the complex harmonic motion of the vocal folds is superposition of a series of tones as even multiples of a basic fundamental frequency (f_o). The (f_o) serves as a carrier wave for the complete series and is perceived as the pitch of the voice. The remainder of the tones in the harmonic series (f_x) provide the unique perceptual qualities of a particular speaker's voice. The laryngeal tone is vastly different from that which emerges from the speaker's lips, however.

A curved line connecting the tops of a harmonic series, as in Figure 2, is called an *envelope* of the spectrum. When an envelope is drawn, the harmonics inside it are referred to as its "fine structure."

The slope of the acoustic envelope is an important consideration. The average slope is about −13 db per octave. This means that the acoustic energy in a particular harmonic is dependent upon its distance from the f_o. Although an infinite number of harmonics is theoretically generated with each glottal pulse, most of the higher ones may be ignored because their energy levels are too low to influence perception of speech unless they are strongly reinforced by resonances in the vocal tract.

Frictional Noise

Frictional noises (*F*) arise whenever structures along the vocal channel are brought close enough together to form a small opening or constriction through which the air stream is continuously forced. Frictional noises can be generated at the glottis of the larynx or at any other place in the vocal tract where structures can be brought close together without closing the passageway completely. These constrictions, often referred to as "hiss" sources, are acoustically observed as having a wide range of frequencies randomly spaced in the acoustic spectrum with no harmonic relationships to each other.

Impulse Noise

Impulse noises (I) are the result of complete, momentary stoppages of the air stream. Three phases may be identified in the generation of impulse noises: placement of the articulators so they stop the air stream, buildup of air pressure behind the valving point, and abrupt release of the compressed air. The phases are referred to as implosion, compression, and explosion, respectively.

The acoustic effect of the implosion and compression phases of impulse noise production is to create a brief period of *pseudosilence* in the output. The explosive release of the air during the third phase is in the form of a transient sound burst with a very abrupt rise time. This noise burst contrasts sharply with the preceding pseudosilence and makes this class of sound readily identifiable.

Cavity Resonance

Cavity resonance modulations reflect the fact that a body which is free to vibrate will have a certain resonant frequency of oscillation. The resonant response of a cavity consists of a range of frequencies clustered around a central peak *frequency* or *pole* (House and Stevens, 1958). The total resonance band around a particular pole is referred to as a *formant*. On each side of the pole the formant slopes off to approach *zero* intensity. The zeroes are called *antiresonances*. These are regions in the spectrum where the cavities actually oppose the vibrational movements being transmitted.

The formants of the vocal tract can be approximated from the theory of standing waves in a tube (Chiba and Kajiyama, 1958). The formants are raised or lowered according to the point where the tongue constricts the passageway. By "tuning" the passageway we can control the poles and zeros of sound passing through it. The shifting relative intensities and peak frequencies of the formants, F_x, when resonant cavities are "tuned" by adjustment of their relative diameters, is seen to be analogous to variations in the fundamental frequency, f_o, achieved by adjusting the tensions in the vocal folds.

We are now ready to consider the total function of the vocal tract as a unified whole. The total vocal process is schematized in Figure 3 by means of an electroacoustic analog model. The symbols P, F, I, and H in the model represent periodic sound, fricative noise, impulse noise, and voiceless hiatus energy transductions, respectively. Cavity resonance transductions are represented by transfer filter functions T_1–T_{17} at different loci along the channel.

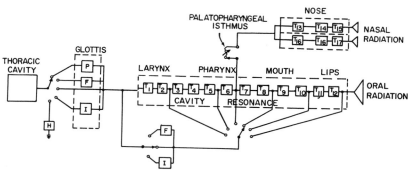

Fig. 3. Block diagram representing an electroacoustic analog model of the speech processes.

The number of filter blocks shown is not intended to be a formal representation of specific resonant cavities. Rather, the series is included to show multiple coupling potentials within the total system. The final emitted signal is thus a composite of the "shaping" of the air stream by all transducers along the vocal tract.

The electroacoustic model has been set in a switching position to generate a periodic tone at the glottis. The other three options at this level are to produce a fricative noise, an impulse noise, a voiceless hiatus, or to simply pass the air stream through the glottis with no resultant sound. The signal from these possible transductions then passes into the larynx, pharynx, mouth, and/or nose for cavity resonance. A parallel route is shown for part of the energy to be deflected into frictional or impulse noise transducers at a higher anatomical level and thence back into the resonators. Entrance into the nasal cavity may be either through an open isthmus between the palate and pharynx or partially obstructed by palate to pharynx approximations, as symbolized by a variable resistor. Infinite resistance from complete palate-pharynx apposition is also possible.

As the switches are presently set, the periodic tone would meet a deflection at about $\frac{2}{3}$ of the distance from the glottis to the lips. The palatal valve is closed. This arrangement would result in production of a sound resembling the /ɛ/ vowel.

Some additional clarification may be helpful with respect to configuration of the acoustic envelope when a laryngeal tone is coupled to the resonant cavities above the larynx. Recall that the complex harmonic series from the larynx has a high frequency drop off of about -12db per octave. If they met the constant diameter assumption, the resonating cavities would have formant poles at approximately 500, 1500, 2500 . . . Hz. When these transducers shown in Figure 4A are coupled together, their energies would summate to produce an envelope like that in Figure 4B. Thus, the envelope from the laryngeal tone would be molded by the series of poles and zeroes added through resonant transductions. The harmonics in the antiresonance areas of the spectrum would give up their energy to adjoining frequencies whose wavelengths fit the configuration of the cavities along the vocal tract. This molding would

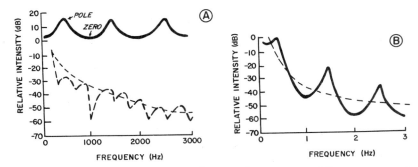

Fig. 4.   Illustration of coupling laryngeal tone to a 17 cm. resonant cavity with a constant cross-sectional area. 3A shows the two functions separately displayed on a single graph. In 3B the two functions are combined. The solid line depicts the resultant configuration of the envelope. The radiation constant is not considered.

continue from cavity to cavity until the formant characteristics of the total resonant channel were imprinted upon the harmonic pattern of the glottal tone. Harmonics in the laryngeal tone which were too low in intensity to be perceptible may in this way be accentuated by cavity resonance and become important components of speech.

Biophonetic Fundamentals

Having developed basic bioacoustic principles as building blocks of human sound, we are now ready to apply them to the phonetic structure of speech. The format of this discussion will be to sketch a series of comparisons between phonetic sound classes. That is, sets of acoustic data will be presented by which a particular class of sounds may be acoustically differentiated from other sets of sound classes insofar as present knowledge permits. In these comparisons we will rely upon what is known about how the human listener uses acoustic information to attack the problem of speech recognition. The present discussion of necessity excludes consideration of a great mass of a priori information used by a listener to make decision about the likelihood of certain phonetic possibilities. Such information includes listener knowledge about what sequences of sounds and words are permitted in his native language (Whorf, 1940), what are the "logical" words that a speaker would be likely to be saying in the particular speaking context(Rapoport, 1953, 1967), what the speaker seems to be "intending" to say (Searle, 1967), and the communicative function of the language he is using (Tannenbaum, 1955).

In 1963, Fry suggested that human recognition of selected phonemes in speech occurs by scanning their acoustic properties and, on the basis of "either-or" decisions, eliminating competing possibilities. These clusters of acoustic specifications were used to define certain *discriminants* which were felt to be the basis of the human ability to separate acoustic stimuli and define certain sets as denoting a particular phonetic element as present or absent at a particular instant in time. That is, if certain acoustic criterion were met, the human listener would have a high probability of selecting one and only one phoneme from other competing possibilities. This framework will be used in the following pages.

Acoustic cues embedded in a particular utterance or in a set of utterances are always relative to each other and to the total signal. Many acoustic differences in frequency, intensity, and duration may be detected by the human listener, sorted out, and excluded as irrelevant or nondistinctive to the task of phonetic discrimination. Other characteristics may distinctively identify a sound pattern. Identification of these distinctive characteristics and their internal relationships to each other is the fundamental goal of this chapter. The acoustic data summarized in the following tables has been limited to that which has been shown to have phonetic relevancy and should be recognized as a very preliminary attempt to unify this still developing body of information.

Eight discriminants will be discussed beginning with contrasts between vowels and consonants and progressing through increasingly finer differentiations among phonetic categories. In general each later discrimination will extend from and subsume the acoustic criteria in the initial categories. For example, within the "consonant" category which itself has certain categorical differences from "vowels" are sounds which have periodicity whereas in others this characteristic is absent. Periodicity, therefore, represents a possible discriminant for consonant sounds. Hearing impaired persons may be expected to have difficulties in discriminating sounds with acoustic contrasts that are too fine to be detected by their auditory system.

Discriminant I. Consonants vs. Vowels

The most fundamental differentiation among sounds of the English language is by consonant and vowel class. Table 3 summarizes the acoustic contrasts between these two phonetic categories.

Examination of Table 3 indicates that periodicity is a constant factor in vowel production and is variably present in consonants. In this classification a sound is interpreted as "periodic" only if it does not contain prominent fric-

Table 3. Acoustic Contracts Between Vowel and Consonant Phonetic Categories

| Category | Transductions | Modulation Characteristics | | |
		Frequency	Intensity	Duration
Vowels	P	Energy concentrated in formants	20–45 db ave. phonetic power	130–360 msec.
Consonants	$\pm P \pm F \pm I$	Broad band, rising F_1 in consonant-vowel transitions.	0.01–16 db ave. phonetic power	20–150 msec.

tional or impulse noises. Thus, it may have periodicity without being classed as periodic. This is shown in Table 4. The periodic-aperiodic contrast allows us to separate all consonants except nasals and glides into a different group than the vowels. Whispered and very breathy speech efforts are also excluded from this rule. The fact that some friction may be present in tense vowels such as /i/ and /u/ is additionally disregarded.

Table 4. Sounds Classified According to Periodicity

Periodic Sounds	Sounds with Periodicity Mixed with Friction and Impulse Noise	Aperiodic Sounds
i, I, ɛ, æ, a	b, d, g	p, t, k
ɑ, ɔ, o, U, u	v, z, t, ʒ	f, s, θ, ʃ
ə, ɜ, ɚ, ɝ, ʌ	dʒ	tʃ
m, n, ŋ		
l, r, w, j		ʍ

The coupled effects of periodicity and cavity resonance are reflected in fine acoustic modulation differences in frequency, intensity, and duration of the vowels. The acoustic energy in vowels is concentrated in low formant bands while the frequency distribution of the consonants tends to be spread throughout the frequency range although it is somewhat more concentrated in the higher frequencies.

The average measured characteristics for vowel frequency and intensity modulations are shown in Table 5. The data concerning the fundamental frequencies, formant frequencies, and formant amplitudes are from the Peterson and Barney (1952) study of 33 men, 28 women, and 15 children. The relative formant amplitudes are from Sacia and Beck (1926) in which the strongest vowel /ɔ/ was arbitrarily assigned a zero decibel level. The three formant bandwidths are the average of three sets given by Fant (1962a). One set was his own, one was from House and Stevens (*JSHR*, 1958), and one was by Dunn (1961). The bandwidths are not as accurate as the other data since they vary widely among different speakers (Dunn, 1963).

A sliding reference system is used for vowel perception. This is shown by the different formant values for men, women, and children, respectively. The typical listener has no difficulty in adjusting his vowel acoustic framework to different speakers even when they are speaking almost simultaneously.

Consonant–vowel transitional cues were shown by Delattre and others at the Haskins Laboratory (1955) to be important in the perception of consonants. They noted that when the second formant is straight, the first formant must have "some degree" of rising transition to the steady state level of the vowel following it, if a consonant were heard at all. In the case of voiced stops the consonant impression was found to be stronger as the first-formant transition was larger.

While formants provide the primary basis for distinguishing among vowels, and the transitional cues influence consonant-vowel discrimination,

Table 5. *Average Measured Characteristics for Vowel Frequency and Intensity Modulations*

Speaker		Fund. Freq. f_o(Hz)	Formant Freq. (Hz)			F Bandwith (Hz)			F Amplitude (dB)		
			F_1	F_2	F_3	F_1	F_2	F_3	F_1	F_2	F_3
i	M	136	270	2290	3010	54	55	170	−4	−24	−28
	w	235	310	2790	3310						
	Ch	272	370	3200	3720						
I	M	135	390	1990	2550	53	69	113	−3	−23	−27
	w	232	430	2480	3070						
	Ch	269	530	2730	3600						
ε	M	130	530	1840	2480	48	69	101	−2	−17	−24
	w	223	610	2330	2990						
	Ch	260	690	2610	3570						
æ	M	127	660	1720	2410	63	81	126	−1	−12	−22
	w	210	860	2050	2850						
	Ch	251	1010	2320	3320						
ɑ	M	124	730	1090	2440	54	57	93	−1	−5	−28
	w	212	850	1220	2810						
	Ch	256	1030	1370	3170						
ɔ	M	129	570	840	2410	43	47	68	0	−7	−34
	w	216	590	920	2710						
	Ch	263	680	1060	3180						
U	M	137	440	1020	2240	40	44	62	−1	−12	−34
	w	232	470	1160	2680						
	Ch	276	560	1410	3310						
u	M	141	300	870	2240	50	49	77	−3	−19	−43
	w	231	370	950	2670						
	Ch	274	430	1170	3260						
ʌ	M	130	640	1190	2390	52	57	89	−1	−10	−27
	w	221	760	1400	2780						
	Ch	261	850	1590	3360						
ɜˑ	M	133	490	1350	1690	44	58	64	−5	−15	−20
	w	218	500	1640	1960						
	Ch	261	560	1820	2160						

laryngeal excitation also affects vowel detection. Wendahl (*JASA*, 1959) showed that when formant positions were held constant while fundamental frequency was shifted, the vowel value judgments varied with different fundamental voice frequencies. Fry et al. (1962) showed that the phonetic context of a vowel strongly influenced vowel perception whereas Eimas (1962) had shown that the effect of context upon the consonants /b,d,g/ was much less than with vowels.

Intensity modulation. Intensity modulations show general marked differences between consonants and vowels. Fletcher (1953) arrived at mean-

ingful intensity contrasts by establishing auditory thresholds for correct identification of certain words, then observing the attenuation in db required to
make the different sounds in these words inaudible. The *average phonetic
power* for sounds thus obtained are summarized in Table 6. The phonetic

Table 6. Average Phonetic Power in db for Vowels and Consonants

Vowels			Consonants					
ɔ 45	o 25	ɛ 22	r 16.00	ʃ 1.80	k 0.30	ʃ —	t —	
ɑ 41	ʌ 24	I 20	ŋ 12.57	tʃ 1.40	t 0.10	ʒ —	θ —	
u 26	e 23	i 20	m 11.67	s 0.90	d 0.08	g —		
			n 11.20	z 0.70	f 0.08	b —		
				dʒ 0.50	v 0.03	p —		

powers of the nasal consonants /m,n,ŋ/ were obtained from data provided by
House (1957) and adjusted to Fletcher's reference levels.[*]

The general intensity of vowels when measured by average phonetic
power is clearly higher than that of the consonants. This difference is especially evident in those consonants that do not have strong periodicity.

Duration modulation. Duration differences between vowels and consonants are somewhat variable. Fletcher (1953), House (1961), and Peterson
and Lehiste (1960) have all published data pertinent to the duration of vowels
in a consonant-vowel-consonant (CVC) environment. These data are compared in Table 7. Although Fletcher's data show somewhat longer duration

Table 7. Vowel Duration in CVC Environment, in Milliseconds

ɑ	305[*]	295[**]	265[†]	i	340	220	207
æ	295	295	284	ɛ	220	205	204
ɝ	330	260	256	ʌ(ə)	280	195	181
ɔ	290	280	250	U	250	170	163
oᵘ	325	270	222	I	210	160	161
u	350	240	235				
eɪ	295	265	200				

[*] Fletcher (1953).
[**] House (1961).
[†] Peterson and Lehiste (1960).

than the other two, they are all in the 200 to 300 msec. range. Some of the
differences among the three studies may be attributed to the different phonetic
environments in which the vowels were placed. House and Fairbanks (1953)
found that different consonant environments have a very dramatic effect on
vowel duration. Vowels placed between voiced consonants were found to be
considerably longer than the same vowels surrounded by voiceless consonants
and those between stop consonants were shorter than in any other context.

[*] Intensity of the nasal sounds were given by House relative to a standard, uncoupled
/i/ vowel. To arrive at a comparable power level, the 20 db level of the /i/ vowel reported by Fletcher was, therefore, subtracted from the intensity levels given by House.

House also pointed out that the tense vowels /i, e, α, and u/ have longer duration than the corresponding lax vowels /I, ε, Λ, u/. This trend is evident in all three of the sets of data listed above with a minor reversal of ε and eᴵ in the Peterson-Lehiste findings. House felt that this shorter vowel duration could be attributed to less physiologic effort needed to speak the lax vowels.

Lehiste and Peterson (1961) identified another important duration contrast within the vowel category. They studied the relative time involved after onset of the vowel until it reached a steady frequency state, the time at this frequency, and the time expended from the steady state to onset of the next sound. These three periods were called "Onglide," "Target," and "Offglide," respectively. The time periods were expressed in percent of the total vowel phonation time. Figure 5 depicts the three relative time periods for the lax-tense vowel contrast. The relative times indicate that in general the lax vowels have a comparatively shorter time on target and relatively longer offglides.

Comparable data concerning consonant duration is not available. Some data, such as that of Lisker (1957) and of Crandall (1925), suggest that vowels have longer duration than do consonants although considerable overlap exists between short vowels such as /I/ and the continuant consonants /s, z/, etc.

Discriminant II. Voiced vs. Voiceless Consonants

The conventional pairing of voiced-voiceless consonants is as follows:

	Stops		*Continuants*	
Voiced		*Voiceless*	*Voiced*	*Voiceless*
b		p	v	f
d		t	ð	θ
g		k	z	s
			ʒ	ʃ

	Affricates	
	dʒ	tʃ

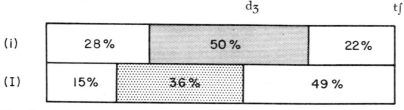

(i)	28%	50%	22%
(I)	15%	36%	49%

Fɪɢ. 5. Relative vowel duration in onglide, target, and offglide for /i/ and /I/ CNC words. (Adapted from Lehiste and Peterson, 1961.)

Six additional consonants used in English are /m/, /n/, /ŋ/, /l/, /r/, /j/ and /h/. All of these except the /h/ are classified as voiced. The known acoustic contrasts are summarized in Table 8.

The principal transduction difference between voiced and voiceless sounds is that voiced consonants have periodicity. This periodicity is most typically detected in a low frequency component called a "voice bar" (Potter et al., 1947) which represents the laryngeal tone. The voice bar is displayed on a sonagram as a combination of the fundamental and the second harmonic in a wide band filter display.

Table 8. Acoustic Contrasts Between "Voiced" and "Voiceless" Consonants

| | | | Modulation Characteristics | | |
| | | | | Duration | |
Category	Transductions	Frequency	Intensity	Total	Voice Onset
Voiced	P + (F *or* I)	Broad band, variable voice bar	0.0 to 16 db ave. phon. power	50–100 msec.	/b/ = 0 msec. /d/ = 0 msec. /g/ = 20 msec.
Voiceless	F *or* I	Broad band, no voice bar	0.01 to 1.8 db ave. phon. power	110–230 msec.	/p/ = 55 msec. /t/ = 70 msec. /k/ = 75 msec.

The perception of apparent periodicity of voiced consonants is not limited to presence or absence of a laryngeal tone.

The contribution of the first formant to perception of "voicing" was observed by Liberman et al. (1963) in synthesized speech by progressively eliminating the vowel transitions following stop consonants. They found that first formant cutbacks "effectively converted voiced stops into voiceless."

The speed of transition of F_1 from the time of its onset to its steady state in a vowel following a stop sound is also related to perception of "voicing." Durand (1956) showed that if this time interval were around 20 msec. the preceding consonant would be perceived as voiceless. An interval of 50 msec. or longer caused a listener to hear the consonants as voiced. These findings are consistent with the observation that voiceless stops attenuate the formants of vowels that follow them.

With fricatives an underlying, low intensity formant pattern is present in addition to the voice bar.

Intensity modulation. The relative intensity of the principal phonemes of English are shown in Table 9 with the intensity of the faintest sound, θ, used as the basis for comparison. The values listed in θ phonetic power level (θ PPL) were obtained by converting the relative phonetic powers given by Fletcher (1953, p. 86, Table 7A) into decibel levels. The absolute value of θ was 0.05 μw.

Table 9. Relative Intensity of Principal English Sounds Derived From Measurement by Fletcher. The Value of θ Was Used as Reference.

Vowels				Consonants									
ɔ	28	e	26	r	23	n	16	t	12	b	8
ɑ	28	ɛ	25	l	20	dʒ	14	g	12	d	8
ʌ	27	u	25	ʃ	19	ʒ	13	k	11	p	8
æ	27	I	24	ŋ	18	z	12	v	11	f	7
o	27	i	23	m	17	s	12	ð	10	θ	1
U	27			t	16						

It may be seen that although eight of the first ten consonants in Table 9 are voiced, intensity contrasts between voice-voiceless pairs show no consistent trends.

Duration modulation. Relative duration may be an important factor in voiced-voiceless consonant distinctions. Denes (1955) separated the final, inharmonic, s-like part of the utterance "the use," as pronounced by a human speaker, from the rest of the word and rerecorded it a number of times to achieve different consonant durations. This "s" sound was then attached to a synthesis of /ju-/. Thirty-three subjects listened to these partially synthesized words and judged whether the word spoken was (the) *use* or (to) *use,* by answering the question: Is it an *s* or a *z*? Denes reported that the perception of "voicing" of the final consonant increased as the duration of the consonant decreased relative to the length of the preceding vowel. When the consonant duration was approximately half that of vowels, essentially 100 percent of the subjects judged the sound to be "z." As duration was lengthened these judgments gradually shifted to "s." Crossover was at a consonant/vowel ratio of approximately 1.0.

Lisker and Abramson (1964) studied periodicity onset time in stop consonant sounds with respect to the instant of the noise burst. Onset was defined as the first vertical striations in a broad band spectrograph after the impulse release of a stop sound. Onset before the noise burst was calculated as negative numbers and called "voicing lead" while onset after the burst was stated as positive numbers and called "voicing lag." Of the four English speakers studied, one consistently produced the initial stops b, d, and g, with voicing lead. The others all produced them with −1 to 0 level and as much as to 22 msec. voicing lag. The /p,t,k/ sounds in initial position demonstrated 20 to 135 msec. voicing lag. Similar relationships were found in sounds imbedded in running speech. Both lead and lag periodicity onset time tended to be somewhat compressed toward the burst, however.

Discriminant III. Continuous vs. Interrupt Consonants

All spontaneous speech contains interruptions. Some of these are voiceless hiatuses that are present as natural boundaries between thoughts expressed, between groups of words spoken on single breaths, or as pauses between words to make the meaning of the words clearer. Other shorter breaks in the speech stream identify certain phonemes of the language. Phonemic interruptions enable us to separate the sounds of the language as follows:

Interrupted Sounds		*Continuant Sounds*	
p : b		f : v	m j
t : d		θ : ð	n r
k : g		s : z	y w
tʃ : dʒ		ʃ : ʒ	l (h)

The members on each side of the dotted line carry the additional voice-voiceless contrasts enumerated in Discriminant II.

Acoustic contrasts between the interrupted and continuant phoneme sets and the voiceless hiatus are shown in Table 10.

Table 10.   Acoustic Contrasts Among Interrupted Sounds, Continuant Sounds, and Voiceless Hiatuses

Category	Transductions	Frequency	Intensity	Modulation Characteristics Duration of Interruption	Duration of C-V Transition
Interrupted	I ± P ± F	—	—	30–100 msec.	40 msec.
Continuant	F ± P	—	—	—	50 msec.
Voiceless Hiatus	H	—	—	110–250+ msec.	—

Examination of Table 10 reveals, as might be expected, that impulse noise is the differential transduction for perception of interrupted sounds. Recall that impulse noise is characterized by a blockage of the air stream, a period of pseudosilence during which pressure is built up behind the blockage, and sudden release of this pressure. The release generates a sharp noise burst. During the period of air stoppage the vocal folds may or may not vibrate. Halle et al. (1957) emphasize that if the pseudosilence is filled by any other sound except the low frequency voice bar, a stop will not be perceived.

Frequency and intensity modulations.   Neither frequency nor intensity modulations have been found to provide differential information concerning interrupted and continuous consonants.

Duration modulation.   The time interval of silence in voiceless hiatuses and pseudosilences in interrupted sounds is important to their differentiation. Liberman et al. (1961) conducted a synthetic speech study designed to measure the influence of the duration of the pseudosilence on identification of /b/ from /p/ in "rabid-rapid" context. They found a reasonably sharp boundary between /b/ and /p/ at about 70 msec. of pseudosilence. Silence intervals of less than 70 msec. precipitated selection of "rabid." After relistening to their stimuli they seemed to detect an additional class of sounds when durations of the silent interval became rather lengthy. Listener judgments confirmed this impression. When the interval exceeded about 110 msec. the /f/ gave way to a new sound, labeled °/p/. This °/p/ approached 100 percent identification at 130 msec.

The 110 msec. silence that Liberman et al. identified may well reflect the lower limit in a voiceless hiatus used for momentary breaks in connected speech. Liberman (1967) observed that 100–150 msec. is the minimum required to bring the vocal folds together and build up sufficient pressure to generate a tone. On the other hand, Fry (1963) has indicated that pauses in speech are typically 250 msec. or greater.

Consonant-vowel transition duration. When a stop consonant is adjacent to a vowel, the valving process is accompanied by rapid changes or *transitions* in the vowel formants. These transitions are important cues for perception of different consonant categories. They also provide important information about the place of articulation, discussed in Discriminant IV.

Transitions of stop sounds, semivowels, and vowels of "changing colors" were studied by Liberman et al. (1963). Their data showed that rapid transitions were typically found with the stop sounds. Transitions were increasingly long for the semivowels and diphthongs. Thus, duration of transition is an important consideration in discrimination and identification of speech sounds.

Discriminant IV. Bilabial, Alveolar or Velar, Place of Articulation

The first three phonetic discriminants presented sound contrasts according to *manner* of production, i.e., periodic-aperiodic, etc. The fourth discriminant focuses attention upon *place* of articulation in three broad categories: (1) those sounds produced by the lips, (2) those by the front of the tongue against the alveolar ridges, and (3) those by the middle and back of the tongue against the palate. The acoustic characteristics identifying these places of articulation are summarized in Table 11.

Table 11. Acoustic Contrasts by Place of Articulatory Contact

Category	Transductions	Modulation Characteristics Frequency of Locus	of Burst	Intensity	Duration
Labial	± P ± I ± F	750–1500 Hz	300–700 Hz	Rel. low in burst	—
Dento-Alveolar	± P ± I ± F	N 1800	3500–4000	Rel. high in burst	—
Palatal-Velar	+ P + I + F	600–2500	600–3000	Rel. high in burst	—

Frequency modulation. Examination of Table 11 indicates that the discriminative information concerning place of articulation is concentrated in frequency modulation. Two types of such modulation have been identified: (1) in transitional cues where consonants and vowels join, and (2) in the frequency of the noise burst for stop consonants.

The formant theory has been shown to be a powerful tool for vowel recognition. In more recent years this theory has been extended to the recognition of consonants. The most significant of these developments has been what is now known as the *locus theory* (Delattre et al., 1955). In the early classical work of Potter, Kopp, and Green (1947) the observation was made that each sound seems to have a frequency "hub" of energy to and from which transitions are made with respect to other sounds preceding or following it. They identified the hub as the key reference point for formant transitions and observed that different speakers have similar hubs for the same sounds.

The locus theory advanced by Delattre and others extended the observations of Potter et al. They use synthetic speech to study the frequencies toward which the transitions of the formants "pointed" and linked the locus of this hypothetical point with specific places of articulation. Thus, they shifted attention to the transitional cues as indices of the consonant hubs. For example, they found that the "best" /g/ is produced by an F_2 transition pointing to a locus of 3000 Hz, the best /d/ to a locus of 1800 Hz, and the best /b/ to 720 Hz. Thus, they observed that whether or not the second formant of the vowel itself was at these levels, the consonant-vowel transition of the F_2 pointed in the direction of such loci. Figure 6 illustrates consonant-vowel transitions and hypothetical locus for the /d/ sound.

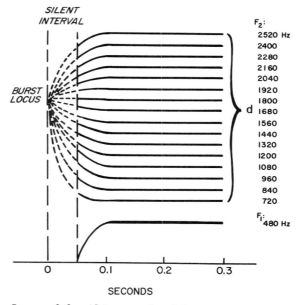

FIG. 6.   Locus of the /d/ extrapolated from consonant-vowel transitional cues. (From Delattre et al., 1955.)

Stevens (Fry, 1963) by and large confirmed the findings of the Haskins group but introduced the following modifications:

1. The bilabial transitions /p,b,m/ range from 750–1500 Hz; however, the locus is never higher than the F_2 of the vowel.
2. The alveolar transition locus /t,d,n/ is relatively fixed at 2000 Hz.
3. The velar transition locus /k, g/ is higher than the F_2 of the vowel but range from 600 to 2500 Hz.

Figure 7 summarizes in hand-painted spectographic form the acoustic cues that distinguish the three sets of consonants in place and manner.

The second means of acoustically separating labial, alveolar, and velar consonants is through identification of the frequency concentration of the noise burst in stop sounds.

The noise burst consists of an abrupt consonant-vowel transient of about 12 msec. that precedes the onset of the transition by about 10 msec. (Hoffman, 1958). Although the spectral distribution of such bursts typically has a rather broad frequency range, the energy tends to be concentrated toward certain resonance centers. Potter, Kopp, and Greene (1947) noted that energy in the noise burst of /p/ is concentrated in the relatively low frequencies and that of /t/ in the high frequencies, while that of /k/ is at a high frequency for the front vowels, e.g., /i/, middle frequency for mid-vowels, e.g., /ʌ/, and at a low frequency for back vowels, e.g., /u/. Liberman et al. (1957) compared the spectral maximum intensity of three classes of stop sounds and found that the labial sounds /p,b/ tended to be about 10 db less intense than the other two sets. The differences were sufficiently stable that /p,b/ intensity contrasts with /k,g/ guided the correct classification in about 85 percent of the cases.

Hoffman (1958) observed that third formant transitions also influenced perception of voiced consonants. He found that an F_3 transition with a locus

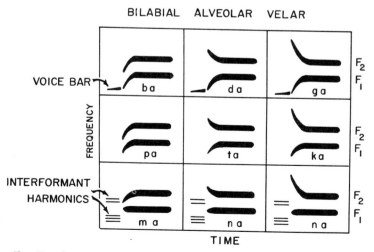

FIG. 7. Hand painted spectrograms contrasting acoustic cues by place and manner of articulation. (Adapted from Liberman et al., 1956.)

above the F_3 target frequency enhanced the identification of /d/ and /g/ identification. Furthermore, he observed that the cues "appear to have independent effects."

Second formant transitional cues are recognized as the principal determinants of place discrimination. The burst frequency and the F_3 transition may then operate as vectors to strengthen or weaken the perceptual pattern.

Discriminant V. Fricative Place of Articulation

Fricatives as a consonant class are characterized by turbulent noise or *hiss* with or without underlying voicing. The sounds in this group are labiodental /f,v/, dental /θ, ð/, alveolar /s,z/, palato-alveolar /ʃ, ʒ/, and glottal /h/. Hughes and Halle (1956) reported that above 1000 Hz "voiced" fricatives do not differ appreciably from "unvoiced" fricatives; therefore, we can limit the following discussion principally to the voiceless fricatives and generalize to their voiced cognates. The glottal fricative is not considered because during its production the cavities are adjusted for the sound following it rather than for the /h/ itself.

Table 12. Acoustic Contrasts by Place of Friction

| Category | Trans-ductions | Modulation Characteristics | | | Intensity Duration (θPPL) |
| | | Frequency | | F_2 Locus | |
		Lower Pole	Spectral Range		
Labiodental (f)	F ± P	6800–8400 Hz	1500–7500 Hz	700 Hz	7 db —
Dental (θ)	F ± P	6000–8400 Hz	1400–7200 Hz	1800 Hz	1 db —
Alveolar (s)	F ± P	3500–6400 Hz	3500–8000 Hz	—	12 db —
Palato-Alveolar (ʃ)	F ± P	2200–2700 Hz	2000–7000 Hz	—	19 db —

Differential cues as to place of articulation of the fricative sounds are given by the frequency of the energy concentration and by the relative intensity.

Frequency modulation. The lower pole of the frequency range provides a substantial means of separating the fricatives from each other. Strevens (1960) found that the fricatives /f/ and /θ/ had turbulent noise spread thinly over wide frequency range with a lower limit of 1400–1500 Hz, whereas Hughes and Halle (1956) found that for "any single speaker" the spectra of /s/ and /z/ showed "consistently higher frequency peaks" than /ʃ/ and /ʒ/. This observation was confirmed and extended by Heinz and Stevens (1961) who used synthesized speech to demonstrate a consistent shift in listener perception progressing from /ʃ/ to /s/ to /f, θ/ in the 6000–8400 range. The addition of low frequency noise accentuated identification of the fricative as /f/ or /θ/.

Separation of the /f/ from the /θ/ can be made on the basis of the consonant-vowel transitions. Harris (1958) suggested that /ʃ/ and /s/ were identified almost solely by their friction portions of the C-V syllable but that /f/ and /θ/ were judged by their "vocalic" or formant portion. Heinz and Stevens supported this viewpoint. They indicated that the F_2 transition of /f/ has a lower frequency, labial locus, whereas the /ʃ/ has a mid-frequency, alveolar locus.

Intensity modulation. /ʃ, s/ and /f, θ/ are also contrasted effectively by intensity. /ʃ/ and /s/ are ranked among high intensity consonants; whereas /f/ and /θ/ have the lowest intensities of any in the language. The difference between the two sets is in the order of 11 db. The voiced cognates of each set show intensity differences in the same direction. Fletcher (1953) observed that in ordinary room noise the θ is barely perceptible to a normal listener at a distance of only 10 feet.

Duration modulation. Duration modulation is not discriminatory among fricative consonants.

Discriminant VI.   *Affricate* vs. *Stop Consonants and Fricatives*

The affricate /dʒ/ and /tʃ/ sounds combine the acoustic characteristics of a stop consonant onset and a fricative termination. Therefore, as shown in Table 13, they contain acoustic characteristics similar to each of the other sets of sounds. /tʃ/ begins with a compression phase similar to /t/ but the compressed air is released through a restricted aperture. Truby (1959, p. 192) emphasized that articulation of the affricates is, however, a single, "physically inseparable" maneuver and that merely because the affricatives are stated to have characteristics of the stops and fricatives is not reason to conclude that they are in actuality a blendlike combination of two phonemes spoken in rapid succession.

Table 13. Affricate vs. *Stop Consonants and Fricatives*

| | | Modulation Characteristics | | | | |
| | | Frequency | | | Duration | |
Category	Transductions	of Low Pole or Burst	Spectral Range	Intensity (re θPPL)	of Noise Rise Time	of Turbulence
Stop	I ± P	300–Hz	Nonrestricted	8–12 db	Abrupt	30 msec.
Affricate	I ± F ± P	2000–2200	Nonrestricted	14–16 db	Intermediate	30–50 msec.
Fricative	F ± P	2200–2700	1500–8000+	1–19 db	Slow	110 msec.

Frequency modulation. Locus of the second formant transition in the affricates is approximately 2000 Hz. This is consistent with the lingua-alveolar articulation although it is slightly lower than the lower pole of fricatives. Otherwise, frequency cues do not provide differential information. The low pole is at a lower frequency level because stop consonants include bilabial phonemes that are not included in either of the fricative categories.

Intensity modulation. Affricate intensity is in the same range as the / ʃ, ʒ/ levels for consonant sounds and considerably higher in intensity than the stops.

Duration modulation. Gerstman (1957) examined the manner of affricate articulation. He found that the principal difference of affricates from stops and fricatives lay in the rise time and duration of the turbulent noise. As shown in Table 13, the rise time of noise is intermediate in affricatives and slow in the fricative sounds. Duration of the turbulent noise is 30 to 50 msec. in affricates and greater than 110 msec. in fricatives. Conversely, both the rise time of the noise burst and the duration of frictional sound is *longer* in affricates than in stops.

Discriminant VII. Nasal Consonants vs. Nasalized Vowels

Nasality is one of the identifying features of the English phonemes /m,n ŋ/ and is variably present in many other sounds of normal and hard of hearing speakers.

In the consonant sounds, nasality is present in the speech spectrum as a characteristic of the laryngeal-pharyngeal-nasal cavity tube with closed oral side branch coupled in varying amounts at the velum. Conversely, nasality in vowel sounds is present in the speech spectrum as a concomitant of the laryngeal-pharyngeal-oral tube with an open nasal side branch coupled in varying degree at the velum.

The palatal valving contributions in the vowels vary with language, with locality, and even with the family or other close social groups (Bosma and Fletcher, 1962). Acoustic contrasts between nasal consonants and nasalized vowels are summarized in Table 14.

Nasal Consonants

Specific acoustic characteristics of nasal consonants have been difficult to isolate. This is not only because nasality varies according to phonetic context but also because the signal is separated into two streams in the nasal chambers which are about 8 inches long. And each chamber is in turn separated into upper, middle, and lower branches by the nasal turbinates. The additional surface area from the irregularities, and the ciliated mucous linings of the walls give these chambers a much higher damping coefficient than that of the oral cavity. Moreover, the oral-nasal shunt may be almost continuously varied during speech by differential placement of the lips and tongue to block the

Table 14.   Acoustic Contrasts between Nasal Consonants and Nasalized Vowels

Category Nasal Consonants	Trans-duction	Modulation Characteristics						Intensity	Duration	
		Frequency								
		F_1	F_2	F_3	F_4	F_2 Transition	Lowest Anti-Resonance		F Transition or On-Glide	Steady State
m	P	300	1000	1300	1950	Labial locus	1000–1200	17 db	50 msec.	30 msec.
n	P	200–300	1050	1450	2000	Alveolar locus	16–3000	16 db	50 msec.	30 msec.
ŋ	P	200–300	1050	1900	2750	Velar locus	5000	18 db	50 msec.	30 msec.
Nasalized Vowels	P	F_1 Suppressed and shifted upward	F_2–F_4 Generally flattened			—	500 Hz	Up to 9.5 db overall reduction	Effect of nasality not established, probably not changed.	

stream at different points and by changing the relative height of the tongue in the mouth in preparation for sounds following the nasal consonants.

Frequency Modulation of Nasal Consonants

The acoustic characteristics of nasal consonants have been investigated in both synthesized and normal human speech. A common finding of these studies is a concentration of energy in the low frequencies. Considerably less agreement is found on location of the upper formants. Through an analog study, House (1957) identified a low frequency at 200–300 Hz and a second prominence near 1000 Hz in all nasal consonants. Fant (1960, p. 147) noted a "dominating intensity" at 250 Hz and low intensity formants at 1000, 2000, 3000, and 4000 Hz and higher formants dependent on the consonant. Thus, a formant for /m/ was identified near 800 Hz, for /n/ around 1000 Hz and for /ŋ/ at 1050 Hz. When all three sounds were combined, the effects of the relatively high damping of the formants and the varying placement of the formants gave rise to an "even distribution" of sound energy between 800 and 2300 Hz with no prominent energy concentration nor deep spectral valleys in any portion of this middle-frequency range.

The effect of the mouth cavity as a side chamber is shown by a shift in the resonance frequencies of the laryngeal-nasal tracts. The oral side chamber also introduces antiresonances into the spectra at frequencies where the energy from the larynx is all trapped in oral shunts. Hattori et al. (1958) used a glass tube with a side branch to demonstrate selective attenuation by antiresonance of a side chamber. The open end of the branch was inserted into a glass cylinder filled with water so that its volume could be regulated. As the glass was lowered and the cavity enlarged, the frequency of the antiresonance seen on spectrographic tracings was lower. Thus, longer side branches have lower antiresonance frequencies.

In the nasal consonants a progressive increase in volume of the oral cavity with concomitant drop in the antiresonance frequency takes place as tongue-palate contact moves from /ŋ/ to /n/ to /m/. House (1957) found the most recognizable, synthetically produced /m/, /n/, and /ŋ/ consonants had antiresonances around 1000, 3500, and 5000 Hz, respectively. Fujimura (1962) found corresponding antiresonances at between 750 and 1250 Hz for /m/, 1450 and 2200 Hz for /n/, and "above 3000" Hz for /ŋ/. He also noted that the antiresonances changed appreciably as the configuration of the oral cavity changed during speech and that they had considerable influence on the formants near them. Other formants remained relatively constant. He found, for example, that the antiresonance of /m/ and /n/ was higher when they were followed by /i/ than when followed by /u/, since the tongue assumed an anticipatory position for the vowel as the nasal consonants were spoken.

The role of the consonant-vowel transition was investigated by Malecot (1956) by separating and interchanging /m,n, ŋ/ segments of words and by splicing these sounds into words before the transition following a burst of /b, d, g/. The results of this study indicated that the primary distinction among the three nasal consonants were made on transitional cues. The nasal formants preceding the consonant-vowel transitions seemed to mask the stop class characteristics remaining in the signal but contributed comparatively little to separation of the specific sounds according to place of articulation.

Nasalization of Vowels

Nasalization of vowels may be most easily interpreted as the variable coupling of a nasal shunt branch onto the larynx-pharynx-oral vocal tract. Four main effects of this coupling have been identified (Schwartz, 1968). The most important of these—and the only set of effects that can actually change perception from a non-nasalized to a nasalized vowel (Delattre, 1958)—are reductions in intensity, increases in bandwidth, and rises in frequency of the first formant. This may be seen in each of the vowels shown in Figure 8.

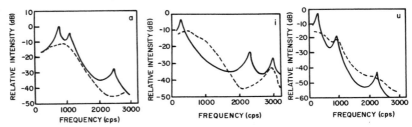

FIG. 8.   Overall spectral contrasts between non-nasalized vowels /a,i,u/. Shifts among the harmonics of a 125 Hz fundamental are shown for /a/. (From Schwarz, 1968.)

Frequency Modulation in Nasalized Vowels

Fant (1960) attributed the change in F_1 of a nasalized vowel to an intersection with the lowest antiresonance of the coupled system. Conversely, House and Stevens (1956) attributed the F_1 effects to damping in the nasal tract. This latter explanation is supported by the fact that efforts of Delattre (1958) to produce nasal vowels with a nasal analog by simply adding a third cavity produced only an additional formant around 1000 Hz with no perceptible vowel nasalization. To produce a nasalized vowel with an F_1 of low intensity, the nasal cavity had to be considerably damped.

The second prominent acoustic feature of vowel nasality is an antiresonance appearing in the spectrum as a result of the nasal side branch. The location of the antiresonance along the frequency line and the magnitude of the attenuation of energy vary with the vowel, the degree of nasal coupling, and the speaker. A sharp antiresonance drop in the spectrum of the vowel /ɑ/ may be seen in Figure 8 at around 2400 Hz. This antiresonance has replaced the third formant. Another may be seen at 2000 Hz in /i/ in place of the second formant.

House and Stevens (1956) compared reduction in vowel intensity as a function of the average area of nasal coupling. They used an electronic analog system with impedances representing velopharyngeal apertures ranging from 0.0 to 3.72 cm². In addition to a general broadening and flattening of the peaks in the vowel spectra they found a differential reduction in overall intensities for different vowels. The maximum reductions in overall level ranged from 5 to 9 db. In associated perceptual studies of synthesized nasal and nonnasalized vowels, House and Stevens found that small amounts of nasal coupling produced marked changes in the spectra and in perceptual identification of nasality in /i/ and /u/. A greater degree of coupling was required to produce comparable changes in /ɛ/ and /ɔ/ and "much greater" changes were needed for /ɑ/.

The third acoustic feature of vowel nasalization is the introduction of "extra resonances" into the acoustic spectrum. The added resonances arise from the superposition of nasal cavity resonances upon the spectrum from the oral tracts. These resonances also vary with the vowel, the degree of coupling, and the speaker. House and Stevens suggested that such resonances may function as "secondary cues" to nasality.

The fourth and final feature of vowel nasality is a shift in the frequency positions of the formants. This shift was mentioned with respect to the F_1. It is found generally throughout other regions of the spectrum also as a result of the changes in relative dimensions of the cavities with nasal coupling.

Intensity Modulation of Nasality

Nasalized vowels and nasal consonants demonstrate intensity levels that are very similar to each other. Thus, the nasal consonants range in intensity (re θ PPL) from 16 to 18 db. Non-nasalized consonants range from 23 to 28 db with a median of 27 db. It may be hypothesized that the loss of vowel intensity of approximately 7 db would bring the intensity of the two sound classes very close to each other and thereby make consonant-vowel differences more difficult to detect.

Duration Modulation of Nasality

This factor has not been investigated; however, no apparent reason exists for this parameter to be changed by nasality other than the fact that a greater flow of air is present in nasalized speech (Warren, 1967). This may precipitate some "choppiness" in output which could be reflected in durational differences.

Discriminant VIII. Glides /j,w,r/ vs. the Lateral /l/

The glides /j,w,r/ and the lateral /l/ have many common phonetic and spectral qualities. They are the only consonants which require a position in immediate contact with the vowel—or with the vowel plus r—in a syllable. And they are the only sounds used in English as the third member of a three consonant cluster (O'Connor et al., 1957). Their acoustic similarities and differences are contrasted in Table 15.

Table 15. Acoustic Constrasts Between /j,w,r,l/

Category	Transduction	F_1	Frequency F_2	F_3	Intensity Re θPPL	Duration F_2 Trans.	Steady State
Glides							
j	P	240–360	2760→1800 (Falling)			100 msec. (Falling)	30 msec.
w	P	240–360	360→1800 (Rising)			100 msec. (Rising)	30 msec.
r	P	120–600	840→1800 (Rising)	1500 F_3 of vowel (Rising)	23 db	100 msec. (Rising	
Lateral							
l	P	360+	840→1800 (Rising)	At F_3 of Vowel (Flat)	20 db	50–70 msec. (Rising)	60 msec.

Frequency modulation. The first formants of /j/ and /w/ were found by O'Connor et al. (1957) to be generally in the neighborhood of 240 Hz. When these sounds were synthesized with lower first formants, they were perceived as *gj* or *bw*. When the first formants were raised above 360 Hz, they lost their identity as speech sounds. Perception of /r/ was relatively independent of its first formant level. The comparatively high first formant of /l/ is important to distinguish it from the nasal consonants.

Changing frequencies in the second formant is a characteristic of all four sounds. Their locus of origin provides a principal differentiating cue. Thus, the bilabial /w/ originates very low at 360–480 Hz and glides upward to around 1800 Hz. Conversely, the palatal /j/ originates near 2800 Hz and glides downward to around 1800 Hz. The two remaining consonants /r,l/ start at 600–800 Hz and rise to 1800 Hz. These two vowels are, however, distinguished by prominent third formants which are different from each other. The third formant of the /r/ begins fairly close to the second formant at 1500 Hz and rises to the F_3 of the vowel. The third formant of the /l/ begins no lower than the level of the vowel third formant and remains flat throughout with no transition shown.

Duration modulation. Two differences are seen in duration of the glides /j,w,r/ and the lateral /l/. Namely, the /l/ has a briefer F_2 transition and both it and /r/ have a longer steady state. The brief steady states has suggested that the /j/ and /w/ sound are very similar to semivowels resulting from a rapid movement from /i/ to /ə/ and /u/ to /ə/ for /j,w/, respectively (O'Connor et al., 1957).

Conclusion

From the foregoing presentation it should be amply evident that for the detection of any phonetic unit a variety of auditory cues are available. The result of this redundancy is that for the listener with normal hearing, speech intelligibility is remarkably resistant to distortion and masking. When any cue is obliterated, he may make use of the remaining acoustic cues as well as of the redundancy of the language to supplement the acoustic signal.

Figure 9 presents a skeleton summary of the frequency and intensity modulation information in the foregoing charts. In this chart the data coincides with sensitivity curves of normal human hearing. The closed-in area indicates the approximate range of sound pressures of the phonetic elements as they would be heard at about 3 feet from the speaker. Since this data has been adjusted to ISO norms, an audiogram of a hearing impaired person may be directly compared to the levels shown. Other charts and tables in the chapter may then be used for further extension of this preliminary scan. It is hoped that this material can provide a basic, working pool of acoustic phonetic information with which the clinician or educator may assess the phonetic implications of hearing impairment and devise better approaches to alleviating the communication barrier.

It is well to remember at this time that the data presented here is from many sources and was originally acquired in many different ways. Much of it was from electrical analogs and speech synthesizers and not drawn directly

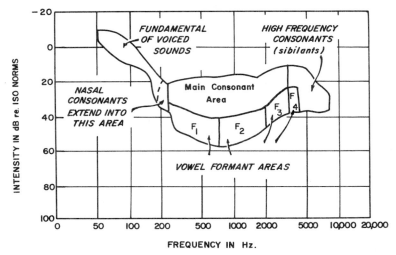

Fig. 9. Intensity vs. frequency distribution of speech sounds in the English language. The closed curves indicate the approximate range of sound pressure at typical speech intensities and at 3 feet from the speaker's lips. The levels are based on ISO norms.

from human speech and thus should be interpreted somewhat cautiously. These limitations should not, however, be allowed to obviate the importance of the information to better understanding of phonetic problems of hearing impaired persons.

References

Bosma, J. F. and S. B. Fletcher. 1962. The upper pharynx, a review. Part II Physiology. Ann. Otol. Rhinol. and Laryngol. 71:134–157.

Broadbent, D. E. and P. Ladefoged. 1960. Vowel judgments and adaptation level. Proc. Roy. Soc. 151:384–399.

Chiba, T. and M. Kajiyama. 1958. The Vowel: Its Nature and Structure. Tokyo: Phonetic Society of Japan.

Cooper, F. S. 1965. Instrumental methods for research in phonetics. Proc. of the Fifth Int. Cong. of Phonetic Sci. Munster 1964. S'-Gravenhague: Mouton & Co.

Crandall, I. B. 1925. Sounds of speech. Bell Technical J., Oct.

Delattre, P. 1958. Acoustic cues in speech. Phonetica 2:108–118, 226–251.

Delattre, P. C., A. M. Liberman, and F. S. Cooper. 1955. Acoustic loci and transitional cues for consonants. J. Acoust. Soc. of Am. 27:769–773.

Denes, P. 1955. Effect of duration on the perception of voicing. J. Acoust. Soc. of Am. 27:761–764.

Dunn, H. K. 1961. Methods of measuring vowel forman bandwidths. J. Acoust. Soc. of Am. 33:1737–1746.

Dunn, H. K. 1963. Acoustical characteristics of vowels. Automatic Speech Recognition. Ann Arbor: University of Michigan Press. P. D–1.

Durand, M. 1956. De la perception des consennes occlusives, questions de sonorite. Word 12:15–34.

Eimas, P. D. 1962. A study of the relation between absolute identification and discrimination along selected sensory continua. Doctoral Dissertation, U. of Connecticut.

Fant, F. 1960. Acoustic Theory of Speech Production. S'-Gravenhague: Mouton & Co.

Fant, G. 1962a. Speech analysis and synthesis. Air Force Cambridge Res. Lab. Tech. Report #62-790. Pp. 32–34, Jan.

Fant, G. 1962b. Sound spectrography. Proc. of the Fourth Int. Congr. of Phonetic Sci. Helsinki 1961. S'-Gravenhague: Mouton & Co.

Fischer-Jorgensen, E. 1954. Acoustic analysis of stop consonants. Mis. Phonetica 2:42–59.

Fletcher, H. 1953. Speech and Hearing in Communication. Princeton, N.J.: Van Nostrand.

Fry, D. B., A. S. Abramson, P. D. Eimas, and A. M. Liberman. 1962. The identification and discrimination of synthetic vowels. Lang. and Speech 5:171–189.

Fry, D. B. 1963. Acoustical characteristics of consonants. Presented at Univ. of Michigan course on Automatic Speech Recognition. Su. 1963.

Fujimura, O. 1962. Analysis of nasal consonants. J. Acoust. Soc. of Am. 34:1965–1975.

Gerstman, L. 1957. Cues for distinguishing among fricatives, affricate, and stop consonants. Doctoral Dissertation, New York University.

Halle, M., G. W. Hughes, and J. P. A. Radley. 1957. Acoustic properties of stop consonants. J. Acoust. Soc. of Am. 29:107–116.

Harris, K. S. 1958. Cues for the discrimination of American English fricatives in spoken syllables. Language and Speech 1:1–7.

Hattori, S., K. Yamamoto, and O. Fujimura. 1958. Nasalization of vowels in relation to nasals. J. Acoust. Soc. of Am. 30:267–274.

Heinz, J. M. and K. N. Stevens. 1961. On the properties of voiceless fricative consonants. J. Acoust. Soc. of Am. 33:581–596.

Hoffman, H. S. 1958. Study of some cues in the perception of the voiced stop consonants. J. Acoust. Soc. of Am. 30:1035–1041.

House, A. S. 1957. Analog studies of nasal consonants. J. Speech Hearing Dis. 22:190–204.

House, A. S. 1961. On vowel duration in English. J. Acoust. Soc. of Am. 33:1174–1178.

House, A. S. and G. Fairbanks. 1953. The influence of consonant environment upon the secondary acoustical characteristics of vowels. J. Acoust. Soc. of Am. 25:105–113.

House, A. S. and K. N. Stevens. 1956. Analog studies of the nasalization of vowels. J. Speech Hearing Dis. 21:218–232.

House, A. S. and K. N. Stevens. 1958. Estimation of formant band width from measurements of transient response of the vocal tract. J. Speech Hearing Res. 1:309–315.

Hughes, G. W. and M. Halle. 1956. Spectral properties of fricative consonants. J. Acoust. Soc. of Am. 28. 303–310.

Joos, M. 1948. Acoustic phonetics. Language Monogr. Suppl. #23, 24:1–136.

Kurtzrock, G. H. 1956. The effects of time and frequency distortion upon word intelligibility. Ph.D. Dissertation, Univ. of Illinois.

Lehiste, I. and G. H. Peterson. 1961. Transitions, glides and diphthongs. J. Acoust. Soc. of Am. 33:268–277.

Liberman, A. M., P. Delattre, and F. S. Cooper. 1952. The role of selected stimulus variables in the perception of the unvoiced stop consonants. Am. J. Psychol. 65:497–516.

Liberman, A. M., P. C. Delattre, and F. S. Cooper, 1958. Some cues for the distinction between voiced and voiceless stops in initial position. Lang. Speech 1:153–167.

Liberman, A. M., P. Delattre, F. S. Cooper, and L. Gerstman. 1954. The role of consonant-vowel transitions in the perception of the stop and nasal consonants. Psychol. Monogr. 68:24–43.

Liberman, A. M., P. C. Delattre, F. S. Cooper, and L. J. Gerstman. 1956. Tempo of frequency change as a cue for distinguishing classes of speech sounds. J. Exp. Psych. 52:127–137.

Liberman, A. M., K. S. Harris, P. Eimas, L. Lisker, and J. Bastian. 1961. An effect of learning on speech perception: the discrimination of durations of silence with and without phonetic significance. Language and Speech 4:175–195.

Lieberman, P. 1967. Intonation, Perception and Language. Cambridge: MIT Press.

Lindblom, B. 1962. Accuracy and limitations of sona-graph measurements. Proc. of the Fourth Internat. Congr. of Phonetic Sci. Helsinki 1961. S'Gravenhague: Mouton & Co. Pp. 189–201.

Lisker, L. 1957. Closure duration and the intervocalic voiced-voiceless distinction in English. Language 33:42–49.

Lisker, L. and A. S. Abramson. 1964. A cross-language study of voicing in initial stops: acoustical measurements. Word 20:384–422.

Malecot, A. 1956. Acoustic cues for nasal consonants. Language 32:274–284.

O'Connor, J. D., L. Gerstman, A. M. Liberman, A. M., P. C. Delattre, and F. S. Cooper. 1957. Acoustic cues for the perception of initial /w,j,r,l/ in English. Word 13:24–43.

Peterson, G. E. 1961. Parameters of vowel quality. J. Speech Hearing Res. 4:10–29.

Peterson, G. E. and H. L. Barney. 1952. Control methods in a study of vowels. J. Acoust. Soc. of Am. 24:175–184.

Peterson, G. E. and I. Lehiste. 1960. Duration of syllable nuclei in English. J. Acoust. Soc. of Am. 32:693–703.

Potter, R. K., G. A. Kopp, and H. C. Green. 1947. Visible Speech. Princeton, N.J.: D. Van Nostrand Co., Inc.

Rapoport, A. 1953. What is information? ECT. 10:247–260.

Richards, D. L. 1964. Statistical properties of speech signals. Proc. IEE 3:941–949.

Sacia, C. F. and C. J. Beck. The power of fundamental speech sounds. Bell System Tech. J. 5:393–403.

Schwartz, M. F. 1968. The acoustics of normal and nasal vowel production. Cleft Palate J. 5:125–140.

Searle, J. R. 1967. Human communication theory and the philosophy of language: some remarks. In F. E. S. Dance (Ed.) Human Communication Theory. New York: Holt, Rinehart and Winston, Inc. Pp. 116–129.

Stevens, K. N. and A. S. House. 1961. An acoustical theory of vowel production and some of its implications. J. Speech Hearing Res. 4:303–320.

Strevens, P. 1960. Spectra of fricative noise in human speech. Language and Speech 3: 32–49.

Tannenbaum, P. H. 1955. The indexing process in communication. The Public Opinion Quart. 19:292–302.

Truby, H. M. 1959. Acoustic-cineradiographic analysis considerations with especial reference to certain consonantal complexes. Acta Radiologica Suppl. 182.

Warren, D. W. 1967. Nasal emission of air and velopharyngeal function. Cleft Palate J. 4:148–156.

Wendahl, R. W. 1959. Fundamental frequency and absolute vowel identification. J. Acoust. Soc. of Am. 31:109–110.

Whorf, B. L. 1940. Linguistics as an exact science. Technol. Rev. 43:61–63, 80–83.

Chapter 7

Linguistics as a Basic Science in the Habilitation of the Hearing Impaired

DAVID M. FELDMAN, Ph.D.

Linguistics is the science of human communication. As such, it is ultimately concerned with the totality of man's system of communicative interaction by means of language in all its forms and varieties. Linguistics, it must be emphasized, is not an instructional method. Rather, it is the system of scientific analysis by which the nature of language systems is revealed. It consists of the application of rigorous scientific procedures to inquire into the essential nature of language and its role in human behavior.

The Linguist's View of Language

All human linguistic systems share certain basic characteristics, all of which are primarily oral and auditory in their nature. That is, all languages make use of the means of sound waves for sending and receiving all messages. Moreover, all languages are structured systems of arbitrary symbolism: that which is symbolized by any given feature of a language is the basic *meaning* of that feature. Language functions on four levels: first, its sound system (*phonology*); second, the system by which these sounds are combined into larger units of meaningful linguistic forms (*morphosyntax*); third, the system of relationships between language behavior and other modes of human behavior (*psycholinguistics*); and fourth, the *lexicon*.

Language, as it functions on each of these four levels, is a system with a very complicated organization. In addition to a certain comparatively small number of recurring speech sounds with varying degrees of intensity and levels of pitch, each language has a large number of morphemes, and an almost infinite number of combinations thereof. The grammatical system of any language, strictly speaking, consists of a number of elements which do not necessarily have "dictionary meaning," but which indicate the function of other elements with which they are combined (for example, our noun-plural affixes written with −s and −es in such words as *cats, boys, boxes;* the past-tense suffix written with −t, −d, and −ed in such verbs as *slept, marked, created;* the definite and indefinite articles; etc.). These elements which indicate grammatical functions are termed "functors"; those which have specific "dictionary meaning" (e.g., *table, smooth, ride,* etc.) are called "contentives." The expressions *functor* and *contentive* are more accurate descriptions of these forms, in that the elements to which they refer are often not really words, but rather affixes or other features which do not occur independently and hence are not normally termed "words."

Languages, also, are largely systems of habits. We acquire very extensive linguistic patterns when we are children, and use them in adult life, without becoming aware of their habitual nature. Thus, our language habits are both below and above our control as individuals: below, in that they are so extensively habitual; above, in that they are not the result of individual choice, but are determined by the entire culture group which uses the language as this usage takes place.

Languages are, then, systems of oral-auditory habits, surrounded by patterned bodily movements and enveloped by a highly systematized pattern of melodic and accentual features, used by humans to convey messages through arbitrary symbolism. Each language differs from every other of the more than 3000 spoken on earth with regard to surface features, such as the particular selection of sounds, sound-sequences, and grammatical constructions. Yet there are some underlying features of structure which are either extremely widespread among the world's languages or may even be considered to be language "universals" (Sapir, 1921). For example, an utterance consisting of a subject and predicate (or entity and event) appears to be a favorite, and possibly dominant, sentence type among a large majority of the world's languages (Bidwell, 1968).

By the age of 12 or 13, the normal individual has a fully developed and functioning linguistic system, although the process of learning a language never really stops. Each person's total set of language habits is termed his *idiolect,* and is peculiar to him as an individual. Although, to communicate, he must use the structural entities and patterns common to his culture group, he develops certain individual characteristics within the permissible variations tolerated by his language which remain so distinctive that no two idiolects are ever identical. In part, this individuality of idiolects is attributable to the physiological fact that no two human beings are identical, while in part also, since each individual has different experiences from those of every other individual, each idiolect is different, at least in slight details, from every other (Hall, 1964).

Because of the great breadth of the field, we must limit our discussion here to those aspects of linguistics which have a direct bearing on the education of the hearing impaired. Surveys of the field of linguistics as a whole exist in a number of sources within the ample bibliography of introductory books in linguistics (Bloomfield, 1965; Bolinger, 1967; Gleason, 1961; Hall, 1964; Hockett, 1958; Hughes, 1962; Robins, 1964).

Linguistic Ontogeny

Perhaps the most consistent single philosophy in the study of the speech and language behavior of the hearing impaired has been the simple contrast between the speech and language phenomena of the hearing impaired patient as opposed to normal. Most of the familiar educational techniques, consequently, have consisted of applying replicas of the order in which hearing infants acquire speech and language to those particular points at which the hearing impaired child's speech and language differed. The implication was, of course, that speech exists ultimately separate from language—a notion that modern linguistics has revealed to be false. The speech-language capacity must be developed simultaneously (Hudgins and Numbers, 1942).

The newborn infant has a specifically human stock of genetically conditioned and transmitted instincts and capacities for language, but development of this capacity depends on participation in language and other communicative systems of his community. The capacity for symbolization (the ability to use one phenomenon to stand for another), the ability to imitate and analogize patterns, and the possession of the organs used for speaking and hearing actually comprise the total list of genetically determined features the infant will require to use in the development of language. The earliest communicative experiences in which the child participates are, however, not linguistic, since they differ from language in several important ways:

1. The signals are not *specialized* i.e., there is a "natural" biological or physical connection between the signal and its antecedents or consequences.
2. The signals have meaning because of some geometric resemblance between signal and meaning. The touch on the shoulder which triggers the child into turning over is a vestige of the full-fledged manipulation.
3. The signals are not transmitted when they are not meant seriously.
4. The understandings between mother and infant are not based on a sharing of repertoires of transmitted signals, but only on the mother's correct understanding of the signals from the child and vice-versa (Hockett, 1958).

This type of nonlinguistic communication between mother and infant is carried on for from 6 months to as much as 20 months. During this period, the use of spectrography can reveal much about defects with relevance to speech, but little here is likely to be conclusive with regard to hearing disorders.

From this point on, however, the development of language in the hearing child as opposed to the hearing impaired child becomes more clearly differentiated: the sharing of communicative systems of child and mother begins because the hearing child starts to *imitate*. At this early level, all we can safely mean by "imitation" is a matching of the contours of perceptible behavior of one organism to those of another. Just how the learning of imitation takes place is not known. Some writers contend that the inception of imitation in any infant is accidental (Carmichael, 1966) while others would support the view that it is part of a general biological predisposition in the human being for language. Of course, language does not stop short at the boundaries of pure speech activity, for, as mentioned earlier, some part of the communicative act is always contained in the kinesic system of the communicators. What is certain, however, is that the production of speech is inseparably connected with the ability to receive speech.

With imitation the crucial factor of *adult misinterpretation* imposes narrowing conditions on the success of the child's efforts by requiring an ever-increasing precision in his own responses and a closer matching of his responses to those of adults.

Through this process of reciprocal imitation, the child eventually develops a repertory of vocal signals which, in sound and meaning, resemble two-word utterances of adult language. These utterances are not, however, really composed of two words, in the technical sense, since they are not used as constituents in building complex messages, according to grammatical conventions, as occurs in adult language behavior. These earliest utterances are, in fact, *holophrases*: not words, but single, indivisible, and uncompoundable signals. Thus, each of the child's utterances consists wholly of signals which have been learned as a whole, in direct or indirect imitation of some adult utterance (Brown and Bellugi, 1966).

The child's repertory eventually comes to include some holophrases which are partially similar in sound and meaning. For example, the child may already use prelinguistic equivalents of adult /³sɪstr¹↓/ and /²sɪstr³↑/, and of /³brʌɚr¹↓/, but not of /²brʌðr³↑/. Each equivalent adult form consists of a recurrent sequence of phonemes with a recurrent intonation. But now comes the most crucial event in the child's acquisition of language: he *analogizes*, in some appropriate situation, to produce an utterance matching adult /²brʌðr³↑/, which he has never heard nor said before.

A child can produce several such analogical formations which meet with no understanding because they deviate too radically from anything in adult speech, before he analogizes his first communicatively successful message. We know that the ability to analogize has become operative, however, when a child says something that he could not have heard from others: frequently a regularization of an "irregular" form of adult speech: *mans* instead of *men* or *hided* for *hid*.

The correlation between the development of phonemic and of grammatical habits is not clear, nor is the mechanism by which phonemic habits begin. The child's earliest phonemic system involves only a few of the contrasts functional in the adult system around him; and only somewhat later does grammatical patterning begin (Berko, 1958). The development of a child's phonemic system from one stage to the next generally takes the form of a splitting of some articulatory range into smaller contrasting subranges: in a range where earlier there was but one phoneme (e.g., /t/ there came to be two: (e.g., /t/ versus /d/). Sometimes there is temporary backsliding. Often, some forms acquired during an earlier stage are not immediately reshaped when the phonemic system is restructured, so that for a while one finds multiple matching of adult phonemes by the child's phonemes. Consonant clusters may be reduced to single consonants, unstressed syllables omitted and single consonants repeated in successive syllables. The end of the process, of course depends upon the phonemic habits of the surrounding adults. Parents understand from context rather than from performance, usually "reading in" articulatory distinctions that the child is in fact not using. This supplies the child both with a model and with a reward for success (Leopold, 1953–54).

Within the age range of from four to seven, the hearing child controls, with only a few exceptions, the basic phonemic system of his language; he handles effortlessly the essential grammatical core; he knows and uses the basic contentive vocabulary of the language. Of course, there is a vast further vocabulary of contentives that he does not yet know, but, as we mentioned earlier, this continues to some extent throughout life.

Ten or 15 years later, an individual undergoes an additional restriction on his adaptability to new local varieties of his own language, although there are many personal differences. Past this age range the adjustment is slower and usually never complete (Hockett, 1958). We have seen, then, that:

> Language depends on the establishment of an autocorrective feedback system to which audition provides the main vehicle for successive approximation to adult models. The hearing child learns to use language long before he learns the grammatical rules. The process is a cumulative one, achieved through infinite redundancies of experience. The deaf child must learn language by special means which require conscious attention. Consequently, language growth for him presents a slow, labored and often frustrating series of experiences (Di Carlo, 1964).

Speech and language in man have their roots in a biologic predisposition for this type of behavior. Physiologically, there seems to be specialized feedback mechanisms that control the smooth operation of voice and speech and we must hypothesize a unique interplay of reflexes that project upon and interrelate the coordinating center of speech activity at various levels of the neuraxis (Lenneberg, 1964).

THE COMMUNICATION PROCESS

In order to understand more exactly how the linguist looks at specific problems in human communication, let us examine a sample speech event. There is a speaker and a hearer. The speaker says something to the hearer. At least 11 steps can be demonstrated in this one simple act of communication (Moulton, 1966; Lashley, 1951).

Idea-Stimulus

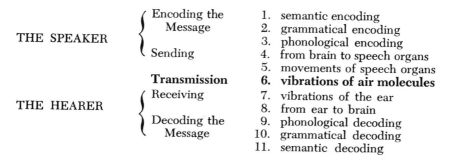

THE SPEAKER	Encoding the Message	1. semantic encoding
		2. grammatical encoding
		3. phonological encoding
	Sending	4. from brain to speech organs
		5. movements of speech organs
	Transmission	**6. vibrations of air molecules**
THE HEARER	Receiving	7. vibrations of the ear
		8. from ear to brain
	Decoding the Message	9. phonological decoding
		10. grammatical decoding
		11. semantic decoding

Understanding

In the six-month-old infant whose communicative pattern we discussed above, the chart is much simpler:

The Communication Process
(in the human infant)

Idea-Stimulus

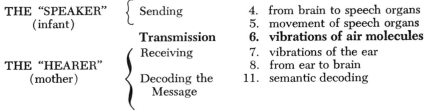

THE "SPEAKER" (infant)	Sending	4. from brain to speech organs
		5. movement of speech organs
	Transmission	6. **vibrations of air molecules**
THE "HEARER" (mother)	Receiving	7. vibrations of the ear
		8. from ear to brain
	Decoding the Message	11. semantic decoding

Understanding

Now, note the following chart in which the speaker's hearing is markedly impaired, but the listener's hearing is not:

The Communication Process
(the speaker has impaired hearing, but the hearer does not)

Idea-Stimulus

THE SPEAKER	Encoding the Message	1. semantic encoding
		2. grammatical encoding (impaired)
		3. phonological encoding (impaired)
	Sending	4. from brain to speech organs
		5. movements of speech organs
	Transmission	6. **vibration of air molecules**
THE HEARER	Receiving	7. vibrations of the ear
		8. from ear to brain
	Decoding the Message	9. phonological decoding (with difficulty)
		10. grammatical decoding (with difficulty)
		11. semantic decoding (inexact)

Imperfect
Understanding

And, finally, another chart in which the speaker has normal hearing but the hearer does not:

The Communication Process
(the hearer has impaired hearing, but the speaker does not)

Idea-Stimulus

THE SPEAKER	Encoding the Message	1. semantic encoding
		2. grammatical encoding
		3. phonological encoding
	Sending	4. from brain to speech organs
		5. movements of speech organs
	Transmission	**6. vibrations of air molecules**
THE HEARER	Receiving	7. vibrations of the ear (impaired)
		8. from ear to brain (impaired)
	Decoding the Message	9. phonological decoding (impaired)
		10. grammatical decoding (impaired)
	BYPASS	11. visual decoding
		12. tactile decoding
		13. semantic decoding (inexact)

**Imperfect
Understanding**

Of course, since language is a fully integrated system of communication, these steps do not represent the virtually simultaneous layering of processes which really occurs in producing or perceiving utterances. Rather, they are an abstract sketch of the organization which is felt to underlie all communicative performance of both speakers and hearers.

When we look at the chart of the infant's communicative pattern, we may be struck by the fact that the message is understood despite the fact that some major steps in the normal language communication system are absent. Of course, this is explained by the fact that these communicative transmissions are nonspecialized as we have already seen. But when we examine the pattern of the full communicative sequence when either the speaker or the receiver has profoundly impaired hearing, we recognize that understanding can be assured only when the visual-tactile supplement is present.

From the linguist's point of view, then, his contribution to the communicative education of the severe to profoundly hearing impaired consists above all in exploiting the visual and tactile media to their fullest and in making the most of the discrete training of residual hearing while dealing fully and accurately with language in accordance with the principles of descriptive and structural linguistics.

Semantic and Grammatical Encoding

We must assume that the speaker, whether or not his hearing is impaired, has some thought or idea which he wishes to communicate to the hearer. Let us assume that he wants to describe the shape of something. We know that within the physical world there are a great number of specifically identifiable shapes. To the geometrist, of course, these shapes can be categorized into a manageable number of basic ones; all others being variations on this one shape; quadrilateral<square, rectangle, etc. In other words, the semantic system of English has many terms for describing shapes. Some are "basic," in the sense that *quadrilateral* is; others are "variants," in the sense that *square* and *rectangle* are variants of *quadrilateral*; and yet others are not really shapenames at all, but are used in this way: *egg-shape, dome, globe,* etc. The speaker in our example, then, who wishes to describe the shape of something must first shape his idea so that it will fit into the semantic system of English shape terms. We call this process *semantic encoding* (Joos, 1958). Any idea that we want to express in a given language first must be encoded within the semantic "slots" recognized by that language, which means that each language community recognizes arbitrary connections between meanings and the specific sign vehicles (utterances) used to express them.

> Once the speaker has found the proper semantic units to express his thought, he must next arrange them in the particular way that his language requires. The scheme by which this arranging is done in a language is called the "grammar" of the language; we may therefore refer to this stage of the speech event as that of "grammatical encoding." For example, if the speakers' language is English, and if he wants to get across the idea of "dog," "man," and "bite"—with the dog and not the man doing the biting—he had to encode it in the order "dog bites man"; the order "man bites dog" gives quite a different message (Moulton, 1966).

The grammatical codes of other languages do not necessarily employ the same devices.

The basic units used in grammatical encoding are morphemes. Morphemes are sequences of sounds which form the smallest element with which recurring meaning can be associated. Moreover, morphemes have characteristic distribution. Thus, the sentence "The cats went running out" contains the morphemes *the, cat, -s, go, PAST, run, -ing, out* in fixed order of occurrence. Occasionally a morpheme may have different phonetic shapes, depending upon its occurrence. In the plurals of *cat, boy,* and *rose*: $/s/$, $/z/$, $/IZ/$ are three of the several possible realizations (allomorphs) of the one plural morpheme {s}. The concept of the morpheme provides an essential stage in revealing how the sound sequences of language are organized in a single ascending hierarchy to the sentence level, for words, sentences, and even entire paragraphs can all be regarded as ultimately being built out of morphemes. *Morphology* is the study of how morphemes are grouped together to make the longer sequences we have mentioned, while *syntax* examines the way in which these sequences of morphemes are grouped together in specific ways to make phrases of various types.

As its basic device for stringing and sequencing morphemes, syntax makes use of the *construction*. A construction is simply a combination of two or more morphemes in order to produce a new, longer form. In this way, "our" and "friend" can be combined into the construction "our friend," which can function grammatically as the subject or object of a predication. Likewise, "read" and "-ing" can be joined into the larger construction "reading." Once the constructions have been formed, they, in turn, can be linked to one another in order to produce longer utterances: sentences. Two types of construction linkages are *coordinating* and *embedding*.

Coordinating implies taking two separate utterances and linking them by means of a functor (such as *and, but, or,* etc.). "He reads poetry" and "He reads novels," are coordinated into the single utterance "He reads poetry and novels." *Embedding* involves taking two or more separate utterances and placing each inside the other successively. For example, "I want him to go" contains two separate basic utterances ("I want" and "he goes") in which the second is embedded into the first, with the resulting changes of surface structure phenomena:

> This is the pen.
> He bought the pen.   >   This is the pen that he bought.

Although space does not permit a complete listing of all the embedding formulas for English, almost all of them follow the general principle that underlies the above examples. Let us look more closely at how we can generalize a single embedding rule from "This is the pen. He bought the pen" > "This is the pen that he bought" which will cover literally thousands of analogous situations. Each sentence contains, in this case, three slots. The first sentence (S_1) has (1) a nominal slot which in this case functions as subject ("this"), (2) a verbal slot ("is"), and (3) a subject slot again, but now functioning as a predicate nominative ("the pen"). We might state these facts as: $S_1 \rightarrow 1, 2, 3$. The second sentence (S_2) has (1) a subject slot ("he"), (2) a verbal slot ("bought"), and (3) a nominative slot, functioning as an object ("the pen"). We might state these facts as $S_2 \rightarrow 4, 5, 6$.

$$\begin{array}{ccc} 1 & 2 & 3 \\ S_1 = \text{This/ is/ the pen.} \end{array} \qquad \begin{array}{ccc} 4 & 5 & 6 \\ S_2 = \text{He/ bought/ the pen.} \end{array}$$

To embed S_2 into S_1, and thus to produce our new sentence (S_3), we follow this formula:

$$S_3 \rightarrow 1 + 2 + 3 + rel + 4 + 5$$

The formula tells us that we eliminate the repetition of the subject (6) and embed S_2 into S_1 by means of a relator (*rel*), which in spoken American English is most frequently *that*.

Linguists call the semantic encoding the *conceptual* (or *deep*) structure of language and the grammatical encoding, the *surface* structure of language. The function of morphology is to create the surface constructions while it is the function of syntax to link conceptual structures with surface structures. Surface structures are normally acquired by the phonologically based system of imitation and analogical creation which we have already discussed, but since, in the hearing impaired, both initial auditory perception for imitation and subsequent auditory acuity for self-correcting analogical feedback are damaged, the visual bypass must be emphasized, and the feel for *language,* as opposed in this instance to *speech,* must be built in by means of techniques such as the visual formulas just presented.

For many years, it was believed that the visual emphasis on language structure involved no more than a linear segmenting of some of the more prevalent simple sentence types in English into a series of morphemes. Indeed, the earliest forms of teaching language structure to the deaf did not transcend the morphological level (Barry, 1899). We taught children to segment an utterance such as "Jane is not there" into its component morphemes in linear order:

Jane + be + PRESENT + not + there.

The effect of these limitations during the considerable longevity of this method was that hearing impaired children rarely succeeded in controlling utterances more than seven or eight morphemes long or complex clause structure. It could not have been otherwise because such a linear listing of morphemes does not transcend any one individual sentence, requiring us to identify the morphemes of every individual utterance in order to achieve a complete listing. What was needed was a means of describing grammar which would transcend the immediate concerns of morphological ordering and would reveal the single, specific system which underlies phrase and clause structure, permitting the hearing impaired child to generate full utterances of complex grammatical structure on the basis of the fundamental, high-frequency constructions of the language, such as in the coordinating and embedding formulas given above.

The first step in this direction was achieved by developing a means of showing the habitual interrelationships of a given set of morphemes; *immediate constituent* analysis. To illustrate how this technique operates, let us begin with the sentence given above: *Jane is not there.* Immediate constituent diagrams (Hockett, 1958; Wells, 1947; Street, 1967) are read from top to bottom in order to reveal the way in which the language combines its morphemes into constructions and then into full-length utterances:

Jane	i–	–s	not	there
		(a)		
		(b)		(f)
(e)		(c)		
		(d)		

We note that each of the boxes (identified here by a letter code) corresponds to a particular construction type:

(a)   simple predicate ("be")
(b)   simple negative predicate ("not be")
(c)   full predicate ("not be there")

(d)   sentence ("Jane is not there")
(e)   subject ("Jane")
(f)   locative modifier of (b) ("there")

The same relationships can also be shown by a tree diagram:

By itself, immediate-constituent analysis tells us that certain morpheme sequences belong together as constituents and that others do not, but it does not show what type of constituent a given sequence is. There is an obvious similarity between diagrams of this type and those once used for teaching grammar in the schools, and this suggests what is needed to complete the analysis: a means of laying out the characteristic functions of the various parts of speech or word classes.

Although there can be no doubt that this technique represents a great step forward in the visual description of grammar, it remains a sentence-by-sentence technique, and, therefore, we still must look beyond to the entire set of possible sentence types in English.

A language must be viewed as a coherent system whose grammar must be all-embracing. For hearing impaired children, the grammar must be written in such a way that it compensates visually for the imitative, analogical, and self-correcting feedback mechanism which is normally accomplished through full hearing. The two essential characteristics of such a grammar for our purposes are that it be: (a) self-confirmatory, and (b) automatic. In the past 10 years, a technique of this type has been developed. We call it transformational grammar and it is now making important inroads on our entire outlook toward the teaching of syntax.

Let us take a passive sentence, "the war was started by the enemy." Transformationally, the sentence is said to have been produced by a specific transformation of an underlying, or *kernel,* sentence: "the enemy started the war." The point is that, generalizing from such an example, one can say, subject to certain statable exceptions, sentences of the passive type can be generated from the active by applying the appropriate transformational formula. The student is expected to learn that there are only two kinds of English sentence types: *kernels* and *transforms.* Thus, rather than concentrating on the linear order of surface elements, such as phonemes and morphemes, as in the initial step, attention is focused on the deep structure rules which are at the core of *language* as differentiated from *speech.* All kernel sentences have a minimum of two parts: a subject (called a noun phrase and abbreviated NP), and a predicate (called a verb phrase and abbreviated VP). The formula for a minimum kernel sentence is S → NP + VP. The economy here is important. Note that this terminology departs from the traditional system of identifying structural parts by *form* (such as noun, pronoun, adjective, etc.) and, instead, focuses on the *function,* resulting in a much closer "fit" to what is actually spoken. Thus, the student learns that the NP can be of any length and complexity, from the simplest: "the man/ate," to the most complex: "the old man whom we saw yesterday on the street/ate." We would not change the structure of the sentence if we substituted "dog" for "man" or "slept" for "ate." Thus, we teach syntax in terms of *functional slots*: a subject slot, a predicate slot, an object slot, a modifier slot, etc. The specific forms, or lexical items, which may singly or in groups realize (or fill) these slots are examined only after the slots themselves are identified and learned. What fills each such functional slot, however, must belong to the same form class as the item in the original slot. One cannot fill the "man" slot with "slept" or the "ate" slot with "dog."

Several separate transformations are possible in each slot so identified. If we examine the sentence "The man buys a book," we immediately identify three functional slots (called "tagmemes"): "man," "buy," and "book," or subject, verb, object. We may, subsequently, vary the slots, by agreement or paradigm, as in, "The men/buy/a book." Or, we may add slots, as in "The men/buy/a book/*together*." We may also delete slots, as in "The men/buy," or expand slots, as in "The *two old* men/*did* buy/a *green* book," etc. In developing language awareness in the hearing impaired child, each vocabulary item is best taught with an immediate identification of the kind of functional slot or slots it can fill. For example, the item "lamp" can be cued visually and, by a consistent use of colored borders or shapes, can be identified as an NP expression. Conversely, "write" can be cued visually but with a consistently different colored border or shape which would automatically identify it as a VP expression.

To continue, we intuitively feel that the two sentences:

(1) The man bought the book.   (2) The book was bought by the man.

are somehow two versions of the "same thing." But if we made diagrams of them using immediate constituent analysis, they would look very different. In (1) the subject is *the man*, whereas in (2) the subject is *the book*. In (1) the verb has an object, whereas in (2) it does not. Even the verbs disagree: *bought* vs. *was*.

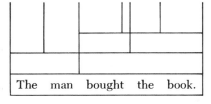   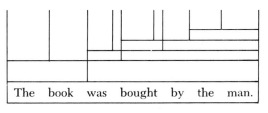

Where we find pairs of sentences like this, we consider one of them as basic (kernel) and the other as derived from it by transformation. Suppose we have 10 active sentences (like *The man bought the book*) and 10 corresponding passive sentences (like *The book was bought by the man*). If all the sentences in each set have different structures, then our learning task will consist of learning 20 sentences. But if we can work out a grammatical rule whereby any given active sentence can be transformed into the corresponding passive sentence, our learning task will be almost cut in half: we shall have to learn only the 10 active sentences plus one transformational rule. Here are some of the most frequent transformations encountered in English:

1. *Order transformations.*   It is often possible to transform the slots of a given utterance into a different order, such as in "He read the book to his mother" > "He read his mother the book."

2. *Full form > substitute form.*

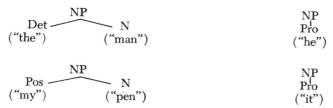

3. *Affirmative* ⟶ *Negative.*

He lives here ⟶ He does not live here.

We shall have more to say about this transformation later on.

4. *Statement* ⟶ *Question.*

He lives here ⟶ Does he live here?

5. *Statement* ⟶ *Command.* In English there is a 2nd person command transformation which consists of dropping the phrase *you will: You will come at six o'clock* ⟶ *Come at six o'clock.* There is also a kind of 1st person plural command, which consists of changing *we* to *let us: We go* ⟶ *Let us go.*

6. *Active* ⟶ *Passive.* This is a type of transformation which we have already discussed: *The man bought the book* ⟶ *The book was bought by the man.*

7. *Statement* ⟶ *Adjectival clause* (i.e., a clause that modifies an "NP"–a "relative clause").

(a) The NP of the first sentence is the same as the subject of the embedded sentence:

We saw *the man* +		We saw the man
The man spoke	⟶	*that/who spoke.*
We saw *the house* +		We saw the house
The house burned	⟶	*that/which burned.*

(b) The NP of the first sentence is the same as the object of the verb of the embedded sentence:

We saw *the man* +		We saw the man
He hired the man	⟶	*(that/whom) he hired.*
We saw *the house* +		We saw the house
He bought the house	⟶	*(that/which) he bought.*

(c) The NP of the first sentence is the same as the object of the preposition of the embedded sentence:

We saw *the man* +		We saw the man *(that/whom)*
He works with the man	⟶	*he works with.*
		We saw the man *with whom*
		he works.

We saw *the house* +	$\longrightarrow$	We saw the house (*that/which*)
He lives in the house		*he lives in.*
		We saw the house *in which*
		he lives.

8. *Statement* $\longrightarrow$ *Adverbial clause.*

I left *then* + *He came*	$\longrightarrow$	I left *when he came.*
I left *beforehand* + *He came*	$\longrightarrow$	I left *before he came.*
I left *afterwards* + *He came*	$\longrightarrow$	I left *after he came.*
I left *nevertheless* + *He came*	$\longrightarrow$	I left *although he came.*
I leave *in that case* + *He comes*	$\longrightarrow$	I leave *if he comes.*
Etc.		

In these last two types of transformations—numbers 7 and 8—the embedded sentence still keeps its essential structure, and its subject and verb still have their normal shapes. There are other types of transformations in English in which these shapes are changed. One example:

She sees him + *He does it* $\rightarrow$ *She sees him do it.*

If we were to continue with further examples of transformations, we would simply be going more deeply into English grammar, and this is not, of course, our purpose. All of these transformational rules are part of the "built-in grammatical code" which we carry around inside our heads, and we can call on them at any time to produce or to understand a brand new sentence (Moulton, 1966).

A transformational statement of the grammar of a language is organized in four main sections. The first describes the kernel utterances, sufficient in number to underlie all possible utterances in the language. The second describes all the potential suprasegmental features which carry meaning as they co-occur with the vowel and consonant sequences of the sentences. The third states all the rules, or formulas, by which the kernel sentences are transformed into the possible structures of English. Finally, the fourth establishes the limits within which a given transformation can be applied to a given kernel utterance.

By applying these techniques to the analysis of each kernel sentence of English, we can build a series of lessons each of which will allow the student to generate more than a thousand sentences, all of which are absolutely accurate.

A. Phrase-Structure Rules (Thomas, 1965)
1. S $\longrightarrow$ NP + VP
2. VP $\longrightarrow$ Aux + V $\pm$ adv.
3. V $\longrightarrow$ V_i
    V_t + NP
    V_c + Adj.
B. Lexicon
NP: boys, girls
Aux: can, should (Aux = "auxiliary" verb)

V_c: be, appear (V_c = "be" type verb)
V_i: play, study (V_i = intransitively-used verb)
V_t: call, tease (V_t = transitively-used verb)
Adj: happy, sad
Adv: now, later

We now work from the bottom of the phrase-structure rules to the top: This is but one of more than 45 possible sentences which this single rule and a vocabulary of only 14 words can produce. Since the vocabulary of the average hearing impaired learner at this point can easily approach 1200 words, one can easily conceive of thousands of utterances being generated by means of this one statement. Of course, it is essential that the learner be aware of the function class of each vocabulary item, as we discussed on page 96.

3. V_t + NP   call the girls
         $V\pm$ (adv)   now
2. Aux + V   should _____
3. NP $\pm$ VP   the boys _____
Terminal string: "The boys should call the girls now."

The importance of this approach to grammar for our immediate purposes can be seen in the following three areas:

(1)   we teach the students to generate unfailingly correct utterances from relatively limited material which can be presented visually and experientially;

(2)   we emphasize the *functional* value of the grammatical forms of the language with minimal reference to their *formal* value; and

(3)   we may remain consistent to our approach from the most elementary to the most complex types of language problems.

Of course, English structure cannot be taught to hearing children in one year, no matter which method we use. It requires a continuing program over a longer period. How much more necessary it is, then, for educational programs for the hearing impaired to continue the language-learning program, at ever more sophisticated levels, over the entire 12-year span of the primary and secondary school.

Today's hearing-impaired student of English should derive from his studies the same values as his hearing counterpart:

1. He should gain an insight into the nature of English and, by the same token, of language in general. He should see the highly systematic nature of the grammar and the essentially simple general structure that underlies and holds together the countless number of possible English sentences.

2. He should develop a concept of grammaticality, what we might call "sentence sense," in order to "feel" the grammaticality or nongrammaticality of an utterance.

3. He should realize that linguistic features such as punctuation and word order, as well as the choice of lexical items, are explicable on the basis of consistent syntactic patterns.

Phonological Encoding

A. *Phonemes and Allophones*

As we have already seen, a newborn child has no experience with or identification of sounds or their relation to processes or objects. A process of learning must take place before hearing becomes an integral part of the human communicative process. The formation of intelligent acoustic behavior takes time, as long as six years in normal language ontogeny. Proof of this is to be found in the fact that it is possible for children to lose the use of articulated language if they lose their hearing even as late as the sixth year (Jellinek, 1948). The effects on language of any cutting off or reduction of auditory stimulation are more or less uniform, regardless of the underlying cause.

As we saw earlier, the sounds of a language are automatically and unconsciously organized by the native speaker into ultimate units, phonemes. In a random recitation of isolated words, such as *full, bird, build,* without the aid of context to help establish meaning, each word can be recognized by the listener only through its sound shape. Thus, the speech sounds themselves convey the maximum amount of information. The central question is: how many units of sound relevant for the discrimination of the samples do the sound shapes of each sample contain? Upon hearing syllables such as *pill* and *bill,* any member of the English-speaking community recognizes that these two utterances mean different things, distinguishable by their initial sounds, /p/ and /b/. As we know, the phonetic nature of phonemes is complex. But the reason why, despite this complexity, the identification of the phoneme is essential, is because both aural perception of meaning and communicative oral behavior depend equally upon the phoneme. The phoneme is the "ultimate unit" of language at the level of its sound system.

· Any such minimal distinction carried by the message is really made up of all the characteristics—acoustic and physiological—which we can identify in the sound: the articulatory positioning of the speech organs, the sound wave produced by the articulation, voicing, nasality, etc. These qualities, when they co-occur simultaneously and thus produce what our ear recognizes as a particular sound, form a phoneme (Jakobson et al., 1967). Any given language has a finite set of distinctive features and also a finite set of rules for grouping them into phonemes and for grouping the phonemes into sequences. Such grouping results in the unique *phonemic patterns* of each language.

Obviously, the human speech organs are capable of producing an almost infinite number of recognizably different speech sounds. Yet, as we know, individual languages in fact contain a relatively small number of phonemes. Generally, the number falls between approximately 20 and 65. Linguistic analysis at the phonemic level is concerned with describing the system whereby this virtually infinite number of articulatory movements produces a limited number of phonemes in a given language and then with how these sounds are grouped into their functional phonemic classes.

To communicate in his language, a given speaker or listener must possess at least the ability to produce and perceive these distinctive sound units, but need not necessarily be able to *transcend* these units. This implies, of course, that the habilitation of deficient speech and hearing can be conceived in two steps: first, the habilitation of oral and aural capacities to the level of the production and perception of these phonemes; then, second, the habilitation of total oral and aural capacities. The first plateau is, in fact, sufficient for the needs of the most basic communicative behavior, and is often as far as we can go in the speech education of some individuals.

Yet another implication here, and one which will be of growing importance in speech and hearing therapy, is that of the speech or hearing impaired bilingual child. Let us take, for example, such a child whose family at home speaks Spanish but in the pursuit of daily tasks, English. In such cases, speech and hearing specialists face a double task, for they must be prepared to bring this patient to the first plateau in both Spanish and English.

Lest one tend to think of the habilitation of the bilingual patient as being more a speech and language problem than one of hearing, let one example suffice to illustrate the importance of this concept in the hearing impaired. English has vowel phoneme /ɔ/ with two allophones, [ɔ] and [ɔ:]. Spanish has no equivalent and its nearest rounded low-mid back vowel phone is /o̞/, which is higher, more posterior, and more labialized than the English phonemes we are discussing. By the inevitable process of language transfer (Weinreich, 1954), the speaker will opt for the nearest Spanish phones: [ɑ] or [o̞]. He, in fact, hears one of these two Spanish phones in the English utterance and, consequently, pronounces English /ɔ/ incorrectly. Thus, the problem is essentially one of auditory discrimination deficiency, and it is this problem of hearing which underlies the articulatory phenomenon of what is commonly called "foreign accent."

One branch of linguistics—sociolinguistics—has dealt extensively with the problems of bilingualism and has demonstrated forcefully that the psychological well-being and intellectual productivity of the bilingual child requires a restoration and maintenance—not the abandonment—of his bilingual capacities. This certainly suggests the need for speech and hearing clinicians and researchers specifically trained in the habilitation of bilingual children with speech and hearing disorders. Because the bilingual communities thus far have tended to localize in specific geographical regions and have not achieved the general economic level at which therapy is sought when a child or adult demonstrates disorders of hearing or language, they have not yet made a noticeable impact on the speech and hearing profession. That they will is only to be expected (Haugen, 1961; Ruke-Dravina, 1967).

Phonemics, of central importance in the speech and hearing sciences, is a contribution of modern linguistic analysis working upward from the basis of pure phonetics in a three-step procedure: articulation features > phones > phoneme classes. If we examine the English words *cool* and *key*, for example, our ear tells us that the initial consonant phoneme /k/, although undeniably the same phoneme in both occurrences, sound slightly different in each of the two words. A more posterior, or velar, articulation is used before /u/ and a more anterior, or palatal, articulation is used before /i/. When we analyze the words *cool* and *key* on the sound spectrograph, we see that the pattern of the initial /k/ is closely adapted to the formants of the following vowels. Anyone could, of course, substitute the more forward [ķ] of *key* for the more posterior [k] of *cool* and the result would be remarkable only in that it would sound as if the speaker has just the slightest touch of a foreign accent. Thus, these two noticeably different varieties of /k/, when interchanged one of the other, do not change the meaning we perceive when we hear an otherwise identical sequence of sounds following. Whether we use the velar or palatal /k/ before the sequence /-úwl/, we will still understand it as meaning "refreshing," or something similar. The linguist gives a name to these types of sounds: *allophones.* Thus, we have, in the examples cited, only one *phoneme*, but two *allophones.*

There are, basically, three types of allophones: (1) phonetically conditioned (such as those we have just seen); (2) positional variants; and (3) free variants.

The positional variant type is exemplified in the English word pair *lick* and *pill.* The fact that there is a perceptible difference between the frontal /l/ and the posterior [ł], sometimes called the "dark" [ł], but one which does not affect our perception of meaning, leads us to classify these as allophones of a single phoneme: /l/. The difference in sound corresponds directly to the position of each allophone in the utterance (in this case, initial and final) rather than to the environment of the following sound (as in *key* and *cool*), and, consequently, are positional variants rather than phonetically conditioned.

The third major category of allophones is the free variant. Take, for example, the utterances /ál/ and /əl/, for *all.* Both are characteristic pronunciations in English and many speakers use both interchangeably. Our ear perceives the difference in each case, of course, but the meaning we perceive remains unaltered. Thus, identifying this alteration as allophonic is automatic. Yet we note that it is neither the position of the sounds in the utterance nor the surrounding phonetic environment, so we cannot classify these allophones as phonetically conditioned or as positional variants. They are in a class of their own: free variants.

In a majority of cases, free variants in the overall pattern of the phonology of a language can be found to be geographically determined and one of the variants is said to be characteristic of one regional dialect as opposed to the other being characteristic of a different area. Sociolinguistics has emphasized that effective communication in given regions depends largely upon the speaker's consistent use of those allophones which are regionally determined. The concept of the social "outsider" in a community is in large part based upon this idea and the social history of the United States offers countless examples of "lack of communication" between native speakers of English when one fails to adhere to the allophonic patterns of the region.

This suggests that yet another area of cooperation between the linguist and the speech and hearing scientist could be direct toward remedying the traditional adherence to a single dialect of English in preparing materials for the speech and hearing impaired, in which all patterns are designed toward recreating the norms of this one dialect. The fact is, however, that the dialect selected is quite often either simply whatever the dialect of the developer of the materials at hand happens to be, or an artifically established norm, such as what we often call "stage pronunciation." Linguistics has demonstrated, through the study of linguistic geography, that no one dialect of American English is absolutely predominant. Thus, the clinician in California would hardly base his work with California patients on, say, the Boston or Houston dialects. Yet despite the obviousness of this, one searches in vain for regionally adapted habilitational materials.

B. *Syllables*

It would be a serious mistake to leave the question of the system of distinctive features in a language only after looking at individual sounds. Linguists do not consider the matter of the sound system of a language fully treated until they have examined the ways in which the language combines individual sounds into meaningful strings. We have already seen how individual distinctive acoustic and articulatory features are aligned into simultaneous bundles called phonemes. Now we must examine how phonemes are concatenated into meaningful, communicative sequences.

In terms of auditory training, of course, these considerations are of great importance. Although in following the dictum that residual hearing must be exploited to its fullest, hearing specialists have developed a wide variety of auditory discrimination materials (Wedenberg, 1951). These are too often based on the single concept of minimal pairs, from the purely segmental point of view. The fact is that human communication, although dependent upon the accurate perception and production of certain isolated sounds, is rarely carried out in such isolated units. The elementary pattern underlying any sequential grouping of phonemes is the syllable. We all are aware, of course, that the ability to articulate individual speech sounds in isolation does not in any way guarantee the ability to articulate these same sounds in sequence. The basic fact underlying the syllable is that the microwatt meter of any acoustic recording device will show definite "peaks" of acoustic energy which correspond in number and sequence precisely with the enunciation of the vocoidal (syllabic) sounds. Stetson (1951) suggests that the syllable is a motor unit, that each syllable is basically a movement complex in which the larger underlying movement is the breath pulse. Every free form in a language (defined as a sequence of sounds which can be bounded by silence) must contain an integral number of syllables. Obviously, the number of different syllables in a language is a small submultiple of the number of syllables, and the number of distinctive features a submultiple of the number of phonemes.

The key concept in syllable structure is the contrast of successive features within the syllable. The one part of the syllable which stands out from the others is the vocoid *vs.* contoid contrast. Using the symbols *C* and *V* for contoid and vocoid, respectively, we may describe the canonical shape of syllables in a language, e.g., *CV, VC, V, CVC,* etc. In contradistinction to *C,* *V* can neither be omitted nor figure twice in the syllable. *V* is always the peak (or highest acoustical point) of the syllable. The syllable boundary will thus fall at the lowest acoustical point. In using the terms *vocoid* and *contoid,* we recognize that the "traditional" vowel sounds are not the only ones which in English can function as syllabic peaks. Consequently, any sound that functions as a syllabic peak is, at that point, *vocoidal,* even though it may not formally be a *vowel.* English /r, l, n/, for example, can function as syllable peaks:

"learn"	/.CVC./	(/lrn/)
"learning"	/.CV.CVC./	(/lr.niŋ/)

C. Stress and Juncture

When we examine a written list of forms such as *protest, concert, permit, invalid, rebel, address,* our tendency is to want to pronounce them all with a higher degree of loudness or intensity on the first syllable. Yet these same forms, when they occur in utterances like "he will protest," "they will concert their efforts," "I won't permit it," "this pass is invalid," "we rebel," "address that letter!" we automatically produce the higher degree of volume or intensity on the second syllable. Of course, this is the familiar case of homonymic nouns and verbs in which the difference in meaning is perceptible only through a phenomenon of *stress.* Smith (1960) provides an entertaining example of the same principle by using the following newspaper headline, written at a time when a high rate of unemployment and a rash of robberies were prevalent:

REPORT NUMBER OF SAFE JOBS HERE

The situation being reported on is ambiguous because different degrees of *stress,* or "loudness," can fall on the words "safe" and "jobs," and, of course, stress is not marked in standard English orthography. Pairs of two-syllable utterances such as *permit* (n.) and *permit* (v.) seem to indicate that English has two degrees of stress: strong (/'/) and weak (/ᴗ/). But if we examine some utterances of three and four syllables, we shall quickly see that there are yet two more intermediate degrees of stress. Let us take the word *conversation* as an example. We immediately identify the third syllable as the most strongly stressed. The final syllable is, for most speakers, the least stressed. But if we listen closely, we will note that the remaining two syllables are not equally stressed: the first is clearly more heavily stressed than the second. The linguist, therefore, distinguishes four degrees of stress: *primary, secondary, tertiary,* and *weak,* in descending order of loudness or intensity. Thus, the linguist marks the stresses of the word *conversation* as follows:

/kàn|vər/séj/šň/

The symbols are:

/ó/ primary
/ò/ secondary
/ô/ tertiary
/ŏ/ weak

Another type of contrast in English is revealed through comparing sequences such as:

nitrate	vs.	night rate
an aim	vs.	a name
that sod	vs.	that's odd

The average speaker hears these pairs as different because of what he might perceive as a short break or silence between the items in the right-hand column, as if they were written: *night + rate, a + name, that's + odd*. The symbol /+/ is called *juncture*. Because, as we have seen, both stress and juncture are often the *only* contrasting feature between otherwise identical utterances, they are *phonemic* and are of as great importance in the communicative string as are the vowels and consonants. Yet for all this, both features are accorded relatively scanty treatment in our present materials.*

D. *Intonation*

Of equal, if not greater, importance as a basis for determining the various grammatical patterns of the language are the seven significant melodic features of language: the four *pitch* phonemes and the three *terminal contour* phonemes. The four pitch phonemes can be symbolized by the numerals 1, 2, 3, 4, with 1 representing the lowest significant pitch level and 4, the highest. Pitch phonemes differ from stress phonemes in that a significant pitch level continues over several syllables, each with its own stress, until another significant occurrence of pitch takes place.

At the end of each sequence of pitches, or intonation pattern, we also notice that our voice may "fade" or "fall away," "rise," or remain relatively sustained. The linguist marks these as /↓/, /↑/, and /|/, respectively. Again, intonation patterns (the combinations of pitch sequences and a terminal contour) are vital carriers of meaning and cannot be overlooked in the education of the hearing impaired. Because, however, the linguist has the means at hand to describe these phenomena visually, there remains little valid excuse for any continued lack of emphasis on them. Note that the immediate basic difference the hearing speaker of English perceives in the meaning of these two utterances, *Johnny ran out* (of the room) and *Johnny ran out* (of money), can be clearly shown:

[2]Johnny ran + [3]out.[1]   (of the room)
[2]Johnny ran [3]out.[1]   (of money)

---

* The details of the exact phonetic nature of stress and juncture are very complex and space does not permit them to be mentioned here.

Thus, intonation signals to use that the words in the sentences form different *constituents* and also that the *relationships* between the constituents are quite different, revealing that phonology is the basic foundation for the study of grammar through such examples as those in which stress differences signaled different relationships between words. But phonology not only helps us by furnishing an unequivocal and formal basis for deciding "what goes with what" *within* the sentence; it also allows us once and for all to decide what a sentence is and when it *ends*. We are no longer forced to "define" a sentence as "expressing a complete thought" or even as something bounded by silence or a "pause." A sentence can now be seen as one of several easily statable sequences of words, phrases, or clauses bounded by certain kinds of intonation patterns (Smith, 1960).

E.   *Rhythm*

In the speech of the severely to profoundly hearing impaired, one of the most consistent findings is a characteristically slow and labored articulatory pattern accompanied by high chest pressure with the expenditure of excessive amounts of breath (Hudgins, 1934). Another is the prolongation of vowels. A third is the addition of superfluous syllables between grouped consonants. These phenomena can be grouped into one larger category: rhythmic abnormalities.

In contrast to some other languages, English is characterized by what has been called *stress-timed rhythm*. This means that it takes about the same length of time to get from one primary stressed syllable to the next, in speaking at a given overall tempo, whether there are no syllables between them or many. If there are none, we slow down our rate of speech slightly; if there are many we squeeze them in fast. To diagram this, we shall use long vertical lines like the bar lines of music before each successive primary stress; these must not be confused with our intonational symbol /||/. The typical timing of two examples can then be shown as follows:

$$^2The \mid \text{bómb} \qquad \mid bléw \; \grave{u}p \; the \mid {}^3stréet^1 \downarrow$$
$$^2The \mid wind \; bl\grave{e}w \mid \acute{u}p \qquad the \mid {}^3stréet^1 \downarrow$$

This type of timing is the rhythmic basis of English verse. The versification makes full use of the availability in English of the stock of small syllables which, in some positions, can carry either secondary stress or no stress at all; in addition, we are accustomed in verse to have some of the syllables carry primary stress. If the versifier requires us to put a primary stress on, say, the first or third syllable of *Rebecca*, we rebel and say his sense of rhythm is poor. But he can quite freely require a primary stress on *and* or *of*, or the like. We should normally say

$$^2and \mid things \; are \mid not \; what \; they \mid {}^3seem^1 \downarrow$$

When Longfellow requires us to say, instead,

$$^2and \; thìngs \mid \acute{a}re \; not \mid wh\acute{a}t \; thèy \mid {}^3séem^1 \downarrow$$

the only uncomfortable distortion is the secondary stress on *things* (Hockett, 1958).

The study of speech rhythm implies a close examination of many additional features which the limitations of space prevent us from investigating in detail. Some of these are (Heffner, 1960):

1. the breath-group
    each such unit between two of which the speaker may pause considerably without destroying the distinctness of his utterance may be called a speech measure (again borrowing our terminology from music), phrase-group or sense group
2. fusion
    within the breath-group a number of different kinds of phenomena of fusion may be observed:
    A. dynamic displacement (omission of juncture)
        i.   *an aim > a name*
        ii. at any rate   /æ.tənɪ.rejt/
    B. doubling (gemination)
        we have various types   /wìjhæv:érjəstajps/
        more likely when primary stress follows
    C. reduction
        we have various types   /wìjhævè ↑ jəstájps/
        more likely when primary stress does not follow
    D. omission
        i.   *I've; I'm; won't.*   "Aphaeresis"
        ii. civilization   /sɪvləzéŝan/   "Syncope"
        iii. one or another   /wənrŋ əðr/   "Apocope"

We have now seen that the simple string of segmental phonemes (vowels and consonants) is only one part of communicative speech behavior and that true human language is not complete until these vital features of stress, juncture, intonation, and rhythm are added to it.

Conclusions and Summary

In this necessarily limited presentation, we have attempted to present an overview of a very few of the concepts and techniques of linguistics which would appear to have the most direct bearing on the education and habilitation of the hearing impaired. By focusing on a functional view of language and its structure, linguistic analysis helps to pinpoint the essential communicative elements of speech and language which form the indispensable core of the system of human communication.

Certainly, it is to be hoped that the linguist and the hearing specialist, given their common areas of interest, will strive to evolve means for closer cooperation and for an open, productive sharing of their theories and methods. Such cooperation begins in the fundamental training of both specialists in which intensive course work in linguistics should form part of the preparation of the hearing specialist and in which work in the pathologies of speech and hearing should be required of the linguist. At the professional level, such cooperation should take the form of sharing research funds and facilities, professional meetings and professional publication media for the mutual advancement of these two closely allied sciences.

References

Barry, K. E. 1899. The Five Slate System. Philadelphia: Sherman.

Berko, Jean. 1958. The child's learning of English morphology. Word 14:150–177.

Bidwell, Charles. 1968. Some typological considerations bearing upon language prehistory. Linguistics 44:5–10.

Bloomfield, Leonard. 1965. Language. New York: Holt, Rinehart and Winston.

Bolinger, Dwight. 1967. Aspects of Language. New York: Harcourt, Brace and World.

Brown, Roger and Ursula Bellugi. 1966. Three processes in the child's acquisition of syntax. In Janet Emig, et al. (Eds.) Language and Learning. New York: Harcourt, Brace and World.

Carmichael, Leonard. 1966. The early growth of language capacity in the individual. In Eric Lenneberg (Ed.) New Directions in the Study of Language. Cambridge: MIT Press. Pp. 1–22.

Carroll, John. 1960. Language development in children. Encyclopedia of Educational Research. New. York: Macmillan.

de Saussure, Ferdinand. 1922. Cours de Linguistique Générale, 2nd ed. Paris: Payot.

Di Carlo, Louis. 1964. The Deaf. Englewood Cliffs, N.J.: Prentice-Hall. P. 87.

Gleason, Henry. 1961. An Introduction to Descriptive Linguistics, rev. ed. New York: Holt, Rinehart and Winston.

Goldstein, K. 1948. Language and Language Disturbances. New York: Grune & Stratton.

Greenberg, Joseph (Ed.). 1966. Universals of Language, 2nd ed. Cambridge: MIT Press.

Hall, Robert A., Jr. 1964. Introductory Linguistics. Philadelphia: Chilton.

Haugen, Einar. 1961. The bilingual individual. In Sol Saporta (Ed.) Psycholinguistics. New York: Holt, Rinehart and Winston. Pp. 395–407.

Heffner, R. M. 1960. General Phonetics. Madison: University of Wisconsin Press. Pp. 173 ff.

Heider, F. K. and G. M. Heider. 1940. A comparison of sentence structure of deaf and hearing children. Psychological Monographs 52.1:42–103.

Hockett, Charles. 1958. A Course in Modern Linguistics. New York: Macmillan.

Hudgins, C. V. 1934. A comparative study of the speech coordinations of deaf and normal subjects. Journal of Genetic Psychology 44:1–48.

Hudgins, C. V. and F. C. Numbers. 1942. An investigation of the intelligibility of the speech of the deaf. Genetic Psychology Monographs 25:289–392.

Hughes, John. 1962. The Science of Language. New York: Random House.

Jakobson, Roman, et al. 1956. Fundamentals of Language. The Hague: Mouton.

Jakobson, Roman. 1964. Towards a linguistic typology of aphasic impairments. In De Reuch and O'Connor Disorders of Language. Boston: Little, Brown.

Jakobson, Roman, et al. 1967. Preliminaries to Speech Analysis. Cambridge: MIT Press. P. 3.

Jellinek, Augusta. 1948. Acoustic education in children. In Emil Froeschels (Ed.) Twentieth Century Speech and Voice Correction. New York: Philosophical Library. Pp. 103–109.

Joos, Martin. 1958. Semology: a linguistic theory of meaning. Studies in Linguistics XIII:53–70.

Lashley, K. S. 1951. The problem of serial order in behavior. In L. A. Jeffress (Ed.) Cerebral Mechanisms in behavior. New York: Wiley. Pp. 112–136.

Lennebèrg, Eric H. 1964. A biological perspective of language. New Directions in the Study of Languages. Cambridge: MIT Press.

Leopold, Werner F. 1952. Bibliography of Child Language. Evanston.

Leopold, Werner. 1953–54. Patterning in children's language behavior. Language Learning 5:1–14.

Luria, A. R. 1947. Travmaticheskaja Afazija. Moscow: Academy of Medical Sciences.

Moulton, W. G. 1966. A Linguistic Guide to Language Learning. New York: Modern Language Association. P. 23.

Robins, R. H. 1964. General Linguistics: An Introductory Survey. Bloomington: Indiana University Press.

Ruke-Dravina, V. 1967. Mehrsprachigkeit im Vorschulalter. Lund: Gleerup.

Sapir, Edward. 1921. Language. New York: Harcourt, Brace and World.

Saporta, Sol (Ed.). 1961. Psycholinguistics. New York: Holt, Rinehart and Winston.

Smith, Frank and George Miller (Eds.). 1966. The Genesis of Language. Cambridge: MIT Press.

Smith, Henry, Jr. 1960. Linguistics: a modern view of language. In L. Bryson (Ed.) An Outline of Man's Knowledge of the Modern World. Garden City: Doubleday.

Stetson, R. H. 1951. Motor Phonetics, 2nd ed. Amsterdam.

Street, J. C. 1967. Methodology in immediate constituent analysis. In I. Rauch, et al. (Eds.) Approaches in Linguistic Methodology. Madison: University of Wisconsin Press.

Thomas, Owen. 1965. Transformational Grammar and the Teacher of English. New York: Harcourt, Brace and World.

Wedenberg, E. 1951. Auditory training of deaf and hard of hearing children. Acta Otolargyngologica suppl. 94:1–129.

Weinreich, Uriel. 1954. Languages in Contact. New York: Linguistic Circle of New York. Pp. 7–12, 63–70.

Wells, Rulon. 1947. Immediate constituents. Language XXIII:81–117.

Chapter 8

Language Development

FREDERICK S. BERG, Ph.D.

Normal hearing children ordinarily learn a verbal language system better and earlier in life than do hard of hearing children. A description of the landmarks and sequence of language acquisition may help us to understand why this should be the case. It may also provide guidelines for planning a remedial program designed to accelerate language development among hard of hearing children.

Language may be defined as the complex system of phonological, syntactical, morphological, and semantical forms by which humans communicate with one another. Characteristically the verbal language system is learned largely through the medium of speech events. However, its refinement ordinarily comes as a result of use of the visual code of reading and writing.

From the earliest stages of linguistic acquisition, an individual comprehends more through the language system than he can express. By age 2, for example, he can follow simple verbal directions given by others but not fully express them himself. At age 6 he may understand over 10,000 words but only speak 2,500 of them. Later in life, his reading vocabulary may exceed 100,000 words but his spoken repertoire consists of only 15,000 words (McCarthea, 1954; Smith, 1926; Templin, 1957).

Language expression, however, seems to facilitate language comprehension. Evidence exists that speech perception is more closely related to speech production than to acoustic correlates of auditory discrimination (Lieberman, 1967). The child who learns to articulate the difficult phonemes may perceive linguistic features better than his peer who has defective speech. Also, the listener who subvocalizes along with the speaker may decode the message better; and the person who learns to express himself well in writing may in turn have become a better reader.

Prelinguistic Utterances

The prelinguistic utterances of the child contribute to his language acquisition. They are the discomfort cries, the comfort sounds, and the vocal play which occur primarily during the first year of life and which precede the emergence of the first words. They include phonetic and prosodic features similar to many of those characteristic of the spoken code of adulthood.

111

Lewis (1951) described the existence of phonetic-like features among infants. He noted, for example, that back-like consonants were associated with the swallowing and belching movements following infant feeding. He observed also that lip consonants were made with articulations of the tongue and lips in anticipation of feeding. Lewis observed also the repetition of identical or similar syllables in the babbling activity of the first year of life. The writer has noted that such syllabic repetitions as "dada" and "mama" often are among the first words uttered by the child because his parents respond in a meaningful way to them.

Vocal activities basic to language development occur as early as the first six months of life. Babbling is prevalent and intonation patterns are evident. The auditory feedback loop is also becoming established as acoustic sensations are linked with tactual and kinesthetic impressions.

Berry (1969) indicates that the infant's prelinguistic utterances are perhaps valuable only as a tuning up and integrating activity upon which true speech depends. Lewis (1951), however, notes that articulatory growth is considerable by the first year of life. By 12 months of age when words begin to emerge, a child might use many vowels as well as the consonants /p/, /b/, /m/, /t/, /d/, and /n/.

Phonological Development

The raw material or sound substance of prelinguistic utterance begins to be classified into a finite set of mutually exclusive classes by the sixth to ninth month of life (Myklebust, 1964). Each class or phoneme emerges in the speech of the child on a more or less developmental schedule.

The emergence of the phonological subsystem of language is a landmark in language acquisition. It signals the *coming to life* of the entire language system which has existed only in potential form previous to this time. It is manifested receptively by the infant's developing repertoire of appropriate responses to the speech signals of others. Phonological emergence is evidenced also by the growth in number and type of speech signals produced by the child.

A determination of whether or not the language system of a child encompasses particular phonemes is difficult to make. Variables such as contexual clues, linguistic redundancy, and childhood uncooperativeness have confounded identification of the existence of phonemes in receptive language responses. What the observer seems to know is that the child is identifying enough of the phonemes to decode the message of the speaker. He does not know which phonemes have become a part of the child's phonological system. Lieberman's (1967) research on intonation and perception does suggest, however, that the initial phonological classifications are suprasegmental rather than segmental.

On the other hand, the emerging expressive language of the young child does not reveal the acquisition of all phonemes that may have been acquired, either. The expressive form of language or speech is motor in characteristic and so complex that it is not usually mastered until at least 8 years of age.

The acquisition of speech is also delayed by such factors as undeveloped auditory perception (Templin, 1957), inconsistent environmental stimulation, and competing psychological and biological priorities.

A description of the manuevering of the vocal organs during adult utterance may clarify the motor task faced by the child in learning to speak. Initially selective respiratory activity produces a controlled exhaled airstream which is needed for the production of long sequences of syllables. As the airstream is exhaled, it is modulated in numerous ways along the vocal tract. Within the larynx it is changed in distinctive acoustic ways so that pitch and intensity phenomena will be produced. Next, the airstream is modified physically by changing relationships of the resonating spaces of the laryngeal, pharyngeal, oral, and nasal cavities. Finally, it is again changed acoustically by a great variety of positionings of the articulators including the oropharyngeal walls, velum, tongue, lips, and mandible. The finished product is a sequence of overlapping movements which modulates one exhaled air stream after another in a manner appropriate to particular social situations. The child's task of learning such complex behavior is that of producing successively closer approximations to the target pattern over a period of eight years.

Notwithstanding these limitations, a longitudinal study of the developing language system of a young child reveals the existence of one phoneme after another. From the emergence of the first words at about one year of age to the near mastery of articulation at age eight years, the phonemes are eventually identified. However, each phoneme of a child is not ordinarily discovered by an observer at its onset of existence. It may have been part of the language system of the child for many months or even years previously, notwithstanding the usual reciprocal relationship between speech reception and speech production. Also, when a phoneme is identified it may not include all its member allophones as yet.

The writer has made a longitudinal recording of some of the intelligible speech responses of one of his sons named Sven. Table 16 reveals a list of words, phrases and sentences containing most English phonemes uttered during the first three years of Sven's life.

By Sven's standards, however, his expanding phonemic system may have included even more classifications than those suggested from Table 16. Sven uttered many additional words that were intelligible within particular intonation contours and social contexts but which contained misarticulations in the positions of the symbols underlined in Table 17.

Table 16. Speech Responses and Emerging Phonemes of Sven During the First, Second, and Third Years of Life

Year	Response	New Phoneme
1	dædæ, mɑmə, bauwau, haɪ, hɛlo, kukɪ	/d/, /æ/, /m/, /ɑ/, /ə/, /b/, /w/, /au/, /h/, /aɪ/, /ɛ/, /o/, /k/, /u/
2	go, no, ɪə (ear), mgoaut foə (for), bip	/g/, /n/, /ɪ/, /ə/, /t/, /f/, /i/, /p/
3	jɛwo (yellow), wet (late), tu, bæŋ, ju fid, bɔɪ	/j/, /e/, /u/, /ŋ/, /ju/, /ɔɪ/

It may be that the great majority if not all of adult phonemes exist in the language system of the 3-year-old child even though his motor speech immaturity precludes observation of them.

Templin (1957) has studied the acquisition of speech articulation by 480 children from three to eight years of age as indicated in Table 18.

The speech utterances of Templin's 3-year olds were essentially intelligible but far from completely articulate. Eight-year-old children, however,

Table 17. *Misarticulations in Speech Responses Made by Sven During the Second and Third Years of Life*

Year	Response
2	hɛlo (hello), luɪs (Louis), ʃu (shoe), noz (nose)
3	θri (three), dʒɚæf (giraffe), sɛvn (seven), ðæts (that's), tʃɝtʃ (church)

Table 18. *Earliest Age at which 75 Percent of All Subjects Produced Each of 176 Tested Sound Elements Correctly (Templin, 1957, p. 51)*

CA	Sound Elements
3	Vowels: ē, ĭ, ĕ, ă, ŏ, ŭ, ŏŏ, ōō, ō, ô, à, ûr Diphthongs: u, ā, ī, ou, oi Consonants: m-, -m-, -m, n-, -n-, -n, -ng-, -ng, p-, -p-, -p, t-, -t, k-, -k-, -k, b-, -b-, d-, -d-, g-, -g-, f-, -f-, -f, h-, -h-, w-, -w- Double-consonant blends: -ngk
3.5	Consonants: -s-, -z-, -r, y-, -y- Double-consonant blends: -rk, -ks, -mp, -pt, -rm, -mr, -nr, -pr, -kr, -br, -dr, -gr, -sm
4	Consonants: -k, -b, -d, -g, s-, sh-, -sh, -v-, j-, r-, -r-, l-, -l- Double-consonant blends: pl-, pr-, tr-, tw-, kl-, kr-, kw-, bl-, br-, dr-, gl-, sk-, sm-, sn-, sp-, st-, -lp, -rt, -ft, -lt, -fr Triple-consonant blends: -mpt, -mps
4.5	Consonants: -s, -sh-, ch-, -ch-, -ch Double-consonant blends: gr-, fr-, -lf
5	Consonants: -j- Double-consonant blends: fl-, -rp, -lb, -rd, -rf, -rn, -shr Triple-consonant blends: str-, -mbr
6	Consonants: -t-, th-, -th-, -th, v-, -v, t̶h̶-, -l Double-consonant blends: -lk, -rb, -rg, -rth, -nt, -nd, -pl, -kl, -bl, -gl, -fl, -sl Triple-consonant blends: skw-, -str, -rst, -ngkl, -nggl, -rj, -ntth, -rch
7	Consonants: -th-, z-, -z, -̶t̶h̶, -zh-, -zh, -j Double-consonant blends: thr-, shr-, sl-, sw-, -lz, -zm, -lth, -sk, -st Triple-consonant blends: skr-, spl-, -spr, -skr, -kst, -jd
8	Double-consonant blends: -kt, -tr, -sp

* hw-, -hw-, -lfth, and -tl are not produced correctly by 75 percent of the subjects by 8 years of age.

seemed to have essentially mastered the articulatory maneuvering required of mature speech.

Syntactical Development

A second landmark in the child's acquisition of language is the emergence of the syntactical subsystem. This aspect of language ordinarily called syntax may be labeled as *combinatorial skill* (McNeill, 1965). It refers to combining words, forming new combinations of words, sequencing different groupings of grammatical classes, and producing new combinations of sentence patterns. Through such combining the child creates sentences, participates in conversation, and describes the world as he comes to know it.

A description of syntactical acquisition requires initially that a distinction be made between language competence and linguistic performance (McNeill, 1965). The former refers to a biological capacity, or inborn set of predispositions, that is present in every neurologically intact human organism. The latter refers to utilization of this capacity through the development of language comprehension and linguistic expression.

The capacity to acquire language may consist of two parts: hypotheses or language universals including basic grammatical relations, and abilities to test hypotheses against parental speech. The capacity for syntactical acquisition may hit a crest at 2 to 4 years of age, decline thereafter, and disappear by adolescence. If this is true, syntactical performance may optimally emerge during the early years of life. Ordinarily, words begin to be combined in syntactical arrangements during the second year of life, and syntactical manipulation is virtually complete by 3.5 to 4 years of age (McNeill, 1965).

Table 19 illustrates Sven's rapid development of syntactical performance from use of single words at 12 months to employment of complex sentences at 36 months.

The psycholinguist views the young child as a fluent speaker of an exotic language, namely his own (McNeill, 1965). On the basis of longitudinal recording, he tries to write successive grammars that represent the syntactical development of the child. The psycholinguist regards these grammars as models of the competence of the child to grasp the structural patterns of sentences. He notes that nearly every sentence is novel rather than imitative. The child, as remarkable as it may seem, is constructing successively more complex grammars by exposure to parental speech.

A child's acquisition of the rules of adult syntax for a particular language is a series of cumulative steps (Lee, 1966). The learning of one step depends upon success at earlier stages. An adaptation of Lee's outline of syntactical development appears in Table 20.

Level I

According to Lee, the first developmental level consists of 2-word combinations called the pivot open class constructions. Illustrations may be noted in Table 20.

Table 19.   Sample Utterances Made by Sven at 6-Month Intervals from 1 to 3 Years of Age

Month	Sample Utterances
12	Mama, bowwow
18	Uppa go
24	I want more.
30	Let Sven go down and iron.
36	When Louis gets big like me, I'll be bigger.

The open class of these miniaturized adult syntactical forms include words for the objects, activities, and attributes of the child's growing world. Referred to as lexical forms, these vocabulary words comprise many thousands of nouns, verbs, adjectives, and adverbs. In Table 20, for example, the open class words include *big, take,* and *truck* in addition to *car.*

The pivot words form a closed class of several hundred highly functional words, usually monosyllabic in form. In Table 20 they include such words as *a, my, no, again, other,* etc. They are typically learned early in life as compared to the many thousands of lexical forms which would require a lifetime to acquire even if no new words were added to the category.

The pivot-open class combinations are not the only 2-word utterances used by the child during his second year of life. Certain utterances called fragments are incorporated into other constructions but do not by themselves expand into sentences. Some of these include prepositional phrases, negatives, and conjunctions such as *to office, not car,* and *and car.* Other 2-word utterances such as *go bye bye* are mere imitations of adult stereotyped phrases. Perhaps the latter type of utterance should be classified as a vocabulary item and not as a construction of the child's grammar.

Level II

The second syntactical level encompasses use of the noun phrase. This construction consists of a series of 3–4 words, in which two or more pivot words occur, each in a special location of the string. Examples of the noun phrase included in Table 20 are *my big car, no more car,* and *the other big car.* In the noun phrase sequence an article or possessive which is produced occurs first, a quantifier second, an adjective third, and noun last.

All but the very last words of noun phrases are pivot words. At this level the pivot words have become differentiated into articles, possessive nouns and pronouns, numbers, or adjectives. In Table 20 *the* is an article, *my* a possessive, *no* and *other* quantifiers, and *big* an adjective.

Both *no more books* and *all more books* fit the order criterion of the noun phrase. However, a child must learn eventually that *all more books* is not socially acceptable. Also, morphologically immature noun phrases like *two big house* and *mine two shoe* are not acceptable for an adult grammar, either.

Table 20. Developmental Sentence Types (Modified from Lee, 1966. Pp. 314–315)

Level	Label	Examples
I	2 word	a car, big car, car broken, not car
II	Noun phrase	my big car, no more car, the other big car
III	Construction	it a car, the car broken, take car again
IV	Kernal sentence	there's the car, the car is broken, I see a car
V	Emerging transformations	is that a car, where is the car, the car and the truck are broken, I don't see a car

Once developed, a noun phrase may take a position in a longer string of words or be removed and replaced by a pronoun. For example, *a big car* might be encompassed by *the man rode in a big car* or replaced by the pronoun *it* in *He enjoyed it*. In the latter instance, our grammar requires that with second presentation and thereafter, *a big car* becomes *the big car*, the noun phrase which is really replaced by *it*.

Level III

The third level of syntax includes the designative, the predicative, and the verb phrase constructions. Examples include *it a car, the car broken*, and *take car again*, respectively. The constructions typically vary from 3–4 words in length but may contain somewhat more words in some instances.

A designative construction consists of an introductory pivot word and a noun phrase. In this construction pivot words include locators such as *here, where*, and *over there*; demonstrators such as *this, those*, and *which*; and identifiers such as *it, itsa*, and *s*. Irregulars such as *itsa* and *s* may either classify a series of adult words for the child or be parts of expanded designative sentences. Often one must conduct a junctural and phonemic analysis to determine whether or not in an example like *itsa car*, a child has said *itsa, sa*, or *it's a*.

A predicative construction is a noun phrase followed by one or more words about it. The predicates of the predicative construction include several grammatical forms: adjective, prepositional phrase, locator, and noun phrase. A child might say, for example, *a man bad, a man at home, a man there*, and *a man you*, respectively.

It is of interest that a locator such as *there* and a demonstrator such as *that* do not share the same privilege of positional occurrence as they did in designative constructions, for example, *there a car* and *that a car*. In the predicative constructions *there* appears at the end position such as *a car there*; whereas *that* is located in the initial position, *that boy Louis*. In the latter example, the predicative construction seems to consist of two consecutive noun phrases *that boy* and *Louis*.

A verb phrase is a verb followed by a noun phrase, a prepositional phrase, a locator, an adverb, or some combination of these forms. An example is *take car again*. A verb phrase, however, often includes a particle such as *down* in *lie down on the blanket*. An example of an extended verb phrase is *look at that thing on me*. It includes a verb, a particle, a noun phrase, and a prepositional phrase.

At times a child may bypass a verb phrase construction to reach the next higher sentence level of syntactical development. For example, he might use a 2-word subject-predicate utterance like *you feed*. In most cases, however, a verb phrase seems to be generated separately from a noun phrase, and the two joined to form a basic kernal sentence (McNeill, 1965).

Stereotyped constructions, or phrases which are oft-repeated without their component parts being understood by the child, also are used at the third level of syntactical development. According to Lee (1966), it is probable that *don know*, or *donno*, or even *I don't know* began as a stereotyped phrase without being constructed from a grammatical system. However, it is difficult to determine whether or not such a phrase is stereotyped or a product of grammatical competence.

Level IV

The fourth level of syntactical development is the formulation by the child of kernal sentences. These include the designative construction, the predicative construction, and the actor-action sentence. Examples included in Table 20 are *there's the car, the car is broken*, and *I see a car*, respectively. These sentences characteristically are three to five words in length. A rationale may exist for lumping the designative and predicative constructions into one category of constructions which incorporates use of *is*. In this way, there would be the *is* kernal sentences and the actor-action kernals, or a two classification fourth level.

The designative sentence may be considered an expansion of the third level designative construction by the addition of *is* between the designative word and the following noun phrase. The words *come* and *go* also have special applications in designative sentences. Examples are *here comes a car* and *there goes a wagon*.

A designative sentence is used by a child to point out or identify an object. It is one kind of simple-active-declarative sentence from which transformations can be evolved. For example, *there is a car* can be changed to *where is a car* or *is there a car*.

The predicative sentence is an expansion of the predicative construction by the inclusion of *is* or *'s*. For example, *this is muffin* becomes *this is a muffin*. It is another type of simple-active-declarative kernal sentence. Emerging interrogative and negative transformations include *is this a muffin* and *this is not a muffin*.

The actor-action sentence is a combination of an independently developed noun phrase and similarly generated verb phrases. This type of sentence, for example *Sven do it,* can be evolved into transformations that indicate further grammatical development.

Level V

The fifth level of syntactical development includes the emerging transformations such as *did Sven do it* and *Sven did not do it.* Such transformations are revealed by the child's substitutions of pronouns for noun phrases, use of interrogatives as mentioned, and employment of *and* to join series of words.

The acquisition of the syntactical system seems to proceed by a categorizing or assigning of class membership to all incoming speech stimuli. The child typically does not memorize sentences uttered by adults. He rather uses a set of rules to understand those spoken by others and to generate both sentences he has heard and many others as well. According to the generative model of grammar (Chomsky, 1957), a child utilizes a combination of generative rules and a heuristic component which determines, through a series of successive approximations, which rules are used to produce a particular sentence (Menyuk, 1964). Through application of this process, the child learns to formulate various sentence types such as affirmative, negative, and imperative constructions. Examples might be *Louis did it, Louis didn't do it,* and *Louis, do it,* respectively.

At the transformational level, more and more complex sentence types are generated by rules for addition, deletion, permutation, and substitution within or among kernal sentences. The rules which apply to one kernal sentence are called simple transformations; those which operate on two or more kernals are termed general transformations.

Menyuk (1964) described transformation structures used by a young child between the second and third years of life. At age 2.0 these included *negation, contraction, relative question,* and *imperative;* at 2.4, *adjective, nominal compound;* 2.6, *possessive, separation, relative clause, conjunction;* 2.7, *infinitival complement, question;* 2.9, *passive nominalization, cause conjunction, conjunction deletion, inversion,* and *do.*

Among some children a period of 60 to 90 days during the third year of life encompasses a considerable progression in the use of transformations. For example, Sven progressed from use of sentences that averaged 2.65 words in length during his 30th month of life to those that averaged 6.50 words during his 32nd month, as may be noted in Table 21.

The sentences of the 30th month were kernal sentences at best. Those employed 60 to 90 days later were substantial transformations. By 36 months, or another 120 days later, Sven was using complex sentences like *When Louis gets big like me, I'll be bigger* and *If I see Daddy, I'll tell him that I want some of that juice again.*

Templin (1957) analyzed 24,000 utterances of 3- to 8-year-old children according to length, grammatical complexity, grammatical accuracy, and parts of speech used. The mean length of utterance varied from approximately 4

Table 21.   Mean Length and Longest Utterance of a Sample of 20 Syntactical Constructions Spoken by Sven During Each of Three Successive Months

Month	Mean Words per Sentence	Longest Generative Construction
30	2.65	That's a hole.
31	4.35	I want a pencil like in Daddy's hand.
32	6.50	I wish we could have two bathrooms, one for men folk, and one for women folk.

words at 3 years of age to 7–8 words at 8 years. During this period a steady increase in the use of more complex and elaborated forms of sentences occurred as well as a consistent decrease in the proportionate use of structurally incomplete but functionally complete utterances. Forty-eight percent of the remarks of the 3-year-old children and 76.1 percent of the utterances of the 8-year-olds were grammatically correct. After the age of 3 the proportion of parts of speech did not change.

Morphological Development

The acquisition of the morphemes of a verbal language system may be viewed in part as the highest level of generative language functioning (Chomsky, 1957). Morphemes, the smallest meaningful units of language, are of two types: bound or free. A morpheme which can stand alone, for example *dark,* is free. A morpheme which cannot appear by itself, for example *er* in *darker,* is bound. Whereas the free morphemes emerge as the first words used by the child, the bound morphemes do not appear with any frequency until well into the third year of life.

Menyuk (1964, p. 110) describes the morphological level of grammar in terms of the application of inflectional rules.

> For example, at the phrase structure level we may choose the sentence Noun Phrase + Verb Phrase expanded into "He play + past tense." At the transformational level we may add by an optional rule the "do" morpheme and derive "He do play + past tense." Then from another optional rule for a question we permute and derive "Do he play + past tense." From a final obligatory transformation we permute tense to attach to "do + and derive "Do + past tense he play." At the morphology level "do" + past tense becomes "did" and the sentence "Did he play?" is derived. In this way the model organizes previously compartmentalized measures of language production into an interdependent sequence of rules.

Inflectional morphemes are bound to nouns, verbs, adjectives, and adverbs. Examples of these are italicized in selected utterances used by Sven during the first six months of the fourth year of life as noted in Table 22.

Table 22. Inflectional Morphemes in Sven's Sentences

Month	Noun	Morpheme Verb	Adjective or Adverb
37	We should go to our relatives, . . .	Louis splash*ed* me . . .	When Louis gets big, I'll be big*ger*.
38	I don't like vegetable*s*.	I slep*t* . . . and open*ed* my eyes . . .	
39	My pant*s* hold me together.	This dog is stand*ing* up.	Glenn's the small*est*.
40	The man*s* are not singing.	I'*ll* come home at three then.	When I get big*ger*, I should have one of those.
41	If you need more groceries, you . . .	I was cry*ing* for awhile.	I'm eating slow*ly*.
42	My teeth are getting worn out.	That surprise*s* me.	I'm getting so tired . . . purple flavor*ed* nestles.

Some of the combinations of bound and free morphemes used by children are generated by grammatical rules but not acceptable by adult standards. Examples of such unusual forms used by Sven were: *The mans are not singing*, 3.4; *That's why I like to go to bed because I don't get any real botherments from Glenn*, 5.1; *Well those car windows have been unconnected*, 5.3.

Berko (1961) investigated the learning of English morphological rules by 4 to 7 year olds. Of 27 comparisons of use of morphological rules, the school age children performed better than the preschoolers did in 26 instances. However, these differences were significant at the .05 level in only 12 instances. The children were presented with a number of nonsense stimuli designed to elicit plurals, verb tenses, possessives, and derivations of compound words. Berko found that the children in this age range responded with clearly delimited morphological rules. Their answers were not always right by English standards but they were consistent and orderly. For example, the children were able to form the plurals requiring the /-s/ or /-z/ allomorphs but did not generalize to form new words in the /-ɪz/ allomorph. The children did, however, add the /-ɪz/ more often to form possessives and verbs. On the verb forms, the best performance was on the present progressive: 90 percent of all children said that a man who knew how to *zib* was *zibbing*. The children did not, however, have complete control in applying the /-er/ and /-est/ to form the comparative and superlative forms. Also, derivation of words was minimally used when inflectional suffixes were competing for attention.

Inasmuch as the mastery of morphological rules and associated syntactical structures is not accomplished during the preschool years, extensive *grammar* instruction is provided as a part of formal schooling. For example, considerable attention is given to the learning of the principal parts of verbs such as: *go, went, gone; lie, lay, lay;* and *grow, grew, grown.* In these instances, however, children generally are unable to test hypotheses to determine the correctness of irregular forms according to adult standards. Learning must depend considerably upon memorization instead.

Semantic Development

Chomsky and Halle (1968) suggest that each sentence may be analyzed as having two components: a surface structure which is the phonetic shape of an utterance, and a deep structure which determines the semantic content. "The grammar of each language relates phonetic representations to surface structures in a specific way; and furthermore, it relates surface structures to deep structures, and, indirectly to semantic interpretations."

From the time that the first words emerge at about 12 months (Darley and Winitz, 1961, p. 289) to the period of late adulthood, a vocabulary of free morphemes is acquired cumulatively by the individual. As members of semantic categories or parts of speech, these morphemes with or without bound morphemes describe the objects, events, and attributes of the individual's growing world. The lexicon or dictionary contains the thousands of lexical or content words as well as the hundreds of function words or functors.

The size of the child's developing vocabulary of comprehension and of expression is impressive. At 2 years of age receptive vocabulary may exceed 1,000 words and expressive vocabulary, about 250 words (Smith, 1926). Similarly at six years of age these vocabularies may be approximately 13,000 and 2,500 words respectively. In her detailed study of 480 young children, Templin (1957) estimated the size of receptive vocabularies of 6, 7, and 8 year olds at 13,000, 20,000 and 26,000, respectively.

In a description of the reading process, Buswell (1959) noted that while the unabridged dictionary contained more than 300,000 words, no one used them all. More than 98 percent of words found in common nontechnical material read by adults were a basic vocabulary of 4,000 words. Seventy-five percent of such reading matter employed only 300 different words, most of which were functors.

Many of the function words have multiple meanings. Simmons (1949) found an average of 4 meanings per word in commonly repeated words of fourth grade arithmetic textbooks. For example, the word *over* could mean *across* in *over the ocean, above* in *over the table, again* in *do it over* and *finished* in *it is over.*

The vocabulary development of the child reveals much about the semantics or meanings derived by the child from his environment. It also provides insight into the realms of reasoning and cognition. The utterances of Sven as noted in Table 23 are provocative.

Summary and Guidelines

In summary, several parameters of language development have been described briefly in this chapter. The development of prelinguistic utterances, as well as the phonological, syntactical, morphological, and semantic subsystems of language, have been outlined. The content of the chapter suggests at least five guidelines that might well be applied to the education of hard of hearing children.

1. The prelinguistic utterances of the hard of hearing child, being basic to the mastery of language itself, should be encouraged from the earliest months of life through the combined use of appropriate sound amplification, natural and contrived situations, and parental verbalization.

2. The hard of hearing child's language acquisition follows biological laws of innate mechanistic maturation rather than the laws of learning. Therefore, it should be facilitated early in life; and longitudinal evaluation of language growth should be applied to such a child to determine whether or not the various levels of syntactical and morphological development are emerging as expected. Ordinarily, syntactical skills exfoliate and selected morphological rules exist by three to four years of age, at which time the normal child exhibits established rules of categorization, differentiation, and transformations (DiCarlo, 1968).

3. During the habilitative process hearing remediation should be conducted to enable the hard of hearing child to perceive the unstressed words and syllables which are linguistically function words and bound morphemes. With just perception of stressed elements, the phonetic shape of the utterance will be restricted and surface and deep structures will be deleteriously affected. Telegraphic language will result in which articles, prepositions, conjunctions, auxiliary verbs, and inflections will be omitted.

4. Reading and writing instruction should constitute an integral part of the habilitative and regular curriculum of the hard of hearing child. It employs a medium which may be perceived notwithstanding hearing impairment. However, it is based upon language acquisition which is developed naturally through hearing.

Table 23. Ten of Sven's Most Interesting Remarks from 36 to 64 Months of Age

Month	Remarks
36	I am not going home because I am going to New York City with Louis Nils Berg.
48	I looked in the microscope and Glenn has chicken pox all over him.
54	My tummy hurts so much it's going to cry its heart out.
56	He's a house hopper. If he was on the pavement, he'd be called a pavement hopper. If he was on the grass, he'd be called a grasshopper like he usually is.
56	I'm so irritated, I'm just frustrated. It astonishes me.
57	I'd like to have an electric motor to widen my shoe when I put my foot into it.
60	When I push the button, I'll go up to the top of the house, or to outer space, or to the top of outer space.
61	I made a rule for myself. When I'm watching TV, do not leave until the program is over. This is the first rule I've made.
62	I lost my mind on projects. I'm not wanting any more projects. My mind is off from the projects. Maybe I'll have some after I see the World's Fair.
64	Well, breakfast is when you wake up, and dinner is before you go to bed, and lunch is in the middle of the afternoon. Lunch is between morning and afternoon.

5. Prosodic and articulatory competence, being supportive of the acquisition of all of the language subsystems, should be encouraged from an early age so that the hard of hearing child progressively approximates target or adult standards of vocal behavior.

References

Berko, J. 1961. The child's learning of English morphology. In S. Saporta (Ed.) Psycholinguistics. New York: Holt, Rinehart and Winston. Pp. 359–376.

Berry, J. 1969. Language Disorders of Children. New York: Appleton-Century-Crofts.

Buswell, G. 1959. The reading process. The Reading Teacher 13:108–114.

Chomsky, N. 1957. Syntactic Structures. The Hague: Mouton.

Chomsky, N. and M. Halle. 1968. The Sound Pattern of English. New York: Harper & Row.

Darley, F. and H. Winitz. 1961. Age of the first word: review and research. Journal of Speech and Hearing Disorders 26:272–290.

DiCarlo, L. 1968. Speech, language, and cognitive abilities of the hard-of-hearing. Proceedings of the Institute on Aural Rehabilitation. Denver: University of Denver.

Lee, L. 1966. Developmental sentence types: a method for comparing normal and deviant syntactic development. Journal of Speech and Hearing Disorders 31:311–330.

Lewis, M. M. 1951. Infant Speech: A Study of the Beginnings of Language. New York: Humanities Press; London: Routledge and Kegan Paul.

Lewis, M. M. 1963. Language, Thought and Personality in Infancy and Childhood. New York: Basic Books.

Lieberman, P. 1967. Intonation, Perception, and Language. Cambridge, Mass.: The MIT Press.

McCarthea, D. 1954. Language development in children. In L. Carmichael (Ed.) Manual of Child Psychology. New York: John Wiley & Sons. Pp. 492–630.

McNeill, D. 1965. The capacity for language acquisition. Research on Behavioral Aspects of Deafness. Washington, D.C.: Vocational Rehabilitation Administration, U.S. Department of Health, Education, and Welfare.

Menyuk, P. 1964. Comparison of grammar of children with functionally deviant and normal speech. Journal of Speech and Hearing Research 7:109–121.

Myklebust, H. 1964. The Psychology of Deafness. New York: Grune & Stratton.

Simmons, A. 1945. Multiple meanings of words in arithmetic textbooks. St. Louis, Washington University: Unpublished Master's Thesis.

Smith, M. 1926. Vocabulary in Young Children. University of Iowa Studies in Child Welfare 3 (5).

Templin, M. 1957. Certain language skills in children. Institute of Child Welfare Monograph No. 26. Minneapolis, Minn.: University of Minnesota Press.

Chapter 9

A Functional Analysis of Behavior*

MARVIN F. DALEY, Ph.D. and
PETER C. WOLFF, Ph.D.

Introduction

Why do organisms behave as they do? This chapter examines variables which are functionally related to behavior, and the empirically derived principles on which these functional relationships are based. Using these principles, a high degree of control over the behavior of organisms can be maintained.

The fundamental assumption underlying behavioral analysis is that any behavior comprising observable recordable events can be measured. Therefore, the description of behavior in scientific terms similar to those used in the natural sciences offers the greatest advantages. Because there is a lawful relationship between the probability of behavior and observable environmental conditions—the independent variables—an experimental analysis of behavior can proceed most effectively by systematically replicating procedural effects and evaluating these effects against a measured baseline of behavior.

The specific characteristics of a behavioral event and its associated probability of occurrence are determined by four main classes of variables: (1) the environmental conditions which precede and accompany the behavior, (2) the special properties of the response—topographical, physiological, etc., (3) the contingencies that operate to relate responses to their immediate and historical consequences, and (4) the environmental consequences themselves.

In the following chapter these four classes of variables are discussed. The first section contains an overview of major procedures to assist in organizing an entry into the literature. In the second section the means for developing, maintaining, and increasing behavior through positive and negative contingencies are examined with emphasis on reinforcement scheduling. In the third section procedures are described for decreasing response rates. The fourth section contains a discussion of the important features of stimulus control over behavior. In the fifth section the setting of momentary response probabilities are examined, and in the sixth section, several very active research

* The authors thank P. Bement, N. Daley, J. Fitch, J. Mahelic, L. Morreau, and P. Pool whose timely and vigorous assistance enabled us to meet the editor's deadline.

areas are outlined with a description of some major developments in the functional analysis of behavior.

Operant Conditioning

Operant conditioning is used to change the strength of behavior which is more complex than respondent or reflexive behavior (Skinner, 1969). Behaviors like verbalizations, motor skills, imitation, cooperation, aggression, love, thinking, reasoning, and conceptualization can be approached with operant conditioning procedures. The procedure was developed by Skinner (1938), who adopted the strategy to provide a functional rather than a mere descriptive analysis of behavior. Skinner's suggestion was to define behavior by its consequences. For example, the consequences of behavior, such as gaining parental attention or obtaining food and drink, define the operant response.

Obtaining liquids for consumption is an example of operant behavior. The young child may simply cry and get the drink, while his older brother may have to pull his mother's apron and say "drink" before he gets the water. His father may have to talk for an hour or more to get out of the house, then drive downtown, park the car, find a sign that says "bar," sit on a bar stool and ask for a specific drink. Skinner would say these behaviors are examples of the same class of operant behavior because they are all maintained by similar consequences. This section will explain how the adult's complex operant behaviors develop out of the relatively simple behavior of the infant.

The basic operant conditioning procedure is to identify consequences or stimuli which strengthen or weaken the probability of behavior. These consequences are of two general types, *reinforcements* and *punishments*. Reinforcements are consequences which increase the frequency or probability of a behavior and which maintain and strengthen behavior. Punishments are consequences which decrease the frequency or probability of a behavior and which suppress and eliminate behavior. Reinforcement procedures employ stimuli like food, good grades, parental praise, or social interactions which are pleasurable to the individual, but they can also employ aversive stimuli like those generated by social bores, undesirable work loads, or getting out of class! The termination of these stimuli strengthens behavior. A behavior could be reinforced by the consequence of getting money, as *positive reinforcement,* or by the consequence of avoiding bankruptcy, which would be negative reinforcement.

Just as there are two fundamental reinforcement procedures, two fundamental punishment procedures can be used. *Positive punishment* involves making a noxious or aversive stimulus the consequence for behavior, while *negative punishment* involves terminating a pleasurable activity after a response. A child's behavior can be suppressed by a spanking (positive punishment) or by taking his toys away for a week (negative punishment).

Table 24 presents the four basic procedures in operant conditioning, the types of stimuli used with them, and the predicted change in the frequency of the behavior.

In operant conditioning it is essential to make the consequence occur immediately after the behavior. This can be done by using stimuli which represent the primary reinforcement or punishment stimuli, and which are easier to administer immediately than are the actual reinforcing or punishing stimuli. For example, the animal trainer says "good" when the dog has successfully executed the trick and the mother says "I'm going to spank you" when she finds her son wetting the living room floor. Because language can be used to represent symbolically many kinds of reinforcing and punishing consequences, secondary reinforcement or secondary punishment is probably one of the important uses of language.

Experimentation with human and animal subjects has revealed that organisms will rapidly learn to respond to symbolic stimuli, but they must still periodically be reinforced or punished with the primary pleasurable or aversive stimuli. Table 25 shows how the same neutral stimulus, a buzzer, can be used to indicate various consequences to an organism, depending on which operant procedure is employed. In the example, food is a primary appetitive or pleasurable stimulus, and a loud noise is a primary aversive or noxious stimulus.

To measure operant behavior the experimenter or clinician must specify the criterion for change in the behavior he wishes to modify. For example, the manipulatory behavior of a rat and the pecking behavior of a pigeon are easily translated into electronic impulses which can be counted and continuously recorded. Verbal behavior can be taped and then analyzed by frequency, intensity, duration, pattern, etc. Consequences can then be made contingent on particular responses and their emission rates can be increased or decreased. The intensity or frequency characteristics of speech can be modified by using aversive and rewarding stimuli, and measurement of the change in rate of these responses constitutes a measurement of operant conditioning.

Table 24. *The Four Basic Procedures in Operant Conditioning, the Types of Stimuli Used with Them, and the Predicted Change in the Frequency of the Behavior*

Procedure	Stimulus Used	Consequence	Predictable Change in Behavior
+reinforcement	Rewarding stimuli	Presentation of stimulus	Increase in the probability of the behavior
−reinforcement	Noxious or aversive stimuli	Termination of stimulus	Increase in the probability of the behavior
−punishment	Primary reward	Termination of stimulus	Decrease in the probability of the behavior
+punishment	Noxious or aversive stimuli	Presentation of stimulus	Decrease in the probability of the behavior

Table 25.

Procedure	Secondary Stimulus Function	Consequence
+Secondary reinforcement	Buzzer is presented after response and is occasionally paired with the primary positive reinforcer, food.	Buzzer becomes a "token" and increases the probability of the response.
—Secondary reinforcement	Buzzer comes on and stays on until the loud noise comes on. If subject makes appropriate response during the buzzer, the buzzer is terminated and the loud noise does not occur.	Buzzer becomes a warning stimulus and enables the subject to avoid the aversive consequence. It increases the probability of the avoidance response.
—Secondary punishment	Buzzer comes on prior to termination of eating opportunity.	Buzzer takes on warning stimulus function and brings about avoidance.
+Secondary punishment	Buzzer comes on after each response and is occasionally followed by the loud aversive noise.	Buzzer takes on a warning stimulus function and brings about avoidance.

Pseudoconditioning, a phenomenon in which a reinforcing or punishing stimulus may activate or sensitize an organism to emit more responses, is possible in operant conditioning as it is in respondent conditioning. The control for pseudoconditioning in operant conditioning is essentially the same as it was in respondent conditioning: the experimenter breaks up the contingency between the operant performance and the consequence. For example, to determine the effect of a food reinforcement on speech emission in a school child, the food should be made contingent on an emission of the appropriate speech signal. If the rate of speech increases significantly, operant conditioning has taken place. In a noncontingent control procedure, the food is given at random intervals regardless of when the appropriate speech behavior occurs. If the rate increases equally under both a contingent and noncontingent condition, pseudoconditioning has occurred. This control procedure is described in detail by Ferster and Skinner (1957) and Wolff (1959).

Operant Conditioning Procedures that Have Been Used to Develop, Maintain, and Increase the Rate of Behavior

Procedures for Shaping and Maintaining Behavior

Operant conditioning principles can be used to shape or create new behavior in a variety of organisms, using the basic strategy of reinforcement of approximations of the desired behavior (Skinner, 1953). This procedure is best illustrated in human subjects by programmed instruction in which the teacher reinforces completion of small tasks, gradually strengthening operant behavior until mastery of the subject matter is attained. The teacher or shaper must arrange the steps in a program so the student can follow each step to the final performance, with each correct response positively reinforced throughout the program (Breland and Breland, 1966; Taber, Glaser, Schaefer, 1965; and Skinner, 1966). Shaping and programmed learning must be tailored to the teacher's or clinician's objectives. In addition, the learner's behavioral repertoire, the skill required, and the types of reinforcers available must be considered in any shaping strategy.

Schedules of Reinforcement

Once an adequate shaping procedure has been established, consideration must be given to maintaining the behavior. Operant conditioning procedures that specify schedules of reinforcement have been developed to maintain high as well as low response rates from a variety of organisms (Skinner, 1938). Intermittent reinforcement can be presented on a fixed schedule, for example, after every 10 responses or after every 10 minutes, or on a variable schedule, with reinforcement after every 10 responses or after every 10 minutes on the average. Experimentation has demonstrated that both fixed and variable reinforcement schedules are effective in maintaining behavior for long periods of time at moderate to high response rates. An excellent interpretive discussion of reinforcement schedules has been prepared by Schoenfeld (1970).

Ratio Schedules of Reinforcement

These schedules depend on the number of operant responses that meet a specific criterion, for example the number of words a child with hearing impairment emits when shown certain kinds of pictures. By reinforcing the organism only after every 5th, 50th, or 500th response on a fixed or variable contingency, high response rates can be generated. Ratio schedules have characteristically produced high rates of response since the faster the organism responds the more reinforcement he will obtain per unit of time. However, the high response ratios usually can only be obtained by a successive approximation procedure, in which a low response requirement is gradually increased until many responses are required to produce reinforcement.

Interval Schedules of Reinforcement

Interval schedules depend on the elapsed time since the last reinforcement. These schedules maintain behavior by reinforcing the organism only for responses emitted after specified periods of time have elapsed. In general, they tend to generate lower response rates than ratio schedules (Ferster and Skinner, 1957).

Differential Reinforcement of Response Rate

Another widely used reinforcement procedure is the differential reinforcement of organisms while they are emitting responses at a very low or
very high rate, the DRL and DRH techniques (Ferster and Skinner, 1957).
For DRL the experimenter designates a certain period of time in which the
organism cannot respond—3 seconds, 10 seconds, 30 seconds, etc. Reinforcement is made available if the organism does not respond until after the
specified period of time elapses. For the first response and thereafter, reinforcement is delivered. If the organism responds within the specified delay
period, the timer is reset and the organism must wait through another complete
cycle. The inter-response times (IRT) are measured on this type of schedule
and are considered the operant response. DRL schedules are the most effective way to generate low rates of response since rate will be a direct function of the delay interval or IRT required for each response.

One effect of reinforcement independent of the response contingency is
the simultaneous increase in the base rates of large classes of behavior. This
phenomenon goes by various names; the most common is "activation." The
DRL schedule, particularly when a component of a multiple schedule, is an
excellent control for determining that the observed rate change is a function of
the reinforcement contingency, and not just generalized activation.

Differential reinforcement of high rate (DRH) schedules are an effective
way of generating rapid bursts of response (short IRT's) (Ferster and Skinner, 1957). The experimenter reinforces the subject for emission of a specified
number of responses in a short period of time, for example, 5 words spoken in
3 seconds. If more responses are required in less time, higher and higher response rates can be generated. DRH schedules of reinforcement result in
response rates similar to fixed and variable ratio schedules.

Schedules of reinforcement which set limits for response rates are also
possible. An organism can be reinforced periodically if his response rate is
above a certain rate and below an upper limit.

Additional Schedule of Reinforcement Procedures

A common procedure is mixing schedules of reinforcement, shifting from
ratio to interval or from interval to differential (Ferster and Skinner, 1957).
The only stimulus feedback available to an organism on a mixed schedule of
reinforcement comes from his own responses and the pattern in which the
IRT's are reinforced.

Another reinforcement scheduling procedure makes some attribute of the
response, such as rate, amplitude, etc., determine the reinforcement density,
magnitude or speed of delivery. Logan (1960) termed this mode of reinforcement "correlated," whereas Lindsley (1963) coined the term "conjugate."
The main advantage to this procedure is that both those values of the intended reinforcing event, which function as reinforcers in any given setting,
and those which do not, are provided within the same procedure.

These *adjusting* or *titration* schedules (Ferster and Skinner, 1957) are valuable in determining the reinforcing properties of a stimulus, for example, in assessing the reinforcement value of food or verbal approval. The adjusting schedule is also valuable in studying drive states. The adjustment can be programmed automatically by the experimenter. When the organism responds at a low rate the ratio requirement between response and reinforcement is automatically lowered. When the organism begins to respond at a high rate the ratio requirement between response and reinforcement is automatically increased. Adjusting schedules represents one attempt to make automatic the shaping of response rates; doing electronically what the good experimenter does by "hand" shaping. Adjusting schedules has almost exclusively involved ratio schedule procedures. Only one attempt to use temporal adjusting schedules has been reported (Wolff and Ulrich, 1966).

Another important schedule innovation is the concurrent schedule of reinforcement (Ferster and Skinner, 1957), which maintains two or more responses. Chicks have been trained to peck a key on a ratio schedule and to chirp at the same time (Lane, 1961). Chimpanzees have been trained to key press (on two different keys) on variable interval and fixed ratio schedules concurrently. This concurrent control of behavior has important implications in human behavior. For example, a person can write and talk on two different variable ratio schedules, and all of us are probably always on one type of concurrent schedule or another. A review article by Catania (1969) gives further details on this important type of schedule.

Accidental Contingencies

Skinner (1948) reported that stereotyped and "superstitious" behavior could be developed in pigeons by periodically reinforcing them with food. The food reinforcement was not contingent on a response but simply dispensed to the bird no matter what behavior was occurring. The pigeons in this experiment developed elaborate stereotyped behaviors like flapping their wings or turning in a circle, and these stereotyped responses were correlated with accidental reinforcement of prevalent pigeon behavior. The behavior would increase in rate and would be likely to be accidentally reinforced again and again until the behavior would become dominant and stereotyped. The development of this type of behavior is "superstitious" because its emission is incidental to obtaining the reinforcement. It parallels many human "superstitions" in which behavior is irrelevant to the consequence, although the organism behaves otherwise.

Herrnstein (1966) further analyzed superstitious behavior by reinforcing pigeons to peck a key on a fixed interval schedule of reinforcement. Once the behavior was established Herrnstein purposefully set up accidental contingencies by making the reinforcement noncontingent and random. The birds still maintained key pecking at a high rate although the rate on the noncontingent schedule decreased in comparison with the rate on fixed interval contingent reinforcement schedule. Herrnstein thus demonstrated that once a dominant behavior pattern is established it requires less precise control through reinforcement for its maintenance. Presumably, if stuttering, slurring of words, and the use of simplified grammatical forms become dominant they may be maintained by infrequent reinforcements and by imprecise contingencies. Herrnstein contends that more precise reinforcement contingencies and more frequent reinforcement are necessary during the initial acquisition of a response than for subsequent maintenance of a response, a hypothesis with important implications for applications of shaping procedures and schedules of reinforcement to human behavior.

Shaping and Maintaining Behavior Through the Use of Noxious and Aversive Stimuli

As indicated earlier, negative reinforcement is also a useful procedure for strengthening and maintaining behavior. Much of our everyday behavior is maintained by escape or avoidance of unpleasant consequences. It has generally been determined from animal studies that organisms must learn to escape noxious stimuli before they can learn to avoid them. While much adult human behavior is the avoidance type, escape behavior can often be observed in social situations. A person with impaired hearing may escape from using speech with low intelligibility by avoiding speaking situations.

Schedules employing negative reinforcement can generate very high response rates. Norton, Daley, and Wolff (1968) trained rats and guinea pigs to respond on fixed ratio schedules in excess of 200:1 to escape from a continuous shock. Dramatic control by negative reinforcement was illustrated when the subjects would respond for several minutes under electric shock for reinforcement by a 30-second period of shock termination. The procedure produced no harmful effects to the animals and their behavior could be maintained with a degree of regularity rivaling that obtained on positive reinforcement schedules.

Traditionally the establishment of terminal responding on a reinforcement schedule is developed by successive approximations of the final scheduling procedure, i.e., gradual increase in the ratio requirement on a fixed ratio schedule. Too rapid an increase in the ratio requirement will disrupt the pattern of behavior and responding may cease altogether. A promising line of investigation combines continuous reinforcement, intermittent reinforcement, reduction of reinforcement density, and successive approximation procedures in shaping schedule performance. All responses initially produce reinforcements, but of a lesser magnitude than those produced by gradually reducing the magnitude of reinforcement for all responses, except the one on the primary contingency. Final performance on the primary schedule is produced by gradually reducing the magnitude of reinforcement for all responses, except the one on the primary contingency. Patterns and rates of responding typical of intermittent reinforcement schedules can be rapidly established with both positive (Huston, 1968) and negative reinforcement III Khalili and Daley, 1968. Khalili, Daley, and Cheney (1969) have labeled this shaping strategy a titration procedure.

The experimental development and maintenance of avoidance behavior has also been dramatic. Belleville, Rohles, Grunzke, and Clark (1963) established elaborate schedules of avoidance behavior in the chimpanzee. Once avoidance behavior becomes dominant, animals will go for several hours without receiving the actual shock. This behavior appears analogous to human behavior such as careful speech articulation in certain situations but not in others, or avoiding certain types of listeners. These behaviors may be maintained for many months or years once they are established, and often only an occasional aversive experience is necessary to re-establish an elaborate avoidance response repertoire.

Sidman (1953) studied another type of avoidance behavior called nondiscriminative avoidance or "free-operant avoidance" (Sidman, 1966). In this procedure no warning or discriminable stimulus is used, and the organism can avoid the aversive consequence only by responding. Rats have been trained on free-operant avoidance schedules to respond at low steady rates, while avoiding over 80 percent of possible shocks. Table 26 summarizes the procedures which have been used to shape and maintain operant behavior. The table also gives some possible applications of the procedures.

Table 26. Procedures and Possible Applications Used to Shape and Maintain Operant Behavior

Procedure	Important Properties
Fixed and variable ratio schedules	High rates of response, with pausing after the reinforcement.
Fixed interval schedules	Increased inter-response-times with an overall increase in response rate as the reinforcement time approaches.
Variable interval schedules	Increased inter-response-times depending on the interval selected. Variable schedules provide an excellent control procedure for establishing base line rates of response because they establish and maintain a steady rate of response.
Differential reinforcement of rates	Most efficient methods of controlling the rate of response or the inter-response-time.
Mixed schedules of reinforcement	Excellent procedure for assessing an organism's motor feedback or "self" feedback system. Organism must rely on his own behavior for regulating his rate of response.
Multiple schedules of reinforcement	Very useful in research. Particularly well suited for analysis of discriminative behavior.
Adjustive schedules of reinforcement	Good method for initially shaping response rates. Also a titration procedure for assessing the effect of variables such as strength of reinforcement or strength of drive.
Concurrent schedules of reinforcement	Useful for maintaining two or more simultaneous operant repertoires.
Escape training and schedules of negative reinforcement	Procedures only recommended when positive reinforcement is not readily available.
Discriminative avoidance training	Can be used to establish "warning stimuli" which then can be used to control the rate of response.
Nondiscriminative avoidance training	A useful technique for studying operant behavior under stressful conditions. This procedure has been used to produce ulcers in primates.

Procedures for Decreasing the Rate of Response or for Eliminating Undesirable Behavior

Nonreinforcement

Extinction, the nonreinforcement of a previously reinforced response, will eventually reduce the frequency of responding to a very low level, but the decrease does not always occur immediately (Kimble, 1961), because the temporal pattern of behavior in extinction depends on the reinforcement history. Extinction is often examined as the rate of decline in response frequency, or the total number of responses emitted before responding ceases or some criterion level is reached. These parameters are used to determine the persistence (or "resistance to extinction") of the response after it is no longer reinforced. In general, schedules of intermittent reinforcement make responding more resistant to extinction, and a large number of previous extinctions will cause extinction to proceed more rapidly. The greater the deprivation over that which prevailed during reinforcement, the slower extinction will be, and the greater the magnitude of the reinforcer and the larger the number of reinforcements received prior to extinction, the greater resistance to extinction. The schedule of reinforcement is by far the major procedural determinant of resistance to extinction. The effects of other variables on extinction behavior are small when compared to the effects of schedules of reinforcement.

For cases in which contingencies maintaining an undesirable response are known, but in which withholding the reinforcer is impractical, reinforcement of alternative responses is a viable alternative to extinction, but it is necessary to strengthen the alternative response with a positive reinforcer which is significantly more potent than the one maintaining the undesired response. This procedure indirectly produces a condition in which environmental control is shifted from the undesirable response to the alternative response.

Punishment Stimuli

In punishment procedures an aversive or noxious consequence is made contingent on a response. The result must be a reduction of response rate.

Azrin and Holz (1966) have described several criteria for an ideal positive punishing stimulus:

1. The punishing stimulus should be measured in accurate physical units to insure reliability and replicability.
2. The punishing stimulus should make consistent contact with the subject. The subject should not be allowed to learn to avoid or escape from the punishing stimulus if it is to be used to eliminate an undesirable behavior.
3. The punishing stimulus should not affect the ability of the organism to respond. That is, it should not physically paralyze the organism. In such a case, response reduction would be a function of disability and not a function of the punishing stimulus.

4. A good punishing stimulus should have the characteristic of being variable over a wide range. Thus the amount of suppression of behavior could be controlled by changing the intensity of the punishing stimulus.

These four criteria can also be applied to negative punishing stimuli. The amount of time out from television or from food can be accurately measured and the time out period could be made consistently contingent on the subject's behavior. Time out from television or from food for short periods would probably not disable the subject and can be varied systematically from a few seconds to several hours. This variation in length of time out from a pleasurable consequence should have a variable effect on the reduction of a response rate (Leitenberg, 1965).

Conditioned Punishment Stimuli

Just as conditioned or secondary reinforcements have proven useful in developing human behavior, conditioned punishing stimuli are helpful in decreasing or eliminating undesirable human behavior. While it is impractical to shock humans or to deprive them of food for long periods of time, human subjects often come into the laboratory or therapy session with conditioned reinforcing and punishing stimuli. Time out or withdrawal of social approval, or threat of a loud aversive noise will serve as conditioned punishing stimuli which will suppress human behavior and lead to a decrease in response rate.

Schedules of Punishment

Punishing stimuli can be presented on an intermittent schedule just as can reinforcing stimuli. Azrin, Holz, and Hake (1963) constructed a fixed-ratio schedule of punishment and found that the frequency of the punished responses was a direct function of the fixed ratio, with smaller fixed ratios leading to greater response reduction. Azrin (1956) found that fixed-interval schedules of punishment led to decreasing rates of response as the time for punishment approached. This is directly opposite of response patterns with fixed interval schedules of reinforcement. Ferster (1958) employed a differential punishment of high rates procedure. Virtually any intermittent schedule which employs reinforcement can also be adopted to punishing stimuli.

Conditioned Stimuli and Suppression of Behavior

Conditioned stimuli can be used to generate emotional respondents which suppress operant behavior (Estes and Skinner, 1941). Brady and Hunt (1951) demonstrated that a buzzer paired with electric shock through classical conditioning could be used later to suppress an operant response, like pressing a lever. The conditioned stimulus presumably elicited anxietylike emotional respondents which were incompatible with the bar pressing operant. Suppression occurred as long as the buzzer was presented; when the buzzer was turned off the bar pressing response reoccurred.

This procedure has had limited application in human studies. A therapist does not usually wish to create anxiety, but an understanding of this procedure is important because many human operants are suppressed by unidentified conditioned stimuli which produce anxiety responses. Desensitization to these stimuli is an important step in eliminating undesirable respondent behavior and in reinstating desirable operant behavior (Wolpe and Lazarus, 1966).

An extensive review of punishment by Azrin and Holz (1966) suggests some techniques for eliminating undesirable behavior:

1. If positive or negative punishment is used, the punishment should be as intense as possible if the undesirable behavior is to be rapidly eliminated.
2. The frequency of punishment should be as high as possible. Continuous punishment is the best procedure. While intermittent schedules of punishment are possible they are not as efficient as continuous punishment in eliminating undesirable behavior.
3. The punishing stimulus should be presented at the strongest intensity at the beginning of conditioning. Gradual introduction of punishment weakens its efficiency in eliminating behavior.
4. The environment in which punishment is to be employed should be constructed so that unauthorized escape is impossible. If the organism is allowed to escape or avoid the aversive consequence through some other response then that response will be strengthened and the behavior to be weakened by punishment will not be affected.
5. Responses maintained by high levels of deprivation are more difficult to eliminate than responses maintained by low levels of deprivation when the same intensity of punishment is used; therefore, weakening the motivation which heightens the response will increase the effectiveness of punishment.
6. An alternative or escape behavior should be provided to enable the subject to avoid making the undesirable and punished response. Thus, for example, if we wished to prevent a child from avoiding speech situations, we could reprimand him when he left the room, and we could reinforce the child if he played in the areas providing speech opportunities.
7. If it is impossible to deliver the primary punishing stimulus after an undesirable response, then a neutral stimulus may be associated with the aversive situation and a conditioned punishing stimulus may be developed. This conditioned or secondary punishing stimulus can be used to eliminate or weaken the behavior.

Stimulus Control

The extent to which an aspect of the environment is followed by the occurrence of an operant response is the extent to which a stimulus has control over behavior. A stimulus may set the occasion for a response. The following account of stimulus control is limited to behavior maintained by positive reinforcement rather than by negative reinforcement and to stimuli that have discriminative rather than eliciting functions.

By far the most frequently employed experimental techniques are those used to study discriminative behavior, i.e., changes in response probability as a function of environmental conditions. Using traditional methodology, the typical laboratory experiment for developing stimulus control over operant behavior is as follows: (1) The pigeon is appropriately deprived of some known reinforcing stimulus such as food. (2) Following a shaping procedure, the animal is trained to peck a key in order to have a few seconds access to a grain hopper, the reinforcement. (3) A red light is projected upon a translucent plastic key mounted on the chamber wall. The experimenter then arranges the contingency that reinforcement-access to food occurs for pecking the key, but only in the presence of this light. The red light paired with reinforcement is the positive stimulus (S+). When the key is illuminated with a green light or negative stimulus (S−), emitting the key-pecking operant will not produce food. The red and green stimulus conditions are then alternated in some convenient manner, usually a short period for S+ and a relatively longer one of the S−. Usually a longer duration is programmed for the negative stimulus because the animal continues to respond when it is present (errors). Often, unreinforced responding in the S− is so high that it is necessary to have extended training in order to reduce error responding to a low rate. Eventually a maximum rate of responding occurs when S+ is present and a low response rate occurs in the presence of the S−. Stimulus control is demonstrated when a wide difference in response rates to the two colored lights occurs (Skinner, 1938).

The reinforcement schedules discussed earlier are procedures which specify how discriminative and reinforcing stimuli will be presented. The traditional procedure is really a multiple schedule in which there is reinforcement in one component of the schedule and extinction in the other. In the multiple schedule procedures, different exteroceptive stimuli are presented successively, and the different rates and patterns of responding in the presence of each stimulus are analyzed.

It is unnecessary to use only the two-component traditional model. Several different types of schedule-controlled behavior may be developed by putting each reinforcement schedule in effect in the presence of a different exteroceptive stimulus. Further, it is unnecessary for the stimuli and their corresponding schedules to be presented in a fixed order or sequence.

Stimulus condition, scheduling procedure, type of reinforcement, and response class are the four variables whose combinations and permutations dictate the degree of complexity which can be arranged in a multiple schedule. Multiple schedules in which reinforced responding occurs are useful for studying variables that might effect discriminative behavior. For further information see Murray Sidman's *Tactics of Scientific Research* (1960), a rather extensive discussion on the use of multiple schedules.

In many practical situations the investigator wants an estimate of the subject's probability of responding to each of two or more simultaneously presented stimuli. The oddity procedure and the matching-to-sample procedure are the most common examples of ways to determine this. For the oddity procedure (Kimble and Garmezy, 1963) it is necessary to determine the relative frequency of responses to the odd stimulus under all possible stimulus combinations. In the matching-to-sample it is necessary for the subject to match the choice stimulus with the standard or sample stimulus. Generally, each appropriate response is reinforced, but it is possible and often quite necessary for discriminative behavior itself to be reinforced according to some intermittent schedule. There are at least three advantages to using intermittent reinforcement in the maintenance of discriminative behavior: (1) the rate of responding can be measured at the same time that discriminative response is being evaluated, (2) the discriminative performance under these conditions shows less variability and greater stability, and (3) the accuracy of a discriminative performance can be improved by using an intermittent reinforcement schedule rather than a continuous reinforcement schedule.

Intermittent reinforcement of the discriminative response enables the experimenter to: (a) maintain discriminative behavior for relatively long periods of time, (b) control the rate at which the discriminative behavior occurs, (c) generate more accurate behavior than a continuous reinforcement schedule, and (d) affect the level of discrimination as a function of the schedule of reinforcement employed.

The traditional procedure discussed earlier is based on the assumption that differential reinforcement with respect to S+ (stimulus correlated with reinforcement) is necessary to establish control over a response along one of the stimulus dimensions. Stimulus control may be acquired over an operant behavior by a variety of methods.

Skinner (1938) was among the first to demonstrate that brightness discrimination could be developed with only a small number of responses emitted to the S−. In order to prevent a high response rate in the negative stimulus, he found it necessary to begin discrimination training immediately after the animal had been conditioned to press the bar. Thus, the point in training where the S− is introduced is critical.

Following Skinner's lead, Terrace (1963a) developed a technique in which the S− is introduced immediately following a few reinforced responses in the presence of S+ (correlated with reinforcement). In order for the stimuli to be maximally different for promoting errorless responding, the initial stages of training required S− to be made drastically different from S+. This was accomplished through varying as many dimensions of the stimulus as possible. Terrace introduced the S− not as a green key as in our example, but rather as a dark one, thereby manipulating both intensity and wavelength. During the first stage, S− was a dark key of short duration introduced early in training, just the opposite of the traditional procedure. The initially short duration that S− remained in effect was then progressively increased until eventually it came to match the duration of S+, at which time the animal was making an errorless light-dark discrimination.

During the second stage, S— was made short again, and the wavelength plus intensity dimensions were progressively increased. In our example, the green illumination would be gradually faded onto the initially dark key until a fully bright green key of short duration was present. During the final stage, the duration of S—, now a bright green key, was progressively increased. The final effect produced, with few error responses, was that the S+ controlled a high probability of responding in its presence, and the S— controlled a low probability of responding in its presence.

In a later study, Terrace (1963b) extended the training to one more dimension. First he developed a red-green light control over the pigeon's key-pecking behavior. Then a vertical line was faded onto one key illumination and a horizontal line faded on the other, and finally, the colors were progressively removed, leaving an errorless performance under the control of the horizontal and vertical line stimuli.

When Terrace (1963a) compared the behavior of birds trained by the errorless method to behavior of birds trained in the traditional manner an important difference appeared. Birds trained by the traditional procedure usually display "emotional" behavior like stamping on the floor and flapping their wings when the S— is presented. In sharp contrast, those receiving errorless training lowered themselves away from the key and stood quietly facing it until the S+ appeared.

The aversive or emotional properties of the S— in ordinary training were investigated by Terrace (1963c) in an experiment using tranquilizing drugs. When animals were trained by both standard and errorless methods, only the discrimination of animals trained by traditional procedures was disrupted after they were injected with very small doses of chlorpromazine. Terrace concluded that stimulus control developed by standard procedures is partially determined by the aversive emotional properties acquired by the S— during training.

Because the traditional manner of training discriminations generates emotional behavior which may seriously retard efficient development of discriminations, error responding should be minimized. Errors indicate that a *stimulus change* has been too rapid, *not* that the student couldn't learn.

Normal children have been employed to develop complex concepts. For example, the alphabet and beginning reading were taught by embedding the letter in a representation of the object itself such as A in apple, H in house, etc. Irrelevant stimuli were progressively faded out until the final letter form alone stood to control the behavior (Evans, 1965). These procedures have been successfully used by Murray Sidman (1966) with mentally retarded persons.

In a rather complex investigation using a matching-to-sample procedure, Hively (1962) studied discriminative responding as a function of type of earlier discrimination training. In this procedure the sample stimulus first appeared directly above the matching choice stimulus and the nonmatching choice stimulus was not presented. Gradually the nonmatching stimulus was introduced with very low intensity, and its brightness gradually increased until it was the same as the matching stimulus. Next, by an approximation (progressive) procedure, the sample-stimulus was gradually shifted to a centered position above the choice stimuli. In the criterion procedure, the sample stimulus was centered above the choice stimuli and the choice stimuli appeared at random in either choice window. An analysis by error favored a lower error rate through training with this progressive procedure.

It is often assumed that an organism either "knows" a discrimination or doesn't "know" it. The dependence of accurate discriminative performance on the schedule of reinforcement used to maintain it suggests this assumption is wrong. If an organism fails to develop a discriminative performance, the organism's history, particularly in connection with the variables indicated in this section, should be examined.

Reinforcement of behavior in the presence of one stimulus increases the tendency to respond *not only* in the presence of that stimulus but also to a lesser degree in the presence of other stimuli. Many authors view discrimination and generalization as competitive processes. Generalization can be expected to occur to stimuli having properties in common with the stimulus that was originally reinforced. Some excellent reviews examine both the theoretical and empirical properties of this intricate behavioral phenomenon, e.g., *Stimulus Generalization* by Mostofsky (1965).

Setting—Momentary Response Probabilities

In the animal laboratories, deprivation and satiation procedures are routinely employed to modulate the effectiveness of reinforcement. A procedure removing or decreasing the rate at which a reinforcing event is provided usually leads to an increase in the reinforcer's effectiveness. As operations, therefore, deprivation and satiation are reciprocals. Other than investigations of repetitive stimulus conditions there has been little research in this area, but deprivation-satiation functions are gradually being identified for nonrepetitive stimuli (Glanzer, 1958; Jones, 1964; Odom, 1964; Gewirtz, 1967).

In human situations the moment-to-moment identification of reinforcing events for a given individual is often the most serious problem a clinician faces. Some decision rules are emerging. Premack (1965) formulated a concept of reinforcement which is beginning to have impact on the field of behavior modification. A report by Daley (1969), supporting Premack's position, has shown that the most frequently occurring behavior in a restricted setting may be arranged in a contingency to reinforce relevant school behavior. A list of possible high frequency behaviors may include: talking; writing; coloring; listening to records; reading; swinging feet; dancing; walking; running; drawing on a board; using a telephone; turning a light switch on and off; playing with puzzles, games, blocks; jumping; drinking; eating candy; swinging; singing; talking to a teacher; looking at reinforcement list; building models; moving chairs; watching movies; watching TV; typing; playing tape recorder; looking at filmstrips; sitting alone; etc. The list will vary, of course, largely depending on age and cultural variables. Older students may suggest items to be placed on the list. All items on the list must be acceptable to the teacher, and to the school. This position will be examined in greater detail under Management Systems.

Applications

The normal development of speech from an operant conditioning point of view. Allport (1924) and Markey (1928) hypothesized that the acquisition of language starts with the infant's babbling behavior and that this babbling behavior is maintained and shaped by auditory feedback. Miller and Dollard (1941) and Mowrer (1950) elaborated this hypothesis in reinforcement terms, stating that the infant, like the talking bird, shapes himself to emit human sounds by repeating babblings which sound pleasing or reinforcing to him. These sounds resemble the reinforcing sounds emitted by the mother and associated with food and comfort, and thus become conditioned positive reinforcers themselves. Spontaneous babbling, which resembles the mother's reassuring words during feeding, actually reinforces the infant to repeat the sound.

Friedlander (1970) has prepared a stimulating argument, based largely upon his listening-preference data with preverbal subjects leading to the conclusion that ". . . receptive language functioning appears to involve processes and variables that lie at the very heart of mental development and the child's successful adaptation to the world of things, the world of people, and the world of action that surround him."

Once the infant begins to make sounds approximating human speech, direct social reinforcement from adults will shape his language behavior. Rheingold, Gewirtz, and Ross (1959) demonstrated that infants of three months could be conditioned to increase the rate of vocalization by social reinforcers like smiles, soothing sounds, or light touches on the abdomen by an adult. When the social reinforcement was withdrawn the rate of vocalization systematically decreased, demonstrating that young infants apparently can be conditioned to vocalize even before they have reached the stage of maximum babbling.

Skinner (1957) describes the development of six basic types of verbal behaviors, the "mand," the "echoic," the "tact," the "textual," the "intraverbal," and the "autoclitic." Mands are emitted under conditions of deprivation or discomfort. According to Skinner, mands are the earliest form of verbal communication. When the infant cries under certain states of deprivation the adult may reinforce him by alleviating the deprivation state. Later the young child may say, "Wa, Wa," for water and still later say, "May I have a drink?" In each case the verbal behavior is shaped and maintained by the verbal community eliminating his deprivation.

The second functional behavioral unit is the echoic response. In an echoic repertoire there is a formal identity between the response produced by the speaker and the discriminative stimulus, or occasion for the response. This repertoire is the basis for many educative functions. For example, a person with a fully developed echoic repertoire can repeat any word he hears. Certainly such a repertoire can be important for developing new complex responses quickly. The reinforcement of the echoic, in contrast to the mand, is of primary benefit to the listener. An echoic repertoire enlarges the child's verbal repertoire for both the community and his mutual benefit.

The tact is determined by a nonverbal stimulus. It is based on the three-part contingency which includes the discriminative stimulus, the operant response, and the reinforcing or punishing consequence. According to Skinner, tact behavior develops later than mand behavior. The young child is socially reinforced for correctly reporting external situations in the environment. For example, if he says "chair" in the presence of a chair, or "bird" in the presence of a bird, he is socially reinforced. The social value of tact responses can be illustrated by such statements as "brother is playing in the street" or "I have wet my pants." Social verification by the parent will lead to reinforcement or punishment depending on the accuracy of the tact response.

A fourth type of verbal behavior discussed by Skinner is the intraverbal response, which is similar to tact responses, but with verbal statements rather than objects or situations serving as discriminative stimuli. Intraverbal behaviors are the operant responses which develop in everyday conversation, and in other important activities like reading. According to most experts, intraverbal behavior is initially echoic. The first attempts at conversation by the young child are often nothing more than imitations of what a parent says. Intraverbal behavior is maintained and shaped through social reinforcements and chaining.

Textual behavior deserves special attention because of its importance to persons with hearing problems. Verbal operant behaviors characterizing the tact are under the control of stimuli usually in one modality, e.g., tactile stimuli in the case of braille. Therefore, the minimal repertoire required is largely a function of the nature of the text. There is no formal structural similarity between the stimulus and the terminal response. Nevertheless, the textual behavior, like echoic behavior, may be reinforced because it helps in the acquisition of other types of behavior.

The final type of verbal behavior considered by Skinner—the autoclitic—is a subtle form of verbal behavior designed to let the listener know about the internal affairs of the speaker. It can be a response such as, "I can't hear you," or it can be a qualifying statement about his own verbal behavior such as "I am not sure it was Johnny." The "I am not sure" response modifies the intensity or certainty of the tact and thus reflects the speaker's estimate of his statement. Autoclitic responses can also be used to modify mands or intraverbals. Such responses as "I think I'm getting hungry" or "I didn't quite hear you" can be used to make other verbal responses more accurate. These operant adjectives are reinforced because they increase the accuracy of communication. The accuracy of responses such as "I think I see a snake about to strike," and "I'm sure it's a snake ready to strike," are demanded by a discriminating society (Skinner, 1957).

While Skinner's classification and description of verbal operants are highly speculative, they provide a useful model for categorizing the development of language within an operant conditioning framework. Much research has demonstrated that adult verbal behavior can be readily modified through social consequences like gestures and speech signifying approval or disapproval. Krasner (1958) and Krasner and Ullman (1965) offer intensive reviews of the ways verbal behavior can be modified in experimental and therapeutic situations.

Imitation is another important behavioral phenomena in the acquisition of speech and language. Miller and Dollard (1941) suggest that imitation is not a primary process, and that it can be analyzed in conditioning terms. They hypothesize that organisms learn to imitate because they were reinforced for imitating the behavior of others. Bandura (1962, 1965) reports an extensive series of experiments on imitation using both adult and child models. Films of models receiving reinforcement and punishment for aggressive acts led to direct initiation of aggressive responses in young children, and the children exposed to models who were reinforced for aggression, displayed more aggression than children who were exposed to models who were punished for aggression. Such behaviors as making moral judgments and rewarding oneself with praise and candy were also imitated directly from models.

Baer and Sherman (1964) found that children would imitate a puppet as a direct consequence of being reinforced for the imitative behavior. When the reinforcement was withdrawn or made noncontingent the imitative response decreased in frequency, a direct verification of the Miller-Dollard hypothesis. Baer and Sherman also found that children would imitate the puppet's bar pressing behavior although they were never directly reinforced for this imitation, and Bandura (1965) reports that children will often imitate a model's behavior without any direct reinforcement for the imitation, a phenomenon which Baer and Sherman (1964) explain as a generalized response. When the reinforcement for the direct imitation was withdrawn their subjects also decreased their generalized imitation responses. It appears that imitative behavior, like other operant responses, can be maintained by only occasional reinforcement and theoretically could be placed on an intermittent schedule of reinforcement.

Bandura's extensive use of models in changing the behavior of his subjects illustrates another important applied principle. Presumably the "model" becomes a discriminative stimulus which sets the occasion for imitative behavior which can be readily strengthened through positive and negative reinforcement.

Studies Dealing With Establishment and Reinstatement of Speech in Mute Individuals

Isaacs, James, and Goldiamond (1960) and Sherman (1963) reinstated verbal behavior in psychotic patients by direct reinforcement. The patients rapidly learned to emit vocal and verbal responses but showed little recovery of speech outside the experimental room. Hamilton and Stephens (1967) presented a training program in which they not only reinstate speech in an emotionally disturbed young woman, but also maintain and shape an elaborate verbal repertoire in a ward situation. During the initial phase of training they conditioned the patient to verbally identify objects and pictures correctly. Thus, they trained the subject to make "tact" type verbal responses.

In the second phase of training they conditioned the subject to emit intraverbal behavior by reinforcing imitations of the experimenter's spoken words. In phase three of the training they required the subject to ask for things like assistance in dressing, or food in the cafeteria, reinstating the subject's "mand" vocabulary. During the final phase of training they required spontaneous verbalizations in the ward and they restrengthened mand and interverbal behavior. The patient eventually manifested a high rate of verbal behavior in the ward environment.

Another direct application of operant conditioning technology to areas of human speech has been the establishing of verbal repertoires in human subjects who have not manifested verbal behavior to any degree. Salzinger, Feldman, Cowan, and Salzinger (1965) report establishing speech in two speech deficient children. They shaped a 3-year-old speech deficient child to emit words by first reinforcing vocal approximations. Vocalizations were reinforced continuously, eventually on a 37:1 fixed ratio schedule. Later in shaping, the child was only reinforced if he emitted complete words. Animal-like cries disappeared from the child's verbal repertoire, probably because of non-reinforcement.

With a second speech-deficient child the experimenter's verbal statements became social reinforcers. By talking to him, the experimenter conditioned the child to emit words, learn grammatical structure and respond to discriminative stimuli. The child also learned new words outside the therapy room.

Kerr, Meyerson, and Michael (1965) established imitative vocal response in a severely handicapped and previously mute 3-year-old girl. First they socially reinforced her for vocalizing, and then faded in vocal discriminative stimuli at a high rate. They trained the child to emit interverbal behavior by reinforcing her vocalizations which followed vocalizations by the therapist. The subject vocalized in response to the experimenter's vocalization 60 percent of the time after just a few hours of conditioning.

Baer, Peterson, and Sherman (1967) conditioned two profoundly retarded children to verbalize using a modified imitation procedure. They first taught the children to imitate nonverbal behavior by using a food reinforcement procedure. Next, they developed imitation chains by adding new imitative behaviors to an already established repertoire. Finally, they interspersed verbal imitation behavior with nonverbal imitation. They found that while the subjects would not imitate verbal behavior directly, they would imitate verbal behavior if it were part of a nonverbal chain. After 20 hours of this procedure, the subjects emitted 10 words.

Lovaas, Berberich, Perloff and Schneffer (1966) established speech in autistic children by first reinforcing all vocalizations the children made. During the next phase of training the children were taught to imitate an adult's vocalization within 6 seconds. Then the child was required to increase his intraverbal output three-fold to be reinforced, and finally, direct imitations of English words were required for reinforcement. After training, the subjects would imitate Norwegian words interspersed with English words although they were never directly reinforced for imitating Norwegian words, again illustrating the generalization of the imitation process.

Other investigators reporting success in reinstating and establishing speech in autistic children and severely mute children are Metz (1965), Hewett (1965), Fineman (1968), and Sapon (1966). Investigators also report teaching normal and retarded subjects grammatical structure through imitation and reinforcement procedures. For example, Guess, Sailor, Rutherford, and Baer (1968) report teaching a 10-year-old severely retarded girl to correctly label new objects with the singular or plural ending, and Hart and Risley (1968) taught disadvantaged preschool children to use descriptive adjectives with noun referents.

Operant conditioning studies have demonstrated that the classes of verbal behavior described by Skinner can be reinstated in older subjects and can be systematically developed in young retarded, autistic, and normal children. Imitation of the development of echoic intraverbal behavior has been an important part of the procedure in many of the studies. Reinforcements have ranged from such primary reinforcements as meals (Lovaas et al., 1966) to such activities as spinning a chain, or listening to music (Hewett, 1965). Surprisingly, few studies (Premack, Homme, Daley) have used a response probability analysis or any other systematic analysis to choose appropriate social reinforcers. Certainly operant conditioning methods offer great promise for problems of mutism and temporary loss of speech.

Programmed Instruction

Skinner (1963b) has defined programming as ". . . the construction of carefully arranged contingencies leading to terminal performances which are the object of education." Programmed instruction is a direct empirical extension of those principles of learning established through the experimental analysis of behavior in the animal laboratories. In directing the learner toward a desired terminal behavior, a precise program will incorporate features of successive approximation (shaping), reinforcement, chaining, generalization, and discrimination training.

Two of the most commonly used programming strategies are (1) the branching program, and (2) the linear program. The branching program (intrinsic), developed by N. A. Crowder allows for response-determined sequencing through a given program, i.e., if a learner proceeds accurately through a given sequence of responses, mastery of a following sequence is assumed, and the learner is rerouted to more advanced material. The use of multiple choice (prompt) questions is frequently identified with this strategy. The linear program (Skinner, 1954) requires that all learners proceed through a fixed sequence in a given program and that each student complete all of the questions in an ordered sequence. The student responds to the stimulus material by filling in blanks.

The RULEG programming strategy (Evans, Homme, and Glaser, 1962) involves the sequential presentation of rules (isolated principles, laws, etc.) and examples (applied generalizations) of these rules. A component of the rule or example is omitted or rephrased, and the learner completes the statement by *filling in* the missing component.

Gilbert (1962) has developed a strategy for the systematic analysis of S-R relationships in the preparation of practice (as contrasted to frame) sequences. This "Mathetics" programming strategy emphasizes the condition under which the desired terminal behavior will occur, and the program sequence tends to maintain generalized application rather than isolated small "bits" of information.

The COREX (COmposite Ruleg Extension, Morreau and Daley, 1970) programming strategy utilizes the "rule-example" presentation format. Incorporated into the sequence, however, are learner-selected responses using multiple choice prompts and learner-constructed examples of the rule in application, which allow for generalization from the unique repertoire of each individual. Because of response variations these responses are evaluated by the learner, utilizing criterion references.

All major behavior programming strategies are extensions of empirically derived laws of behavior. The chief advantage of programming instruction is the employment of scientifically sound learning strategies which lead to assessment and evaluation in terms of performance outcomes. Other advantages include: (a) the learner can proceed at his selected rate; (b) the learner can proceed autonomously; (c) the learner receives immediate feedback on the accuracy of his response; (d) the learner proceeds through a specific, empirically-based sequence; and (e) the learner is reinforced for his task behavior.

Management Systems

Token reinforcement systems have been used to develop and maintain useful human behaviors in a variety of settings. Tokens are tangible objects (poker chips, coins, credit cards) or symbols (gold stars, dash marks, points) which have little intrinsic reinforcing power but which become secondary reinforcers when paired with the opportunity of exchange for reinforcing objects or activities (Skinner, 1953). Token reinforcement systems, sometimes called token cultures or token economies, assume characteristics of any economy, such as inflation, hoarding, borrowing, lending. The tokens are delivered immediately upon performance of specified target behaviors by a person (Garms and Brierton, 1967) or mechanical dispenser (Sapon, 1967) and are usually accumulated until the time of exchange. In all cases, the tokens are artificial devices and the intent is to replace the tokens with naturally reinforcing events or objects.

The use of tokens to modify behavior has many advantages: (1) token delivery can be made an immediate consequence of behavior more conveniently than primary reinforcers, (2) token systems can make use of reinforcing events which already exist in a setting, but which have little influence on the target behaviors (Clark, Lackowicz, and Wolf, 1968), (3) tokens may be stored easily and do not spoil, (4) in a delayed exchange, the behaviors of many Ss may be managed simultaneously because of the convenience of token delivery (Hamblin and Buckholdt, 1969), (5) Ss may be fined a number of tokens as negative punishment for inappropriate behavior, and (6) token reinforcement systems may be employed in a large variety of situations with both adults and children.

Institutional settings have provided many opportunities to use token economies to alter patient behaviors. From 1962–1968 Ayllon and Azrin (1968a) investigated techniques for finding and maximizing the effects of reinforcers. The investigators instituted several token economies in a ward of female patients to overcome the patients' resistance to typical hospital procedures (Ayllon and Azrin, 1968b). Chronic schizophrenic and brain damaged males in a VA hospital were used as Ss in a token culture which was designed to increase their abilities to help themselves, interact with fellow patients, and attend scheduled events more regularly (Atthowe and Krasner, 1968). Garms and Brierton (1967) investigated the variables that influence behavior in token reinforcement systems, particularly those variables correlated with decreases in performance. The Ss were male mental retardates in Dixon State School; target behaviors were improvements in personal care and maintenance of Ss' rooms. Steffy (1968) controlled aggressive behavior of young women who were disrupting a token economy system being used with severely regressed patients in a mental hospital.

Token reinforcement systems have also been used effectively in home and educational environments. The frequency of assaultive behaviors by a 6-year-old boy upon his 3-year-old brother was reduced by using a token system (O'Leary, O'Leary, and Becker, 1967).

A target behavior may be simple, as in the study by Zimmerman, Zimmerman, and Russell (1968) in which the authors increased the frequency of following instructions, using retarded boys as Ss. In other cases, the goal behavior may be quite complex; improvement of academic performance was the target behavior of a study conducted by Cohen, Goldiamond, and Filipczak (1967) in the National Training School for Boys. Clark, Lackowicz, and Wolf (1968) increased the achievement scores of female adolescent dropouts in a remedial education-job program, using an amount of backup reinforcement (money) alterable only within a very narrow range. The modification of verbal behavior of socioeconomically disadvantaged nursery school children was the objective of a study by Sapon (1967) who found that these children did not differ much from middle-class children in their responses to token reinforcement.

Sloane and MacAulay (1968) have compiled reports on the use of operant procedures in remedial speech and language training, including the use of token reinforcement systems with retarded pupils. Token economy and auditory control were used to modify behavior of mute autistic children by Hingtgen and Coulter (1967). Gray and Fygetakis (1968) trained preschool dysphasic children in a variety of linguistic performances using a combination of programmed instruction and token reinforcement.

Token reinforcement and other management systems are easily adapted to a wide range of situations and, when appropriately designed, are most effective in shaping desirable behavior. Bibliographic information is available in a single source compiled by Barnard and Orlando (1967) containing 840 entries.

Another major break-through in behavior management has evolved out of the work of David Premack (1965). Premack developed a reinforcement concept which states, ". . . for any pair of responses, the more probable one will reinforce the less probable one" (Premack, 1965, p. 132). An important corollary is the "indifference" principle, which states that the reinforcement value of an event is independent of the parameters producing response probability—*any* behavior can be used as a reinforcer of *any* lower probability behavior at the instant that the behavior is a higher probability one.

An impressive array of scientific experiments has contributed to this conceptualization of reinforcement, but the most exciting and useful development has been the systematic application of the "differential probability principle" to human behavior in educational settings. The mechanical dependency on candy or trinkets as "reinforcers" is broken, and it is now necessary only that each student's most frequently emitted responses be identified for use as reinforcers. Homme, and others (1963), have effectively modified behavior of nursery school children, preschool non-English speaking Indian children (Homme, 1965), adolescents (Homme, 1964), and young nontalking retarded (Homme, 1966) children. He has also successfully applied contingency management to school-like tasks (Homme, 1964, 1965) and problem behavior (Homme et al., 1963; Homme, 1966).

Daley, Holt, and Vajanasoontorn (1966) focused their research activity on a technique in which high probability responses were depicted in a menu (Addison and Homme, 1966). They examined several ways of managing contingencies between high and low probability response classes, and strengthening or developing behavior important to academic or acculturation processes of trainable mentally retarded. Following this earlier study, Friar (1969) showed that with standard materials for moderately retarded children in small classes it was possible to engineer increases and decreases in both academic and nonacademic response classes. In another experiment, Daley and Holt showed that it was possible to employ a menu of limited potential activities as a device for fading low probability task behavior into high probability reinforcing behavior. Investigations in which response probabilities are systematically adjusted so they may be used in consequating a natural contingency are of great significance in the design of new educational ecologies.

References

Addison, R. M. and L. E. Homme. 1966. The reinforcing event (re) menu. NSPI Journal 5(1) pp. 8–9.

Allport, F. H. 1924. Social Psychology. Boston: Riverside Press.

Anger, D. 1963. The role of temporal discriminations in the reinforcement of Sidman avoidance behavior. Journal of the Experimental Analysis of Behavior 6:477–506.

Atthowe, J. M., Jr. and L. Krasner. 1968. Preliminary report on the application of contingent reinforcement procedures (token economy) on a "chronic" psychiatric ward. Journal of Abnormal Psychology 73(1):37–43.

Ayllon, T. and N. H. Azrin. 1968a. Reinforcer sampling: a technique for increasing the behavior of mental patients. Journal of Applied Behavior Analysis 1(1):13–20.

Ayllon, T. and N. H. Azrin. 1968b. The Token Economy: A Motivational System for Therapy and Rehabilitation. New York: Appleton-Century-Crofts.

Azrin, N. H. 1956. Some effects of two intermittent schedules of immediate and non-immediate punishment. Journal of Psychology 42:3–21.

Azrin, N. H. and W. C. Holz. 1966. Punishment. In W. K. Honig (Ed.) Operant Behavior: Areas of Research and Application. New York: Appleton-Century-Crofts.

Azrin, N. H., W. C. Holz and D. F. Hake. 1963. Fixed-ratio punishment. Journal of the Experimental Analysis of Behavior 6:141–148.

Baer, D. M., R. F. Peterson, and J. A. Sherman. 1967. The development of imitation by reinforcing similarity to a model. Journal of the Experimental Analysis of Behavior (10):405–416.

Baer, D. M. and J. A. Sherman. 1964. Reinforcement control of generalized imitation in young children. Journal of Experimental Child Psychology 1: 37–49.

Bandura, A. 1962. Social learning through imitation. In M. R. Jones (Ed.) Nebraska Symposium on Motivation. Lincoln: University of Nebraska Press. Pp. 211–215.

Bandura, A. 1965. Behavioral modification through modeling procedures. In L. Krasner and L. P. Ullman (Eds.) Research in Behavior Modification. New York: Holt, Rinehart and Winston.

Barnard, J. W. and R. Orlando. 1967. Behavior Modification—A Bibliography. Nashville, Tennessee: George Peabody College for Teachers. Eric ED 018–028.

Bechterev, V. M. 1932. General Principles of Human Reflexology. New York: International.

Belleville, R. E., F. H. Rohles, M. E. Grunzke, and F. C. Clark. 1963. Development of a complex multiple schedule in the chimpanzee. Journal of the Experimental Analysis of Behavior 6:549–556.

Brady, J. V. and H. F. Hunt. 1951. A further demonstration of the effects of electro-convulsive shock on a conditioned emotional response. Journal of Comparative and Physiological Psychology 44:204–209.

Breland, K. and M. Breland. 1966. Animal Behavior. New York: Macmillan Co.

Catania, A. C. (Ed.). 1969. Contemporary Research in Operant Behavior. Dallas: Scott, Foresman.

Clark, M., J. Lackowicz, and M. Wolf. 1968. A pilot basic education program for school dropouts incorporating a token reinforcement system. Behavior Research & Therapy 6(2):183–188.

Cohen, H. L., I Goldiamond, and J. Filipczak. 1967. Maintaining increased education for teenagers in a controlled environment: Case II-model project. Report given at the American Orthopsychiatric Association, Inc., Washington, D.C., March 20–23, 1967.

Daley, M. F. 1969. The reinforcement menu: Finding effective reinforcers. In J. D. Krumboltz and C. E. Thoresen (Eds.) Behavior Counseling: Cases and Techniques. New York: Holt, Rinehart, and Winston.

Daley, M. F. and G. L. Holt. 1969. Systematic probability reversal and control of behavior. Prepublication manuscript.

Daley, M. F., G. L. Holt, and C. Vajanasoontorn. 1966. Reinforcement menus in the instruction of mentally retarded children. Proceedings of Far West Laboratory for Educational Research and Development, November 1966.

Estes, W. K. and B. F. Skinner. 1941. Some quantitative properties of anxiety. Journal of Experimental Psychology 29:390–400.

Evans, J. 1965. Personal communication.

Evans, J. L., L. E. Homme, and R. Glaser. 1962. The ruleg system for the construction of programmed verbal learning sequences. The Journal of Educational Research 55(9):513–518.

Ferster, C. B. 1958. Intermittent reinforcement of a complex response in a chimpanzee. Journal of the Experimental Analysis of Behavior 1:163–165.

Ferster, C. B. and B. F. Skinner. 1957. Schedules of Reinforcement. New York: Appleton-Century-Crofts.

Fineman, K. R. 1968. Visual color reinforcement in establishment of speech in an autistic child. Perceptual and Motor Skills 26:761–762.

Friar, C. M. 1969. Behavior modification of trainable mentally retarded children. Doctoral Dissertation, Utah State University.

Friedlander, B. 1970. Receptive language development in infancy: Issues and problems. Merrill-Palmer Quarterly.

Garms, R. and G. Brierton. 1967. A token reinforcement project with retardates. Unpublished manuscript, Dixon State School.

Gewirtz, J. L. 1967. Deprivation and satiation of social stimuli as determinants of their reinforcing efficacy. In J. P. Hill (Ed.) Minnesota Symposia on Child Psychology, Vol. 1 Minneapolis: University of Minnesota Press.

Gilbert, T. F. 1962. Mathetics: The technology of education. The Journal of Mathetics 1:7–74.

Glanzer, M. 1958. Curiosity, exploratory drive and stimulus satiation. Psychological Bulletin 55:302–315.

Gray, B. B. and L. Fygetakis. 1968. Mediated language acquisition for dysphasic children. Behavior Research & Therapy 6:263–280.

Guess, S., W. Sailor, G. Rutherford and D. M. Baer. 1968. An experimental analysis of linguistic development. The productive use of the plural morpheme. Journal of Applied Behavior Analysis 1(4):296–306.

Hamblin, R. L. and D. Buckholdt. 1969. Structured exchange and childhood learning: Ghetto children. Report #2, Unpublished manuscript, CEMREL.

Hamilton, J. W. and L. Y. Stephéns. 1967. Reinstating speech in an emotionally disturbed, mentally retarded young woman. Journal of Speech and Hearing Disorders 32:383–389.

Hart, B. M. and T. R. Risley. 1968. Establishing use of descriptive adjectives in the spontaneous speech of disadvantaged preschool children. Journal of Applied Behavior Analysis 1:109–120.

Herrnstein, R. J. 1966. Superstition: A corollary of the principles of operant conditioning. In W. K. Honig (Ed.) Operant Behavior: Areas of Research and Application. New York: Appleton-Century-Crofts.

Hewett, F. M. 1965. Teaching speech to an autistic child through operant conditioning. American Journal of Orthopsychiatry 35:927–935.

Hilgard, E. R. 1931. Conditioned eyelid reactions to a light stimulus based on reflex wink to sound. Psychological Monographs 41 (184):1–50.

Hingtgen, J. N. and S. K. Coulter. 1967. Auditory control of operant behavior in mute autistic children. Perceptual & Motor Skills 25(2):561–565.

Hingtgen, J. N., S. K. Coulter, and D. W. Churchill. 1967. Intensive reinforcement of imitative behavior in mute autistic children. Archives of General Psychiatry 17:36–43.

Hively, W. 1962. Programming stimuli in matching to sample. Journal of the Experimental Analysis of Behavior 5:279–298.

Homme, L. 1964. A demonstration of the use of self-instructional and other teaching techniques for remedial instruction of low achieving adolescents in reading and mathematics. U.S. Office of Education, Contract No. OE-4-16-033.

Homme, L. 1965. A system for teaching English literacy to preschool Indian children. Westinghouse Research Laboratories Contract 14-30-065001506. Bureau of Indian Affairs, Final Report, October 11, 1965:1–15.

Homme, L. E. 1966. Contingency Management. Newsletter, Section on Clinical Child Psychology, Division of Clinical Psychology, American Psychological Association 5(4).

Homme, L., P. De Baca, J. Devins, R. Steinhorst, and E. Rickert. 1963. Use of the Premack principle in controlling the behavior of nursery school children. Journal of the Experimental Analysis of Behavior 6:544.

Honig, W. K. 1966. Introductory remarks by W. K. Honig (Ed.), Operant Behavior: Areas of Research and Application. New York: Appleton-Century-Crofts.

Huston, J. P. 1968. Reinforcement reduction: A method for training ratio behavior. Science 159:444.

Isaacs, W., T. James, and I. Goldiamond. 1960. Application of operant conditioning to reinstate verbal behavior in psychotics. Journal of Speech Disorders 25:8–12.

Jones, A. 1964. Drive and incentive variables associated with the statistical properties of sequences of stimuli. Journal of Experimental Psychology 67:423–431.

Jones, M. R. (Ed.). 1968. Miami symposium on the prediction of behavior 1967: Aversive stimulation, Coral Gables, Florida: University of Miami Press.

Khalili, J. and M. F. Daley. 1968. Titrated negative reinforcement procedure for scheduled escape behavior. Paper presented at AAAS, Pacific division.

Khalili, J., M. F. Daley and C. Cheney. 1969. Titrated negative reinforcement procedure for generating escape behavior, Journal of Behavioral Research, Methodology and Instrumentation (8):293–294.

Kerr, N., L. Meyerson, and J. A. Michael. 1965. Procedure for shaping vocalizations in a mute child. In L. P. Ullman and L. Krasner (Eds.) Case Studies in Behavior Modification. New York: Holt, Rinehart and Winston.

Kimble, G. A. 1961. Hilgard and Marquis' Conditioning and Learning. New York: Appleton-Century-Crofts.

Kimble, G. A. and N. Garmezy. 1963. Principles of General Psychology. New York: Ronald Press.

Krasner, L. 1958. Studies of the conditioning of verbal behavior. Psychological Bulletin 55:148–170.

Krasner, L. and L. P. Ullmann (Eds.) 1965. Research in Behavior Modification. New York: Holt, Rinehart and Winston.

Lane, H. 1961. Operant control of vocalizing in the chicken. Journal of the Experimental Analysis of Behavior 4:171–177.

Leitenberg, H. 1965. Is time-out from positive reinforcement an aversive event? Psychological Bulletin 6:428–441.

Lindsley, O. R. 1963. Experimental analysis of social reinforcement: Terms & methods. American Journal of Orthopsychiatry 33:624–633.

Logan, F. A. 1960. Incentive: How the Conditions of Reinforcement Affect the Performance of Rats. New Haven: Yale University Press.

Lovaas, O. I., J. P. Berberich, B. F. Perloff, and B. Schneffer. 1966. Acquisition of imitative speech by schizophrenic children. Science 151:705–707.

Markey, J. F. 1928. The Symbolic Process. London: Routledge & Kegan Paul.

Metz, J. R. 1965. Conditioning generalized imitation in autistic disorders. Journal of Experimental Child Psychology 2:389–399.

Miller, N. E. and J. Dollard. 1941. Social Learning and Imitation. New Haven: Yale University Press.

Morreau, L. and M. E. Daley. 1970. Principles of Behavior for Classrooms. New York: New Century.

Mostofsky, D. I. (Ed.). 1965. Stimulus Generalization. Stanford: Stanford University Press.

Mowrer, O. H. 1950. Learning Theory and Personality Dynamics. New York: Ronald Press.

Norton, R., M. F. Daley, and P. C. Wolff. 1968. The effects of bar-holding and rapid ratio shaping on fixed-ratio escape responding. Psychonomic Science 11:165–166.

Odom, R. D. 1964. Effects of auditory and visual stimulus deprivation and satiation on children's performance in an operant task. Journal of Experimental Child Psychology 1:16–25.

O'Leary, K. D., S. O'Leary, and W. C. Becker. 1967. Modification of a deviant sibling interaction pattern in the home. Behavioral Research & Therapy 5:113–130.

Pavlov, I. P. 1927. Conditioned Reflexes. Trans. & Ed. by G. V. Anrep. London: Oxford University Press.

Premack, D. 1965. Reinforcement theory. In D. Levine (Ed.) Nebraska Symposium on Motivation. Lincoln: University of Nebraska Press. Pp. 123–188.

Rheingold, H. L., J. L. Gewirtz, and H. W. Ross. 1959. Social conditioning of vocalizations in the infant. Journal of Comparative and Physiological Psychology 52:68–73.

Salzinger, K., R. S. Feldman, J. E. Cowan, and S. Salzinger. 1965. Operant conditioning of verbal behavior of two young speech-deficient boys. In L. Krasner and L. P. Ullman (Eds.) Research in Behavior Modification. New York: Holt, Rinehart and Winston.

Sapon, S. M. 1966. Shaping productive verbal behavior in a non-speaking child: A case report. Georgetown University Monograph Series on Language & Linguistics 19:157–175.

Sapon, S. M. 1967. Contingency management in the modification of verbal behavior in disadvantaged children. Presented at the meeting of the American Psychological Association in Washington, D.C. on September 1, 1967.

Schoenfeld, W. N. 1970. The Theory of Reinforcement Schedules. New York: Appleton-Century-Crofts.

Sherman, J. A. 1963. Reinstatement of verbal behavior in a psychotic by reinforcement methods. Journal of Speech and Hearing Disorders 28:398–401.

Sidman, M. 1953. Avoidance conditioning with brief shock and no extroceptive warning signal. Science 118:157–158.

Sidman, M. 1960. Tactics of Scientific Research. New York: Basic Books.

Sidman, M. 1966. Avoidance behavior. In W. K. Honig (Ed.) Operant Behavior: Areas of Research and Application. New York: Appleton-Century-Crofts.

Sidman, M. and L. T. Stoddard. 1966. Programming perception and learning for retarded children. International Review of Research in Mental Retardation 2:151–200.

Skinner, B. F. 1938. The Behavior of Organisms: An Experimental Analysis. New York: Appleton-Century-Crofts.

Skinner, B. F. 1948a. "Superstition" in the pigeon. Journal of Experimental Psychology, 38:168–172.

Skinner, B. F. 1948b. Walden Two. New York: Macmillan.

Skinner, B. F. 1953. Science and Human Behavior. New York: Macmillan.

Skinner, B. F. 1954. The science of learning and the art of teaching. Harvard Educational Review 24 (2).

Skinner, B. F. 1957. Verbal Behavior. New York: Appleton-Century-Crofts.

Skinner, B. F. 1963a. Operant behavior. American Psychologist 18:503–515.

Skinner, B. F. 1963b. Reflections on a decade of teaching machines. Teachers College Record 65:168–177.

Skinner, B. F. 1966. An operant analysis of problem solving. In B. Kleinmuntz (Ed.) Problem Solving. New York. John Wiley.

Skinner, B. F. 1969. Contingencies of Reinforcement: A Theoretical Analysis. New York: Appleton-Century-Crofts.

Sloane, H. N. and B. D. MacAulay. 1968. Operant Procedures in Remedial Speech and Language Training. Boston: Houghton-Mifflin.

Spence, K. W. 1956. Behavior Theory and Conditioning. New Haven: Yale University Press.

Steffy, R. A. 1968. Service applications: psychotic adolescents and adults, treatment of aggression. A paper delivered at APA convention in San Francisco, Sept., 1968.

Taber, J. I., R. Glaser and H. H. Schaefer. 1965. Learning and Programmed Instruction. Reading: Addison-Wesley.

Terrace, H. S. 1963a. Discrimination learning with and without "errors." Journal of the Experimental Analysis of Behavior 6:1–27.

Terrace, H. S. 1963b. Errorless transfer of a discrimination across two continua. Journal of the Experimental Analysis of Behavior 6:223–232.

Terrace, H. S. 1963c. Errorless discrimination learning in the pigeon. Effects of chlorpromazine and imipramine. Science 140:318–319.

Ulrich, R., T. Stachnik, and J. Mabry. 1966. Control of Human Behavior. Greenview: Scott, Foresman.

Wickens, D. D. and C. D. Wickens. 1940. A study of conditioning in the neonate. Journal of Experimental Psychology 26:94–102.

Wolff, P. C. 1959. Subcortical electrical stimulation in primates: Differential behavioral effects with operant conditioning schedules: Doctoral Dissertation. University of Houston.

Wolff, P. C. and R. E. Ulrich. 1966. A DRL schedule with temporal adjustment. Psychological Reports 19:579–584.

Wolpe, Joseph and A. A. Lazarus. 1966. Behavior Therapy Techniques. New York: Pergamon Press.

Zimmerman, E. H., J. Zimmerman, and D. Russell. 1968. Differential effects of token reinforcement on attention in retarded students instructed as a group. Paper presented at the meeting of the American Psychological Association in San Francisco, Sept., 1968.

Chapter 10

Counseling

E. WAYNE WRIGHT, Ed.D.

The term *counseling* connotes many things to many people. Not only are there differences among professional counselors and psychologists as to the most appropriate or generally acceptable definition of counseling, but the lay public is even further confused regarding *counseling* and *counselors* by the frequent use of this increasingly popular concept and title outside the traditional, helping professions. For example, trained specialists in the fields of counseling, guidance, psychology, social work, psychiatry, and other professionally oriented clinical services are generally recognized as practitioners of counseling and/or psychotherapy; yet the training, theoretical orientation, job function, and interviewing approach of these specialists are often quite different. At the same time, attorneys at law, court justices, ministers and others are often called upon for *counseling*, while at other times they are seen more in the role of *giving counsel,* the latter role and relationship connoting something quite different from the former.

Even more confusing (and somewhat distressing to the professional counselor) is the current and misleading use of this term for *real estate counselors, financial loan counselors, investment counselors,* etc., this usage obviously referring to businessmen and business dealings rather than to professional practitioners of the *healing arts.*

It is the viewpoint of this chapter that much of what is being done under the title of counseling cannot really be considered counseling as it has been traditionally defined and conceived by professional counselors. This does not mean that other kinds of interpersonal relationships are not helpful. On the contrary, many people do not require counseling (or therapy) as such, but might well be helped by some other type of relationship. Also, counselors perform many tasks and utilize other kinds of processes which are not counseling in the true sense of the word. Since counselors are often expected to show evidence of the supposed or potential benefits of counseling, it is important that the counselor have a clear understanding, in his own mind at least, of the basic ingredients of *counseling,* as distinct from the various non-counseling functions generally associated with the counselor's role and with other kinds of interpersonal relationships.

155

A Definition of Counseling

Counseling can occur spontaneously or as a planned, scheduled interview, but is more than a casual, unstructured conversation. It can be initiated at the request of either the counselee or the counselor, or as a result of a referral by someone else; but the counseling session has relatively specific goals and operational guidelines. It may involve a relationship between only two people (the counselor and the counselee) or between a counselor and a group, but the essential nature of effective counseling relationships remains much the same.

Tyler (1961) believes that "the psychological purpose of counseling is to facilitate development," and she defines counseling as ". . . a process designed to help a person answer the question, 'What shall I do?'" Elaborating on this definition, Tyler says, "The counseling process is one through which individuals are enabled to make good choices and thus improve their relationships to the world and to their fellowmen . . ." (p. 17). She qualifies the concept of counseling, however, by adding that:

> When a counselor helps a client decide what to do, it does not mean the counselor gives him advice or tells him what he *should* do. There may be occasions when this is the best way to proceed, but generally speaking a person facing a choice where he must take responsibility for the counsequences needs to be given an opportunity to do his own thinking rather than to have someone do it for him. This is where the professionally trained counselor differs from the man on the street. To the average person counseling is practically synonymous with advising. To the counselor it is quite a different procedure (p. 13).

Blocher's (1966) concept of "developmental counseling" supports Tyler's notion that the aim of counseling is to facilitate personal growth, but he puts it in terms of helping an individual (the counselee) "to maximize his possible freedom within the limitations supplied by himself and his environment." For Blocher, developmental counseling ". . . aims at helping an individual become aware of himself and the ways in which he is reacting to the behavioral influences in his environment. It further helps him to establish some personal meaning for his behavior and to develop and clarify a set of goals and values for future behavior" (p. 5).

Blocher suggests, as two aims of counseling, the "maximizing of human freedom," and the "maximizing of human effectiveness." His point of view is based on the premise that "the effective human being strives for control over those aspects of his environment that he can manipulate, and for control over his affective responses to those aspects of his environment that he cannot" (Blocher, 1966, p. 6). Counseling, thus conceived, attempts to help the counselee in several ways: (1) to make optimum use of his personal and environmental resources for effective problem solving, (2) to make appropriate choices, (3) to change inappropriate behavior, and (4) to improve interpersonal relationships. To achieve these outcomes, the counseling process should be distinguishable from other kinds of conversations and/or social relationships, with the *uniqueness* of counseling centering primarily in the nature of the counseling relationship itself, in the relative specificity of goals for the interview and in the training and skills of the counselor for facilitating personal growth. The uniqueness of counseling relationships, as suggested here, is further implied in Blocher's discussion of his position, in which he indicates that counseling is ". . . a planned, systematic intervention in the life of another human being aimed at changing that person's behavior" (Blocher, 1966, p. 13).

Guidance-Counseling-Therapy

A long-standing problem in attempts to define a *pure* concept of counseling centers in the purported similarities and/or differences between counseling and psychotherapy. A similar problem, but one that seems to receive less attention, is that of distinguishing counseling from its close associates in the field of education, i.e., *guidance* and *teaching*. In the opinion of this writer, it is easier to distinguish counseling from guidance and teaching than it is to distinguish counseling from therapy, although some differences in the latter two processes can also be noted.

The problem is, that in spite of reported benefits of counseling and guidance, there have also been many reported failures. Counselors often attempt to implement various kinds of counseling and guidance programs, and to work with various types of problem students, only to abandon their efforts—either because they feel uncomfortable and lacking in clinical skills, or because, for other reasons, they fail to achieve the outcomes for which they had hoped. Pointing out this dilemma in reference to *group* counseling, Goldman (1962) suggests that failures of this sort are often due to the counselor's ignorance regarding basic differences in content and process of the various functions he is called upon to perform. In other words, what a counselor *does* (the process) must be appropriate for the type of content he wishes the counselee to discuss and also for the kinds of behavioral outcomes he wishes to effect. Thus, if a counselor expects to help a counselee change behavior, improve self-concept, develop insight, etc., all of which are typical counseling goals, it is important that he utilize a *counseling* process rather than some other process, e.g., guidance or teaching, since the latter processes are not particularly compatible with desired counseling content and/or counseling goals.

Goldman (1962) and Mahler and Cladwell (1961) have outlined several levels of discussion topics (*content*) and of leader style (*process*) for distinguishing group counseling from other group processes, i.e., *teaching, guidance, therapy;* and the distinctions suggested by these writers are equally applicable for individual counseling as they are for group process. Basically, it is assumed that each of these several processes is expected to be a learning experience for the client. In teaching, as in guidance, the content of what is learned is basically *external* to the learner. However, in counseling and in psychotherapy, the content of learning is essentially *internal* to the learner.

For example, content that is basically external in nature includes such topics as instruction about school subjects (reading, mathematics, science), general orientation and information about school, discussion of the world of work, etc. On the other hand, content that is *internal* to the individual focuses more specifically on his personal needs, feelings, or problems which may have brought him to the counselor. When the counselor helps to keep the focus on internal content, it increases the probability that the individual will learn something about himself, i.e., his abilities, interests, feelings, "hangups"; and only as he learns about himself is he able to evaluate himself and his opportunities, make choices and decisions about his life and consider alternative behaviors for solving the problems confronting him. Conversely, talking about external content, i.e., things or people outside himself, does not require the counselee to assimilate the discussion material in terms of his own problems and areas of needed help. Neither does it require him to make appropriate choices or move toward needed changes in his own behavior.

Topics such as the improvement of study habits, choosing a vocation, finding a job, getting along with others, understanding oneself, and so forth, may or may not provide internal content, depending on the *process* employed by the counselor. While such topics *can* have personal meaning for the counselee, they do not necessarily require personal reference, even though the discussion may sound related to personal problems or feelings. Content such as this lends itself very easily to "academic" discussions and presentation of external information. Such topics are often considered in typical guidance units presented in the classroom by teachers and/or counselors. If the content of these topics is seen primarily as *informational* or *orientational* in nature, the process is more likely to be considered guidance or teaching. Only as the individual is helped to internalize the content and to use the external information for evaluating personal goals, making decisions, or finding solutions to personal problems can the process be considered counseling in the real sense of the term.

Differences between counseling and psychotherapy are not as easily made in terms of content and process, since the content of both is essentially internal, and the process, for many counselors and therapists, is very much the same. In fact, many practitioners and writers consider counseling and therapy almost as synonymous concepts, and often these two terms are used interchangeably (Rogers, 1942, 1951). The point of view here is that counseling and therapy can be viewed primarily as difference in *degree* rather than kind. Proponents of this particular point of view categorize counseling-therapy differences on a continuum in terms of (1) the level of presumed stability (integration) of the client, and (2) the consequent length and depth of treatment required.

In an effort to resolve the counseling-psychotherapy question and to bridge the gap between these two traditional ends of the therapeutic continuum, Brammer and Shostrom (1968) have defined a body of knowledge which they feel is common to both counseling and psychotherapy, and they present counseling and therapy as overlapping concepts, not only in terms of the processes themselves, but also in terms of the professional competence required for each. In their schema, counseling is characterized as *educational, supportive, situational, problem-solving, conscious awareness, emphasis on "normals,"* and *short-term.* Psychotherapy is described by the words *supportive* (in a more particular sense), *reconstructive, depth emphasis, analyt-*

ical, focus on the unconscious, emphasis on "neurotics" or other severe emotional problems, and long term (p. 7). Blocher (1966) suggests similar differences between counseling and therapy.

Regardless of how the counselor views these two processes and his competence for each, most counselors will inevitably be faced with cases which require skills beyond superficial counseling or informationally oriented guidance functions. Therefore, it is this writer's opinion that counselors should acquire the professional competence to understand and work effectively with a broad range of psychological problems and personality dynamics. This practical reality is pointed out by Stewart and Warnath (1965) as follows:

> The school counselor must be an adequate diagnostician so that he can make appropriate referrals; however, the referral sources mentioned in many counseling tests do not exist in the real world of most small towns. Thus, the counselor is often faced with two alternatives: to do *something* for the disturbed student in his present environment with the resources available to him or to send him off to a state hospital, which may be no more than an overcrowded custodial institution (p. 273).

This point of view is further emphasized by Albert (1966), who concludes:

> Whether he is a "psychotherapist" or not, the counselor may often find himself required to deal with situations that *should* be met with psychotherapeutic skills. . . . Since each client is, to a greater or lesser degree, an integral unit, all of his activities reflect and are reflected by all parts of him. Excluding the unconscious, the defensively repressed, the irrational (which are part of *every* personality, however minimal or well compensated) from the remedial efforts is excluding the parts which, even in "normals" may relate most actively to the difficulties under treatment. In more severe cases, such exclusion is like treating a brain tumor with a cold compress.

Space does not permit further elaboration on this particular point here, but the reader will find additional clarification regarding some differences and similarities of counseling *vs.* psychotherapy in the treatment of this topic by Perry (1955).

The Nature of Therapeutic Relationships

It is probably true that not all therapy is therapeutic, and that everything therapeutic is not necessarily therapy. However, research in counseling and psychotherapy has identified some common elements which are felt ·to be essential for effective, therapeutic relationships. In reviewing these common elements, and for the remaining discussion of this chapter, counseling and psychotherapy will be considered as being essentially synonymous processes.

It should be recognized at the outset of this discussion, that any expectations on the part of a counselor for effecting a therapeutic relationship with a counselee presumes several basic conditions: (1) a felt need for help on the part of the client, wherein the client's anxiety about a problem exceeds his resistance to change, (2) sufficient competence (or clinical skills) on the part of the counselor for coping with the client's problem(s) and emotional needs, (3) some sort of interpersonal bond and psychological interaction between counselor and client, and (4) the ability and the opportunity for both to share reciprocal communication.

Since the purpose of this chapter is to discuss general concepts of counseling as applicable to hard of hearing clients, it is recognized that counseling the hard of hearing does present additional problems and limitations regarding shared communications; and some of the special problems in counseling with such handicapped clients are discussed later in this chapter. At this point, however, suffice it to say that counseling and therapy, generally, and the potential for establishing any sort of therapeutic relationship presupposes a minimum level of cognitive and effective communication between counselor and client.

Clinical practitioners and theorists have long been interested in finding the "right" or "best" techniques of counseling and therapy. In earlier literature, the writings of Rogers (1942), Williamson (1950) and others (Snyder, 1945; Thorne, 1944) promoted two primary philosophical counseling camps which were supposedly at opposite ends of a theoretical continuum, and which became known as the *nondirective* and *directive* philosophies of counseling, respectively. Rogers also referred to his nondirective approach as *client centered* counseling (1951). The primary issue between these two extreme positions centered in the amount of control or direction the counselor should be expected (or even have the moral right) to exercise over the client. Counseling theorists subsequently aligned themselves and their respective counseling techniques somewhere along the directive-nondirective continuum; and much research of the 1940s and 1950s attempted to prove the superiority of each approach, presumably at the exclusion of the other (Porter, 1950; Rogers, 1951; Rogers and Dymond, 1954; Williamson, 1958).

As the directive-nondirective controversy has evolved, and particularly during the past several years, research in various counseling methodologies has produced two relatively consistent conclusions, which, in the opinion of this writer, have contributed significantly to current thinking about essentials in counseling effectiveness. One conclusion has been that no single, theoretical approach seems to be "best" or "right" for all clients or in all settings. Instead, demonstrated differences in counseling effectiveness have apparently been due more to the counselor's personal qualities and to his general effectiveness *as a person* in relationship to the client, rather than to any specific "techniques" or given theoretical approach (Blocher, 1966, p. 143; Brammer and Shostrom, 1968, p. 170; Tyler, 1961, Pp. 244–283, 291–292).

A second factor that has emerged consistently in the literature of the past decade has been an increasing awareness of the *relationship* between counselor and client as the primary criterion for therapeutic outcomes. Reviewing the literature in support of this concept, Brammer and Shostrom (1968) have summarized the views of many current theorists in saying that "the heart of the therapeutic process is the relationship established between the counselor and client." " . . . We are becoming more and more convinced that the relationship in psychotherapy and counseling is a curative agent in its own right" (p. 160). For Carl Rogers, the essence of successful relationships centers primarily in the *attitudes* of the participants and in the manner in which the participants communicate their attitudes to one another.

Following his earlier writings and research with client-centered therapy (Rogers, 1942, 1951; Rogers and Dymond, 1954) Rogers synthesized, in a number of position papers, three basic conditions which he considers essential for effecting client learning and growth. Referring primarily to counselor attitudes, Rogers (1954, 1957) called these basic conditions "congruence," "unconditional positive regard," and "empathic understanding." (See Blocher, 1966, p. 144.) The same factors have also been referred to in other sources in terms of (1) genuineness and transparency, i.e., trust, spontaneity, realness, openness, and lack of facade; (2) acceptance, liking, and caring, i.e., warm regard for the client as a person of unconditional self-worth; and (3) a continuing desire on the part of the counselor to understand, i.e., having and communicating a *sensitive empathy* with the client's feelings and communications (Rogers, 1957, 1961).

That the therapeutic conditions postulated by Rogers have withstood the test of many research investigations and theoretical confrontations is attested to by the recent writings of Truax and Carkhuff (1967). Summarizing much theoretical literature and relevant research findings regarding counseling and therapy relationships, Truax and Carkhuff indicated that:

> Despite the bewildering array of divergent theories and the difficulty in translating concepts from the language of one theory to that of another, several common threads weave their way through almost every major theory of psychotherapy and counseling, including the psychoanalytic, the client-centered, the behavioristic, and many more eclectic and derivative theories. In one way or another, all have emphasized the importance of the therapist's ability to be integrated, mature, genuine, authentic or congruent in his relationship to the patient. They have all stressed also the importance of the therapist's ability to provide a non-threatening, trusting, safe or secure atmosphere by his acceptance, non-possessive warmth, unconditional positive regard, or love. Finally, virtually all theories of psychotherapy emphasize that for the therapist to be helpful he must be accurately emphathic, be "with" the client, be understanding, or grasp the patient's meaning (p. 25).

Since the scope of this chapter does not permit a more thorough treatment of these relationship factors, the reader who wishes to become more conversant with these concepts, and, hopefully, to increase his skills for therapeutic interpersonal encounters is encouraged to consult the several references cited above. In addition, a most helpful discussion of the concept of empathy in counseling will be found in the following work by Buchheimer (1963).

It should be recognized that providing the kind of relationship suggested here is not always easy. But one's ability to genuinely *be* this kind of person apparently distinguishes, quite conclusively, between his potential effectiveness or ineffectiveness as a counselor. Truax and Carkhuff (1967) state this conclusion quite firmly, as follows:

> Counselors and therapists who offer high levels of empathy, warmth, and genuineness produce positive changes in their clients, while therapists who offer low levels of these "therapeutic conditions" produce deterioration or no change

in their clients. These central ingredients of empathy, warmth, and genuineness do not merely represent "techniques" of psychotherapy or counseling, but are interpersonal skills that the counselor or therapist employs in applying his "techniques" or "expert knowledge," whether he be a psychotherapist, a vocational rehabilitation counselor, or a personal counselor (p. 2).

In other words, if the counselor is to be "genuine" and "real" in demonstrating these kinds of personal characteristics in his interpersonal relationships, it would seem that he must personally possess and practice these qualities more as a *way of life,* than merely as a *bag of tricks.*

The integrative approach presented by Brammer and Shostrom (1968) can help beginning and experienced counselors, alike, to bridge the gap between the interpersonal relationship skills which should be part of the counselor's personal makeup—and the traditional, externally oriented, and technique-centered strategies counselors employ. Such a merger has long been needed between theories which stress only the counselor's attitudes, with the additional contributions to be made by the diagnostically oriented techniques of other therapeutic approaches. As Brammer and Shostrom put it, "Counseling Psychology incorporates traditional counseling and assessment with newer emphasis on self actualization and improving human effectiveness" (p. 5).

Pointing out that helping relationships evolve through stages, Brammer and Shostrom suggest that the counselor must be able to grow in his ability to extend and share more and more of himself as the relationship matures.

> The nature of the emotional interaction appears to be a key variable determining the quality of the relationship or encounter. . . . First he reacts at a friendship level, as one liking certain qualities in the other and experiencing pleasure at the meeting. Secondly, he reacts at a genuine personal encounter level disregarding qualities he may like or dislike in the client. Then he reacts at a deeper level of loving concern for the other person's welfare. . . (p. 162).

> The most reasonable goal seems to be that the counselor get emotionally involved to the extent necessary to keep the client emotionally involved, but the counselor's keen interest in helping be tempered with a reserve and distance so that the counselor can accept attitudes and feelings expressed by the client without reacting personally to them (p. 163).

> . . . The psychotherapist's task, therefore, may be seen as establishing whatever relation the client is able to make, solidifying it, gradually freeing it of unrealities and teaching the client the dynamisms thus disclosed (p. 160).

In addition to their focus on relationship skills, Brammer and Shostrom also give specific helps regarding interview techniques; but they support the position presented here, that so-called *techniques,* as such, are regarded only as implementations of the counselor's attitudes toward the client and as facilitators of those elements which are felt to be inherent in the relationship itself.

Counseling the Hard of Hearing

Knowledgeable counselors and psychologists recognize that hard of hearing subjects present some unique problems beyond the normally hearing client.

However, the basic principles of treatment, in terms of helping or therapeutic relationships remain much the same (see *Hearing Loss . . . A Community Loss*, 1958, p. 87–95). For this reason, the following discussion does not emphasize presumed differences of hard of hearing cases, but attempts, instead, to show that the emotions and self-image of hard of hearing youth are much the same as other counseling cases—albeit, the hearing disabilities may well magnify such emotions and incapacitations.

If such an assumption is tenable, cases involving hard of hearing and/or speech problems are particularly appropriate subjects for the type of therapeutic relationship being suggested here; and it would follow that any *unique* aspects of such handicapped subjects center more in the counselor's ability to communicate a therapeutic relationship than in any special treatment methods indicated for this particular type of client. That this conclusion has been reached also by hearing and speech therapists, quite independent of counseling psychologists, is shown by the writings of Backus and Beasley (1951), Webster (1966) and others (Levine, 1960; Vaughn, 1967).

At the same time, however, it should be noted that counseling or psychotherapy with hard of hearing subjects does require an area of knowledge and professional skill somewhat outside the typical training of counseling psychology. For example, the practitioner with hard of hearing clients must not only understand the dynamics of behavior and personality development as required for typical in-depth counseling, but he must also be more skilled than usual in transmitting genuine, emotional warmth and understanding—by *nonverbal* as well as verbal means. In addition, he should, ideally, have training and background for understanding the causes and nature of auditory disabilities, and for working specifically with individuals so afflicted (Vaughn, 1967, pp. 57–58).

While it is not within the scope of this chapter to discuss, at length, the desired training of counselors, several approaches to training seem feasible for individuals who expect to work extensively with hard of hearing subjects: (1) primary training as a professional counselor or psychologist, with additional orientation and clinical internship with hard of hearing cases; (2) primary training in audiology and speech pathology, with additional training and a clinical internship in counseling psychology; or (3) professional practice in an interdisciplinary clinic, wherein specialists from each of the appropriate disciplines are available for broad diagnostic and treatment capabilities as required in each case, and where hearing specialists and counseling psychologists can work together as co-therapists when indicated.

Emotional Characteristics of Hard of Hearing Subjects

Aside from the expected difficulties in verbal communication which are associated with auditory disabilities, the individual with moderate to severe hearing loss is often characterized by feelings of loneliness, isolation, fear, inadequacy, inferiority, negative self-worth, rejection, helplessness, and hopelessness. Some also feel considerable bitterness and resentment about their handicap (see *Hearing Loss . . . A Community Loss*, 1958, pp. 92–93; Vaughn, 1967, pp. 144–145, 183–190; Wright, B., 1960, pp. 13, 41–52, 61). Individuals who experience such feelings tend to be more "on guard" than usual about themselves and their interpersonal relationships; and prolonged emotions of this sort inevitably lead to personal-social behavior often characterized by depression, hypersensitivity, social withdrawal, submissiveness, and/or apathy (Levine, 1960, pp. 61–62).

Many hard of hearing subjects attempt to deny or "cover" their disability and are, therefore, perceived by others as being immature, indifferent, hostile, or stubborn (Vaughn, 1967, p. 135; Wright, B., 1960, pp. 42–43). The hard of hearing child, for example, may adapt to his hearing deficiencies as he grows, without realizing the nature of his problem. As a result, he may experience more rejection than warranted from parents, teachers, and peers, either because he does not hear requests made of him, or because he attempts to fake his way through social situations at home, school, and elsewhere (Levine, 1960, p. 67).

Because of these enhanced emotional barriers (either perceived or real) the hearing problem, and any consequent language impairment, only complicate the already difficult process of establishing a trusting relationship between counselor and counselee—or between the normally hearing adult and the hearing impaired child. In addition, the realities of the hearing loss and any attendant language disabilities often present many other limitations for this person in terms of educational, vocational, and social opportunities. These limitations are not only difficult for a counselor to point out to the client without seeming discriminatory, but facing and accepting these realities of life squarely, and learning to adjust to restricted life goals without bitterness or pessimism could not help but be an even more painful and difficult task for the counselee. In some instances, hard of hearing subjects are reluctant to attempt, or even consider educational, vocational, and social goals for which they might well have the potential. Others either do not realize their limitations, or they refuse to admit any limitations, and, therefore, encounter repeated disappointments and frustration in constantly striving toward unrealistic goals.

Counseling Objectives

Counseling with the hard of hearing individual, as with any counselee, needs to be oriented to social realities, as well as to the intellectual, emotional, and physical capabilities of each client. Basically, the intent of counseling is to help the counselee make appropriate decisions and to initiate appropriate behavior in light of available information about him and his environment. Referring to educational programs for hard of hearing subjects, Vaughn (1967) outlined the objective as helping the student "explore the breadth and diversity of opportunities available to him." She added that support programs should be designed to "enable subjects to develop both socially and emotionally," since these appear to be prime factors in personal motivation, interpersonal relationships, successful employment, independence, adjustment to realities of life, and improved self-concept (p. 44).

In many ways, the counselor serves as an intervener in the counselee's life style, and thus as a change agent. As such, the counselor has an opportunity to provide hope and direction to the discouraged and/or the disabled. Although many counselors resist the inference that they exercise influence over their clients, it is the position of this practitioner that the counselor *can*, *does*, and *should* influence the counselee toward the "best" possible goals and behavior for him.

Often the client moves in "good" directions with minimum influence from the counselor. At other times, however, it may mean that the counselor exerts considerable influence, either overtly or covertly, to get the client to do what the *counselor* thinks will be best for him. This does not usually mean that the counselor makes decisions for the client, or that the counselor robs the client of his right to make his own decisions. On the contrary, most counselors agree that the counselee should be helped to make his own decisions; however, most counselors also have a built-in, theoretical bias—which says, in effect, that they have failed in counseling if the client makes unrealistic choices, or if he does not improve his behavior along socially acceptable dimensions. Such a bias or point of view suggests that client feelings and behavior are "best," or more appropriate and potentially helpful when they are (1) growth facilitating in terms of improved self-concept and strengthened interpersonal relationships, (2) personally and socially valued, and (3) realistic in terms of the client's assessed capabilities and opportunities.

Counselor Expectations and Persuasion

Restating the research conclusions from counseling literature, client progress toward desired outcomes seems to depend more on the counselor's attitudes toward his client and on the counselor-client relationship than on any other variables. In effect, the successful counselor-client relationship establishes conditions, not only for a climate in which the counselee can explore his feelings and experiment with behavioral changes, but it also presents a "significant other" model (the counselor) which the counselee learns to trust and to imitate. Either directly or indirectly, intentionally or unintentionally, the counselor thus becomes an influence for client change: and cases are usually considered successful or unsuccessful in terms of the amount and the direction of change evidenced by the client. According to Bednar (1969) and Bednar and Parker (1969), improved client behavior results when "the client accepts the counselor's frame of reference as valid for understanding his own behavior and believes it will be of help to him."

The implication is that, in successful cases, the counselor's attitudes and proffered relationship elicit from the counselee a sense of trust and faith in the counselor, and a subsequent willingness of the counselee to accept the counselor's explanations about the problem, as well as his recommendations for coping differently with it. Support for this kind of persuasion-expectation implication is found in earlier writings of Jerome Frank (1961), who suggests that the "healing powers" of counseling and psychotherapy may result more from the client's expectations of improvement (faith) than from the treatment method used. More recently, a number of other writers have demonstrated a positive relationship between the counselor's expectations for client improvement and the actual improvement made by the client (Bednar, 1969; Goldstein, 1960, 1962; Goldstein and Shipman, 1961; Rosenthal and Jacobsen, 1968). The research reported by these authors indicates that client expectations for improvement are influenced primarily by the counselor's feelings about and expectations of the client.

With such an hypothesis sounding somewhat analogous to "faith healings," it is not surprising that this phenomenon has also been referred to by Rosenthal (1968) as a "self-fulfilling prophecy." He writes, "One prophesies an event, and the expectation of the event then changes the behavior of the prophet in such a way as to make the prophesied event more likely" (p. 49).

Discussing this concept in reference to experimenter effects in research, both with humans and with rats, Rosenthal indicates that the self-fulfilling prophecy is brought about by two types of experimenter (counselor) expectations. One expectation, he says, occurs only in "the eye, the hand, and the brain of the researchers," or, for example, in the counselor's attitudes toward, and mental expectations of the client. The second type of expectation, Rosenthal says, is "the result of the interaction between the experimenter and the subject . . ." (p. 47). He adds,

> Quite unconsciously, a psychologist interacts in subtle ways with the people he is studying so that he may get the response he expects to get. This happens even when the person cannot see the researcher. And, even more surprisingly, it occurs when the subject is not human but a rat (p. 47).

Referring to teacher-pupil expectations, Rosenthal's research showed that teachers not only altered their teaching style according to their perceptions of their students, but that they also communicated their expectations both orally and visually, even though quite unconsciously. In all cases reported, when the teachers had favorable expectations of their students, these expectations were communicated in ways which facilitated increasing learning beyond that attained by equally-able pupils who were viewed with less favorable expectations. Translating Rosenthal's research into counselor-client relationships, the therapeutic essentials emphasized throughout this chapter, i.e., *counselor congruence, positive regard for the client*, and *empathic communication*, take on additional meaning.

Even more supportive of the persuasion-expectation dimension is the research in nonverbal communication discussed by Mehrabian (1968). Making a distinction between *verbal* communication (words) and *vocal* communication (tone, feeling, etc.), Mehrabian indicates that "the verbal part of a spoken message has considerably less effect on whether a listener feels liked or disliked than a speaker's expression or tone of voice" (p. 53). He reports further that communication is judged more accurately when the verbal and vocal components of a message agree (congruence), and that when these two aspects of speech give contradictory messages, the *vocal* component has the greater impact. Therefore, how the counselor perceives and feels about a client is likely to be communicated to the client, with or without accompanying words. The same principle, also, is apparently true for parents' feelings about their children, since Mehrabian reports that the degree of a child's emotional disturbance is influenced by the total amount of positive or negative feelings communicated to him. If so, this notion lends further credence to the curative properties previously attributed to the "positive regard" feelings of a counselor for his client.

In addition to the verbal and vocal aspects of communication, Mehrabian discusses still other, more subtle cues that are often given in a spoken message. Since hard of hearing individuals will undoubtedly be sensitive to and "on the look out" for any subtleties communicated to them, especially nonverbal cues, it is important that the counselor be aware of the nuances of communicated speech, and of their implied meanings. Among the cues that Mehrabian considers significant and which he discusses from the findings of several research studies are: timing of verbal responses, length of utterances or silences, speaking directly versus indirectly to the person, facial expressions, touch, changes in body position, posture, a relaxed versus tense feeling, looking into the other person's eyes, and positive versus neutral tone of voice.

Other resources materials which should help the reader develop a better understanding of nonverbal communication in counseling will be found in the following works (Kagun, 1967; Lifton, 1966).

In summary, the accumulative evidence of the research reported above can be stated as follows: (1) if a counselor has faith in himself and in the theoretical framework (counseling model) he has developed for interpreting human behavior, and (2) if the client has faith in the counselor, then, (3) the client can be helped, directly or subtly, to accept the counselor's conceptual framework and ultimately to move in the directions being cued by the counselor's expectations of him. A more thorough, and thought-provoking discussion of this viewpoint will be found in the "cognitive-behavioral" counseling model presented recently by Lewis (1969).

Assuming that the counselor will focus primarily on the emotional and social problems attendant to the client's auditory disabilities, and not on the medical aspects or auditory condition itself, the mutual faith and expectations for client improvement expressed in the counseling framework described above will provide a base for the handicapped individual to gradually view himself more positively and to learn improved ways of coping with his behavioral choices and feelings. If the counselor has sufficient professional stature and a personal demeanor which invites confidence in his expertise, the counselee can be helped to grow, in some measure, even when reality dictates limited goals and when client progress is slow and difficult. Beyond his own clinical competence and image, the research findings in support of this point of view, i.e., counselor persuasion and expectations, suggest further, that in cases which might ordinarily be viewed with "guarded prognosis," the counselor might be well advised to nurture the kind of faith in the client which, according to the Bible, can move mountains (Matthew 17:14–20).

Benefits of Multiple Counseling

Working with adults and older youth obviously involves a direct relationship between counselor and client; and this relationship can be provided either on an individual basis, or through group counseling with several clients simultaneously. When the hard of hearing subject is a young child, however, the counselor will usually find it necessary and more fruitful to work with the parents of the child, or else to involve the parents and child together. In many instances it will be most helpful to work with the entire family as a group. In either case, *group* counseling, particularly with handicapped persons, can provide benefits not available through individual counseling alone (Hansen et al., 1967; Vaughn, 1967; Wright, E. W., 1959, 1968).

The objectives of group counseling, i.e., to effect therapeutic encounters and, thus, improve the counselee's relationships and behavior are much the same as is individual counseling—except, that in the group setting the counseling now utilizes the power of *multiple* relationships in the group, rather than merely the one relationship between counselor and counselee.

In this sense, the counselor serves as a facilitator of group interaction and increased interpersonal bond among the group participants; and depending on the makeup of the group, a given counselee can be helped to deal more directly with the "significant others" in his life. The group setting thus provides an environmental milieu in which to observe not only the counselee's self-perceptions and responses to his environment, but also the attitudes and reactions of parents and reactions of parents and peers toward the counselee. Both are important variables in helping the counselee to feel better about himself, to function better, and to utilize his environmental resources optimally.

Inasmuch as each individual is raised from infancy in social settings (groups), it is logical that groups form a reality oriented setting for individuals to work out their personal-social problems and life goals. Further, how one behaves toward others in a group counseling situation is a fairly accurate index of how he deals with problems and people outside the counseling group. Therefore, the opportunity for first-hand observation of individuals and relationships in the group provides the counselor, counselee, and other group members with evaluative data for seeking solutions to the problems confronting each member of the group.

One important aspect of the group process is implied in the term, "multiple counseling," which some have proposed as an alternative for the term group counseling (Wright, 1958). For this writer, the term *multiple counseling* connotes the fact that group members serve as "multiple counselors" for one another—by assisting each other in the expression and clarification of feelings, by helping interpret the meaning of what is said, by giving and receiving honest "feedback," by exerting group influence on individual behavior, and by helping to establish norms for group behavior.

Research reported by Hansen, Zimpfer, and Easterling (1967) lends support to the concept and terminology of "multiple counseling," as well as to the other benefits usually attributed to the *group* process itself. Investigating the relevance of relationship conditions in multiple counseling to the change in self-concept congruence of secondary students, these authors reported the following conclusions: (1) when the group atmosphere is good, the group members have a better chance for growth. Students who perceive the other group members, including the counselor, to be genuine, accepting and understanding, have a better chance for personal growth than when they perceive the group as offering a poorer relationship; (2) the perceived relationships offered by group members may be more meaningful than the relationship with the counselor. Students who perceived other group members offering a positive relationship made greater gains in self-concept congruence than those perceiving a negative relationship, and this was more true for group relationships than for the counselor-client relationship in the group; (3) students perceiving a negative condition being offered from the group showed deterioration in self-concept congruence; and (4) students expecting a positive relationship with the counselor made significantly greater gains in self-concept congruence than students expecting a negative relationship. Also, students who expected a poor relationship actually perceived what they expected.

Each of the findings reported by Hansen, Zimpfer, and Easterling also contributes additional support to the *relationship* orientation presented throughout this chapter; and it is not difficult to recognize the implications of these research outcomes in terms of the potential benefits to be derived from a multiple counseling approach when the counselor involves the parents and/ or peers in the counseling situation with hard of hearing youth. For example, counseling with the parents of hearing impaired youth, particularly in cases of very young children and those with severe handicaps, will usually be essential for arriving at a realistic program of action between parents, teacher, rehabilitation agencies, etc. In many such cases, the parents and family of a disabled child need help in evaluating their feelings and responses to the child, in establishing a positive atmosphere generally, and in developing greater congruence between their verbal and emotional communications to the child. Over-protective parents will also need help in facilitating the self-confidence, maturation, and relative independence of the handicapped child.

Benefits of family counseling, with parents and children together, include the following: (1) it requires the parents to involve the child more in decisions that affect him, (2) it enables the counselor to influence improved parent-child interactions, and (3) it allows both the parents and the child to know exactly what the counselor says and does with the other—thus minimizing any parent-child competitiveness for the counselor's exclusive support, or any concern over the confidentiality of information that each brings to the counseling situation.

Group, or multiple counseling has still other advantages for working specifically with hard of hearing and otherwise handicapped subjects. Involvement of the hard of hearing counselee with a group of peers, both normally hearing and hearing impaired, forces him to relate more than he might ordinarily do with others around him. The need for this is evidenced in the educational project reported on by Vaughn (1967), who indicates that a high percentage of hard of hearing subjects were uncomfortable identifying both with the normally hearing world and with the deaf. This was particularly true with subjects who had severe hearing loss but who had developed oral communication skills. While they did not feel equal to normally hearing associates, they did not like to identify with deaf people who used manual communication. Use of the group relationships available in a multiple counseling setting enables such a person to "find himself," and hopefully to bridge the gap he is experiencing between the hearing and nonhearing worlds.

Not only is it therapeutic for the handicapped individual to receive understanding and support from others who have problems, but it is also therapeutic for the individual to become "other-centered" in getting outside himself to *give* support *to* others. In this sense, group counseling can capitalize on the heterogeneity of the group participants to help the normally hearing and hard of hearing subjects learn to respond more comfortably with each other. Those having difficulty relating to both worlds would, thus, be expected by the group to give help to, and receive help from both worlds; and as each individual learns to accept others in the group, he becomes more accepting of himself, also. In the process, members of the group provide various models as "living witnesses" to encourage the more severely handicapped and less oral; and oral subjects who sign can serve as interpreters between the hearing impaired and normally hearing participants.

Effective multiple counseling requires three things of the group participants: (1) individual involvement, (2) group interaction, and (3) mutual assistance (Wright, 1968). Stated another way, Hill (1966) discusses three basic dimensions which he found to increase the therapeutic potential of a group: (1) member centeredness, (2) interpersonal threat, and (3) patient-therapist role taking. Elsewhere (Wright, 1968), this writer has summarized the meaning of Hill's three dimensions as follows:

> *Member centeredness* means that the group discussions focus on topic persons in the group or on group relationships rather than on subject matter or "things" outside the group, i.e., on internal, rather than external content. The more a group deals with "member centered," rather than "non-member-centered" topics, the higher the group is rated for member-centeredness.

> *Interpersonal threat* is seen as an important factor in the group process because of the impact that group members have on one another when they are willing to take some risk of being exposed. Most group behavior represents resistance, or "guardedness"; and only as members become more "open" and "vulnerable" with each other is there greater opportunity for them to make some investment in "trusting" relationships. This means that for a group to get beyond mere intellectual discussions and to realize the therapeutic value of interpersonal impact on each other, members must be helped, at some point, to give up their traditional "cover" and undertake some measure of interpersonal risk. To do so usually requires that a person is either talking about, or *to* someone in the group, or about himself.

> The dimension of *patient-therapist role taking* requires that group members learn not only to "share" the leader with others in the group, but also that they become willing to accept "treatment" from other group members as well as from the counselor. Many individuals in counseling or therapy do not recognize or feel a real need for help. Accepting help from other "sick," or equally unstable persons is even more difficult. Similarly, when one is insecure about

himself and his own problems, it is difficult to be "other-centered" and oriented toward helping others. One unique aspect of the group counseling process is that it provides opportunity for, and to some extent requires, this kind of other-centeredness and sharedness of responsibility and concern for each other. Counseling groups can only attain optimum therapeutic potential as the group members are willing, able, and assisted to assume this kind of patient-therapist role taking.

Conclusion

At this point, the reader might well be asking, "so now that we have a *theory* about counseling, how do we actually make it work?" "What are the best techniques?" The awareness that many readers would like a "cookbook" of counseling techniques causes me some uneasiness in knowing that the present chapter probably does not fulfill such an expectation. However, I have resisted a technique-centered orientation because of a strong personal belief that the counselor, *as a person,* constitutes the most important variable in counseling. In other words, the counselor *is* technique (see Williamson, 1962). Not only does he provide a personal model, which the counselee can accept or refute as he evaluates his own values and goals, but the counselor is often expected by the counselee and others (even though somewhat un-realistic and naïve at times) to be sufficiently omnipotent and omniscient to transcend many of the normal barriers to problem solving and individual growth.

The point of view expressed in this chapter suggests that the effective counselor will, ideally, possess many of the qualities exemplified by the Love of Christ, i.e., maturity, stability, wisdom, sound judgment, understanding, patience, tolerance, caring for others, etc. At the same time, he must interpret reality correctly to the counselee, and somehow influence the counselee toward socially appropriate goals and behavior; and it is this latter expectation of the counselor which suggests a second dimension of the kind of love modeled by Christ, i.e., direction and influence, judging and evaluating, encouraging and exorting, setting of approved goals, limits and controls, at times *requiring* appropriate behavior, and when appropriate, chastising as needed, to dis-courage inappropriate behavior. That the counselor is expected to accomplish all this in an atmosphere of relative freedom and interpersonal safety, and without judgmental attitudes, moral preachments, or personal rejection, places considerable responsibility on the counselor. It is no small wonder that many writers have been concerned about the counselor's apparently conflicting roles (Bentley, 1968; Perez, 1965; Williamson, 1958, 1964a, 1964b, 1966; Wrenn, 1962; Vance and Volsky, 1962).

Obviously, before a counselor can be an effective change agent with others, he must begin by sharpening himself as *the* therapeutic tool. Since most psychological (or emotional) problems of people are considered to stem from difficulties in earlier or present-day interpersonal relationships, Kovacs (1966) says that we can help such people "come to terms with their own chronic flight from intimacy" only if we are able to "lay aside the phony, self-protecting emphasis on techniques which guard us and our boundaries. . . ."

Thus, the therapeutic potentialities inherent in the *person* of the counselor, "as technique," can be summarized by Kovacs' (1966) well-expressed description of psychotherapy, as follows:

> Psychotherapy, for me, is not something that one person, the therapist, does to another, the patient. It is a living human relationship in which, if successful, both persons grow and change: where who is the expert at any moment may change is locus; where the experiencing that each does of their relationship together must be treated which equal respect and attempts at understanding . . . and where the needs of the therapist matter as much as the needs of the patient. . . .

> . . . I question the utility not only of the concept of "treatment" but of neurosis itself. For me there are only people—not diagnostic categories—people inclined, bent, scarred, and struggling on in a fashion which is uniquely *them* in the face of inevitable destructive experiences which life can and does bring to us all. For me, then, psychotherapy is not the application of a technique to the treatment of a neurosis, psychosis, or character problem but rather the therapist's participation in the patient's attempts to understand the course of his life's journey and his often self-defeating reactions to it, in helping to impart the courage to tolerate its present pains undisguised, and in selecting future paths which, with good fortune, will lead to greater fulfillment.

> . . . There is an implicit assumption that participation in the immediacy of real personal encounters can have a growth promoting effect on the persons involved, given a commitment to observe, to learn, and to profit therefrom.

References

Albert, G. 1966. If counseling is psychotherapy—what then? Personnel and Guidance Journal 45:124–129.

Backus, A. and J. Beasley. 1951. Speech Therapy With Children. Boston: Houghton-Mifflin.

Bednar, R. L. 1969. Persuasibility and the power of belief. Unpublished manuscript. Arkansas Rehabilitation Research and Training Center, University of Arkansas.

Bednar, R. L. and C. A. Parker. 1969. Client susceptibility to persuasion and counseling outcome. Journal of Counseling Psychology. In press.

Bently, J. C. 1968. The Counselor's Role: Commentary and Readings. Boston: Houghton-Mifflin.

Blocher, D. H. 1966. Developmental Counseling. New York: Ronald Press.

Bordin, E. S. 1968. Psychological Counseling, 2nd Ed. New York: Appleton-Century-Crofts.

Brammer, L. M. and E. L. Shostrom. 1968. Therapeutic Psychology, 2nd Ed. Englewood Cliffs, N.J.: Prentice-Hall.

Buchheimer, A. 1963. The development of ideas about empathy. Journal of Counseling Psychology 10(1):61–70.

Frank, J. 1961. Persuasion and Healing. New York: Schocken Books.

Goldman, L. H. 1962. Group counseling: content and process. Personnel and Guidance Journal 40(6):518–522.

Goldstein, A. P. 1960. Patient expectancies and non-specific therapy as a basis for (Un) spontaneous remission. Journal of Clinical Psychology 16:399–403.

Goldstein, A. P. 1962. Therapist Patient Expectancies in Psychotherapy. New York: Macmillan.

Goldstein, A. P. and W. G. Shipman. 1961. Patient expectancies, symptom reduction and aspects of the initial psychotherapeutic interview. Journal of Clinical Psychology 17:129–133.

Hansen, J. C., D. G. Zimpfer, and R. E. Easterling. 1967. A study of the relationships in multiple counseling. Journal of Educational Research 60(10):461–463.

Hearing Loss . . . A Community Loss. 1958. Washington, D.C.: American Hearing Society.

Hill, W. F. 1966. Hill Interaction Matrix. Los Angeles: University of Southern California, Youth Studies Center.

Kagun, N., D. R. Krahtwohl, et al., 1967. Studies in Human Interaction. East Lancing: Michigan State University, Educational Publication Services, College of Education.

Kovacs, A. L. 1966. Further remarks on psychotherapy as an intimate relationship. Psychotherapy: Theory, Research and Practice 3. (Quotations for this chapter were taken from a reprint of Kovacs' article in Applications of Reality Therapy: A Book of Readings. Mink, Becker and Zaslaw (Eds.).) Morgantown: West Virginia University. Pp. 271–274.

Levine, E. S. 1960. The Psychology of Deafness. New York: Columbia University Press.

Lewis, E. 1969. Unpublished manuscript. In press for publication.

Lifton, W. M. 1966. Symposium on nonverbal communication in group counseling . . . How the silent client communicates. Unpublished paper. American Personnel and Guidance Association.

Mahler, C. A. and E. Caldwell. 1961. Group Counseling in the Secondary Schools. Chicago: Science Research Associates.

Mehrabian, A. 1968. Communication without words. Psychology Today 2(4):53–55.

Perez, J. F. 1965. Counseling: Theory and Practice. Reading, Mass.: Addison-Wesley.

Perry, W. G. 1955. On the relation of psychotherapy and counseling. Annals of the New York Academy of Sciences 63:396–407.

Porter, E. H. 1950. An Introduction to Therapeutic Counseling. Boston: Houghton-Mifflin.

Rogers, C. R. 1942. Counseling and Psychotherapy. Boston: Houghton-Mifflin.

Rogers, C. R. 1951. Client Centered Therapy: Its Current Practice, Implications, and Theory. Boston: Houghton-Mifflin.

Rogers, C. R. 1954. Some hypotheses regarding the facilitation of personal growth. Paper given at Oberlin College, 1954. In On Becoming A Person. Boston: Houghton-Mifflin. 1964. Pp. 31–38.

Rogers, C. R. 1957. The necessary and sufficient conditions of therapeutic personality change. Journal of Consulting Psychology 21:95–103.

Rogers, C. R. 1958. The characteristics of a helping relationship. Personnel and Guidance Journal 37:6–16.

Rogers, C. R. 1961. On Becoming a Person. Boston: Houghton-Mifflin.

Rogers, C. R. and R. F. Dymond. 1954. Psychotherapy and Personality Change. Chicago: University of Chicago Press.

Rogers, C. R. and B. F. Skinner. 1956. Some issues concerning the control of human behavior. Science 124 (3231):1057–1066.

Rosenthal, R. 1966. Experimenter Effects in Behavioral Research. New York: Appleton-Century-Crofts.

Rosenthal, R. 1968. Self-fulfilling prophecy. Psychologist Today 2(4):44–51.

Rosenthal, R. and L. Jacobson. 1968. Pygmalion in the Classroom. New York: Holt, Rinehart and Winston.

Snyder, W. U. 1945. Dr. Thorne's critique of nondirective psychotherapy. Journal of Abnormal and Social Psychology 40:336–339.

Stewart, L. H. and C. F. Warnath. 1965. The Counselor and Society. A Cultural Approach. Boston: Houghton-Mifflin.

Thorne, F. C. 1944. A critique of nondirective methods of psychotherapy. Journal of Abnormal and Social Psychology 39: 459–470.

Truax, C. B. and R. R. Carkhuff. 1967. Toward Effective Counseling and Psychotherapy. Chicago: Aldine Publishing Co.

Tyler, L. 1961. The Work of the Counselor, 2nd Ed. New York: Appleton-Century-Crofts.

Vance, F. L. and T. Volsky. 1962. Counseling and psychotherapy: Split personality or Siamese twins? American Psychologist 17(8):565–570.

Vaughn, G. R. 1967. Education of Deaf and Hard of Hearing Adults in Established Facilities for the Normally Hearing. Pocatello: Idaho State University.

Webster, E. J. 1966. Parent counseling by speech pathologists and audiologists. Journal of Speech and Hearing Disorders 31:331–340.

Williamson, E. G. 1950. Directive vs. non-directive counseling. California Journal of Secondary Education 25:332–336.

Williamson, E. G. 1958. Value orientation in counseling. Personnel and Guidance Journal 36:520–528.

Williamson, E. G. 1962. The counselor as technique. Personnel and Guidance Journal 41:108–111.

Williamson, E. G. 1964a. Counseling as preparation for directed change. Teachers College Record 65:613–622.

Williamson, E. G. 1964b. The counselor should not sit in judgment. Unpublished paper. In press. University of Minnesota.

Williamson, E. G. 1966. Value options and the counseling relationship. Personnel and Guidance Journal 44:617–623.

Wrenn, C. G. 1962. The Counselor in a Changing World. Washington, D.C.: American Personnel and Guidance Association.

Wright, B. A. 1960. Physical Disability—A Psychological Approach. New York: Harper & Row.

Wright, E. W. 1959. Mutliple counseling why? When? How? Personnel and Guidance Journal 37:551–557.

Wright, E. W. 1958. The content and process of group counseling with Job Corps youth. Unpublished paper. University of Oklahoma, Job Corps Staff Training Center.

Chapter 11

The Potential of Current Trends in Public Education for the Hard of Hearing Child

CLIFFORD J. LAWRENCE, Ed.D. and
MIRIAM B. KAPFER, Ph.D

The most important trend on the current educational scene is the fact that individualized instruction and learning is at last beginning to be *implemented* in schools rather than just talked about. For the first time, the public schools have within their grasp the necessary scientific, electronic, and technological tools and methods for educating students as *individuals*. It now becomes a matter of incorporating these exciting educational possibilities into the educational programs of all schools so that the innovations of today become the commonplace educational realities of tomorrow.

The changes resulting from individualized approaches to education for the "normal" child also have profound implications for the education of the hard of hearing student. For example, if enrolled in an individualized public school program, the hearing handicapped child can live at home rather than being institutionalized, he can learn to function effectively within a modern school environment, he can associate with normal hearing students, and he can have the success experiences in learning that are essential to the development of a healthy self-concept, both as a student and later as an adult.

Before examining further the potential of public education for the hard of hearing child, it is necessary to consider at least three prior questions: (1) What are the philosophical, historical, and legal precedents which place the education of the hard of hearing student within the province of public education?; (2) What provisions are currently being made for the hard of hearing in the public schools?; and (3) What are the most significant and adaptable of the many innovations presently being developed in public education? Thoughtful answers to these questions are vital if the most promising trends in current public education are to be made productive for the child with special problems resulting from hearing loss. It is obvious that the educational programs designed specifically for the hard of hearing must be as inventive and forward-looking as possible if these children are to keep pace in an increasingly complicated and rapidly changing world.

175

Public School Responsibility and Provisions for
Educating the Hard of Hearing

The complex nature of hearing disability mandates a broad and equally complex scope of educational approaches. The following paragraphs focus on the problems, first, of whether public education should be responsible for the specialized educational programs required by the hard of hearing, and, secondly, whether public education presently is doing an adequate job in this area.

Philosophical, Historical, and Legal Precedents

The development of public education in the United States has been based on a democratic belief in the worth of each individual. This belief has undergirded our public school system since its beginning; yet children whose needs could not be readily served in the regular classroom were at first exempted or excluded from school. Through the years, however, and particularly since the beginning of the present century, the new horizons opened by psychology and other branches of behavioral science have expanded the possibilities of program development for all types of children in the public schools. More surely today than ever before, a first-rate public education is considered the right of all American children, whether or not they may be handicapped by social conditions, by economics, by geographic location, or by an actual physical disability such as hearing loss.

Historically, education in the United States has evolved from largely church-supported and church-related patterns transplanted to the Americas from Europe. In the early New England towns, the education of the young, both in religious and secular areas, was thought to be highly important. Initially, however, the colonial educational system at elementary as well as more advanced levels was basically voluntary, both in terms of attendance and support. When it became evident, due to difficult pioneer conditions, that these voluntary efforts were not sufficient to insure adequate religious education for the young, church leaders appealed to the colonial legislature of Massachusetts for support in providing better educational programs. Thus, in 1642 and 1647, the civil authorities of Massachusetts enacted two laws which represent the first state-level action on the American continent ordering all children to be taught to read (Cubberley, 1948). These precedent-establishing laws provided the basis for the state, rather than the federal government, to serve as the agency responsible for the control of education in the United States.

In recent years, however, the federal government has vastly increased its school activity, particularly in the area of educational funding. For example, federal funds for educating handicapped children increased from approximately $1 million to more than $78 million in the 10-year period between 1958 and 1968. Federal efforts focused on providing equal educational opportunities for all children have undoubtedly opened the door for the initiation and improvement of many educational programs specifically designed for handicapped students.

Current Public School Provision for the Hard of Hearing

A 1966 National Education Association study of programs for handicapped children in school systems enrolling 300 or more pupils revealed that fewer than 50 percent of the districts (and then principally the larger ones) made provision for children with hearing disabilities. Among that minority of districts that did report programs for the hearing handicapped, many children were taught at home by specialists or sent out of the district to special schools rather than receiving instruction within the regular routine of the public schools (NEA Research Bulletin, 1967).

Such studies underline the fact that hard of hearing children often face two equally undesirable educational alternatives; either they are enrolled in classes for normal hearing children (without being provided with special assistance), or they are taught at home or placed in special schools intended for the profoundly deaf because no appropriate hard of hearing programs within regular public school schedules are available. This dilemma for the hard of hearing was further described in a statement prepared for the Maryland Commission on the Educational Needs of Handicapped Children:

> The case for the deaf child is one thing; the case for the hard of hearing child is another. This [the hard of hearing child] is the youngster who fifty years ago might have been considered to be profoundly deaf but today, with modern techniques of diagnosis and modern hearing aids, is classed as hard of hearing. This is also the youngster with a moderate hearing loss who years ago might have been contacted by shouting at him at the top of the lungs but today can have his hearing loss reasonably compensated for by a good hearing aid. These youngsters are betwixt and between the more profoundly hearing handicapped and those who have no hearing losses at all. Few of our public school systems have provision for the proper handling of these hard of hearing youngsters since their needs are not as profound as those of the more severely handicapped and not as easily identified. These hard of hearing youngsters can become deaf adults merely for the lack of attention to their educational and emotional needs (Fellendorf, 1966).

Thus, although some progress has been made in meeting the educational needs of children with moderate auditory and speech difficulties, the greatest progress has been made in providing instruction designed for the more severely handicapped. The moderately handicapped child who could function well within the regular school setting with the aid of some special help is the one who usually is not receiving the additional assistance he needs. Substantial efforts at educational program development and improvement within the public schools should be directed toward this type of child.

Educational Change—Current Trends

In the opening paragraph of this chapter it was noted that the single most important current trend in education today is the *actual implementation of individualized systems of instruction and learning* in certain lighthouse schools across the nation. Such implementation stands in vivid contrast to the time-honored and thoroughly entrenched group-paced instructional methods which have characterized education for years. Why should individualized programs be of any greater significance today than 10, 20, or even 100 years ago? What events have occurred to make true individualization more feasible as well as of greater necessity during the current period than ever before?

The Origins of Educational Change

Impetus for current educational innovation and change in the United States can be traced to the decade of the 1940s. The war years brought an obvious and immediate need, particularly with reference to the training and skills required by the defense and military complexes, to revolutionize and systematize traditional approaches to teaching and learning. Following the war, these new approaches gradually began to have an effect on general public education. Other post-World War II circumstances—marked by events such as the G.I. Bill, the appearance of the first of many "new" curricula, and the launching of Sputnik— introduced a new era in education. In the broadest sense, these years can be identified as an era of change. In general, the change has focused on the importance of the individual and his unique needs, on improving the means and materials of instruction in order to better meet the needs of the individuals in a rapidly changing world, and on improving the means of evaluating both the educational system and its products.

However, emphasis on the need for educational planning and evaluation related to individual needs has, perhaps, identified as many problems as solutions. Teachers and administrators have discovered that educational programs originally designed for simplicity of administration and instruction are often not the same ones which best meet the unique needs of students. As a result, educators have had to face two important facts: first, that the learning patterns of students vary tremendously, and second, that the schools must assume responsibility for designing instructional programs which will accommodate this variety in learning styles.

The Components of Effective Educational Change

During the past few years the "knowledge explosion" has brought not only increased emphasis on an expanded *need* to acquire knowledge but also increased attention to the *means* by which it is acquired. The methods of instruction have shifted from group-paced, rote learning of printed materials to a wider variety of individualized approaches and media. Emphasis on inquiry learning, creativity, and conceptualization, rather than on the amassing of factual information, is the theme of the day.

Other aspects of education have also changed. Organization and staffing patterns such as flexible scheduling and team teaching have opened new educational horizons. Instructional materials such as textbooks, supplementary reading materials, films, recordings, maps, and models have increased dramatically in quantity, quality, and variety. Instructional television, computerized instruction, and programmed materials of various types represent newer technological means of helping students achieve their educational objectives.

And the process of stating educational objectives has, itself, undergone change. The emphasis has moved from broad, general goal statements to more specific or "behavioral" objectives which serve both as better guides to program development and as more effective means of evaluating educational results. Such behavioral or learning objectives (in which specific behaviors under given conditions at particular performance levels are defined) are basic to many of the newer "hardware" and "software" approaches to the improvement and individualization of instruction and learning.

In too many schools throughout the country, however, this deluge of technological, theoretical, and practical innovation has simply been *added to* existing classroom practices and materials. In a few schools, by contrast, teachers and administrators are utilizing the systems approach in order to *integrate* essential educational changes with existing instructional patterns. The four basic elements being considered by such educators in their use of the systems approach to educational change are (1) architectural patterns, (2) organizational patterns, (3) staffing patterns, and (4) curricular patterns. These four components of change will be discussed in the following paragraphs.

Architectural patterns. The need in individualized programs for both teachers and students to work together more effectively and to work with media of all types more efficiently was recognized early by school facilities designers. Technological advances such as carpeting, climate control, nearly windowless construction, and operable acoustic walls are combining to encourage the design of large, open, instructional and learning areas. The need for easy access to the school instructional media center, coupled with an equal need for continuous movement of students between such a center and classroom areas, is resulting in the design of large circular buildings with media centers located in the middle.

Classroom walls are coming down (or not being built in the first place) as educators are recognizing (1) the values of team teaching and differentiated staffing, (2) the fact that classrooms built for 30 students are either too large or too small for many productive learning activities, and (3) the related fact that lecturing to students in groups of 30 or more is often the least useful mode of teaching and learning. In cases where lecturing is appropriate, large group areas are being designed for more profitable use of teacher time as well as for greater student comfort and sight-sound access to the lecture material. Small group areas are being created to provide much needed space for discussion-oriented learning experiences.

Of even greater importance is the creation of independent study areas in which students can interact with each other, with teachers, and with media of all types in order to achieve the student's objectives for his learning. It is in independent study areas and situations that teachers are developing more fully their skills as consultants to learners and managers of the learning process. In fact, the instructional media center, in which individual students can use such materials as books, prints, 35 mm slides and film strips, 16 mm films, video and audio tapes, and diversified realia, is becoming so important to independent study that this center is beginning to dominate school facilities design.

In general, architectural patterns in the public schools are evolving into open instructional areas which are flexible enough to facilitate changing organizational patterns, staffing patterns, and curricular patterns. Only in this way can schools built in the 1970s accommodate innovative programs of the 1980s, 1990s, and beyond.

Organizational patterns.   This topic is an extremely broad one which includes such relatively new concepts as nongradedness, multigrading, daily-demand scheduling, computer scheduling, student learning teams, the extended school day and school year, and vertical designs including the 4-4-4, 5-3-4, and other patterns. Each of these ideas, individually and in combination, has great potential for individualized programs of instruction.

The decades of the 1950s and 1960s have been marked by departures from the administratively convenient lock step of cataloging students by age for purposes of placing them in groups of 30 with one teacher at a time. In the attempt to move away from such traditional organizational patterns, however, the bandwagon approach has been common and, often, little genuine change in teacher and student behavior has resulted. For example, educators have been dismayed over the fact that simply changing the manner in which students are organized does not necessarily change what happens behind closed classroom doors.

However, with insightful leadership, organizational changes *can* create a climate which stimulates curriculum revision along individualized lines. Organizational changes can assist educators in thinking of students as individuals rather than as self-contained classroom units of 25 or 30. As a result, educators can be encouraged to organize curricular materials for individualized learning rather than for group-paced instructional techniques in self-contained classrooms operated under traditional schedules.

It is important to remember that the teacher and student behavior changes required by individualized instructional designs are dependent on a variety of other changes in the educational system. As one educator stated recently, "These changes literally cannot take place within an educational system bound by the constraints of the traditional classroom, the traditional school day and the traditional administration of the traditional educational system (Seidel, 1969). In other words, successful educational innovation that leads toward individualization must involve a thoroughgoing and coordinated approach to educational change rather than piecemeal or superficial attempts at changing only the organizational patterns of schools.

Staffing patterns.   One of the most important recent developments in staffing has been the increased emphasis on teacher specialization and collaboration. The term "team teaching" was invented to label resulting changes in the working patterns of teachers. This term has become all-inclusive in meaning because of the great variety of ways in which teachers have found themselves working together. The particular patterns of team teaching that have evolved, however, are far less important than the fact that teams of teachers are learning to share responsibility for the educational program of a given number of students.

A primary result of the teaming of teachers has been the realization that they must communicate among themselves with a degree of clarity, openness, and detail not required by the self-contained classroom approach. Such communication, although often difficult for teachers in its initial stages, has been very productive in generating modifications in instructional programs. It has also necessitated the provision of team planning time, thus effecting changes in organizational patterns. Finally, the renewed emphasis on staff communication has provided administrators with functional groups in which they can more readily lead teachers in determining the need for and direction of educational change.

A second important result of the teaming of teachers has been the recognition by school boards, administrators, and teachers that some form of differentiated staffing is needed. Differentiated staffing is a means for providing meaningful role alternatives based on responsibility and productivity. For example, a school might be staffed with (1) an instructional team which analyzes individual student needs, prepares appropriate learning materials and projects, and prescribes learning programs; (2) a guidance and evaluation specialist who diagnoses pre-instructional behavior and provides for continuous feedback of learning data to the instructional team; (3) an instructional materials specialist who provides media of all types as well as instruction in the skills needed by students for information retrieval; (4) a variety of instructional technicians (para-professionals) who assist and advise students, monitor student progress, and provide encouragement and reinforcement for positive student behavior; and (5) an instructional leader who is responsible for educational management and who assists the staff in program development.

Staffing patterns are changing in order to provide more humanized learning environments for students through the process of individualization. In such environments, the teacher's role, rather than being one of disseminating information, is becoming one of facilitating or managing a total milieu for learning. In this role, the teacher functions as a catalyst for inducing the learning process. He helps the student determine the objectives and tools needed for the student's learning. This new role is essential if the focus of education is to move from learning more and more factual information to the development of the skills and attitudes necessary for lifelong learning.

Curricular patterns. The trend toward adapting curricular patterns to individualized needs has occurred as a result of several forces. The first of these is based on a very common and obvious problem. How can the teacher in the regular classroom, with 30 or more students whose IQs may range from 80 to 130, whose achievement levels may vary from 4 to 6 years in each subject area, and whose disabilities may include hearing difficulties as well as mild visual, physical, and emotional handicaps, meet the individual curricular needs of each of the 30 children during the school day? The answer is obvious—he cannot come close to doing so unless he makes use of some form of individualized instruction.

A second force for change in the curriculum has occurred as a result of "knowledge explosion." New knowledge is presently being developed at a rate so rapid that the total amount of existing knowledge doubles every 7 years. In the face of this rapidly increasing body of subject matter, educators must accomplish at least three tasks. They must be more selective about *what* each child is required to learn, they must insure greater *efficiency* in the teaching and learning processes, and they must place greater emphasis on the acquisition of the *skills needed to learn*. Each of these can be provided for in the newly emerging patterns of individualized instruction.

A third force for change in the curriculum has been the realization that making changes in architectural patterns, organizational patterns, and even staffing patterns will not automatically result in truly individualized programs. As a result, educators have begun to recognize the need for unique curricular materials and strategies designed to translate traditional curriculum guides and teacher lesson plans into the kind of student lesson plans that will serve as vehicles to guide the student in his learning. Examples of such vehicles, or individualized learning packages, include the University of Pittsburgh's Individually Prescribed Instruction (IPI), Westinghouse's Teaching-Learning Units (TLUs), Nova's Learning Activity Packages (LAPs), Duluth's Student Learning Contracts (SLCs), and the Kettering Foundation's UNIPACs. Such individualized curricular materials generally include some or all of the following ingredients: (1) concept, skill, and value statements; (2) behavioral objectives; (3) pre-, self-, and post-assessment methods; (4) media and activities of all types; and (5) quest or inquiry study for enrichment in depth or in breadth.

A fourth important force for individualization in the curriculum is the recent rapid advance in computer technology. The greatest potential of the computer in individualized instructional systems appears to lie in the two related areas of *assisting* instruction and *managing* instruction. Computer-assisted instruction (CAI) is basically a means for "automating the programmed learning process by using a computer as a substitute for the classroom instructor" (Persselin, 1969). Computer-managed instruction, on the other hand, "deals with automating the broader aspects of selecting, planning, and arranging individual learning experiences, the testing and evaluation of achievement, student counseling, etc." (Persselin, 1969). While large-scale implementation of CAI is not yet economically feasible in most school districts (Kopstein and Seidel, 1968), systems of computer-managed instruction appear to be economically practical on a widespread basis in the near future (Persselin, 1969).

One of many possible examples of computer-managed instruction is the "instructional management system" devised by System Development Corporation (System Development Corporation, 1968). In a plan designed to aid teachers in monitoring and managing individual student progress, the teacher administers frequent tests which are keyed to behaviorally defined objectives and are printed on machine readable forms. The computer analyzes the student responses on examinations and generates reports to the teacher. These reports provide an evaluation of pupil achievement of stated learning objectives, and suggest additional media and activities for students who do not meet expected performance levels.

Closely related to the idea of computer-managed instruction is a broad and relatively new concept known as the "systems approach." As applied to education, the systems approach is a means of specifying, organizing, and controlling the complicated interactions of all of the different elements involved in educational planning. This is done with a view to making teaching and learning as relevant and complete as possible with respect to the learning objectives of individual students. Obviously, the systems approach to education can be utilized either with or without the computer; the important aspect of this approach is not its degree of technical complexity but rather its effectiveness as a decision-making tool in individualizing instruction.

In short, individualized learning packages, programmed learning, computer-assisted and computer-managed instruction, data retrieval systems, instructional television, and sophisticated types of instructional methodology such as simulation and role playing are revitalizing educational programs throughout the country. While no panaceas are being claimed by knowledgeable proponents of any one of these ideas, viable modifications and alternatives to existing, traditional curricular patterns are beginning to emerge.

A Practical View of Implementing Change

As noted in the preceding section, prototypes of all of the necessary components for implementing needed educational change in the public schools are currently available. The technology and diagnostic techniques needed to meet the educational needs of individual students are within the grasp of educators. It is now primarily a matter of producing and installing these components and systems on a large-scale basis.

In the past, many educators have erroneously assumed that teacher and administrator behavior could be modified by the simple process of introducing new approaches. Change in human behavior, however, is usually not that easily accomplished. In fact, Carlson (1965) noted that in many cases in which educational innovation required different approaches to instruction, teachers actually modified the new procedures in order to maintain older patterns of teaching.

What are the factors, then, which must be reckoned with before the impact of educational change can be felt in the public schools nationwide? At the most obvious level, the primary factors which seem to support the status quo in education include the large geographic size of the United States, its population distribution, and its enormously varied and complex systems of educational organization and control (Rushing, 1969).

At a more vital level, however, the most significant obstacle to progress appears to lie in the human sphere. As a college president stated recently,

> People—their philosophies, prejudices, experiences, and desire for security—prove much more resistant to change than any other element in education. Tomorrow's schools will become a reality only when attitudes are changed (Rushing, 1969).

Other educators have made similar observations. For example, Bienenstok (1965) stated:

> Innovations by their very nature pose a threat to the stability and continuity of an ongoing system. Any change of any consequence requires some shifts in habits, beliefs, and attitudes, very often in patterns of behavior learned in emotionally compelling ways.

This problem has also been clearly described by McPhee (1967):

> Our individual enthusiasm for a specific change is usually inversely proportional to how much we ourselves must change. We desire it greatly, in and for others. We praise change for others, but seldom value changes for ourselves.

Thus, those concerned with public education for normal as well as handicapped children must realize that the pace of educational innovation depends to no small degree on the extent to which educators can be induced to modify their behavior and beliefs in accordance with changing educational roles, values, and attitudes. Such modifications, obviously, are far from simple to achieve and must be planned for carefully. It is evident that educators of the hard of hearing must approach program design and implementation armed with all of the information, techniques, and skills currently available.

Implications for the Hard of Hearing

Permanently impaired hearing leaves an imprint on the child's total development and adjustment. The effects of hearing loss pervade all communications, including speaking, reading, and writing, as well as hearing. These factors, accompanied by what research has shown concerning the psychological characteristics of the hard of hearing child, present a challenging task for educators in the public schools.

Many of the changes now taking place in school districts across the country strongly imply the need for change in instructional programs for the hard of hearing. It is important to realize, however, that only legitimate change, and not "educational tinkering" or name changing, has any real implication for the education of the hard of hearing. Individualized programs which result in genuine continuous progress education, for example, are especially vital to the hearing handicapped child because they can provide him with needed success rather than debilitating failure experiences. The specific learning objectives, teaching strategies, and learning materials that are appropriate for one hard of hearing child are probably not appropriate for another. The needs of these children, therefore, can be met only by dynamic, personalized programs geared to their individual capabilities and potentialities.

The Importance of Diagnosis and Teacher Education

Prior to enrollment in school, every child should have a thorough examination by a physician. If a hearing loss is discovered, any educational difficulties anticipated as a result of the loss must be identified. For example, it should be recognized that a child may hear well a few feet from a speaker but may not hear well at a distance. He may hear normal speaking sounds in a quiet room but be unable to hear speech in a noisy situation. He may hear some types of voices better than others or he may hear with amplification but not without it. Once specific hearing difficulties are identified, then the techniques, materials, and facilities needed to compensate for the difficulties can be determined.

The duties involved in properly diagnosing and handling hearing handicapped children make it essential that every educator have certain basic information about hearing disabilities. Obviously, the otologist, the audiologist, and the speech pathologist must consider the educational meaning of hearing handicaps; but, in addition, unless the regular classroom teacher or teaching team—those who work most directly with the youngster during the major portion of his school hours—understands the educational implications of such handicaps, the child may join the ranks of the educationally retarded or become a school dropout. Therefore, a basic responsibility of teacher training institutions and, ultimately, of school districts must be to provide all instructional and para-professional personnel with sufficient training to recognize symptoms of hearing disability and to be familiar with techniques of instruction that will minimize the child's handicap.

The Importance of the Behavioral Approach

The practice of stating learning objectives in terms of student behaviors has been mentioned previously as an important aspect of several current trends in public education. Efforts to improve and individualize instruction through, for example, combinations of multimedia experiences (Stepp, 1968), computer-managed instruction, or the new approaches to "software" including any of the forms of individualized learning packages all require objectives stated with greater precision than was common a decade ago. Thus, educators have found it necessary to redefine broad educational goals in terms of the specific behaviors desired of the learner.

Where do behavioral objectives fit into the educational program for the hard of hearing child? If a primary educational goal is to equip the hard of hearing child to function effectively in a normal society, than it behooves educators to define in specific terms the behaviors that indicate the student is capable of fulfilling this role. What specific or unique experiences will help him develop the skills necessary to exhibit this behavior pattern? Which of these experiences can occur within the regular classroom? Which require special instructional materials and equipment? The educator must work closely with the hearing specialist to find answers to these questions—answers that can provide the basis for program development for the hard of hearing child.

Solutions to questions such as these can also provide insight into the importance of the new student roles that are emerging as a result of behavioral approaches. Individualized programs based on behavioral objectives allow the learner to participate in selecting or formulating his own objectives for learning, to assist in determining his own learning sequence and learning media, to engage in self-directed study and self-monitored learning, and to exhibit generally increasing levels of independence and responsibility for his own education. It is important to recognize that these new student roles have perhaps even more significance for the handicapped child than for the normal child because of the handicapped child's more complicated needs for independence and achievement.

The Importance of the Continuous Progress, Multimedia Approach

Individualized, continuous progress programs in the public schools permit the hard of hearing child to enter the curriculum at his own achievement level, to work in a nongraded situation with children of varying ages, and to progress to more advanced content, materials, and activities when *he*, not a given group, is ready. Thus, he is spared the psychological disadvantage of being labeled an "underachiever" as well as the related social handicap of being placed in a traditional classroom situation which is one to two years lower than that of his theoretical grade placement.

Research conducted over recent years on the nature of the hearing impaired child has shown him to be typically less well-adjusted and less socially competent than children with normal hearing. As a result of the common coupling of a continuous progress plan with some form of team teaching or differentiated staffing, the hard of hearing child is exposed to several, perhaps even·many, adult leaders rather than just the one teacher present in the self-contained classroom. At the same time, the chances of severe emotional and academic problems resulting from spending an entire year in a single classroom with a single teacher with whom he may have a "personality conflict" are reduced to zero. In a differentiated staffing situation, the hard of hearing child has multiple adult models upon which he can build his own socially acceptable behavior patterns, as well as with whom he can learn to relate on personally and psychologically satisfying levels.

Research has also shown that hearing deficiencies affect academic performance more in the verbal and abstract areas than in any other. This fact renders the multimedia aspect of a continuous progress program of considerable importance for the hard of hearing child. When the teacher is no longer the chief disseminator of facts and information (usually in aural form), and when many other visual or audiovisual means for obtaining the same information are provided, the hard of hearing child's opportunities for learning become nearly equal to those of the normal hearing child. For example, the familiar suggestion of "preferential seating" (as one of the possible adjustments for the hearing handicapped child in the regular classroom) becomes superfluous when all children have equal access in an instructional materials center to headphones attached to recordings, 16 mm films, filmstrips with sound, and many other forms of alternative media. Likewise, when large-group question and answer sessions are replaced by small-group discussions, "preferential seating" for the hearing handicapped child becomes unimportant because all children are preferentially seated.

Obviously, all of these factors—continuous progress programs combined with differentiated staffing and learning media of all types—are important for the education of the normal child; but, they are vastly more meaningful in the public school experiences of the handicapped. They allow the hard of hearing child to be integrated with normal hearing children and, thus, to become a successful part of the regular school environment, while still permitting him to receive the special training in audition, speech, language, or lip reading that he may need.

Summary

The lag that has existed in providing meaningful and effective programs for hard of hearing children in the public schools will continue until educators in the schools and on university campuses recognize the tremendous potential for special education of the instructional tools and techniques being developed almost daily. As a result of these new media and methods, the educational programs of the future for the hard of hearing child can be launched with full knowledge of a child's disabilities and their probable effects on his capacity to learn and adjust in a school setting. This knowledge, in turn, will be the basis for determining appropriate educational and social experiences.

In essence, effective public school education for the hard of hearing child is dependent upon individualized public school education for all children. In other words, if the public schools nationwide were actually individualizing their programs using all of the means currently available to them, the hard of hearing child would have no difficulty performing successfully in such programs.

In summary, upgrading the education of the hard of hearing requires the integration of many diverse ingredients. First, teachers and administrators must be attuned to change and must be able to use educational innovations wisely. Second, public schools and universities must provide training in the latest uses of technology. Third, teachers of the hard of hearing must have the skills and information needed to truly understand the problems and the disabilities of the individual child. Fourth, educational programs must focus on the unique needs of the individual student. These four are among the most important ingredients in programs designed to help the hard of hearing child develop the skills, understandings, and attitudes necessary to function capably in a hearing world.

References

Bienenstok, Theodore. 1965. Resistance to an educational innovation. The Elementary School Journal LXV:420.

Carlson, Richard O. 1965. Adoption of Educational Innovations. Eugene, Oregon: University of Oregon Center for the Advanced Study of Educational Administration. Pp. 83–84.

Cubberley, Ellwood P. 1948. The History of Education. Boston: Houghton-Mifflin Co. Pp. 363–366.

Fellendorf, George W. 1966. Statement of George W. Fellendorf before the Maryland Commission to Study Educational Needs of Handicapped Children. Washington, D.C.: Alexander Graham Bell Association for the Deaf, Inc. P. 10.

Kopstein, Felix F. and Robert J. Seidel. 1968. Computer-administered instruction versus traditionally administered instruction: economics. AV Communication Review XVI:147–175.

McPhee, Roderick F. 1967. Planning and effecting needed changes in local school systems. In Edgar L. Morphet and Charles O. Ryan (Eds.). Planning and Effecting Needed Changes in Education. Denver: Publishers Press, Inc. P. 183.

Persselin, Leo E. 1969. Systems implications for secondary education. Journal of Secondary Education XLIV: 159–166.

Programs for handicapped children. 1967. NEA Research Bulletin XLV:115–117.

Rushing, Joe B. 1969. Tomorrow's schools—the elements are all here. Educational Media 1:4–6.

Seidel, Robert J. 1969. Is CAI cost/effective? The right question at the wrong time. Educational Technology IX:21–23.

Stepp, Robert E. 1968. Educational media and deaf education: the emerging literature. In Harriet G. Kopp (Ed.) Curriculum: Cognition and Content. Washington, D.C.: Alexander Graham Bell Association for the Deaf, Inc. Pp. 101–110.

System Development Corporation. 1968. Progress Report for the Instructional Management System. Santa Monica, California: System Development Corporation. Pp. 1–13.

PART III

CLINICAL AND EMOTIONAL
CONSIDERATIONS

Chapter 12

The Case History Interview

CARL W. FULLER, Ph.D.

A case history is clearly an essential part of every clinical examination. However, the literature of speech pathology and audiology does not appear to emphasize the use of the case history as a clinical tool. One of the most widely used texts, that by Van Riper (1963), concentrates its discussion of the case history into one-and-a-half pages of an appendix. A similar treatment of the topic is used by Berry and Eisenson (1956). Van Riper and Irwin (1958) and Johnson et al. (1967) do not mention case history at all. Milisen (1957) discusses methods of obtaining history information and presents questionnaires for use with various types of speech disorders, but his discussion suggests, as does Bangs' (1961), that the role of the history is only to provide, in Bangs' words, "pertinent background information."

The viewpoint expressed in this chapter is that the history comprises *foreground* information, that it is a part of the child himself and not just a backdrop against which the picture of the child is sketched. The history is an examining device, not simply the collecting of certain facts preceding an examination. The examination defines the child at a point in time and space; the history describes the directions and dimensions of his physical and psychological movement to the point at which he is examined. The history foretells the examination's findings; the examination adds insight to historical information. Each acts to illuminate the other.

The Objectives of the Case History

Certain general objectives of the history tend to be common to all examinations. The case history interview may be regarded as incomplete if these objectives are not reached.

First, the history should *provide a clear picture of the child's developmental progress from birth to the present.* One purpose of the developmental history is to define the child's *rate* of development, with its implications for intellectual capacity, for motor skills, and for adequacy of environmental stimulation.

A second purpose is to identify the child's *pattern* of development—the ways in which he has conformed to, and has seemed to deviate from, normal

191

expectations. These deviations may relate to tempo, e.g., faster or slower than normal; or to quality, e.g., awareness of toilet needs at the normal age but abnormal fear of the commode.

A third purpose of the developmental history is to note the child's *age* when deviations from normal expectations were first observed. Obviously such times are often causally related to the developmental anomaly. In many cases this aspect of the developmental history will indicate how perceptive the parents or the family physician was with respect to the child's failure to make normal developmental progress.

Fourth, the developmental history has the aim of *identifying the influences*, organic and environmental, which might have had traumatic effect upon development in general and audition in particular. Such physical events as infectious disease and such psychic disruptions as separation of the parents may be relevant in this respect.

A second general objective of the case history is to *describe the effects of communication handicap upon interactions between the child and his environment*. The description represents the culmination of the developmental picture achieved by meeting the first objective. For this purpose the history should describe the child's social relations with the various members of his family, with his playmates and schoolmates, and with persons outside the family. Particular emphasis should be placed on the manner in which he achieves both verbal and nonverbal communication and on his reactions to success or failure in communication. In brief, this section of the history describes what kind of person the child is, in contrast to the developmental aspect of the history which traced how the child reached his present status.

A third general objective of the case history is to *establish a hypothesis for definition and treatment of the child's hearing disability*. A detailed history will identify those events in the child's life which seem to be causally related to his communication deficit. It will suggest behavioral patterns which have diagnostic significance. It may provide evaluation of the effects of whatever treatment has been attempted. In synthesizing these data, the clinician will begin to anticipate the most probable findings of his direct examination. If the examiner starts his examination without having learned from the history what kind of problem he is most likely to face, then the history has not achieved this objective.

Finally, the case history interview has the objective of *establishing a basis for counseling parents regarding future management of the child*. It may be taken for granted in practically all cases that the information contained in the case history is obtained from parents and that parents will be given responsibility for acting on the recommendations for follow-up management after the clinical examination has been completed. An important function of the case history interview is to provide the clinician with an impression of how diligent and dependable the parents are likely to be and of what problems they themselves may have or introduce into the overall management of the child. The interview should, therefore, be utilized to define parental anxieties about the child, to determine what the expectations and ambitions of the parents may be about the child's immediate future and ultimate achievement, and to assess the extent of the parents' understanding of the child's problems. It is particularly important for the interview to reveal to the examiner how the parents have defined to themselves what they want the examination to accomplish. Parents are sometimes reluctant to accept recommendations evolving from an examination which does not meet their anticipations.

To sum up, the general objectives of the case history interview will have been met if the history answers four questions: What kind of person is this child now? How did he come to be this way? What does the clinical examination need to accomplish? What kind of people are the parents and what help do they require?

In addition to the above general objectives each interview will have specific objectives which will lead to greater or lesser emphasis on different aspects of the history content. The audiologist engaged in a hearing aid evaluation of a child known to be hard of hearing will be interested in a somewhat different set of historical facts than the audiologist conducting a diagnostic audiological assessment. The school administrator trying to decide on the appropriate classroom placement for a child entering school will want different information than the vocational counselor assessing an older child whose classroom education has been essentially completed. A language pathologist engaged in a diagnostic study will ordinarily require a more comprehensive behavioral history than an otologist similarly engaged. Research studies might probe deeply into some aspects of auditory behavior while ignoring others of importance to clinical practitioners. The structure and content of the specific case history will, therefore, be dependent on the particular interests and requirements of the examiner conducting the interview.

The Content of the Case History Interview

Because of the varying needs of different clinicians it is not possible to enumerate explicit case history questions which will have universal application, with the possible exception of such vague inquiries as, "How well does your child hear?" Van Riper (1963), Milisen (1957), Berry and Eisenson (1956), and Myklebust (1954), among others, have published history questionnaires; Myklebust's is specifically designed to elicit a "differential" history for use in the diagnostic examination of children with auditory disorders. Such questionnaires may be helpful in keeping inexperienced clinicians "on the track" and in reminding them of the material to be covered, but they tend to be cumbersome and inflexible with their unspoken requirement that every question be answered and every blank be filled in. It is impossible to predict the exact course of an interview; compelling the interview to follow the ordered structure of a predesigned questionnaire tends to stifle spontaneity, to reduce rapport, and to limit the flow of information. If the primary purpose of the interview is to fill in blanks, the questionnaire should be mailed to the informants in advance so that they can fill in the blanks at home.

The interviewer will usually succeed in accumulating information he needs if he keeps clearly in mind the general objectives discussed above and whatever specific goals may be set for a particular examination. In other words, the interviewer should concentrate, not on what he should ask, but on what he needs to know. The following categories of information will contribute significantly to an understanding of the child.

A. Birth History

This includes the mother's pregnancy and labor, and the delivery and neonatal course of the child. Unusual conditions occurring during the mother's pregnancy (illness, injury, prolonged emotional tension in the mother); traumatic labor or delivery (prematurity, Caesarian section); unusual appearance, physical condition, or behavior of the newborn (cyanosis, cleft palate, excessive sleepiness) should be noted, even if the clinician is unsure at the time of their possible clinical significance. He may achieve some insight into their clinical significance by asking how other people acted: "What did your doctor say about that? How was the baby treated for that?"

B. Medical and Health History

The child's experience with injury, illness, and surgery should be recorded. If the child's condition required hospitalization, his age at the time, the length of hospital stay, the child's reaction to separation from the parents and vice-versa may be worthy of note. Changes in the child's behavior, particularly in communication skills, during and/or following illness should be thoroughly investigated. In this connection it should be noted that few parents regard otitis media as an illness. The questions, "Have you ever taken your child to a doctor? What for?" are more likely to elicit a history of otitis than the question, "What illnesses has your child had?"

C. Developmental Landmarks

As many may be listed as are found useful. Typically these include the ages at which the child was able to sit unsupported, walk unsupported, say his first word, use sentences routinely, and care for himself at the toilet. Was the child markedly different from the norms for these achievements? Was he markedly different from his siblings? What were his parents' expectations for these behaviors? What were their feelings when the child failed to meet their expectations?*

*The questions listed here and in following sections are intended to suggest the subject matter to be covered, not the phraseology to be employed. The specific questions listed may not be relevant in some cases; in other cases they will only introduce a much more detailed inquiry.

D. *Family History*

List names and ages of people in the immediate family constellation, the child's place in the order of siblings, the presence of speech and hearing disorders in other members of the family, including grandparents, parents' siblings, and their children. The socioeconomic status of the family and the educational achievement level of the parents should be recorded. Note how the parents have reacted to the child's handicap and what kinds of pressures may have been exerted by other members of the family to induce the parents to take certain courses of action to help the child. How have the parents responded to these pressures?

E. *Social-Psychological History*

This is concerned with the child's temperament and personality. Is he placid, aggressive, fearful, passive, inventive, friendly, assaultive, etc.? Has he had difficulty eating, sleeping, getting along with playmates? Is he afraid to leave his parents? Has this behavior changed with age? What indications are there that these problems or characteristics are associated with parental anxieties, changes of residence, other sources of emotional tension, etc.?

F. *Auditory History*

Note the specific age at which the child's hearing loss was first suspected, and why. When and how has the child's hearing been tested, by whom, with what results? What educational, as opposed to medical, treatment has been attempted, with what success? What experience has the child had with amplification, in what form, at whose recommendation, with what results? What changes have been observed in the child's response to sound over the years?

G. *Speech and Language History*

Has the child ever talked? How did he use his voice before he began to say recognizable words? What has been the rate and pattern of language development? Was speech development interrupted after having started normally? What other modes of communication has the child used? What have the parents done to teach the child to talk? What professional assistance have they had in this effort, for how long, on what schedule, with what success? What has been the effect of the child's communication difficulties on his relationships with adults, peers, school achievement, social relationships generally?

H. *Motor History*

Have motor skills developed at a normal rate? Did the child have difficulty with sucking, chewing, swallowing, sitting, walking, manipulation of
toys, feeding, or dressing himself? Did motor disability appear after an illness? What treatment was provided, with what success? What is the medical
diagnosis, if any, of motor problems exhibited by the child?

I. *Educational History*

What formal schooling has the child had? What preschooling? Starting
when? Particularly, what specific teaching has been given him in language,
speech, speechreading, auditory training? How has he responded to this
teaching? What have the parents done at home to supplement teaching done
elsewhere? What problems have they encountered in their efforts to teach
the child at home?

J. *Current Status*

The history in each of the foregoing areas logically culminates in a statement of how the child behaves *now*. From the synthesis of these statements
the clinician should be able to draw a reasonably clear picture, seen through
the parents' eyes, of the child he will examine. Usually by the time the interview has progressed to this point the clinician will also have a clear impression
of the parents, of the extent and realism of their concern for the child, and of
the general directions his counseling will take when his examination of the
child has been completed. He may wish to corroborate these impressions by
asking the parents questions like, "Of the problems you have mentioned, which
gives you the most trouble?" Or, "which would you like to take care of first?"
To complete the picture of current status, the clinician may wish to utilize a
standardized measuring instrument such as the Vineland Social Maturity Scale
(Doll) or the Verbal Language Development Scale (Mecham).

Other Sources of Historical Information

Though the interview may be the primary source of history data, other
sources of information should not be neglected. The child's pediatrician or the
family physician often can give a more precise and reliable account of the
childs' illnesses and the treatment thereof than can the parents. The results of
otologic examination and treatment would be of special interest. If the child
has been tested previously, or has been taught in a clinic, rehabilitation center,
or school, these agencies may be requested to send summaries of their test
results and observations. Older children with sufficient verbal skill may be
asked to write an autobiography; in such a case it should be emphasized to

the child that what is desired is the story of his experiences with and his feelings about his hearing problem, not a review of vacation trips he has taken or wild animals he has seen.

It may be necessary to secure from the parents a signed statement authorizing other agencies and individuals to release confidential information about the child. The names, titles, and addresses of the people to whom the authorizations should be sent should be obtained from the parents at the time of the first interview. It may be possible to obtain some of this information in advance by requesting the parents when they are notified of the child's appointment to ask for the information to be forwarded. For example, the appointment letter may include one or more copies of a summary questionnaire which the parents can distribute to physicians, school officials, or other agencies for them to fill out and return directly to the examiner.

The Tactics of the Case History Interview

Bingham and Moore (1959) emphasize that an interview is a situation in which two or more personalities, the interviewer and the informant(s), interact; the outcome of the interview depends upon the nature of that interaction. Clearly, the interviewer cannot conduct the interview as though he were buying merchandise from a coin vending machine, putting questions into one slot and getting answers out of another. He will be bored by some of his informant's statements, frustrated by others, amazed at times, even angered now and then. He must remember that the interview may produce these and similar reactions in the person he is interviewing. Some of these reactions may promote the progress of the interview; obviously others will impede it. In any case the interviewer must assume responsibility for achieving the dynamic relationship with the informant which will lead to a reliable, relevant, and comprehensive case history. Some precautions taken in advance, though they will not guarantee success, will at least minimize the factors which may obstruct it.

The Approach to the Interview

1. Review the information already available. Be familiar with the correspondence which might have accumulated, with any difficulties which might have interfered with scheduling the examination, with previous clinical findings and treatment, if reports are on file, and with any other "previous" information which will help to define the forthcoming clinical task.

2. "Know thyself." The clinician should know his strengths and his limitations as an interviewer. He should try to remove the influence of philosophical bias from the course of questioning. The clinician who favors an organic explanation of communication disorders may not even ask the questions which would reveal psychogenetic elements in the history. His attitudes largely determine the quality of the interaction mentioned above; he should know what these attitudes are and be aware of their influence on the progress of the interview.

3. Set a comfortable scene. The interview should be conducted in a room which insures comfort and privacy. If the parents being interviewed have brought children with them, provision should be made for care of the children. It is almost impossible to proceed with an interview when a child's parents are concerned about his "getting into things." The atmosphere should be that of a mutually supportive attempt to share information, not that of a cross-examination.

4. Be prepared to keep track of what you learn. Recording may be done on the spot as information is acquired or later from memory, but the decision as to which method to use should be made in advance. Sullivan (1954) found that taking notes during the interview distracted him from the observation of subtle behavioral nuances which were often as meaningful as the patient's words. Johnson, Darley, and Spriestersbach (1963) advocate the use of a shorthand system or a telegraphic code; alternatively they suggest the use of a tape recorder. Probably no one system will have equal value for all clinicians. The procedure adopted may well be governed by the adequacy of the interviewer's recall. If he knows his own capacity for recalling accurately the content of the history after the interview is finished, he will know what and how much to record at the time his questions are answered.

The Technique of Inquiry

1. Start where you are. If information about the child has been made available prior to the interview, start with what is known. "I understand that Dr. X thinks your child has a hearing problem" or some such statement will establish a point of departure. If no advance information is available, simply ask in a straightforward manner what the child's communication problem is.

2. Learn as early as possible what the parents expect to gain from the examination. It should be clear to the parents that the interviewer is seeking information which will help him help them and not just for its own sake or for his private uses. It is easier to make this connection clear if the interviewer knows what the parents expect the examination to accomplish.

In some cases the interviewer will perceive rather early that the examination should be directed in a somewhat different direction than that initiated by the parents' complaint. An audiologist, for example, checking the performance of a school age child's hearing aid may suspect after a few questions that the school placement rather than the hearing aid ought to be changed. This does not license him to abandon the goal of the original examination, but it requires him to broaden the scope of his interview so as to encompass information relevant to his changed perception of the problem. At the same time, he should communicate to the parents that he sees the situation in a different way than they had originally defined, now that he knows more about it, and, therefore, he must ask some additional questions to clarify his understanding.

3. Follow the lead of the informant in shifting from topic to topic. This does not mean that the interview must proceed willy-nilly, but simply that

what the informant says can usually be utilized for transition to the next topic when discussion of the last is finished.

In answer to the question, "What kind of speech problem does your child have?" a mother answered, "Well, he just doesn't talk. I have taken him to several doctors, and one says he doesn't hear and another says he is retarded, and I don't know what to believe. I took him to Miss _____ for speech therapy, but she said she wanted him to be examined here first." This statement provides "take-off" points for the health history, the developmental landmarks, the history of speech and language development, the auditory history, and the educational history. It also helps to define the goals of the examination. Transition from one topic of the history to another usually seems more natural when it is based on previous statements that when it is accomplished by the abrupt introduction of entirely new subject matter.

4. Try to head off irrelevant discussion. This becomes a problem only when the interviewer cannot decide whether the topic is irrelevant or not. Grandmother's experiences with an old fashioned hearing aid are probably irrelevant; the way the child's siblings talk may not be. The interviewer will have to decide on the spot whether he needs to know more about the siblings. If he decides that he doesn't, he should not hesitate to suggest that the interview should concentrate on the child being examined.

Some informants never seem to "turn off." Once started, they provide a running narrative, sometimes coherent sometimes not, which covers all aspects of the child's life. The interviewer may be tempted to interrupt this flow, if only to give himself time to properly record the data, but he should not suggest disapproval of the parent's verbosity. An answer is not necessarily irrelevant just because the question has not yet been asked.

In fact, the inability of a parent to sense and follow the structure of the interview may be of paramount clinical significance. Is incoherence a consistent feature of the parent's thinking and behavior? If so, what does that imply for the child's diagnosis and treatment? Does the parent go off on tangents as a defensive maneuver to fend off threatening anamnestic material? Is irrelevance a sign of impaired mental function?

Obviously these questions have significant implications for the future management of the child. While filing them away for future reference, however, the interviewer must get on with the history project, and he, therefore, may need to intervene to bring the interview back to its plotted course.

5. Maintain a respectful attentive attitude. The interviewer should listen to replies with the same intense interest he would like the parents to pay to his questions. His interest should not be restricted to the verbal content of the replies. The parent's tone of voice, shift of glance, mannerisms of movement and posture, and other nonverbal behavior may be highly revealing and will be missed if the interviewer is not alert. His own tone of voice and use of gesture should not suggest disapproval or scorn of the parents or the child; thus he must be attentive to himself as well as to his clients.

6. When recording information, make a clear distinction between probable fact, e.g., the child was toilet trained by 4 years of age; parental judgment, e.g., the child was hard to toilet train; and interviewer judgment, e.g.,

the mother used poor techniques in toilet training. Some overall estimate of the reliability of the history should be attempted. If it is considered unreliable, verification of it should be attempted through other sources of information.

7. Avoid phrasing questions in a way that puts parents on the defensive. Many parents volunteer their feeling that they are in some way responsible for the plight of their handicapped child. These guilt feelings are seldom realistic; there is no need for the interviewer to add to them. Such a question as "Why did you wait so long to get a hearing aid for your boy?" is unnecessarily accusatory. The desired information can be obtained without imputing negligence to the parents. Simmons (1968) advocates avoidance of phraseology which implies "bad" traits in the child and suggests the use of "open-ended" questions instead. For example, the question, "How does your child get along with other children?" is preferable to "Is your child mean to other children?"

8. Avoid argumentative discussion with the informants. The interviewer should not allow himself to be drawn into intrafamily squabbles or into making statements which can be used by one parent to ally himself with the interviewer against the spouse. If the relationship between the parents is abrasive, they should be interviewed separately. One should note, however, whether argumentative parents are directing their hostilities primarily at the interviewer, at each other, at the child, or possibly at other members of the family. The future management of the child may require the interviewer eventually to make a decision which puts him on one side of a family quarrel. He should try to learn before he joins the fray who is fighting whom, and why.

9. Avoid direct counseling during the interview. Many parents are so eager for help that they punctuate the interview with requests for advice. In answer to the opening question, "How would you describe your child's hearing problem?" one woman answered, "My doctor says he is deaf from the measles. How much will a hearing aid help him?" The only reasonable thing to do with such replies is to defer them, pleading ignorance of the child, with a promise to return to them for further discussion after the examination has been completed.

Secondary Implications of the Case History Interview

In addition to its primary role as a device for obtaining and recording certain information the case history interview can serve other functions which are secondary to the purpose of the interview but not unimportant to the welfare of the client. The first of these is what might be called a "public relations" function. Ordinarily the case history interview is the first setting in which the client and the examiner have an opportunity to establish a clinical relationship. The willingness of the client to accept the findings of the examination and to act on the recommendations for treatment may well hinge on whether or not he feels that he himself has been fairly and competently examined during the history-taking. The history interview thus lays the groundwork for all that follows, not only in terms of understanding the child but also with respect to the parent's attitude toward the examiner and possibly toward the profession he represents.

Secondly, the case history interview may function as a counseling device. It was advocated earlier that the parents not be counseled directly during the interview; that is, direct answers to direct questions requesting advice usually should be avoided. Nevertheless, it is often possible and desirable to suggest by indirection, by manner and phraseology, that there is a different, better way for the parents to do things. In asking questions which ostensibly search for further information about problem behavior in the child, the interviewer may at the same time suggest to perceptive parents an effective technique for dealing with that behavior, e.g., "Some parents have dealt with that problem by doing thus and so. Have you tried that?" The counseling effect of the interview need not be limited to episodic situations. It is not unusual for a mother, during the administration of the Vineland Social Maturity Scale, to smile sheepishly and admit, "I really do baby him, don't I. I never realized." Thus, she and the interviewer learn at the same time that she may be unduly solicitous of the child.

A third secondary function of the case history interview is that of a prognostic device. The direct examination of the child may provide a more realistic basis for predicting his future than does the history. The history, on the other hand, in combination with the counseling which follows the direct examination, is the primary—perhaps the only—setting which allows the examiner to estimate the strengths and weaknesses of the parents. Since the younger the child the more critical the role of the parents in his therapeutic management, the assessment of the parents' feelings for each other and for the child, their insight into the nature of his communication problem, their capacities for further effort on his behalf, will have an important influence on the statement of the prognosis. Thus, the case history interview, recognizing that "the child is father of the man," helps to record his future as well as his past.

References

Bangs, Tina E. 1961. Evaluating children with language delay. Journal of Speech and Hearing Disorders 26:6–18.

Berry, Mildred F. and Jon Eisenson. 1956. Speech Disorders: Principles and Practices of Therapy. New York: Appleton-Century-Crofts.

Bingham, Walter Van Dyke and Bruce Victor Moore. 1959. How to Interview, 4th Rev. Ed. New York: Harper & Row.

Doll, Edgar A. Vineland Social Maturity Scale. Minneapolis: Educational Test Bureau.

Johnson, Wendell, et al. 1967. Speech Handicapped School Children, 3rd Ed. New York: Harper & Row.

Johnson, Wendell, Frederic L. Darley, and D. Spriestersbach. 1963. Diagnostic Methods in Speech Pathology. New York: Harper & Row.

Mecham, Merlin. Verbal Langauge Development Scale. Minneapolis: Educational Test Bureau.

Milisen, Robert. 1957. Methods of evaluation and diagnosis of speech disorders. In Lee E. Travis (Ed.) Handbook of Speech Pathology. New York: Appleton-Century-Crofts.

Myklebust, H. R. 1954. Auditory Disorders in Children. New York: Grune & Stratton.

Simmons, James E. 1968. Interviewing. In Morris Green and Robert J. Haggerty (Eds.) Ambulatory Pediatrics. Philadelphia: W. B. Saunders Co.

Sullivan, Harry Stack. 1954. The Psychiatric Interview. New York: W. W. Norton.

Van Riper, Charles. 1963. Speech Correction: Principles and Methods, 4th Ed. Englewood Cliffs, N.J.: Prentice-Hall.

Van Riper, Charles and John V. Irwin. 1958. Voice and Articulation. Englewood Cliffs, N.J.: Prentice-Hall.

Chapter 13

Differential Diagnosis

CARL W. FULLER, Ph.D.

The identification of a child with a hearing loss would seem at first glance to be a fairly straightforward matter. In practice, as every clinician knows, the task of testing hearing in children is often arduous, the results sometimes perplexing. The audiological evaluation of children is difficult for a variety of reasons.

First, the complexities of some hearing test procedures are difficult even for adults to cope with. They may require comprehension of verbal instructions, spoken responses to test stimuli, intent and sustained attention to confusing listening tasks, and acceptance of varying degrees of physical discomfort over an extended period of time. In children the difficulties inherent in the testing itself may be compounded by immaturity, apprehensiveness, inadequacy of verbal communication, presence of physical handicap other than hearing loss, reduced attention span, and so on. The full battery of tests available for analysis of adult auditory behavior can rarely, if ever, be applied to the diagnosis of hearing impairment in a child.

Secondly, children are rarely able to describe the nature of their subjective auditory experience. This is information which is particularly valuable to the clinical audiologist, it may be uniquely important in determining the site and nature of the auditory lesion. The child's ability in this regard will be gravely limited when he is of preschool age, when the onset of hearing loss is early in life, and when the hearing disorder is severe enough to interfere with speech and language development.

Thirdly, some children display the two most conspicuous behavioral effects of hearing loss, namely, inattentiveness to sound and deviant growth of verbal communication skills, even though they, in fact, have normal hearing acuity. They may participate willingly in audiometric test procedures but give such inconsistent responses that the audiogram is unreliable. They may respond to audiometric stimuli in a way which is inconsistent with their responses to the ambient acoustic environment. They may be acutely responsive to some sounds while remaining apparently oblivious to others. Whatever peculiarity of auditory behavior these unusual children exhibit, the audiologist seldom is successful in defining it with standard threshold audiometry.

These considerations have impelled audiologists to search for techniques that have special application to the needs of children. On the one hand, they have devised test procedures which are more interesting to children than the rather formal impersonal procedures used with adults and, therefore, more likely to elicit the child's cooperative participation in the test. On the other hand, they have tried by so-called "objective" techniques such as EDR and EEG audiometry to achieve valid test results with procedures which presumably require no cooperation at all. At the same time they have had to rely on observation of the child's nonauditory behavior to confirm and validate audiometric indications of hearing impairment. Finally, they have had to justify a diagnostic impression of normal hearing not demonstrable by audiometry in children with abnormal indifference to auditory stimulation. Or, to put it somewhat more precisely, audiologists have had to develop a rationale for distinguishing between children with peripheral hearing loss and children with other problems which produce behavior mimicking peripheral hearing loss. One such rationale is the concern of this chapter.

Audiometry remains the *sine qua non* of a diagnosis of hearing loss. As Davis says, "The key to direct diagnosis and proper handling is the correct assessment of the degree of peripheral auditory impairment, i.e., to determine whether the child fails to respond to acoustic signals because auditory nerve impulses never reach the brain or because something interferes with the will to respond, or both" (Davis, 1965).

Continuing advances in technique and technology have steadily lowered the age at which reliable threshold measurement can be accomplished. There is widespread agreement that air conduction pure tone thresholds, at least, can be obtained on a majority of 3-year-old children and on many $2\frac{1}{2}$ year olds. A variety of screening procedures have been developed for detection of hearing loss in younger children down to the neonatal period (Davis, 1965; Downs and Sterritt, 1967; Wedenberg, 1956).

Nevertheless, as noted above, there remains a group of children whose audiometric responses, if any, are highly questionable indices of auditory acuity. Deprived of his primary diagnostic tool, the threshold audiogram, how is the audiologist to differentiate hard of hearing children from those children who have normal hearing but do not respond normally to sound? Even if he is able to obtain a tentative measurement of hearing threshold, how can he assess its validity?

The method advocated here was originally described by Myklebust (1954) who suggested analysis of the total behavior pattern of the difficult-to-test child. Behavioral analysis, including but not restricted to the child's behavior on hearing tests per se, will usually allow the audiologist to infer whether the child truly has a peripheral hearing loss.

The rationale for a diagnostic examination based on differential analysis of behavior may be summarized as follows:

1. The various conditions, e.g., peripheral hearing loss, which produce abnormal auditory behavior in children have pervasive effects upon the organism which produces changes in other (i.e., in addition to auditory) areas of behavior as well;

2. The resulting patterns of behavior are characteristic of the condition producing them and tend to be exhibited in some measure by all individuals sharing that condition;

3. Systematic analysis of the behavior pattern exhibited by an individual with disordered hearing will, therefore, reveal the underlying cause of his auditory disability;

4. The individual with impaired function of the peripheral organ of hearing may thereby be differentiated from individuals whose ears function normally but whose auditory behavior is distorted by some other involvement.

The word "behavior" as it is used here has the broadest possible connotations. At one extreme it refers to the child's random activity in unstructured play and at the other to his responses to the systematic stimulation procedures of threshold audiometry and psychometry. It includes affective interaction, motor performance, and communication.

Furthermore, behavior tends to be exhibited in recognizable *patterns*, not as isolated bits and pieces of stimulus-response combinations. The total pattern of the hard of hearing child's behavior, for example, is diagnostically meaningful, whereas a single item of behavior, e.g., failure to react to a particular acoustic stimulus, is not necessarily so.

Differential diagnosis based on behavioral signs does not obviate the need for threshold audiometry. In fact, hearing test procedures, whether they utilize standard audiometric techniques or not, are essential to an evaluation of how the child responds to sound and uses it for adaptation to the environment. A diagnosis of hearing loss must demonstrate that the child has elevated hearing thresholds. By the same token, audiometry should establish the presence of normal hearing acuity to justify a definite diagnosis of a disorder other than hearing loss (Rosenberg, 1966).

In effect, the differential diagnosis establishes a probability that a child suffers from a stated handicap; this probability should be supported by test data and the findings of physical examination. Thus, a child who reacts only to high intensity sounds *may* have a hearing loss. If the lack of response to low intensity sounds fits into a pattern including peculiar vocal quality, slow development of speech, and reliance on visual communication, the probability of hearing loss is enhanced. Otological and audiological findings must also be indicative of hearing loss to establish a definite diagnosis.

It is apparent that audiometry, as a specific mode of observing auditory behavior, and the differential analysis of behavior patterns can be mutually supportive and confirmatory. The more a child's behavior suggests "hard of hearingness" in other respects, the more confidence the audiologist will have in an audiogram which indicates poorer than normal thresholds. Conversely, if audiometry indicates one level of hearing acuity and other aspects of behavior suggest a markedly different level, the clinician has reason to suspect the validity of his hearing test or of his behavioral analysis, or both.

Myklebust originally described the behavior patterns associated with deafness, aphasia, "psychic" deafness, and mental deficiency. McHugh, in a commentary accompanying an illustrative film contrasted the behaviors of deaf, "brain-injured," autistic, and mentally retarded children (Davis, 1965). Kastein and Fowler (1964) compared children in ten different diagnostic categories on seven behavioral variables. The present discussion will concentrate on behavior that can be categorized for convenience under four headings: response to sound, use of voice, use of vision, and social-emotional behavior. With respect to these categories of behavior the child with a peripheral hearing loss will be compared to the child with cerebral dysfunction and to the emotionally disturbed child.

The descriptions are presented as though each child has a "pure" disorder; such is not always the case, of course. The hearing impaired child may be emotionally disturbed, the child with cerebral dysfunction may have a hearing loss, etc. In addition a child's behavior may be altered by fatigue, medication, unfamiliarity with his surroundings, and other factors so that he may not display the behavior which is typical for him on every occasion. This emphasizes the value of extended observation and exploratory teaching, as advocated by Bangs (1961), so that behavioral variations over time can be noted.

Typically the question of how well a child hears arises early in his life when his parents become disturbed by his delayed development of speech and his failure to respond appropriately to their speech. Among children who use verbal communication routinely, whether they are hard of hearing, brain-damaged, or emotionally disturbed, threshold audiometry is rarely more difficult than it is with a normally hearing child of the same age. The task of differential diagnosis is, therefore, primarily concerned with young children who have severe limitations of language development and speech usage. For this reason the constellations of behavior described below should be thought of as applying primarily to nontalking children between 2 and 6 years of age. The concepts expressed with respect to these constellations are applicable, however, to older children, particularly among children who are speechless. Behavioral observations may be utilized less frequently for differential diagnosis in older children, if only because older children are more amenable to threshold audiometry. They can still serve a role in validating audiometric findings, however. The audiologist who knows that he is testing an emotionally disturbed child, for example, will probably be more cautious in accepting the accuracy of his audiometry than he would be if this complication were not present.

In reviewing the behavioral descriptions which follow, certain precautions should be kept in mind. First, not every child in a given diagnostic category will exhibit every behavioral sign which is listed as characteristic of the group in that category. Not every hard of hearing child has unusual voice quality, for example; this will depend upon the degree and type of hearing loss, especially for low frequency hearing. Nor will every child who exhibits a particular kind of behavior act that way all the time. A child who is easily distracted by background sounds is not *equally* distracted by all sounds. To observe that a specific sound did not distract the child does not negate the observation that he is auditorily distractible. With reference to each item the central question is whether it can be considered representative of the child's habitual mode of behavior.

Second, it is reiterated that the diagnostic significance of these observations rests upon whether they can be synthesized into a pattern. The absence of a particular behavioral item from a given child's repertoire of behavior does not necessarily exclude him from the diagnostic category of which that item is characteristic. It is the constellation of signs that counts, not the presence or absence of any particular one.

Third, behavioral signs will be intermixed in a multiply handicapped child. The task of differential diagnosis is difficult enough in a child with a single disorder. In the multiply handicapped child it may be extraordinarily complex. Therefore, behavioral observation should be conducted with great care over an extended period of time, and the audiologist should be very sure of his ground before making a categorical statement as to how well the child hears.

Fourth, behavior which points strongly in the direction of cerebral dysfunction or emotional disturbance does not necessarily rule out hearing loss. The only conclusive evidence of normal hearing is a reliable audiogram showing normal thresholds. On the other hand, a diagnosis of emotional disturbance or cerebral dysfunction may explain why a child's audiogram suggests hearing loss even though the rest of his behavior does not. The validity of the audiogram rests in its correlation with the overall behavior of the child.

The Constellations of Differential Diagnostic Behavioral Signs

The Child's Use of Audition

In general, the *hard of hearing* child uses the sounds that he can hear in the same way that a normally hearing child does. He likes to hear. He produces sounds for the sake of hearing them, of playing with them, of using them as a means of achieving interaction with his companions. The louder the auditory stimulus, the more conspicuous is his response. He will try to imitate, when he is asked to, those sounds which he can hear. If he can't hear the stimulus he is asked to imitate, he may indicate puzzlement, or signify that he doesn't know what to do. When audiometry is attempted, he will try, though not always successfully, to follow instructions. If audiometry can be done, the child usually will have clear-cut threshold levels for the test stimuli, though this may be difficult to observe in children under 2 years of age. Often if the examiner delays the presentation of a test tone, the child will gesture as though to say, "Turn it on. Let me hear it." His apparent thresholds for pure tones correspond to his threshold responses to white noise, octave bands of noise, voice, and other test stimuli. When his attention is caught by a sound, he localizes and investigates the source; he may try to manipulate the sound-making device and produce the sound himself. When he is familiar with a given sound, he will attend to it or ignore it according to his understanding of the instructions given to him by the examiner.

The *child with cerebral dysfunction* tends to be inconsistent in his response to sound. His thresholds apparently fluctuate; it seems hard for him to maintain his attention to the test stimulus or his interest in the test procedure. During audiometry, if it can be done at all, he seems to be relatively good at responding to a tone that is diminishing in intensity and relatively poor at detecting a tone that is increasing in intensity from below the descending threshold; the gap between descending and ascending thresholds thus tends to be inordinately large (15 db or more)—the examiner wonders which one to credit. This child often has difficulty localizing the source of sound. He may respond better to low intensity than to high intensity sounds, being quickly aware of the former but not even startled by the latter. He adapts readily to a given stimulus, acting as though it is no longer interesting to him after a few presentations. For this reason standard pure tone audiometry is difficult; he stops listening for the test tone before his threshold has been defined. Much of the time he responds more readily and consistently to voice or noise than to pure tones. He is also more likely to respond to a sound which is familiar to him than to a novel sound; sound-making toys brought from his home may be the most effective stimuli. It is usually more difficult to elicit a response to sound when he is playing intently; the more engrossed he becomes in a visual task, the "deafer" he acts. Thus, his responses improve—that is, he responds to a greater variety of sounds at lower intensities—when he is in a sound-proofed room devoid of toys. Even here, however, his first responses are the most conspicuous; adaptation still occurs with repeated stimulation.

The *emotionally disturbed child* also tends to give inconsistent responses to most sounds, but he may show a special interest in a particular sound, e.g., a siren, and respond consistently to it. He tends not to play with sound unless it is produced by an object having peculiar emotional significance for him. This play is usually repetitive, stereotyped, and egocentric. The child's interest in sounds is not increased by amplification; in fact, he may appear to be angered or confused when stimulation at high intensities is attempted, but he still will not utilize the sound as a signal for communication with the environment. He may actively reject sound by putting his hands over his ears, by striking a sound toy from the examiner's hand, or by turning away from the examiner or the sound source. He often betrays his awareness of sound by delayed response—though seeming to ignore a sound toy, for example, when it is used by the examiner, he returns to it later and warily, even surreptitiously, manipulates it to make the sound again.

The auditory behavior of these children is summarized in Table 27.

The Child's Use of Voice

The *hard of hearing child* characteristically uses his voice to communicate. At the least he simply vocalizes for attention, at best he talks. When his loss is mild to moderate and has a "flat" audiometric configuration, or when low frequency hearing (up to 750 Hz) is within the normal range, his voice is melodious, widely ranging in pitch, loudness, and inflection. When the low

*Table 27. Contrast of Auditory Behavior of Children with Hearing Impairment, Children with Cerebral Dysfunction, and Children with Emotional Disturbance**

Hearing Impairment	Cerebral Dysfunction	Emotional Disturbance
Clearcut threshold for auditory stimuli	Inconsistent response, with apparent fluctuation of threshold	Inconsistent response; uncooperative in formal audiometry.
Responds better to high than to low intensity sound	Frequently responds better to low than to high intensities	Responds best to sounds which have emotional significance for him; may not give a startle response to very high intensity sounds
Usually tries to imitate sounds which he can hear	May refuse to imitate, or acts as though not knowing what is expected; vocal imitation often grossly inaccurate	Refuses to imitate; may resent imitation of his vocalizations by others
Tries to listen; gets pleasure from auditory experience; likes to play with sound toys	Poor listener; rapid adaptation to a given stimulus; easily distracted by irrelevant sounds	May actively reject direct auditory stimulation (e.g., put hands over ears); may show fleeting interest in acoustic events; no general interest in acoustic environment
Reasonable correspondence between threshold audiogram and other aspects of auditory behavior	Threshold audiometry often unreliable; audiogram frequently incompatible with responses to environmental sounds	Threshold audiometry may be impossible, except by EEG
Readily shows awareness of both voice and pure tones at suprathreshold intensities	Responds better to voice than to pure tones	Voice is least effective auditory stimulus

Adapted from Myklebust (1954, pp. 352–3).

*From Green, M. and M. Haggerty, R. J., Eds. *Ambulatory Pediatrics*, Philadelphia, W. B. Saunders Co., 1968.

frequency loss exceeds 40 db with greater loss at high frequencies, or when the threshold audiogram is flat but thresholds are elevated more than 50 db, voice quality suffers, becoming more and more "deafy" as degree of hearing loss increases. Pitch and loudness changes become less conspicuous, inflection patterns less subtle. Whereas the vocalizations of the child with a mild to moderate loss often have the prosodic patterns of speech even though no words are recognizable, those of a child with a severe loss assume more of a grunting or squealing nature, more often monosyllabic, less musical. Upon request he usually will imitate the vocalizations of others when he can hear them; when he cannot hear clearly or at all, his attempt to imitate is controlled by his lipreading. If he imitates, the accuracy of his imitation improves when he has an opportunity to lipread and when amplification is provided. His speech is usually misarticulated, and the articulation errors agree generally with predictions made from the audiogram. His articulation is more easily corrected when he uses a hearing aid or lipreading or both.

The *child with cerebral dysfunction* tends to have normal voice quality and variety even when he lacks speech, though this generalization may not apply to low level mental retardates, who sometimes display peculiar vocal quality and monotony or may be mute. If vocal imitation can be elicited at all, this child will likely imitate low intensity speech sounds with the same accuracy as he will high intensity sounds; the accuracy of his imitation will not be markedly improved by his opportunity to lipread. His articulation errors do not bear a clear relationship to his apparent auditory thresholds. Echolalia is frequent, but is seldom heard when the child responds appropriately to a verbal command. Conversely, if echolalia occurs, comprehension seems not to.

The *emotionally disturbed child* seldom uses his voice to control the environment. His spontaneous vocalizations tend to be significant to himself but not communicative to others. If he has meaningful speech at all, it tends to be free of articulatory defect. His vocalizations may be peculiar in phonetic content but normal in vocal quality and in variety of pitch and loudness. Echolalia is frequent. If the child's vocalizations are imitated, he will be indifferent on the one hand, startled and anxious on the other. If he is asked to imitate, he is indifferent; occasionally he may be angrily negativistic. One gets the impression that his voice is of no use to him at all.

The vocal behavior of these children is summarized in Table 28.

The Child's Use of Vision

The *hard of hearing child* tends to rely primarily upon vision for adjustment to the environment; this becomes more conspicuous as the hearing loss becomes more severe. His reliance on vision leads him to use gesture as the primary code of communication; even when he uses his voice for communication, it often has only a supportive role for the primary gesture. This child is adept at interpreting the gestures of others. He may be seen in play or during tests "talking to himself" on his hands. He is alert to movement around him; it is difficult to escape his notice. He watches faces—he may even pull a parent's face around toward him so that he can watch the parent talk or have the parent watch him. His own face is a mirror of his thoughts and feelings; it is easy to follow his thinking because it is so clearly on display. If this characterization were to be condensed into one word, the word for the hard of hearing child would be "visual."

The *child with cerebral dysfunction* is also highly visual in his orientation, but not in the systematic purposeful manner of the child with a hearing loss. His use of gesture is limited to simple pointing plus such conventional and uncomplicated gestures as shaking or nodding the head for yes and no and waving the hand for goodbye. The brain-damaged child's gestures do not acquire the pictorial and symbolic elaboration achieved by the hard of hearing child. He is alert to the visual environment but in a helter-skelter fashion, turning his attention from one thing to another, seemingly without trying to understand the first. His visual distractibility, sometimes though not neces-

Table 28.   *Contrast of Vocal Behavior of Children with Hearing Impairment, Children with Cerebral Dysfunction, and Children with Emotional Disturbance**

Hearing Impairment	Cerebral Dysfunction	Emotional Disturbance
Uses voice to get attention and to influence environment; vocal patterns may indicate mood	May use voice to influence environment, depending on IQ and symbolic integrity; autistic vocalization and mutism in low IQ's	Vocalizes primarily for own pleasure; projective use of voice may be elicited from child under stress
Peculiar voice quality; pitch monotony; "deafiness" more conspicuous with greater severity of hearing loss	Usually normal quality and variety of voice, but deviant voice in low retardates	Usually normal quality, but limited phonemic variety
Imitates other voices when he can hear them; accuracy of imitation improves when given opportunity to lipread	May not be imitative; if so, imitates soft voice as well as loud; no conspicuous improvement in imitation with lipreading	Refuses to imitate; may act startled and anxious if his own vocalizations are imitated
Articulation of speech tends to agree with predictions from threshold audiogram; articulation best with "visible" speech sounds, poorest with voiceless high frequency consonants	Articulation patterns not clearly related to apparent hearing thresholds; articulation accuracy not related to "visibility" of speech sounds	Frequently has normal articulation, if he talks at all; may say relevant words, phrases, sentences once, never repeat
Echolalic for words and short sentences in early stages of language learning, not otherwise; articulation errors of spontaneous speech are present in echoed speech.	Frequently echolalic for words, pitch and rhythm patterns, loudness and stress patterns; articulation of echoed speech often better than that of spontaneous speech	Frequently echolalic, even when no spontaneous speech is present

Adapted from Myklebust (1954, pp. 352–3).

*From Green, M. and Haggerty, R. J., Eds. *Ambulatory Pediatrics*, Philadelphia: W. B. Saunders Co., 1968. Reprinted by permission of the publisher.

sarily combined with auditory distractibility, repeatedly leads to interruptions of tasks he has started. His hypersensitivity to visible objects and events, nevertheless, is accompanied by superficiality of observation, so that his use of visually acquired information may be ineffectual or incorrect. His face reflects strong emotion—fear, anger, joy—but lacks subtlety; his face may tell you what he is feeling but not what he is thinking. Similarly, he is not acute in interpreting the facial gestures of others; though he looks *at* people readily, he does not look *into* faces as the hearing impaired child does. He seldom demands that people look at him.

The *emotionally disturbed child* tends to be uninterested in his visual environment, frequently even acting unaware of it. He ignores his surroundings, except for the few objects which may attract his attention. These exert a fascination which seems out of proportion to their inherent value as toys—

a doorknob, a piece of string, a reflection, a pilot light, his fingers. He does not look at faces except with an occasional fleeting glance; he is not responsive to facial expressions of others. Even when his head is held between the hands, his eyes escape direct contact. His own facial expression is impassive. He does not gesture to others from a distance; he may pull another by the hand to indicate his desires. When doing this he treats the hand as though it were an independent object in and of itself; the person to whom the hand is attached is irrelevant to him. He may produce gestures which are significant in a psychiatric sense, revealing his mood or desires, but these gestures do not seem to be produced with the deliberate intent of influencing others.

The visual behavior of these children is summarized in Table 29.

The Child's Social-Emotional Adjustment

The *hard of hearing child* is sensitive to his social environment and makes an effort to play an appropriate role in the social situation as he is able to define it. He is sensitive to the feelings and apparent wishes of others. He

Table 29. *Contrast of Visual Behavior of Children with Hearing Impairment, Children with Cerebral Dysfunction, and Children with Emotional Disturbance**

Hearing Impairment	Cerebral Dysfunction	Emotional Disturbance
Compensatory use of vision for environmental orientation; active visual scanning of environment	Conspicuous visual distractibility	May act unaware of events in visual environment
Watches faces closely, especially after speech teaching is started; alters own behavior in response to changes in facial expressions of others	Has normal attentiveness to faces (low IQ's may ignore faces); may miss significance of facial expression	Ignores faces; eye contact fleeting or impossible
Communicates by gesture; invents symbolic gesture; successfully interprets gestures of others; may use gestures to "talk" to himself	Superficial use of gesture, seldom symbolic; effective interpretation of gestures of others tends to be limited to concrete gestures, such as pointing	Sparse use of gesture, which, when present, tends to have only autistic significance
Skill with visual play materials (blocks, jigsaw puzzles, etc.) appropriate to age	May have difficulty with visual play materials because of visual perceptual confusion (difficulty matching forms and colors, copying geometric forms, etc.); use of toys tends to be unimaginative	Often uninterested in visual play materials; may have intense interest in, and attachment to, a particular object of peculiar emotional interest, e.g., string; precocious ability to assemble jigsaw puzzles in early infantile autism

Adapted from Myklebust (1954, pp. 352–3).
*From Green, M. and Haggerty, R. J., Eds. *Ambulatory Pediatrics*, Philadelphia, W. B. Saunders Co., 1968. Reprinted by permission of the publisher.

likes to display his accomplishments—the doll he dressed, the puzzle he assembled, the picture he colored. When he is frustrated in these activities, he takes the object to an adult and asks for help. He shows pleasure in the accomplishments of others. He engages in cooperative play in a manner appropriate to his age. He is organized and systematic, purposeful in his own actions and attentive to the purposes of others. He tries to anticipate what is expected of him. He modifies his behavior to suit the expectations of others, and he continually monitors the environment to determine whether it is expressing approval or disapproval of him.

The *child with cerebral dysfunction* is disjointed in his behavior, lacking in internal controls. He is the victim of his own impulsiveness, repeatedly coming into conflict with his environment because he can't sense, or can't remember, or can't respect the limitations of behavior the environment wishes to impose upon him. He "goes off half-cocked." He moves too much, too far, too fast. He is "a bull in a china shop," but he doesn't realize how abrasive he is until the environment "cracks down" on him; then he seems surprised—he didn't know that he was out of bounds. He likes toys, but he flits from one to another without fully exploiting any of them. His emotions are close to the surface; he is easily pleased and quickly angered, but his pleasure does not lead to cooperation and his anger does not lead to hostility. A one-word condensation for this child is "disorganized."

The word for the *emotionally disturbed child* is "lone wolf." Whereas the brain-damaged child is exasperating because he requires so much supervision, the emotionally disturbed child is exasperating because he is indifferent to the supervision given to him. He simply ignores his environment; he rejects contact with it. He will not admit others into his play; he doesn't attend to the play of others. To him other people are objects, occasionally useful, seldom interesting. He makes no display of affection, he is unmoved by affection shown him. Like Old Man River he don't do nothin' or say nothin', he just keeps rolling along. He is engaged with his own preoccupations; about the rest of the world he couldn't care less.

The social-emotional adjustment of these children is summarized in Table 30.

It was suggested in the chapter on the case history interview that one of the functions of the case history is to establish a diagnostic hypothesis which is tested by the procedures of the direct examination. The history does this in two ways: first, by establishing the existence of conditions which are known to be associated with the occurrence of hearing loss, cerebral dysfunction, or emotional disturbance. This comprises such events as maternal rubella in early pregnancy, neonatal jaundice, epilepsy, severe parental neglect, etc. Second, the history elicits a description by the parents or other informants of the way the child behaves at home.

When the clinician knows in advance what behavioral signs are most likely to be diagnostically meaningful, he can direct his interrogation to the objective of obtaining an explicit description of the overall pattern of behavior. His question to the parents may be in the form, "How does your child react to the following sounds?" or "How does your child get along with other chil-

Table 30. *Contrast of Social Adaptation in Children with Hearing Impairment, Chlidren with Cerebral Dysfunction, and Children with Emotional Disturbance**

Hearing Impairment	Cerebral Dysfunction	Emotional Disturbance
Behavior generally well organized, purposeful; sensitive to social environment	Behavior often disorganized, haphazard; tasks started and left incomplete; abrasive to social environment	Ignores social environment; behavior satisfies autistic purposes, not related to surrounding activity
Quick to sense feelings of others; adjusts behavior accordingly	Relatively obtuse to feelings of others; may try to adapt to feelings of others, but cannot sustain	Insensitive to feelings of others; treats people as objects
Usually likes other children; interacts with them appropriate to age	Usually likes other children; tends to play alongside rather than with them	Ignores other children; "lone wolf"
Heightened motor activity, but usually with definite objectives	Often hyperactive, fidgety; much movement without apparent purpose	May exhibit bizarre postures and movements; stereotyped play with fingers and other parts of body
Attention span normal for age; attentiveness determined by interest value of play materials or activity	Short attention span, regardless of activity; attentiveness improved by control of environment to reduce unessential stimulation	Not interested in usual play materials or activities, but may maintain attention for unusually long time in activity having autistic significance
Normal emotionality for age	Emotional lability without depth of affect; "catastrophic breakdown" under stress	Emotionally bland, no affective display

Adapted from Myklebust (1954, pp. 352–3).
*From Green, M. and Haggerty, R. J., Eds. *Ambulatory Pediatrics*, Philadephia: W. B. Saunders Co., 1968. Reprinted by permission of the publisher.

dren?" When the parents answer, he should ask himself, "Is that the way a hard of hearing child behaves? Does that behavior suggest cerebral dysfunction?" As the behavioral picture emerges, he can be more and more specific in his questioning until he is satisfied that he has a coherent account of the child's behavioral interactions at home, or at least until he is satisfied that further questioning will not add clarity to the picture. The case history is, thus, the first step in the behavioral analysis.

The Use of the Case History in Differential Diagnosis

The core of the clinical examination is, of course, the measurement of the child's hearing. It is obvious from the foregoing, however, that the analysis of the child's response to sound is aided by analysis of his responses to all aspects of his environment. Indeed, a failure to analyze the total behavior pattern may well lead to a misinterpretation of the audiometric findings. The clinical examination, therefore, should not be restricted to threshold and supplementary audiometric procedures, but instead should permit the broadest possible range of behavioral expression by the child. By so doing, the clinician gives himself an opportunity to make a more comprehensive analysis of the child's use of acoustic information and a more reasoned judgment about the validity of his hearing tests.

It is not the intention of this chapter to teach the audiologist how to diagnose cerebral dysfunction or emotional disturbance in children. There are children with central nervous system pathology and with emotional disturbance who do not behave in the ways described above. In most cases they also do not behave in ways which simulate hearing loss. Thus, they do not present a diagnostic problem to the audiologist.

In the cases that do raise a question as to the adequacy of their hearing, a differential diagnosis derived from behavioral signs will assist the audiologist in identifying hard of hearing children. It will also alert him to the possible presence of complications of hearing loss in multiply handicapped children, and it hopefully will prevent him from being led astray by the red herring of poor response to sound in a child whose hearing acuity is normal. This chapter is written with the conviction that the way the child uses his eyes, his hands, and his heart will help the audiologist decide how he is using his ears.

References

Bangs, Tina E. 1961. Evaluating children with language delay. Journal of Speech and Hearing Disorders 26:6.

Davis, H. 1965. The young deaf child: identification and management. Acta Otolaryngologica Supplem. 206.

Downs, Marion P. and Graham M. Sterritt. 1967. A guide to newborn and infant hearing screening programs. AMA Archives of Otolaryngology 85:37.

Frisina, D. R. 1963. Management of hearing in children. In J. Jerger (Ed.) Modern Developments in Audiology. New York: Academic Press.

Kastein, Shulamith and Edmund P. Fowler. 1965. Differential diagnosis of communication disorders in children referred for hearing tests. AMA Archives of Otolaryngology 60: 468.

Myklebust, H. R. 1954. Auditory Disorders in Children. New York: Grune & Stratton.

Rosenberg, Philip E. 1966. Misdiagnosis of children with auditory problems. Journal of Speech and Hearing Disorders 31:279.

Wedenberg, E. 1956. Auditory tests on new-born infants. Acta Otolaryngologica 46:776.

Chapter 14

The Psychological Examination

McCAY VERNON, Ph.D.

Certain crucial considerations are fundamental to the psychological examination of the hard of hearing child, considerations which are not generally of primary significance with the normally hearing youngster. A failure to be aware of these considerations can result in gross psychodiagnostic errors of tragic consequence to the child, his parents, and all involved in the rehabilitation process.

The first of these hinges upon the relationship of the hard of hearing child's auditory impairment to his language functioning. In many cases hard of hearing children will appear to the psychologist to be capable of hearing well enough to converse with little difficulty, especially in the relatively quiet one-to-one situation of most clinics or offices. This kind of superficial observation frequently masks the role hearing loss has had in language development of the child. Often these children are unable to understand well in groups or in places where there are background noises. Their hearing thresholds may fluctuate. They may have gone through their early years (which are crucial for language development) without a hearing aid. In some cases their hearing loss may have been greater during preschool years. These factors are discussed thoroughly elsewhere in the book. *Their primacy to the psychologist is that these conditions often lead to a language deficiency in the hard of hearing child that is due, not to a lack of intelligence or to psychopathology, but simply to a lack of adequate auditory input of language.* The hard of hearing child generally has not had the exposure to language that his normally hearing peer has had.

This problem is best illustrated by the following example. The author was called upon to examine a patient at a hospital for the mentally retarded. This youth who had been in the hospital several years had received an IQ of 50 on the Stanford Binet, a verbal test, resulting in a diagnosis of mental retardation. On at least one occasion he had also been classified as sufficiently schizoid and withdrawn to require treatment as mentally ill. When given a nonverbal measure, the WISC Performance Scale, the youngster achieved an IQ above average. Interviewing indicated that most of the alleged withdrawal and constriction were actually a combination of a failure to hear conversation and a language retardation. Transferred to an educational program for hearing impaired children, he made rapid academic and social gains. Later this young man was admitted to college.

Unfortunately, cases of these kinds of misdiagnoses are not unusual. **The** reason underlying the errors is almost inevitably a failure of the psychologist to recognize that the language deficiency of the hard of hearing child may be totally unrelated to his intelligence and may mime personality pathology that is not present. The child's flat affect, nonresponsive remarks, and apparent withdrawal may be based on the reality factors of the child not clearly understanding the examiner and/or a history of not being able to grasp spoken language. Often the child copes with this by either keeping quiet or by trying to dominate the conversation in order to avoid having to understand that which is unclear. Many of these children have learned to handle their hearing loss by becoming masters of the neutral response, smiling, saying yes, and periodically nodding their heads in the affirmative. These techniques are often remarkably effective in unintentionally misleading psychologists and others into thinking there has been understanding and full communication when actually the child has unknowingly used a series of sort of "Rogerian" type reflective responses to conceal his inability to understand. It is important that psychologists be alert for this type of response.

With these introductory concepts as a frame of reference, certain general principles for psychodiagnoses with hard of hearing children will be presented. Following this the eight major components of a full psychological evaluation will be discussed.

General Principles

1. Psychological tests or interviewing procedures which depend upon the use of verbal language to measure intelligence, personality, or aptitudes may be measuring the hard of hearing child's language deficiency due to his deafness, not his actual mental capacity or psychodynamics. The situation in some cases is analogous to giving an immigrant whose primary language is German a test battery and interview in English. He could have the intellect of Einstein, yet test scores would probably indicate retardation and psychopathology.

While some hard of hearing children function linguistically and in oral communication in essentially the same manner as the normally hearing, in an appreciable number of cases they are psychodiagnostically more like deaf youngsters. They are in a marginal area between hearing and deafness. It is, therefore, crucial in a psychological evaluation that they be given tests appropriate for deaf persons as well as tests for persons with normal hearing. Where significant differences appear between the sets of test responses they frequently show that the child did better on the nonlanguage measures appropriate for deaf persons. It is these findings which should be judged the more valid in such a circumstance.

2. Whenever possible, instructions and verbal test items should be given to the hard of hearing child in writing as well as orally. For example, most of the verbal subtests of the Wechsler should be typed on index cards with a separate card for each item. In instances where both the hard of hearing child and the psychologist understand fingerspelling and the language of signs this effective means of communication should be used. These procedures do not in

any way eliminate the factor of level of linguistic skill but they do reduce the obstacle oral communication presents for many hard of hearing children. The psychologist may also repeat the questions or have the child repeat them to show he has understood.

3.   Complete and valid psychodiagnostics with hard of hearing children often require more time than is true with normally hearing youth (Brenner and Thompson, 1967). This fact must be accounted for in scheduling and planning. Often several test sessions are required, especially if Rorschach and TATs are to be administered.

4.   Test scores on preschool and early school age hard of hearing children tend to be extremely unreliable. Low scores in particular should be viewed as questionable in the absence of supporting data (Smith, 1967; Vernon and Brown, 1964). Case histories are essential.

5.   Tests given to hard of hearing children by psychologists not experienced with the hearing impaired are in general subject to appreciably greater error than is the case when the service is rendered by one familiar with hearing impaired children.

6.   There are many circumstances which can lead children, especially the hard of hearing, to function below capacity on tests. Thus, there is far more danger that a low IQ is inaccurate than that a high one is wrong.

7.   Tests that emphasize timed responses usually do not yield as valid findings as those that do not. The attentive set of the hard of hearing youngster toward timed tests is frequently to finish as quickly as possible even if answers are random and, therefore, meaningless (Hiskey, 1966).

8.   Group testing of hard of hearing children is a dubious procedure which at best is of use only as a gross screening device (Hiskey, 1966; Lane and Schneider, 1941; Levine, 1960, p. 221; Myklebust, 1962). Even tests such as the Stanford and Metropolitan educational achievement tests which are designed to be used on a group or individual basis, should be given individually.

Components of the Psychological Evaluation

A complete psychological evaluation of a hard of hearing child should include all or parts of the following information.

1.   A measure of intelligence
2.   An evaluation of personality structure
3.   A test for brain damage
4.   A measure of educational achievement
5.   An appraisal of communication skills
6.   Aptitude and interest testing
7.   Case history data
8.   Report of a physical examination

In many cases all of these data may not be needed or, if needed, can be obtained in part from school records or sources other than the psychological examination.

Intelligence Testing

It is especially important to a hard of hearing child that he be given an individual measure of intelligence. Often his speech and language problems and his inability to understand classroom lectures and discussion result in academic retardation and psychosocial problems and are frequently misconstrued by teachers and others to indicate a lack of intelligence. Hence, a valid measure of the child's intellectual capacity can be of tremendous value.

To obtain an accurate IQ requires that both performance and verbal scales be administered. When there are significant discrepancies between these, the differences usually consist of higher scores on the performance scales. This usually means that the results on the performance measures are the more valid. The verbal scores often reflect the language handicap resulting from the hearing loss, not intelligence level.

Table 31 lists some appropriate performance scales for hard of hearing children who have language retardation due to their hearing problem. Care has been taken to omit those tests whose items are nonverbal but which require extensive verbal instructions as these are obviously inappropriate. An additional reference of special value for those testing preschool hard of hearing children is in Smith's (1967) article.

Table 31. Evaluation of Some of the Intelligence Tests Most Commonly Used with Hard of Hearing Children Having Language Limitations Similar to Those of Deaf Children

Tests	Appropriate Age Range	Evaluation of the Test
1. Wechsler Performance Scale for Children (1949)	9 years to 16 years	The Wechsler Performance Scale is at present the best test for hard of hearing children ages 9–16. It yields a relatively valid IQ score, and offers opportunities for qualitative interpretation of factors such as brain injury or emotional disturbance (Wechsler, 1955, pp. 80–81). It has good interest appeal and is relatively easy to administer and reasonable in cost.
2. Wechsler Performance Scale for Adults (1955)	16 years to 70 years	The rating of the Wechsler Performance Scale for Adults is the same as the rating on the Wechsler Performance Scale for Children.
3. Wechsler Preschool and Primary Scale of Intelligence Performance Subtests (Wechsler, 1967)	3 years, 11 months to 6 years, 8 months	This scale is not as good for use for the hard of hearing children as the other Wechsler Scales. Picture Completion and Mazes are difficult to explain nonverbally. Other performance subtests are excellent. Standardization seems a little high.
4. Leiter International Performance Scale (1948 Revision)	4 years to 12 years (also suitable for older mentally retarded deaf subjects)	This test has good interest appeal. It can be used to evaluate relatively disturbed hard of hearing children who could not otherwise be tested. This test is expensive

Table 31—Continued

Tests	Appropriate Age Range	Evaluation of the Test
		and lacking somewhat in validation. In general, however, it is an excellent test for young hard of hearing children. Timing is a minor factor. One disadvantage is in the interpretation of the IQ scores because the mean of the test is 95 and the standard deviation is 20. This means that the absolute normal score on this test is 95 instead of 100 as on other intelligence tests. Scores of 60, for example, therefore, do not indicate mental deficiency but correspond more to about a 70 on a test such as the Wechsler or Binet. Great care must be taken in interpreting Leiter IQ scores for these reasons.
5. Progressive Matrices (Raven, 1948)	9 years to adulthood	Raven's Progressive Matrices are good as a second test to substantiate another more comprehensive intelligence test. The advantage of the Matrices is that it is extremely easy to administer and score, taking relatively little of the examiner's time and is very inexpensive. It yields invalid test scores of impulsive hard of hearing children, who tend to respond randomly rather than with accuracy and care. For this reason, the examiner should observe the child carefully to assure that he is really trying.
6. Ontario School Ability Examination (Amoss, 1949)	4 years to 10 years	This is a reasonably good test for hard of hearing children within these age ranges.
7. Hiskey-Nebraska Test of Learning Aptitude (Hiskey, 1966)	3 years to 17 years	This is a revision of the earlier (1955) version. Basically it is a sound, useful test, but somewhat weak with children 3 and 4 years of age.
8. Chicago Non-Verbal Examination (Brown et al., 1947)	7 years to 12 years	This test rates fair if given as an individual test; very poor if given as a group test. The scoring is tedious and reliability is rather low.
9. Grace Arthur Performance Scale (Arthur, 1947)	4.5 years to 15.5 years	This test is poor to fair because timing is heavily emphasized; norms are not adequate, and directions are somewhat unsatisfactory. This test is especially unsatisfactory for emotionally disturbed children who are also hard of hearing. With this type subject, this test will sometimes yield a score indicating extreme retardation when the difficulty is actu-

Table 31—Continued

Tests	Appropriate Age Range	Evaluation of the Test
		ally one of maladjustment. It is also poor for young hard of hearing children who are of below average intelligence because they often respond randomly instead of rationally.
10. Merrill-Palmer Scale of Mental Tests (Sutsman, 1931)	2 years to 4 years	The Merrill-Palmer is a fair test for young hard of hearing children but it must be adapted in order to be used and would require a skilled examiner with a thorough knowledge of hard of hearing children.
11. Goodenough Draw-A-Man Test (1926)	8.5 years to 11 years	Directions are very difficult to give young children in a standardized manner. Scoring is less objective than would be desired, so this test is relatively unreliable. It does, however, have some projective value in terms of personality assessment.
12. Randalls Island Performance Tests (1932)	2 years to 5 years	This is one of the few nonverbal instruments available for measuring preschool children. It consists of a wide range of performance and manipulative tasks which, used by a competent examiner, provide diagnostic and insightful information. This test is relatively expensive, but valuable.
13. Dr. Alathena Smith's Test for Preschool Deaf Children (Smith, 1967)	Preschool: 2 years to 4 years	This test is not officially on the market but the dissertation which contains the necessary information can be obtained from Dr. Smith at the Tracy Clinic. The test materials are available in most psychologists' offices and Dr. Smith gets excellent results with the test. It is the only intelligence test for deaf or hard of hearing children in this age range which is well standardized on a large sample.
14. Vineland Social Maturity Scale	1 year to 25 years	This is a questtionable test for hard of hearing children generally but can be used for extremely difficult to test, emotionally disturbed youngsters. It is given by asking the parents questions on the development of their child. The norms of this test have to be adapted for the hard of hearing because many of the questions involved such things as the onset of speech, length of sentences, vocabulary, etc. This test is inexpensive and can be given to otherwise untestable children.

Personality Evaluation

Personality evaluation is inherently a far more difficult task than intelligence testing. With the hard of hearing child the problem is greatly compounded because almost all psychodiagnostic instruments and interview techniques require verbal and/or oral communication. For some hard of hearing children this may present no major obstacle but for most it does. The examiner must be aware of and sensitive to this possibility and not misconstrue reactions due to communication difficulty as symptoms of psychopathology. For example some uneducated hard of hearing youths' writing may reflect marked confusion and disassociation. Instead of indicating an equally deranged thought process these writings usually reflect a language disability. There have been cases where a diagnosis of schizophrenia was made primarily due to bizarre written communications which were due to hearing loss, not to psychosis.

One way to minimize the chance of this kind of error is to administer academic achievement tests. If they establish a reading and vocabulary level high enough to permit paper and pencil tests or other verbal measures, then these may be used with some assurance. However, as Rosen (1967) has shown, often hearing impaired youth who have academic achievement scores within the stated reading levels of the personality tests such as the Minnesota Multiphasic Personality Inventory (MMPI) are not able to understand the test items. This is due in part to the idiomatic expressions common to the MMPI but not usually included in academic achievement tests. The MMPI and California Personality Inventory (CPI) should be used only with those of high school age whose reading achievement is near grade level.

A useful general rule for psychological evaluation is to start with the least threatening procedures. Aspects of the evaluation involving oral communication or verbal functioning should be kept until last. For example, it is good to begin with the Bender Gestalt or Draw-A-Person. This procedure enables the child to develop a feeling of accomplishment and pleasure in the task. At the same time it provides the psychologist an ideal circumstance for establishing rapport.

The possibility of psychogenic hearing loss must be given consideration in personality evaluation. In some cases it represents a defense against an admission of the presence of other reasons for academic failure. Often children who have had a history of ear problems may fixate on the mechanism of functional hearing loss in times of stress. In other cases minor losses will be magnified by the child. When suspected, it should be brought to the attention of the audiologist with whom a diagnosis and treatment plan can be developed.

Table 32 provides some specific information on some of the more popular personality tests and their use with the hearing impaired. The reference by Brenner and Thompson (1967) offers additional information of value.

Test for Brain Damage

Many of the causes of hearing loss are also causes of brain damage and resulting learning disabilities (Vernon, 1961). For example, conditions such

Table 32. Some Personality Tests Used with Hard of Hearing Youth

Tests	Appropriate Age Range	Evaluation of the Test
1. Draw-A-Person (Machover, 1949)	9 years to adulthood	This is a good screening device for detecting very severe emotional problems. It is relatively nonverbal and is probably the most practical projective personality test for severely hard of hearing children. Its interpretation is very subjective and in the hands of a poor psychologist it can result in rather extreme diagnostic statements about hard of hearing children.
2. Thematic Appperception Test (TAT) or Children's Apperception Test (CAT) (Stein, 1955)	Can be used with hard of hearing subjects of school age through adulthood who can communicate well orally or can communicate very well in written language or the language of signs.	This is a test of great potential, if the psychologist giving it and the hard of hearing subject taking it can both communicate with fluency in oral (or manual) communication. It is of very limited value otherwise unless the subject has an exceptional command of the English language and can write his responses.
3. Rorschach Ink Blot Test (Rorschach, 1942)	Can be given to hard of hearing subects as soon as they are able to communicate fluently orally (or manually) or if they can communicate with exceptional skill in writing.	In order for the Rorschach to be used it is almost absolutely necessary that the subject taking it be fluent in oral communication. It would be possible with a very bright hard of hearing subject who had a remarkable proficiency in English to give a Rorschach through writing, but this would not be very satisfactory. A Rorschach can be administered in the language of signs.
4. H.T.P. Technique (Buck, 1949)	School age through adulthood	This is a procedure similar to the Draw-A-Person test. It requires little verbal communication and affords the competent clinician some valuable insight into basic personality dynamics of the subject.
5. Rotter Incomplete Sentences Blank (Rotter & Rafferty, 1950)	At least fifth grade reading level	Useful with subjects who understand the vocabulary of the test. Many hard of hearing youth do not. Some experienced examiners substitute simple terms for some of the complex ones on the test.
6. Make-A-Picture-Story-Test (MAPS) (Schneidman, 1952)	About same as TAT and CAT above, except that it is somewhat less verbal	Basically the same as the CAT or TAT except that there are actual figures and a stage which can be moved about and grouped in ways that are indicative of social and personality dynamics.

as prematurity, maternal rubella, complications of Rh factor, meningitis, and genetics which are leading etiologies of auditory deficits, are major causes of other central nervous system damage (Vernon, 1967 a, b, c, d, e, & 1968). Obviously, if one part of the system, the auditory nerve, is damaged, there are greater probabilities that other areas will be involved. For this reason a thorough evaluation of a hard of hearing child should include psychological testing for brain damage.

This testing must always be done with a full awareness of the severe limitations of psychodiagnostic instruments for detection of brain damage. They are but one of many kinds of data including neurological examinations, electroencephalograms, and medical histories which are usually required to make conclusive diagnosis except with children where the damage is gross as in hemiplegias, athetoid cerebral palsies, and advanced chronic brain syndromes. Unfortunately, neurological examinations and electroencephalograms are also limited in their diagnostic potentials. Hence, the psychologist should use the best instruments available to him, report his findings conservatively, and refer to other disciplines for further clinical investigation when warranted.

The relatively high prevalance of brain damage among hard of hearing children is a fact. The development of effective educational and other therapies for these children is contingent upon identification and delineation of the problem. Table 33 lists some tests relevant to this purpose.

Educational Achievement Measurement

A full psychological evaluation of a hard of hearing child should include an assessment of educational level. A major reason for this is the prevalence of academic difficulty among these youngsters. The most appropriate tests for obtaining this information are the Metropolitan and the Stanford. The former has norms for hearing and deaf subjects. Although both tests are easy to administer, the examiner must make certain that the child understands and successfully completes the sample items for each subtest. Another crucial point in using these or any other achievement tests is to choose a battery that is at a level appropriate to the person being tested. If, for example, a person who is reading at the first grade level is given the Advanced Battery of the Stanford he will often test well above first grade level due to the scoring procedures being based on this battery not being administered to those far below high school academic achievement.

In interpreting results of achievement testing with the hard of hearing, it is important to keep in mind not only the average achievement levels for the normally hearing but also those for the deaf and more severely hard of hearing. These are as follows: only about 5 percent of graduates from day and residential schools for the deaf attain a tenth grade level in educational achievement, 41 percent seventh or eighth grade, 27 percent fifth or sixth grade, and approximately 30 percent are functionally illiterate by present governmental standards (McClure, 1966).

Table 33. Tests for Brain Injury

Tests	Evaluation of the Tests
1. Wechsler Performance Scale	Pattern analysis of these scales is of controversial validity as a diagnostic tool. There is fairly general agreement, however, that in the hands of a capable clinical psychologist a partial qualitative type of diagnosis is possible.
2. The Diamond Drawing from the Stanford-Binet	Has good validity, is generally available, can be easily administered.
3. Bender-Gestalt	This test seems to have possibilities, but scoring norms are inadequate and, at present, its interpretation is rather subjective. The Koppitz system is of value in objectifying scoring.
4. Goodenough Draw-A-Man Test and Machover Human Figure Drawing Interpretations	Listed together for convenience, these measures, particularly the latter, reveal symptoms such as impulsiveness, rigidity, anxiety, and perceptual difficulties, but here again, scoring for brain injury lacks standardization.
5. Ellis Test	Has definite possibilities, but lacks validation.
6. Marble Board	Potentially excellent, but very hard to get. Scoring instructions are inadequate.
7. Hiskey Blocks	Require a great deal of visualization and abstract ability and are of value for this reason.
8. Rorschach	Its use requires not only competence in the use of the test, but also a fluency in the use of the oral communication used by the hard of hearing. Results reported where these conditions are not met are of highly dubious validity.
9. Kohs Blocks	These are similar to the block design subtests of the Wechsler, but are more extensive. A qualitative diagnosis is possible, but norms are lacking for organic involvement.
10. Various measures of motor ability and development	Among these would be the railwalking test, tests of laterality, and certain items on the Vineland Social Maturity Scale that pertain to motor development.

Evaluation of Communication Skills

It is in the realm of communication that hearing loss presents its major handicap. For this reason, it is important that an evaluation include an assessment of communication skills. The speech pathologist and audiologist have the primary responsibility for diagnosis in this area and are professionally prepared as experts. However, psychologists should make certain observations of communicative functions.

There are three aspects of communication that should be appraised in a hard of hearing person. First is the ability to read and write because those are primary determinants of educational and vocational potential. Educational tests will provide reading levels. Sentence completion, or several of the verbal subtests of the Wechsler in addition to their clinical data, will yield a reasonably accurate picture of writing skills.

Speech and speechreading are the other key parts of communication to be evaluated. These skills have considerable potential to the hard of hearing child at school and later in the world of work. Psychologists can only assess in practical lay terms the intelligibility and pleasantness of the speech. These should be noted in the child's report.

Speechreading skill is a more complex function to measure. Audiological specialists are needed to do this thoroughly. However, it is important for the psychologist to report the extent to which the youngster is able to understand what is said in a one-to-one situation. It is also helpful if note can be made of the relative degree to which the youngster depends upon visual clues (speechreading) as contrasted to using his residual hearing. From such information the child's ability to communicate in groups can be estimated. One way to get some of this information is for the psychologist to cover his mouth or ask the child to turn his back during conversation.

Aptitude and Interest Testing

A basic part of a complete psychological evaluation for older youth is aptitude testing, i.e., finding the particular abilities that a person may have. As there are hundreds of tests for this, it is not feasible to list or discuss them individually. Both Levine (1960) and Myklebust (1962) survey this area relative to the hearing impaired with excellence and completeness. However, certain information about the following three general areas of aptitude is often of great value because these kinds of abilities are directly related to the types of work done by the more communication limited hard of hearing adults: (1) manual dexterity; (2) mechanical aptitudes; and (3) spatial relations.

It is important in selecting from the many measures of aptitude available to choose some tests that are not primarily dependent on language for either their directions or administration.

Interest tests are almost without exception highly verbal. Thus, they generally cannot be used effectively with all hard of hearing persons. There are pictorial tests purportedly designed for use with those who are profoundly hearing impaired, but they are narrow in scope and offer limited data to a psychological evaluation. It can be stated categorically that interest tests are rarely of value unless reading skills are of high school level.

It would be inappropriate to discuss tests without mention of the General Aptitude Test Battery (G.A.T.B.). As now constructed this test discriminates against a language impaired person. Hence, with the exception of certain parts, it yields more misinformation than help. A new version has just been completed which is specifically for the hearing impaired. It is available through the Rehabilitation Services Administration.

Case History Data

The past is still the one best predictor of the future. For this reason complete background information on a child, especially if he is hard of hearing and may not be accurately evaluated with regular psychological procedures, is of extreme importance. Illustrative of just how essential case history data are is that the best psychiatric and psychological evaluations are often based 75 percent upon background information. Parental interviews are extremely valuable, offering among other things, an insight into the parents' and the child's acceptance of the hearing problem.

Audiological Reports, Physical Examinations, and Medical History

The findings of the audiologist and the speech pathologist are basic to a meaningful psychological evaluation of a hard of hearing child. They address themselves directly to an important part of what is generally integral to the child's problem. As this area is thoroughly covered in other chapters of this book, it will not be further elaborated here.

It is often extremely beneficial to a psychologist if he can obtain some data of a hard of hearing child's physical condition and medical history. Especially useful is data about etiology of hearing loss. As noted before, many of the causes of impaired hearing also result in brain damage, learning disability, visual problems, seizures, mental retardation, aphasia, motor deficiency, orthopedic difficulties, cardiac anomalies, and behavior disturbances (Vernon, 1967, a, b, c, d, e, and 1968). These conditions are obviously highly relevant to a child's functioning and to a meaningful psychological evaluation. They are best understood if medical data are available.

By inter-relating IQ, educational, and other facts about a hard of hearing child, it is possible to derive a picture that reveals the role played by his hearing loss. If the youth's profile is similar to that of the normally hearing, his loss and the way it has been coped with is not particularly disabling. By contrast, if the profile is similar to that of a deaf child, then the loss has had major effects on communication, language development, and education. Appropriate planning for the two kinds of children vary drastically; what would be constructive for one might be devastating for the other. A psychological evaluation which does not fully address itself to this issue has failed to serve one of its major functions. The issue cannot be handled without comprehensive information. Short cuts will not suffice and hasty, inadequately done evaluations are actually unethical and wasteful of human resources.*

Differential Diagnosis

This popular but somewhat redundant term is most relevant to the psychologist working with multiply handicapped hard of hearing children in terms

---

*All of these eight aspects of a psychological evaluation are not necessary for every hard of hearing youth nor is it essential that the psychologist be the one who obtains all of the information. It is important, though, that the psychologist have complete data and that he be able to integrate the diverse information. Every psychologist and clinic should have the release and request forms needed to obtain these kinds of information.

of the problem of distinguishing between deafness, autism, mental retardation, brain damage, and schizophrenia or determining the extent to which aspects of these major pathologies are present. Those with experience in hospitals for the retarded are aware that these facilities often have entire units where there are children with symptoms characterizing one or more of these five conditions, yet who cannot be clearly diagnosed. For example, the author once tested a hearing impaired son of a deaf minister who got perfect scores on the WISC Block Designs, who could take apart and reassemble clocks and watches, and who wired his room with all sorts of intricate lighting and switching devices. However, his overall IQ scores on a series of six different IQ tests was never over 60, his behavior was bizarre, and he was not acceptable to any school. On several occasions he had been in hospitals for the retarded. He had at various times been diagnosed retarded, autistic, schizophrenic, brain damaged, and deaf. In large educational programs serving the deaf at least one extreme case of this type per year is generally seen and a number of similar, but milder cases are evaluated.

The full answer to the differential diagnostic problem of severely involved hard of hearing children lies far beyond the scope of this paper. For that matter, neither the methods of diagnosis nor appropriate therapies are known. Multidisciplinary techniques and full case histories are obviously essential. Evoked potential audiometry in particular may be useful in terms of assessing hearing in some of these very complex cases.

Pragmatics and Psychodiagnostics in Schools

In addition to the technical and theoretical problems of psychodiagnostics with hard of hearing children, the school psychologist faces a serious practical dilemma. How should he report diagnostic findings in a way that is both beneficial to the child, in the school's interest, and yet fully conveys the psychologist's knowledge about the child. This very difficult task centers in part around whether or not to label pathology.

Unfortunately, at the present stage in understanding human learning and how to teach, educators are rarely able to cope constructively with hard of hearing children who are aphasic, schizophrenic, autistic, severely brain damaged, etc. Hence, to label a child in this way on school reports is unlikely to help him. Instead it quite often stigmatizes him. Such labels may be grasped by teachers and administrators in order to rationalize failure to provide the best possible academic and vocational opportunity for these "diagnosed children." Rarely are pathological diagnostic terms used as the basis for constructive therapies or remedial programs because such programs are, for the most part, yet to be developed. *Psychologists, though often quick to label children in these ways, rarely if ever assume responsibility for specifying in operational terms what can be done mainly because they do not always know what to do.* Unless they can suggest a realistic therapy or a feasible referral source where it is available, labeling is not necessarily constructive.

Another example of potentially destructive labeling occurs in the reporting of psychosexual development. Psychologists, especially those who may be struggling with their own problems in this area or who are anxious to impress others with their understanding of psychodynamics, will often report possible latent homosexuality in a hard of hearing youth or else will describe guilt or anxiety over masturbation or fantasy life. As some or all of these traits are normal in adolescents, as well as being present in many adults, there is little value and great potential harm describing a child to a school staff in these terms. More importantly, when these kinds of descriptions are sent to teachers and administrators, many of whom may be unmarried middle-aged persons, the child is often perceived of as some sort of depraved sexual monster. As such he arouses all sorts of anxieties and resultant hostile rejecting behavior in his teachers.

Psychological reports should state a child's assets as well as his problems. When possible, specific constructive suggestions are of value, especially ways in which the child's strengths can be utilized more effectively.

Summary

Some general principles of psychological evaluation with hard of hearing children have been discussed, principles that attempt to adjust evaluation procedures to the role hearing loss plays in psychological functioning. Eight major areas of information required for evaluation have been delineated. Attention has also been given to the problem of differential diagnosis and some practical aspects of school psychology.

Throughout the chapter emphasis has been placed on the crucial necessity to understand the function hearing loss plays in language development and communication. A full grasp of this and its relationship to psychological evaluation procedures and the interpretation of their results is the substance of meaningful psychodiagnostics with the hard of hearing.

References

Amoss, H. 1949. Ontario School Ability Examination. Toronto: Ryerson Press.

Arthur, G. 1947. A Point Scale of Performance Tests (Rev. Form II). New York: Psychological Corp.

Brenner, L. O. and R. E. Thompson. 1967. The use of projective techniques in the personality evaluation of deaf adults. J. Rehabilit. Deaf 1:17–30.

Brown, A., S. Stein and R. Rohrer. 1947. Chicago Non-Verbal Examination. New York: Psychological Corp.

Buck, J. 1948, 1949. The H. T. P. technique, a qualitative and quantitative scoring manual. J. Clin. Psychol. 4, 1948; 5, 1949.

Doll, E. A. 1947. Vineland Social Maturity Scale: Manual of Directions. Minneapolis: Educ. Test Bur.

Goodenough, Florence. 1926. Measurement of Intelligence by Drawings. Chicago: World Book Co.

Hiskey, M. S. 1955. Nebraska Test of Learning Aptitude for Young Deaf Children. Lincoln: Univ. of Nebraska Press.

Lane, Helen S. and J. L. Schneider. 1941. A performance test for school age deaf children. Amer. Ann. Deaf 86:441.

Leiter, R. 1948. The Leiter International Performance Scale. Chicago: Stoelting.

Levine, Edna S. 1960. The Psychology of Deafness. New York: Columbia Univ. Press.

Machover, Karen. 1949. Personality Projection in the Drawing of the Human Figure. Springfield, Ill.: Charles C Thomas.

McClure, W. J. 1966. Current problems and trends in the education of the deaf. Deaf American, 8–14.

Myklebust, H. 1962. Guidance and counseling for the deaf. Amer. Ann. Deaf 107: 370–415.

Raven, J. 1948. Progressive Matrices. New York: Psychological Corp.

Rorschach, H. 1942. Psychodiagnostics. Berne, Switzerland: Hans Huber.

Rosen, A. 1967. Limitations of personality inventories for assessment of deaf children and adults as illustrated by research with the MMPI. J. Rehabilit. Deaf 1:47–52.

Rotter, J. B. and J. E. Rafferty. 1950. The Rotter Incomplete Sentence Blank. New York: The Psychological Corp.

Schneidman, E. S. 1948. Make a Picture Story (MAPS) Manual. New York: Teachers College (Bur. Publ.).

Smith, Alathena J. 1967. Psychological testing of the preschool deaf child—A challenge for changing times. Proceedings of International Conference on Oral Education of the Deaf, June 1967 1:162–181.

Stein, M. I. The Thematic Apperception Test. Cambridge: Addison-Wesley.

Sutsman, Rachel. 1931. Mental Measurement of Pre-School Children. Yonkers-on-Hudson, New York: World Book Co.

Vernon, J. 1961. The brain injured (neurologically impaired) child: A discussion of the significance of the problem, its symptoms and causes in deaf children. Amer. Ann. Deaf 106:239–250.

Vernon, M. 1967a. Characteristics associated with post rubella deaf children. Volta Rev. 69:176–185.

Vernon, M. 1967b. Rh factor and deafness: The problem its psychological, physical and educational manifestations. Exceptional Children 38:5–12.

Vernon, M. 1967c. Prematurity and deafness: The magnitude and nature of the problem among deaf children. Exceptional Children 38:289–298.

Vernon, M. 1967d. Tuberculous meningitis and deafness. J. Speech & Hearing Disorders 32:177–181.

Vernon, M. 1967e. Meningitis and Deafness. Laryngoscope 77:1856–1874.

Vernon, M. 1968. Current etiological factors in deafness. Amer. Ann. Deaf, March: 1–12.

Vernon, M. and D. W. Brown. 1964. A guide to psychological tests and testing procedures in the evaluation of deaf and hard of hearing children. J. Speech & Hearing Disorders 29:414–423.

Wechsler, D. 1955. Wechsler Adult Intelligence Scale. New York: Psychological Corp.

Wechsler, D. 1949. Wechsler Intelligence Scale for Children. New York: Psychological Corp.

Wechsler, D. 1967. Wechsler Preschool and Primary Scale of Intelligence. New York: Psychological Corp.

Chapter 15

Planning Educational Programs and Services for Hard of Hearing Children

BARRY L. GRIFFING, M.A.

A clear concept of hard of hearing children is a necessary prerequisite to the development of appropriate programs and services for them in the public schools. Educators have been faced with a variety of definitions attempting to define hard of hearing children. Definitions have been so extreme that a given child had to be considered either deaf or hearing. In other instances, definitions have been so lacking in precision that some children with minimal losses of no functional significance are included in the population of hard of hearing children. These polarized or vague definitions have not provided the educator with adequate direction for identification, program planning, and staff development purposes.

Jerome Schein suggested that a behavioral description of hard of hearing children be developed instead of continuing to use inadequate definitions (Schein, 1964). ". . . rather than define . . . we should describe it . . . we need not dissipate substantial energy in what may turn out to be a mere quibbling over terms. A description in some detail of children now in schools and classes for the hearing impaired will be very useful in itself, and it will also lead most naturally to an empirically derived classification system best fitting the facts."

E. W. Johnson (1967), a clinical audiologist, reinforces Schein's suggestion by advising that we look at the child, not the audiogram. He states, "It is how the hearing impaired child functions, not the degree of his hearing loss which should determine the type of educational system to which he is assigned."

Educational Description

The educationally hard of hearing child should be described according to the parameters that affect the educational programming. These include the following basic items:

1. Onset of hearing loss.
2. Extent and configuration of the hearing loss.
3. Auding ability (interpretative function in utilizing residual hearing).

233

4. Nature and extent of delayed speech and language development resulting from the hearing impairment.
5. Developmental growth potential in the areas of receptive and expressive communication skills.
6. Potential for learning (intelligence, emotional status, social maturity, level of educational achievement, motor development and perception level).
7. Existence of secondary handicapping conditions.

Educational Program Planning

For the most part, comprehensive educational programs designed to meet a range of needs of hard of hearing children have been nonexistent. In the public school, elementary or secondary school, administrators have had a limited number of alternatives for educational placement for hard of hearing children. In some instances administrators are forced to place hearing impaired children in regular classes with no specialized help readily available.

In a good number of states, the only alternative available for the youngster with impaired hearing whose placement in a regular class is questioned is enrollment in a state residential school, a special public school, or special day class for the deaf. Administrators of schools or classes for the deaf have been reluctant to accept such children since they recognize the needs of hard of hearing children to be significantly different from the needs of deaf children. Yet, to refuse such children admission to programs for the deaf leaves the youngsters facing possible exclusion from formal education or continued frustration in regular classes with no special help.

To be placed in a program designed for deaf children is perhaps as difficult for many hard of hearing children as being placed in a class with normal hearing children. Being in a school for the deaf, the hard of hearing child is encouraged to emulate his deaf peers and before too long many of these hard of hearing children may have assumed behavioral characteristics of deaf children. The phenomena that occurs is much like Ross and Calvert (1967) discuss in explaining what they call the self-fulfilling prophecy of deafness:

> . . . that by either labeling a person as "deaf" or responding to people with different degrees and types of loss as if they were "deaf," the outcome is behavior in the predicted direction. That is, the degree and type of residual hearing is ignored in fact if not in theory, since it would follow that "hearing" is irrelevant in a "deaf" individual. If residual hearing is ignored, it cannot be effectively utilized, and the child's behavior and achievement then become consistent with the hypothesis of "deafness." The root of the problem appears to lie in the very human propensity to describe attributes by polar opposites and to assign common characteristics to those placed at one pole or the other.

Those hard of hearing children unable to develop the behavioral attributes of deaf children to a satisfactory level are not usually accepted by deaf children as belonging and are continually frustrated.

It becomes clear that for hard of hearing children a regular class placement with no special help and placement in a school for functionally deaf children are somewhere at the extremes of a continuum of services required to serve the differential needs of hearing impaired children and youth.

Primary Considerations

There are a number of important considerations when envisioning a comprehensive educational program for educationally hard of hearing children. The major ones are discussed below.

Instructional Alternatives

A comprehensive program for hard of hearing children must have the capability of providing a variety of instructional alternatives in order that the varying needs of the children may be appropriately served. A careful differential diagnosis and thorough educational evaluation will bring to light the sometimes subtle but crucial differences among hard of hearing children. Understanding these differences leads naturally to an educational program that provides a variety of instructional alternatives.

Vital to the concept of instructional alternatives is a distinction between children being *eligible* for placement in a program for the hearing impaired and that of particular placements being *suitable* to the needs of those children. A given child may be considered as having *eligibility* by residing in the appropriate attendance area, being of legal school age, and having had some diagnosis of a hearing impairment. *Suitability,* on the other hand, must give full consideration to the particular needs and abilities of individual children and must weigh carefully the type of placement apt to be most beneficial to those children being placed. Suitability requires educators to periodically reassess the appropriateness of a given instructional placement for children. As children mature, grow, and change it is professionally proper that those responsible reconsider the context for learning and the inputs being provided.

A recent national conference on day programs for hearing impaired children and youth gave some attention to the concept of instructional alternatives. Frisina (1968) outlined eight alternatives which a diagnostician seeks when looking for placement for a given child:

Full-time educational programs for profoundly deaf children
Full-time special classes for hard of hearing children
Part-time special help for selected profoundly deaf children
Part-time special help for hard of hearing children

> Full-time educational programs for multiply handicapped deaf children
> Part-time and full-time opportunities for hard of hearing multiply handicapped children
> Special programs for mentally retarded deaf children
> Special programs for emotionally disturbed deaf children

Some states have made efforts to provide a range of instructional alternatives. In California, for example, there are the following possibilities in providing educational services to hard of hearing children (California, 1967):

1. Full-time special schools
2. Full-time special classes
3. Part-time special classes
4. Part-time regular classes
5. Full-time regular classes with supplemental aid
6. Full-time regular classes with scheduled remedial assistance
7. Special program of individual instruction
9. Full-time preschool classes
9. Special individual preschool instruction in the school or home
10. Special cooperative program between the school and the Department of Vocational Rehabilitation

Planning for a variety of instructional placement alternatives for the educationally hard of hearing must consider at least six kinds of programs:

Special Assessment Class—to provide an appropriate diagnostic and evaluative situation for preschool and kindergarten age hard of hearing children. In this setting, a skilled teacher of children with impaired hearing provides intensive auditory training, speechreading, and speech development. Continuing diagnostic and educational evaluation can be carried on in this portion of a program. This type of program can be carried out in the school or in the home.

Dunn (1968), among others, has stressed the importance of a diagnostic type of instructional setting. He states: "Different modalities for reaching the child would also be tried. Thus, since the instructional program itself becomes the diagnostic teaching, failures are program and instructor failures, not pupil failures. . . . This diagnostic procedure is viewed as the best available since it enables us to assess continuously the problem points of the instructional program against the assets of the child."

Individual Instruction—to provide school or home instruction for infant and preschool age children and to provide orientation and guidance for the parents. This area of educational service to hard of hearing children is perhaps the one in which the greatest intervention might occur. It can link the medical diagnostic effort, audiological hearing assessment effort, and the educational planning. Moreover, it provides the only avenue by which the majority of parents can be guided in the language development task that confronts many hard of hearing children.

Counseling of parents of hard of hearing children can establish good understanding of the dimensions of hearing, and knowing the implications of impaired hearing can assist parents in setting realistic goals for the child and themselves. It will assist them in creating a responsive communication environment for the child.

Integrated Program of Instruction—to provide the educationally hard of hearing the initial participation in regular classes with normal hearing peers. In this type of setting, a sufficient number of children should be assigned to a single school to warrant the full-time assignment of a special teacher for communication skills training. Such a teacher spends a portion of her time in closely coordinating the educationally hard of hearing child's participation in specific regular classes.

Integrated Program of Instruction—Resource Services—to provide those placement opportunities for the educationally hard of hearing children to be enrolled in "their" own regular classes. In this type of setting, the specialist teacher of the hard of hearing provides special communication skills training for less time than in the integrated program based with a class in a single school. The training is less uniform; that is, some children may receive daily contact with the special teacher for periods of time and not so often as others.

Remediation—Orientation—to provide intensive correction and development of communication skills for those hard of hearing children who require only short-term help. This level of service has shown to be of value to the accidental loss of hearing cases and in providing supplemental help to pupils who transfer to the program. Included in this effort is diagnosis and assessment for children beyond preschool-kindergarten ages.

Regular Classes—to provide a placement for those hard of hearing children who gain maximum benefit from educational amplification and who have developed satisfactory oral and communication skills; both receptive and expressive skills.

This placement is a crucial one for hard of hearing children and should be made only when the individual hard of hearing child may be assured of reasonable success. Key considerations are:

1. The student is able to participate at or near the grade level of the regular class in using the receptive and expressive skills—speech-reading, speech, language, reading, and writing.
2. The student's level of social and emotional maturity is at least equal to that of the students in the regular class to which the assignment is to be made.
3. The student gives attention to the job at hand and follows directions well.
4. The student is sufficiently independent, self-confident, and determined to function successfully in the regular class program.
5. The student's ability to learn, as indicated by the results of a standardized test, is average or above average.
6. The student's chronological age is within two years of the average age of the students in the regular class or classes for which part-time assignment is considered.
7. The students in the regular class will accept the hard of hearing student as a member of the class and treat him with respect and consideration.

8. The teacher of the regular class understands the problems faced by a hard of hearing student assigned to the regular class and is prepared to help the student solve his problems.
9. The enrollment of the regular class is sufficiently limited to permit the teacher to have opportunity to provide the special help needed by the hard of hearing.
10. Appropriate sound amplification is available for his use in regular classes.
11. The family of the hard of hearing student is interested in having him assigned to regular classes, will help him with his home assignments as much as it is possible and advisable to do so, and will help him to solve any problems he may encounter in adjusting to the environment of the regular class.
12. The hard of hearing student is willing and reasonably eager to accept an assignment to a regular class or to more than one such class (Hayes and Griffing, 1967).

Hard of hearing children enrolled in regular classes will probably need some preference in seating in classrooms, quality educational amplification, and will likely benefit by a "buddy" system to assist with notes and certain procedures.

All hard of hearing children placed in regular classes should have their placement evaluated periodically. These children should not be "dropped" from the concern of the special education supervisor.

Instructional Staff

There is no general agreement among professionals as to what sort of preparation is required for those teaching hard of hearing children. Some would argue that the preparation provided for teaching the deaf is the most appropriate. Others would stress the areas of training provided speech correctionists and personnel working in areas of hearing conservation. Berg and Fletcher (1967), urge that the skills of the clinical audiologist and clinical speech pathologist can make a positive contribution to the education of the hard of hearing.

Berg and Fletcher (1967) give good direction stating the best of several disciplines will be needed. They offer a title for the "new" specialist—*Educational Audiologist*. The concept implicit in this suggested title is that of utilizing the training from the audiologist, the teacher of the deaf, the speech correctionist, and others. Basically, hard of hearing children in public schools will be getting their academic training in classroom settings. It follows, then, that their teachers will need to be qualified classroom teachers prepared to teach specified grade levels or designated subject matter areas. In addition to this, these teachers are going to be required to assist in refined evaluation strategies relating to learning disabilities contingent to children's impaired hearing. They will need to have skill in creating or assisting others to create a positive learning climate for language development and for the growth of essential verbal skills.

The following areas suggest the breadth and concentration which will be required to adequately serve the needs of these children and youth:

a. Identification, assessment, and placement of children with hearing impairments including audiology, interpreting hearing loss, and hearing conservation.

b. Bases of language, hearing and speech including anatomical, physiological, neurological, psychological, and physical aspects.

c. Principles of educational amplification including aspects of physics of sound, prescriptive amplification techniques, and types of educational amplification for instructional purposes.

d. Methods of teaching language to hearing impaired including theoretical framework of language development and linguistic problems inherent in hearing impairments.

e. Communication theory, psychological processes in communications, methods of teaching both receptive and expressive modes of communication (auditory training, speech, speech-reading, reading, and writing).

f. Study of children and adolescents with emphasis on physical, motor, social, intellectual, and emotional growth and development as these relate to the problems of personal adjustment and education of hearing impaired children and their families. Guidance and counseling methods.

g. Fundamentals of elementary and/or secondary education including curriculum, instructional theory and strategy, and evaluation of instruction.

h. Evaluating instruction including current principles, procedures, techniques and instrumentation, especially those relating to language, hearing, and speech for children and youth.

i. Relationship of hearing impairment in children and youth with multiple physical or mental handicapping conditions.

j. Practice teaching in a variety of designs—individual, small group, and regular classroom.

Few of the suggested areas of competency are mutually exclusive. There should be as close a relationship among the areas as possible in order that the training effort does not become fragmented.

Supervision of Instruction

An essential element of any special education program is a leadership role that works directly with the teachers of educationally hard of hearing children. Griffing (1968) has described the role and function of supervisors of instruction for deaf and severely hard of hearing as follows.

Supervision of Instruction. Services provided for classroom teachers of the deaf and severely hard of hearing which relate to improving the instructional program. The key services in such supervision include educational objectives, planning for instruction, instructional design, instructional techniques, facilities and materials for instruction, evaluation of learning, and continuing professional growth of teachers.

Supervisor of Instruction. A professional person qualified as both a teacher of the hearing impaired and as a supervisor of instruction whose primary responsibilities are to assist classroom teachers of the deaf and severely hard of hearing improve instructional programs. This professional role is viewed as being distinctively instructional in nature, rather than being administrative.

Supervision, as viewed distinctive from administration, requires that the supervisor be trained in both the education of the hearing impaired and supervision. It is important that this person have had at least five years of practical experience in teaching hearing impaired children and youth.

Teachers of hearing impaired children list the following personal qualities as important for a supervisor with whom they would prefer to serve: dependability, efficiency, flexibility, enthusiasm, resourcefulness, sincerity, vision, and common sense. Interestingly enough, more teachers felt that common sense was the single most valuable trait (Griffing, 1968).

Educational Evaluation and Placement

Accurate and comprehensive educational evaluation is required for all hearing impaired children. In securing data, educators and other specialists should clearly differentiate among the following evaluation purposes. It makes considerable differences in the quantity and quality of data needed:

1. To determine pupil eligibility for special services.
2. To determine initial and preliminary placements, i.e., program suitability.
3. To determine suitability of present placement relative to other placement alternatives.

In general, educational assessment of educationally hard of hearing children should be given attention to the following areas: (1) general information; (2) developmental and personal history; (3) medical and visual examinations; (4) otological and audiological reports; (5) psychological examinations; (6) educational history and cumulative record; and (7) school progress notes.

The areas of concentration in the case study should include the following:

1. Family Information
2. Birth History
3. Legal Information
4. Medical History
5. Genetic Development
6. Emotional Adjustment Evaluation
7. Auditory Behavior
8. Language Behavior
9. Educational History
10. Testing Information and Results

a. Sensory
b. Intelligence
c. Language
d. Motor
e. Emotional
f. Social Maturity
g. Educational Achievement

11. Conclusions
12. Recommendations

School districts and county superintendents providing programs for the educationally hard of hearing should establish policies and procedures concerning evaluation and placement of such children. These should clarify the authority of the evaluation, composition of evaluation and placement terms, their procedures including lines of communications. A key line of communication that must be clear is the transmittal of information and the receipt of information between the team and the parents or guardians of hearing impaired children.

The administrative head of the school district or the county superintendent of schools should designate members of an evaluation and placement team. Two considerations are crucial in the formation of the evaluation and placement team: greatest possible continuity and highest level of professional competency.

Members of such teams may include the following professionals, but need not be limited thereto:

1. The Director of Special Education
2. A Credentialed School Psychologist
3. A Licensed Physician (Otologist)
4. A Certified Audiologist
5. A Supervisor of Instruction—Hard of Hearing
6. Teacher of the Hard of Hearing
7. A Building Principal (or Counselor)

Regular classroom teachers, guidance counselors, school nurses and others may be included on the Educational Evaluation and Placement Committee and can be especially important team members in determining program placement suitability.

Curriculum

A curriculum, in broad terms, may be defined as the educational experiences that children have in school. The curriculum is developed in light of the goals of education as set by society in general, the methods and tools developed by those concerned with the learning process and children, and the nature of the learners themselves.

The goals of education for educationally hard of hearing pupils are essentially the same as those for normal hearing children. The curriculum for normal hearing pupils is appropriate for educationally hard of hearing pupils insofar as it meets their educational needs. Its appropriateness is determined by the extent to which it recognizes the effects of impaired hearing on child development and learning and the extent to which proper adaptations have been provided in methods, techniques, and tools of instruction.

Because impairment of hearing restricts the normal development of both receptive and expressive language, curricular considerations for educationally hard of hearing pupils must reflect a foundation or core of language acquisition and development. This means considerable emphasis on reading, writing, speaking, listening, auditory training, and speechreading for all hearing-impaired pupils in all subject areas at all levels of learning.

There are some states in this country where the law mandates which subjects or courses of study shall be taught in the public schools. The curricular content, except for a few areas such as music, does not differ for educationally hard of hearing children. Differences do occur in the methods of instruction, rate of progress in subject matter disciplines, the relationship of content material to the language development needs of educationally hard of hearing children, the emphasis upon important communication skills, the emphasis upon consistency and continuity of instruction, and the necessity of giving considerably more attention than usual to the lives of these children before they come to formal instruction programs and during out-of-school hours. In essence, the fundamental concern with curriculum by those organizing and planning instruction for hearing impaired children is *how* educational goals are to be achieved.

By one or several of the instructional alternatives of a special educational program, the effect of hearing impairments can be minimized and to a degree overcome. Inherent in such a program is intensive and highly technical instruction in basic tool skills which are of critical importance to the educationally hard of hearing child. These are: (1) language; (2) speech-reading; (3) speech; and (4) auditory training.

How these "fit" into a curriculum plan is illustrated by the accompanying diagram (McDonald, 1964):

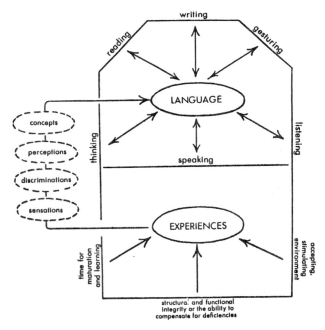

Foundation of language development. (From Eugene McDonald. *Articulation Testing and Treatment: A Sensory-Motor Approach.* Pittsburgh: Stanwix House, Inc., 1964, page 67.)

Promotion of Home-School Cooperation

Every effort should be made to coordinate school and home activities by establishing good communication between parents and teachers, psychologists, and school administrators. This is necessary so that parents may be acquainted with the educational goals established for their child; it is equally important for them to learn how to help the child accomplish these goals in purposeful activities outside the classroom. Contacts between the home and school can be accomplished in many ways—scheduled parent-teacher conferences; prearranged home visits; phone calls; and written communications sent by mail, pinned to the child's clothing, or handed to the parent by the bus driver.

As school personnel communicate with parents, they need to consider several basic facts (Hayes and Griffing, 1967):

1. Parents are by far the most important persons in the life of a hard of hearing child.
2. Parents are not prepared to accept a child who is not perfect, even though it is estimated that one child in every ten is physically, mentally, or emotionally handicapped.
3. Parents want to be good parents, although sometimes they are not.
4. Parents often have much greater capabilities than professionals attribute to them.
5. Parents need and urgently want help.
6. Parents learn chiefly through participation in the habilitation program of their child.
7. Both parents and professionals can learn much about children with handicaps by working together.

Although it is important for teachers to establish positive and strong lines of communication with parents and to help them understand and accept their child, the extent to which an individual teacher can undertake parent counseling has to be determined by the administrator or supervisor of the program. The wise teacher, when a particular problem posed by a parent is beyond his depth of training and experience, makes an appropriate referral. Psychologists and counselors may be used to advantage in the parent counseling program. Regularly scheduled and well-planned parent-teacher conferences can be a most effective medium of communication with parents.

Summary

In this chapter stress is given to the refinement of an *educational description* of the hard of hearing child being served in the public schools. With careful and accurate diagnosis and educational evaluation comes the development of *instructional alternatives* to serve their individual needs. The program placement for any given hard of hearing child must give some assurances that it is a suitable one in terms of the needs. A number of instructional alternatives were suggested that would serve preschool, elementary, and secondary age hard of hearing children.

Whether or not a group of hard of hearing children are served by a full-time special teacher, a resource teacher, or an itinerant teacher, these specialists are required to be highly trained professionals who work in cooperation with medical persons, other teachers, administrators, and other agency personnel. The training required by a teacher of the educationally hard of hearing will not follow existing categorical training programs.

Curriculum for the hard of hearing child will need major emphasis upon receptive and expressive communication and language development. How this is to be done is conditioned by the setting; that is, in which type of program the child is served. It will not be the same strategy in a regular class as it would be in a special class and it will vary according to learning level.

Coordination and program direction in promoting quality educational services for hard of hearing children will not likely occur if left to random administration. It is imperative that public school programs for hearing impaired children be provided the professional leadership of a full-time supervisor of instruction. It is with this leadership that instructional alternatives will emerge, that proper evaluations are conducted, that qualified teachers are serving the children's needs, and that creative curriculum and instruction will prevail.

References

Berg, Frederick S. 1966. Communication training for hearing impaired adults. The Volta Review 68:346.

Berg, Frederick S. and Samuel G. Fletcher. 1967. The hard of hearing child and educational audiology. Proceedings of International Conference on Oral Education for the Deaf. Washington, D.C.: Alexander G. Bell Association, Pp. 874–885.

California Administrative Code, Title 5: Education. 1960. Distributed by the California State Department of Education. Sacramento. Pp. 105–106.

California Education Code (1967 Edition). 1967. Compiled by George H. Murphy. Sacramento: California State Department of Education. Pp. 346–347.

Dunn, Lloyd M. 1968. Special education for the mildly retarded—Is much of it justifiable? Exceptional Children 35(1):5–22.

Frisina, Robert. 1968. Diagnostic evaluation and placement. National Research Conference on Deaf Programs for Hearing Impaired Children. Washington, D.C.: Alexander G. Bell Association. Pp. 113–120.

Griffing, Barry L. 1968. Supervision of instruction: guiding innovation and change in instruction for deaf children. The Volta Review 70(9):678–684.

Hayes, Gordon M. and Barry L. Griffing. 1967. A Guide to the Education of the Deaf in the Public Schools of California. California State Department of Education. Pp. 26–27.

Johnson, E. W. 1967. Let's look at the child not the audiogram. The Volta Review 69(5):306–310.

McDonald, Eugene. 1964. Articulation Testing and Treatment: A Sensory-Motor Approach. Pittsburgh: Stanwix House, Inc.

Ross, Mark and Donald R. Calvert. 1967. The semantics of deafness. The Volta Review 69(10):644–649.

Schein, Jerome D. 1964. Factors in the definition of deafness as they relate to incidence and prevalence. Proceedings of the Conference on the Collection of Statistics of Severe Hearing Impairments and Deafness in the United States. Bethesda, Maryland: U.S. Department of Health, Education, and Welfare, Public Health Service. Pp. 28–32.

Chapter 16

Utilization of Educational Media in the Education of the Acoustically Handicapped Student

ROBERT E. STEPP, Ph.D.

The array of instructional materials available today for teaching the hearing impaired is vastly different from what was used 10 years ago. Even during the short span of another decade, the variety of learning resources and the accessibility of these learning resources will make drastic changes in the teaching-learning process of handicapped children. The process will shift heavily toward the independent acquisition of knowledge by the student and will move away from dependence on his teacher for the major presentation of the lesson. In other words, learning will become more a responsibility of the student. The teacher in this type of educational environment will become the learning mentor, serving as a guide, counselor, and director of the learning experience.

Introduction

What learning experience? For years we have read and talked about individual differences and the unique needs of each child, yet we proceed to group children for teaching and administrative convenience with only slight attention to the abilities of the individual. Even teachers of the hearing impaired, with small classes of 6 to 10 children, with unlimited opportunities for individualization of instruction, concern themselves too much with establishing traditional homogeneous groupings. The teacher of the future must be capable of prescribing learning tasks needed by each student in a logical program that will insure his successful learning experience.

What learning task? Every instructional unit and each instructional increment within the unit should be broken down into learning tasks. "What must the learned do in order to accomplish the desired growth or change?" is the significant question. Is the learning within the cognitive, affective, or psychomotor domain? That is, are you dealing with facts and information, values and emotions, or skills and manipulative dexterity? Once identified, every learning task must be described or stated in behavioral terms. Under what

245

conditions is the learning to take place? What is the learner to do when he demonstrates his understanding or competency? How will you, the teacher, know when the learner has attained the goal and has achieved the level of accomplishment specified in the behavioral objective? Behavioral objectives must be stated in terms and requirements that are measurable. How else will you know to proceed to new ideas or to recycle for further study? The most difficult decision that the learning mentor (teacher) makes is to prescribe the behavioral objectives of the next learning task for each child.

The prescriptive program, then, becomes the teacher's instructional strategy. This strategy includes recognition of the teacher's role as the learning mentor, utilization of educational media as learning resources, selection of the environment in which the learning activities are to be performed, and determination of the student's learning tasks by which he progresses and develops intelligently, both emotionally and physically. Basic to the strategy will be the concept of individualized learning. Educators of the hearing impaired have neglected the importance and satisfaction of independent study for these handicapped children and at the same time have failed to provide the full advantage of the social interaction of children studying together. Too often a group of hearing impaired children sit together while one at a time, each child in turn interacts only with the teacher. Individualized learning, the prescription of learning for each child, does not mean the exclusion of group learning or interaction. Instead, it should capitalize on group learning when appropriate, along with independent study and tutorial experience when these methods are appropriate. This is why the teacher is now being called a learning mentor. This is why the learning mentor must have an instructional strategy.

The strategy includes new roles and functions for educational media. This chapter treats this topic extensively. Perhaps two points should be stressed in this introduction. Educational media are no longer "aids" to teaching; nor are they materials employed exclusively by teachers in their presentations. Educational media are now, or should be, an integral part of all learning tasks. The second point is that educational media are the communication modes of the younger generation. They feel as comfortable with a camera as we, the older generation do with a pen. The computer will be as commonplace to them as the typewriter is to us. This awareness on the part of the learning mentor of new frontiers in educational technology opens many avenues of creative expression for students and expands the instructional strategies of the teacher. Educational media, in many forms, offer the educator, for the first time in history, the opportunity to prescribe and individualize instruction to the unique needs of each child.

Where should the learning task take place? Traditionally one would quickly reply, "In the classroom, of course." For the past several decades instruction has been molded to fit into four walls of a room and student response shaped to fit an $8\frac{1}{2}$ x 11 piece of paper. Again, it is educational media and technology which are helping to break this mold. This classroom of the future may not have walls; it may be the community; it may be a complex of experience spaces or workshops. It may not be geographical or architectural in concept at all, but simply a form of intellectual exposure to informational sources from electronic distribution systems. Regardless of its shape or form, the environment within which the learner's experience is to take place should be appropriate, complementary, and supportive to the learning task. Education of the hearing impaired has been noted for its small classrooms, its complacency with only enough space for grouping the students in a semicircle, and its limited opportunities for a variety of learning activities. If the student is truly the learner, and if the processes or activities of learning have any bearing on his intellectual development, the surroundings in which he learns must be considered. The independent study carrel, a cubicle in which the student has privacy and security, is one of the emerging changes in learning spaces. Specially designed rooms for large group and small group instruction are also receiving architectural attention. An electronic environment, with each student having his own overhead projector (such as developed by Dr. Raymond Wyman, University of Massachusetts) (Wyman, 1968), or some form of electronic intercommunication between students (such as personal television monitors (Kopp, 1966) or computer consoles) (Moore, 1965), may be the breakthrough that is needed to accelerate the education of the acoustically handicapped to new levels of achievement. In the past, not enough attention has been given to the environment in which the learning is to be acquired and the assessment of its success made. The learning mentor must select the learning site as carefully as she selects the content, resources, and activities.

Repeatedly, mention has been made of the learning activities or experiences which the student must have in order to learn. Reference is being made to what the learner is doing during the process of learning. Is he sitting? listening? reciting? writing? marking X's in a workbook? drawing lines between diagrams? matching pictures? or filling in blanks? Is he answering true or false? saying yes or no? giving other one word replies? What are the learner's contributions to the learning task, how demanding are these requirements, and how involved is he? Is the learning activity appropriate to the learning situation? The writer has had numerous opportunities to visit many classrooms for the hearing impaired from coast to coast. The similarity of instruction observed is amazing. Equally amazing, if not shocking, was the observation that in a majority of visitations it was the teacher who was having the learning experience. She selected, utilized, and handled all the learning resources. She operated all equipment and dominated the situation. She often proceeded to answer her own questions and frequently used her position in the center of a semi-circle as a focal point for repeating one student's answer to another student or, as one might say, functioning as a verbal switchboard relaying messages that should have been interactions and dialogues between the students.

In order to learn, when does the task demand some of the more important thinking skills as identified by Project LIFE?

1. Making associations
2. Making comparisons and contrasts
3. Making analogies
4. Arranging in logical sequence

5. The ability to classify and make generalizations
6. Detecting absurdities
7. Matching
8. Making discriminations
9. Groupings
10. Making inferences
11. Drawing conclusions
12. Extricating the meaning of a new word from context
13. Reasoning
14. Making a judgment
15. Predicting the outcome of a given event
16. Meaningful completion of pictures or situations (Pfau, 1969)

In order to learn, when does the student become more deeply involved in the learning experience by:

1. Drawing or sketching his ideas
2. Constructing a model
3. Manipulating devices
4. Making his own transparencies
5. Taking his own slides
6. Shooting his own 8 mm film
7. Producing his own television program with videotape
8. Designing the learning materials for another child

For years educational media specialists have concentrated on perfecting the teacher's selection, utilization, and application of media toward the improvement of her performance. Although this is an essential element in becoming a professional learning mentor, not enough attention has been given to the student's design, creation, selection, utilization, and application of educational media. We must keep reminding ourselves that instructional resources are for the learner and not the teacher. What must the learner *do* in order to learn is probably the most critical judgment that the teacher must make in the formation of her instructional strategy.

Overview of Media

Before pursuing the discussion of what these changes will mean to education of the hearing impaired, perhaps an overview of educational media is in order. These instructional resources offer unique contributions toward acquisition of information, development of concepts, realistic simulation of experiences, performance of skills, and actual involvement in the learning exercise. These contributions will vary according to the functions required of the media, and the extent of involvement will be dependent on the type of learning activity to be performed by the student.

Activities Leading to Learning

Thinking, Inquiring, Discovering, Speaking, Discussing, Conferring, Editing, Listening, Aural Discriminating, Interviewing, Audio Recording, Reporting, Reading (words, symbols, pictures), Writing, Outlining,

Constructing, Creating, Designing, Drawing, Sketching, Painting, Lettering, Labeling, Diagramming, Graphing, Charting, Mapping, Visual Storyboarding, Photographing, Filming, Video-recording, Editing,

Collecting, Classifying, Displaying, Showing, Manipulating, Demonstrating, Observing, Watching, Witnessing, Experimenting, Researching, Problem Solving,

Dramatizing, Role Playing, Acting, Singing, Dancing, Pantomiming, Traveling,

Imagining, Visualizing, Organizing, Summarizing, Accounting, Computing, Testing, Judging, Evaluating

From the above list and more activities that the reader might add may be selected the experiences that will provide for the learner the type of involvement appropriate and essential for the student to learn and perform the learning task. Dr. Alan Leitman, Director, Early Childhood Education Study, Education Development Center, Newton, Massachusetts, states the importance of active learning this way:

> Production is a basic theme for learning in school. Only when a class is a workshop where tools and raw materials are organized and available can a child learn to make the decisions that he must make to build and explore the things that bring the success that builds his sense of competency. Learning to plan, organize, communicate, work with others are underpinnings that make the skills he will learn truly useful. A classroom organized as a workshop will be a hive of activity but the school and the community will be available to the student workers to gather information, ideas and questions that will be brought back to the smaller community of the classroom as food for thought, discussion and production of things, plays and books (Leitman, 1968).

When the learning task is determined first and the proper learning activities prescribed, the learning mentor has little difficulty in deciding on the appropriate instructional materials. The learning situation actually specifies the type of educational media required for each known student and his needs. Although the selection of the learning resource is secondary to the specification of the learning exercise, the prescription of the precise media is as significant as any decision made in the learning process.

Educational Media Leading to Learning

Textbooks, Supplementary Books, Reference Books, Indexes, Documents, Dictionaries, Encyclopedias, Newspapers, Magazines, Clippings, Duplicated Materials, Programmed Materials (Self-instructional),

Graphs, Charts, Diagrams, Illustrations, Maps, Globes, Flat Pictures, Posters, Cartoons, Comics,

Photographs, Slides, Filmstrips, Transparencies, Microfilms, Microcards, Stereographs, Radio, Recordings (Tape and Disc), Motion Pictures (8 mm and 16 mm film), Telecasts, Videotape Recordings, Electronic Video Recordings,

Puppets, Models, Mock-ups, Collections, Specimens, Realia, Instructional Displays,

Consumable Supplies, Construction Materials, Free and Inexpensive Sponsored Materials

Surely from this vast assortment of communicative media it is possible to convey to handicapped children any concept desired. The learning mentor may not have accessibility to the precise medium needed in each case, but one of the major tasks of the learning mentor is to constantly and consistently collect and assemble the required learning resources. Circumstances will necessitate the substitution of one medium for another, resulting in a compromise of learning results, but this situation should not continue year after year as has been the case in many schools for the hearing impaired.

Mediaware Leading to Learning

Boards of Education

Chalkboards, Flannel Boards, Peg Boards, Electric Boards, Bulletin Boards, Hook 'n Loop Boards, Magnetic Boards, Game Boards

Iconographic Devices

Slide Projectors, Motion Picture Projectors (16 mm, 8 mm), Overhead Projectors, Microprojectors, Television Receivers, Filmstrip Projectors, Opaque Projectors, Microscopes, Projection Screens (Fixed and Portable)

Auditory Devices

Record Players (16 rpm, 33⅓ rpm, 45 rpm, 78 rpm), Tape Recorders (1⅞ ips, 3¾ ips, 7½ ips, 15 ips), Tape Recorders (Cartridge, Cassette), Radios (AM, FM), Audio Card Players and Recorders, Language Laboratories, Public Address and Sound Systems

Production Devices

Lettering Sets, Dry Mount Presses, Transparency Printers and Developers, Photographic Copiers, Still Cameras (35 mm, Press), Motion Picture Cameras (16 mm, 8 mm), Videotape Recorders, Paper Cutters, Laminators, Slide Copiers, Duplicators (Spirit, Mimeograph, Electronic), Graphic Arts Tools and Instruments, Audiotape Recorders

Self-Instructional Devices

Slide Viewers, Filmstrip Viewers, Listening Posts and Stations, Cartridge Load Projectors (Still and Motion), Cassette Load Recorders, Reading Pacers and Controllers, Programmed Teaching Machines, Computer Consoles

Once the learning task is defined, the learning activity prescribed, and the educational media specified, the selection of the equipment is automatic. The hardware (equipment) must match the software (material) which has already been determined. So often this process has been mistakenly reversed. Equipment is purchased, made available, and the teacher is instructed to "see what you can do with this." Equipment is the last item to be selected in planning the instructional strategy.

The term "Mediaware" in the preceding title was coined by Dr. Raymond Wyman, Director, Northeast Regional Media Center for the Deaf, University of Massachusetts, and is most descriptive for the audiovisual hardware which can be distinctly associated with educational media (Wyman, 1969). The term identifies the equipment that a school must possess if a media program is to be an integral part of the learning process and essential to the implementation of the curriculum.

Another factor in determining the role that media play in the learning process is the content itself. Is the instructional idea a verbal one? Can the thought be developed by a form of discourse? If so, what learning activities should be prescribed? What media should be used? Perhaps the following might assist the learner:

Verbal Experiences

Activities	*Media*	
Speaking	Lectures	Pamphlets
Listening	Discussions	Correspondence Courses
Writing	Books	Programmed Instruction
Reading	Periodicals	Records
Recording	Manuals	Tape Recordings

Not all ideas are verbal in concept. If the instructional idea is a visual one, let's not talk about it; let's show the student what is meant. For visual ideas, these learning activities and materials might be utilized to assist the learner.

Visual Experiences

Activities	*Media*	
Diagramming	Charts	Bulletin Boards
Sketching	Graphs	Flannel Boards
Animating	Maps	Films (8 mm, 16 mm)
Photographing	Transparencies	Television
Viewing	Photographs	Video Recordings
Recording	Slides	Visitations
	Filmstrips	

There is no reason to read about a subject or observe situations depicting it if the best learning results could be achieved through actual participation. In these instances, maybe these experiences are the ones required of the learner.

Manipulative Experiences

Activities		*Media*	
Handling			
Practicing		Models	Realia
Demonstrating		Mock-ups	Demonstrations
Constructing		Specimens	Construction Tools
Assembling			and Materials
Arranging			
Classifying			

If your strategy is to simulate a real experience, you must first analyze the learning problem, identify the learning tasks, plan the sequence of events, select the communicative media, construct the environment or facilities, and determine the degree of involvement expected of the learner. The degree of involvement is dependent on the types of responses that are to be elicited from the student. The realism of the simulation, the type of mediated instruction, and the form of assessment mode all affect the sophistication of the plan.

Simulation study may be used because it:

1. Puts the child in a learning situation which actually is not available to him because of distance or time.
2. Gives the child, in independent study, the illusion of one-to-one interaction with a tutor.
3. Lets the student see the inside workings of objects and situations that simply are not observable naturally because of size, intervening structure, or other restrictions.
4. Gives the opportunity for a student to imagine himself temporarily in the situation of another person . . . subject to stimuli, pressures, and limitations to which he, as himself, is not accustomed.
5. Gives the opportunity for vicarious learning experience which would be too dangerous, too expensive or inappropriate because of age or sex in actuality.
6. Frees the acoustically handicapped student to proceed with his education without waiting on an adult for his lesson.

Simulated experiences often involve simultaneously the three categories just described: verbal, visual, and manipulative. But simulated experiences function at a higher order of perception because of the design of the educational media being employed and the intent of the instruction. Forms of educational media which offer unlimited opportunities for simulation might be classified as follows:

Simulated Experiences

Verbalizing	8 mm films in cartridges (silent and sound)
Interacting	Television programs and systems
Conversing	Magnetic and electronic video recordings
Visualizing	Programmed learning materials
Observing	(teaching machines)
Witnessing	Multi-media units or kits
Manipulating	Audio recordings
Dramatizing	Dial-access auditory training systems
Performing	Computer systems
	Electronic systems
	Mediated instructional programs

No educational media programs or simulation studies can completely replace real life experiences. Every possible opportunity should be provided for the handicapped child to experience, at first hand, situations which will give long lasting impressions of the world and its people. Sometimes, however, the vicarious experience is more educational because of its direct focus on the specific objective. On other occasions, educational media serves a unique function by preparing the student for his real experience or field trip and media can be equally effective when utilized for follow-up activities of these experiences. Again it is the responsibility of the learning mentor to know where the media experience is more valuable than the real life experience and when the reverse is true.

Multi-Media Approach

Since it is very difficult to separate learning into the above identified discrete activities, a varied approach may be necessary. Current terminology would express this idea as being a multi-media approach. This means the selection and utilization of any and all resources required to provide for the learner an understanding of a specific instructional idea. The implication is that the resources are selected to benefit the learner, not to assist the teacher. The combination of these resources into a multi-media unit may be the most effective means of teaching the acoustically handicapped.

Mr. Robert J. Schmitt, formerly Supervisor, County-Wide Program for the Deaf, Houston Independent School District, Houston, Texas, summarized the advantages of this correlated use of media as follows.

The multi-media approach is an attempt:

1. To increase the use and effectiveness of coordinated visual stimuli in the classroom,
2. To provide more appropriate vocabulary and language in the same amount of time with the invaluable aid of the overhead projector,

3. To use various new media to provide ample, interesting repetitions which are necessary for learning,
4. To supply opportunities which permit the deaf child to practice and then use the language.

Thus, the multi-media approach in the classroom for the deaf is an attempt to teach more language to children in a shorter period of time and thereby provide them with more education (Schmitt, 1966).

The multi-media approach provides for the learner multiple opportunities to comprehend the concept being studied. It is the selection, coordination, sequence, integration, and combination of the educational media into an instructional plan that benefits the learner. As the learning mentor analyzes the instructional situation, she must ask herself several questions.

For the student's learning, is it necessary to:

1. Display materials for prolonged study?
2. Include auditory experiences?
3. Picture an object or scene for detailed study?
4. Visualize a concept or situation for observation?
5. Outline or give continuity to a variety of situations?
6. Stimulate exercises and experiences?
7. Participate in the actual performance or experience?
8. Allow the student to be creative in his response?
9. Select a specific location where the learning is to take place?

Your choice of the educational media in answer to the above questions depends on your instructional objectives and the individual needs and capabilities of your students. The choice of the mediaware is based solely on the plan of the program and the materials being used. For example you might select:

For Display: Chalkboard, bulletin board, flannel board, posters, hook and loop board exhibits.
For Audition: Speech, audio recordings (reels, cassettes, cards, discs), auditory training units.
For Symbology: Charts, graphs, maps, diagrams, cartoons, comics.
For Iconography: Slides, filmstrips, pictures, study prints, illustrations.
For Observation: Films (16 mm and 8 mm), television, videotape recordings, electronic video recordings.
For Coordination: Overhead transparencies, texts, manuals, workbooks.
For Simulation: Models, mock-ups, programmed learning materials, computer assisted instruction.
For Application: Demonstrations, performance, field trips, realia.
For Creation: Multi-media student productions and response modes.
For Environment: Classroom, laboratory library, study carrel, home, community.

Learning resources are available to enable a teacher to structure a learning experience in whatever mode of reception would be the most effective for the learner to gain understanding. One problem is that these resources are not accessible in sufficient abundance. Although the technology does exist and a great variety of materials is on the market, schools for the deaf have not provided these resources for teachers and students. Dr. John A. Gough and Dr. Gilbert Delgado writing about "Some Problems in Audio-Visual Education for the Deaf" stated:

> There is a certain irony in the fact that although most educators of the deaf are aware of the important role of vision in the education of children, audiovisual instruction in most programs for the deaf is relatively insignificant. The eyes are the expressways in most learning processes of the deaf. Other senses play a part, but the main non-stop route is sight. . . .
>
> The consequent failure to utilize educational tools that could, with some modification, have significant impact on the deaf person's development accentuates the comparatively regressive situation in which the deaf find themselves in modern society (Delgado and Gough, 1965).

It can be assumed, at the present writing, that teachers will have only limited access to all these desirable resources. This being the case, every teacher should organize his own instructional system utilizing what resources are available. If you must be restricted in your selection, you should at least have a means of handling each media function. Perhaps you don't have access to one each of these projectors (slide projector, filmstrip projector, opaque projector, and overhead projector), but you should arrange for at least one means of projecting still pictures for detailed study. What facilities do you have for auditory training? Maybe you don't have a language master recorder, a tape recorder, a record player, and an amplifying unit, but provision should be made for at least one device which will permit the establishment of an auditory training program. How do you plan to show motion? Is your display area large enough and in the proper location to be an instructional *billboard* rather than decorative space? If the real experience is not possible, how do you plan to simulate it? How do you intend for the students to indicate their understanding? Are you allowing them to be creative in their responses? What freedom of expression are you giving them? Most important of all, which medium are you employing as your unifying force, the tying link that holds the various media into a cohesive unit? The multi-media unit must be carefully planned and programmed to be effective.

Some of these resources offer greater teaching potential than others. It is probably dangerous to single out any particular type of media for special mention because it is impossible in this chapter to identify all of the resources currently being successfully used in teaching the hearing impaired. Nevertheless a few types do deserve special attention.

Of all the newer media devices now being used, probably the one projector that offers the greatest assistance to the teacher and, thereby, the learner is the overhead projector. Its location at the front of the class, its efficient light source which does not require room darkening for projection, its flexibility of presentation make the overhead projector an ideal tool for teaching the acoustically handicapped person. Of significance is the fact that the students can speechread their teacher without interruption, which was not the case when the teacher turned to write on the chalkboard. Some of the advantages of this projector are stated by Alice A. Kent, Supervisor, East Cleveland Classes for Hearing Impaired Children, East Cleveland, Ohio:

> In any given classroom some children will excel in lipreading, some in reading, others may have better ability to understand language through their hearing and still others will seem to have more ability to derive meaning from words and the syntax of words. Our initial efforts toward using the overhead projector as an effective teaching tool were directed toward devising a technique that would help overcome these individual differences so as to enable teachers to instruct whole classes more effectively.
>
> We wanted a technique that would serve to improve all of the receptive language arts skills for children who were ready to embark on an expansion of knowledge in different learning areas such as social studies, science, mathematics, and literature.
>
> We wanted a technique that would improve the skills involved in expressive communication—writing good language, spelling and speech.
>
> We wanted a technique that would not penalize a child for errors in comprehension but would rather give each an opportunity to experience success according to his own ability.
>
> And finally we wanted a technique that could provide practice for an entire class at one time, but at the same time allow each child to produce according to his own degree of ability (Kent, 1966).

A second type of media that deserves special mention is motion pictures. The film medium is also undergoing a change. Not only have filmed materials improved in content and photographic quality, they have also reached a new dimension. The home-movie size (8 mm) film has invaded the classroom. Both silent and sound 8 mm films are being produced for use in the classroom for group teaching and in the study carrel for independent learning. These films which are usually film loops (the beginning and end are spliced together) and may be loaded in cartridges, are short, sequential visual lessons, each on one instructional idea. More than 10,000 titles of 8 mm films are currently on the market. Eight millimeter films, designed specifically to assist in the instruction of speechreading, have been produced at the Midwest Regional Media Center for the Deaf, University of Nebraska, for distribution by Media Services and Captioned Films. The time is coming when the student will be able to select films for independent study as readily as he now selects books. Mrs. Joan Forsdale describes the potential of this medium in her statement:

> As Marshall McLuhan, Director of the Center for Culture and Technology at the University of Toronto, has recently been making familiar to an ever widening audience, media may profitably be viewed as extensions of our senses. They give us more power over our environment, as do the more commonsense supplementers, such as binoculars or radio or headlights for everyone, and as do a hearing device, a leg brace, or eyeglasses for the handicapped. By, in their own way, increasing the amount of information available to us, the media enable us to exploit more fully the senses which work well for us, and help us to make the most of the senses whose strength is limited. Film, then clearly has a place among the devices that we use to extend our control over our environment. Eight millimeter makes it possible for any child

to be on his own in learning from the moving images; it enables the handicapped child to do the same thing. Both the sameness and the independence are important to him. It puts him on his own in an area where he has never been able to be independent before. And on his own is where he needs and wants to be (Forsdale, 1966).

Another form of the newer media which also "puts the learner on his own" is programmed learning. Programmed instructional materials may be used with or without teaching machines. When teaching machines are used, the program takes the form of a printed scroll, a sequence of pages, microfilm, filmstrips, slides, magnetic tape, or cards. The most sophisticated example is computer-assisted instruction. Without a machine, the programs generally are printed in book (or booklet) style even though the format is completely different from regular books. The content or lesson of the program is broken down into small learning increments so that the student may literally teach himself. In brief, the procedure is as follows, wrote Dr. Adrian Sanford, President, Educational Development Corporation:

> As the learner proceeds through the material, he exposes a trial situation to himself. He then makes his choice based on his knowledge or on sheer guess. He then confirms for himself the degree of accuracy of his choice. At this time he discovers an error on his part and further discovers what his incorrect choice would logically lead to. Moreover, he learns privately. And this becomes important in easing his tension that may have developed from habitual error-making and external correction. He repeats this procedure over material that becomes increasingly challenging, or covers a wider scope or both (Sanford, 1966).

The very design and purpose of programmed learning make it uniquely suitable for teaching the acoustically handicapped. One word of caution is in order. For programmed learning to make its greatest contribution to the education of the deaf, special programs will have to be prepared. Project LIFE, Language Improvement to Facilitate Education of the Hearing Impaired, sponsored by Media Services and Captioned Films, is one example of such development. Dr. Glenn S. Pfau, Director, stated these basic purposes:

> After a comprehensive survey of the profession of deaf education in 1963, it was concluded that a project should be initiated to develop supplementary language instructional facilities and methods. It was decided that these should attempt to (a) increase significantly the language learning rate of primary and intermediate-aged prelingually deaf children and (b) upgrade the language skills of the postlingually deaf and severely hard of hearing. Since expressive language is contingent upon a well developed and functional receptive language, it was reasoned that the latter should first be the Project's primary concern (Pfau, 1969).

These study materials have been basically produced as programmed filmstrips although a limited number of programmed auditory tapes and films have been developed. These are supplemented by specially prepared illustrated children's story booklets, concept-oriented picture dictionaries, and workbooks. Each program is very complete and comprehensive in order for the student to proceed on his own under the supervision of his teacher.

Mr. Robert K. Lennan, Teacher, California School for the Deaf, River-side, reports the successful use of programmed instructional materials for emo-tionally disturbed deaf boys. He writes:

> The programmed format was selected as the medium of instructional materials for several reasons:
> 1. Because of the widely divergent educational backgrounds of the children a high degree of individualized instruction was necessary. Programmed materials provided an independent activity which would reinforce the con-cepts taught by the teacher and permit the children to work at their own pace. They also served a diagnostic function in indicating areas where additional instruction was needed.
> 2. Programmed materials provided the child with the many repetitions neces-sary for the development of language concepts through a series of small, logically arranged visual stimuli. In this way the visual input channel was effectively employed to provide a partial substitution for the auditory channel through which language development takes place in a hearing child.
> 3. These materials were consistent with the use of behavior modification techniques being used since they provided immediate knowledge of results and positive reinforcement for correct responses (Lennan, 1969).

He concluded his report as follows:

> The response of the children to these materials was most gratifying. Unable to sit at their desks for more than a few minutes at a time when they first entered the program they were now working diligently for periods of as long as thirty minutes in activities which they found both interesting and rewarding. The effectiveness of these materials in accomplishing the purpose for which they had been designed was shown by the performance of our students during the periodic evaluations by their teachers.
>
> The development of programmed materials requires a great deal of time and work but the end result is well worth the effort involved not only in terms of its effectiveness as a teaching tool but also in terms of the changes it brings about in the teacher's effectiveness in planning and her perception of her role in carrying out her instructional program (Lennan, 1969).

One of the newer forms of educational technology needs special mention in this section. Reference is being made to the computer.

> Although computer-assisted instruction bears some resemblance to pro-grammed instruction, one feature sets it apart in a significant manner: CAI individualizes—rather than merely "personalizes"—instruction. This means that course materials can be presented to the student in response to his individual progress rather than in an inflexible predetermined sequence (Rathe, 1969).

Mr. Gustave H. Rathe, Jr., Director of Education, Data Processing Division, IBM, made this distinction in a paper he prepared for the 1969 Lincoln Symposium. There are 11 ways in which a student may interact with a com-puter:

1. Drill	7. Simulation
2. Practice	8. Fact finding
3. Problem review	9. Computation
4. Diagnosis and preparation	10. Logical problem solving
5. Tutorial	11. Exploration
6. Gaming	

Of interest to educators of the acoustically handicapped is the fact that the computer does not discriminate against students because of their handicaps. Mr. Rathe describes the following scene:

> As I strolled around this novel classroom, I was struck by the fact that no two lessons flashing on and off the screens were at exactly the same point. The computer to which the terminals were connected had picked up where each pupil left off the lesson before, and was now proceeding at individualized paces. On one screen a picture of a boy climbing a tree was displayed with the request that the student underline, with a light pen, the sentence of four shown that best suited the picture. At another terminal a girl was carrying on a "dialogue" with the computer by pecking out on the typewriter answers to questions that appeared on the screen. And at still another station, a boy was using his light pen to match words with picture images.

> The above scene was part of an experimental computer-assisted instruction (CAI) English course conducted at an elementary school in California. The youngsters in this case were third graders with no hearing disabilities. But the participants in the class could just as well have been deaf students; and if they were, the description of the scene would have been exactly the same.

> Computer-assisted instruction has extraordinary potential for deaf students. Perhaps the primary advantage of CAI in teaching the deaf is that it does not discriminate between the deaf and the non-deaf. As a result, it offers the potential for deaf students to attend regular schools along with youngsters who possess normal hearing; it eliminates the need for special training on the part of teachers who will work with these students; and it opens up the utilization of a greater number of teachers and teaching approaches to bring deaf students up to the level of others in their age group (Rathe, 1969).

In the future the computer, along with other new forms of electronic equipment will join the present array of educational media and forms of educational technology to offer greater opportunities to the learner through the multi-media approach.

Teacher Relationship to Media

The multi-media approach, with its dependence on educational media as the basic learning resources, requires new instructional methods and procedures, as well as different and varied roles for the teacher. There are three distinct relationships that exist between teachers and media in the teaching-learning process. As previously stated, every teacher should have a select set of resources to assist her in communicating with students. Another way to express the same idea is to say that every teacher should have available for her use the learning resources that will enable her to conduct a carefully planned program of instruction—or that will enable her to develop a system of instruction for the learner. Media have a unique role to play in planning such programs of instruction. The teacher has her choice of not employing media at all, using the media herself, or allowing the media to extend her teaching. The three relationships simply stated are: teacher without media; teacher with media; and teacher within media.

Teacher Without Media

This is an instructional situation in which verbal discourse (lecture, conversation, discussion, questioning, writing) are considered to be adequate and effective means by which the student learns the topic at hand. (Note: Adequacy of any instructional method or mode of communication should never be judged by the assistance that it provides the teacher—only as to its effectiveness in benefiting the learner). Although we live in a highly verbal society and our educational program is dominantly an oral one, situations in which the teacher does not employ media are very rare. This statement is based on a broad definition of the word *media*. When a teacher has selected a textbook for the course or subject that she is teaching, she is using media. When she turns and writes on the chalkboard, she is using media. When she refers to a specimen or the real object, she is using media. In the introduction to the final report of the 1966 Lincoln Symposium, the writer of this chapter expressed the thought this way:

> It is difficult to envision a teacher of the deaf working without media. The lecture, a discussion or conversation with the student receiving the message by speechreading, fingerspelling, or both, would qualify as a teaching act fitting this category. If the teacher's voice is amplified and the students are wearing headsets, the teaching act is now employing media. If the teacher is using objects, flash cards, or any of the many and varied types of learning resources, media are being utilized. There are times, of course, in the development of language skills when the student's ability to comprehend spoken discourse must be verified. The true test of his language competency is communicating with other people in a highly visual world but one which is predominantly orally structured. Communicating in the classroom without the use of media, although essential to the normal development of the child, often is more of a testing function than a teaching function (Stepp, 1966).

Teacher With Media

It is evident that the most common relationship of the teacher to media is this second category. Teachers are becoming more adept at using the great array of learning resources that technology has provided. Reference has been made already to the various display boards (chalkboards, flannel board, bulletin board, etc.) and to the various materials that require some form of projection (slide projector, filmstrip projector, opaque projector, overhead projector, motion picture projector, etc.). One of these devices, the overhead projector, is rapidly becoming the right arm of the teaching profession. As mentioned earlier many schools have already reached a goal of one overhead projector and screen in every classroom. Teachers, who are fortunate enough to have their own overhead projector, have reached such a point of dependence on this teaching tool that they now wonder how they ever taught without one. This is truly an example of teacher with media. The teacher's use of study prints, slides, filmstrips, films, tape recordings, to name a few, in her presentation of subject matter is also an example of the teacher with media.

The utilization of media as a form of presentation has been probably the most common function of learning resources and also the role in which the teacher has felt most comfortable.

Teacher Within Media

The newest relationship, and one which holds considerable promise in education of the acoustically handicapped is media functioning as a teacher. One familiar example is educational television. Momentarily, or at least for the duration of an education program, the television teacher takes over the instruction of the student. This does not mean that the classroom teacher is abdicating her role as the student's teacher. It only indicates that the classroom teacher has called on a resource person, the television teacher, to teach for her. Programmed learning is another example of the teacher within media. The author of the programmed text, manual, or program has designed his materials of instruction in such a manner that the student may proceed to teach himself. A good unit of instruction, following the principles of programmed learning, will permit the learner to proceed at his own pace, verify the correctness of his response as he proceeds, and gain a level of understanding about the topic as an independent learner. The author of programmed learning materials is the teacher within the media. Motion picture film, particularly the new 8 mm films in cartridges, offers many opportunities for the teacher to be within the media. The film productions of Dr. Frank Withrow (Withrow, 1966–67) formerly Director of Research and Clinical Services at the Illinois School for the Deaf, and similar work (Stepp, 1965) of the writer have employed this technique in providing speechreading practice and instruction to young deaf children.

Another recent development which demonstrates the concept of the teacher within media is the use of a computer as a teaching machine. An excellent example of this application is the talking typewriter invented by Dr. Omar K. Moore, Social Psychologist, University of Pittsburgh. The interconnection of the typewriter with a computer enables the child to carry on a dialogue with the computer. By pressing the keys the child responds to the computer program. Although this system is based primarily on an auditory stimulus, the program does have visual capabilities. Dr. Moore discussed the application of this instructional system with deaf students in his paper which he prepared for the 1965 Lincoln Symposium (1965). Extensive research on the use of the computer as an instructional device is being conducted by Dr. Patrick Suppes at Brentwood School, East Palo Alto, California, and the mathematics program prepared under his direction is being tested with the acoustically handicapped at the Kendall School for the Deaf, Washington, D.C. One hundred and seven pupils ranging in age from 9 to 21 years are using CAI on a daily basis at this school. The students work at teletypes that are connected by leased telephone lines to the computer in California. One overwhelming reaction is the high motivation of the students to work at the teletype machines. Behrens, Alprin, and Clack report the evidence of this motivation from observing the students and teachers working with the system. The highlights are:

> No child refuses to come for CAI. The learner nearly always shows disappointment and anger when for some reason they cannot use the teletypes on a given day. Some children actually use their recess time to work on the teletypes.
>
> The concentration of students is almost total as they are working through a lesson. Their faces reflect this concentration as well as their frustration and self-disgust at mistakes and triumph at success. . . .
>
> High motivation also results in an amazing ability to stick with problems. Several children have continued to work hard on lessons even though they were getting *NO* problems correct. . . .
>
> Another valuable reaction is increased maturity towards learning, especially towards tests and errors. Children may do poorly on a pre-test. They bring the test to their teacher, demanding to be taught this new concept. Often they are angry with the teacher for not teaching it in the first place. . . .
>
> The teacher reactions have also been very positive. They feel their children learn new concepts more easily in class because they know they will have the same problems on the computer. Teachers have stated that they are teaching more and faster in order to stay ahead of the computer. . . .
>
> Teachers have had to adjust to the system in the above ways. But in other ways they are making the system work for them. For example, they use the pre-tests diagnostically to determine exactly the strengths and weaknesses in a given child. They can measure progress more exactly and serve individual needs more efficiently. . . .
>
> Finally, students faced with story problems on the machine seem to be able to handle language which defeats them entirely in the classroom. In general, the children accept more frustration and "NO" responses from the teletypes than they can from their teachers (Behrens et al., 1969).

Allowing educational media and the accompanying educational technology to become an additional teacher could be one of the major breakthroughs in the education of the acoustically handicapped. More research is needed in how to incorporate the teacher within the medium successfully.

Student Relationship to Media

If the teacher has three possible relationships with media, does the student also have these same relationships? The answer is, "*Yes, he does.*" If his teacher uses media (teacher with media or teacher within media), of course the student has a receptive involvement with media. The question here is "What opportunities does the student have to use media as one of his means of expression?"

Student Without Media

As before, this relationship refers to verbal feedback (recitation, discussion, answering, questioning, writing) or situations in which no forms of media are utilized. These procedures reward, or at least give the advantage to, the learner who has a high order of verbal ability. If education is to provide an equal opportunity to all and if the educational process is to discover the potential of each individual learner, then various modes of communication should be employed and new units of measurement explored, especially for the hearing impaired.

Student With Media

One area that holds considerable promise in the learning interchange between student and teacher is the provision to the student of the entire array of learning resources now used by the teacher. If the teacher believes that these materials are essential to her communication with the student, why aren't similar materials necessary for the student to use in communicating with his teachers and fellow students? What level of response can a low-verbal ability student achieve when given the opportunity to express himself through non-verbal materials? In the past the chalkboard, flannel board, and bulletin board have been common tools for both the teacher and student. Now student-designed and -produced transparencies for projection on the overhead projector are becoming common. Teachers who are using this method of visual reporting have indicated that students who were previously silent and inattentive have become interested and responsive. Mounting pictures for sequential storytelling, narrating films, explaining filmstrips, and designing charts or graphs are all examples of what a student might do to communicate with others. The hearing impaired child, particularly, needs several channels of communication. Media can serve this function and interestingly enough language development can be accelerated through this process (Laird, 1969).

Student Within Media

As a matter of fact, media can serve this third function so realistically that it is now possible for media to represent the student and to "speak" for him. Recording a report on audio magnetic tape for playback in class is an example of the student within media. At the time of his actual report, the recording makes the presentation. The videotape recording may serve this same purpose in visual form and may be more practical for the acoustically handicapped student. A series of 35 mm slides taken by the student and selected for a visual report is another possibility. Recently 8 mm motion picture cameras have become so simple to operate that even a child can create his own movies. Storyboarding, planning the visual sequences, and writing the script for an 8 mm film or a videotape recording, may be one of the best possible situations for language development. When the students also shoot and edit the production, additional comprehension results. An interesting application of the use of the videotape recording in language instruction was described by Mr. Rod Laird, Assistant Superintendent, Wyoming School for the Deaf, at the 1969 Summer Educational Media Institute at the University of Nebraska.

Mr. Laird selects a brief story unfamiliar to his students. He directs the students through a simple dramatization of the story without their having read it, and records the action by videotape. Then he superimposes the written story on the tape as captioning. The students read the story for the first time from the videotape, while their own dramatization makes the meaning of words and phrases perfectly clear. They are subsequently given a purely verbal, written test for comprehension. Mr. Laird reports extremely gratifying improvement in comprehension, with high motivation as an added benefit (Laird, 1969).

Experimentation is underway to study what content and sequences a handicapped child might include in his own film. What will the deaf child attempt to communicate when he is freed from his limited verbal vocabulary. Will this creative experience stimulate him to be more vocal and give him cause for developing a more expressive verbal language? Placing one's self within the media and communicating one's thoughts through representative materials is an educational experience that every student should have. For the hearing impaired student, this is a must.

Systems Approach

The principles of programmed learning form a logical basis for all teaching and learning. Sequential instruction, involvement of the learner, confirmation of his response, and reinforcement of the learning exercise are all features that are associated with good teaching. Such a planned course of instruction leads logically into a systems approach.

The blending of teacher or student presentations with simulation studies; the development of teacher presentation coordinated with student independent study; the implementation of individually prescribed instruction; and the structuring of tutorial, drill, and dialogue programs into one learning continuum may be the beginning of the application of the systems approach to the education of the acoustically handicapped student. The interaction of all influences (educators—family, classroom—home, school—community) with the capabilities of educational technology may provide the basis for a new consortium of instructional strategies. Educating children with auditory disorders is already a "system," but in most instances it has not benefited from the analysis and synthesis that are associated with the systems approach. Dr. Robert Heinich defines the systems approach to education as being an operational system which "synthesizes and inter-relates the components of a process within a conceptual framework insuring continuous, orderly, and effective progress toward a stated goal" (Heinrich, 1966). He further identifies three steps in the process.

> First, we have to go through a systems analysis, taking the system apart. Second, we resynthesize the system putting it back together in a more meaningful way. Third, a process called anasynthesis, which is the interaction between synthesis and analysis. Now, all of this occurs through a certain conceptual framework (Heinrich, 1966).

A systems approach deals with the management of instructional problems and studies where mediated teachers (teachers within media) and classroom teachers complement and cooperate with each other. Although a well-planned and designed instructional system will function without a teacher's constant supervision, its success with each student is highly dependent on the ability of the learning mentor to know when to employ mediated instruction and when to utilize her own talents as the teacher. If the learning objectives can be specified and the learning tasks identified, an instructional system can be devised to assist the learner in achieving the stated objectives. Although educators of the hearing impaired have repeatedly stated and restated educational objectives over the years, they have failed to break down the learning activities into finite student performance tasks which could be analyzed as requiring either the human instructional component or the mediated technological component.

Educators of the hard of hearing have attempted a modified systems approach in conducting an auditory program. For example, it has become standard practice to employ sound amplification while teaching the hearing impaired. This procedure may vary from individual hearing aids, to wire connected sound systems, to loop antennae transmission systems. Selected lessons are given, confirmation supplied, and reinforcement provided. Educators of the hearing impaired are in constant search for new and improved auditory training equipment. When do we design auditory systems that will provide this training as independent study? The electronic equipment and technology are already available. Dr. Robert Frisina, Vice President, National Technical Institute for the Deaf, closed an address with these comments:

> In conclusion, it should be emphasized that in order for maximal educational benefits to accrue in each child, there must be assumed among other things an understanding of the auditory system of the deaf individual, an awareness of available auditory devices at a given point in time and knowledge of what is optimum for the individual's residual auditory potential, a critical analysis of the reason for pursuing each task included in the total educational program for each child, thereby determining the rationale for employing the auditory channel and quantification of results of different approaches in order to provide new directions in the use of media in the education of deaf children (Frisina, 1966).

It is interesting that, although the deaf student learns through his eyes, no visual training program has yet been devised that begins to compare with the auditory training program. Dr. Harriet Kopp, Principal, Detroit Day School for the Deaf, reflects this thought when she said,

None of us, hearing or deaf, uses the visual system to its maxium potential. The deaf *must* make more efficient use of their prime receptor. We have accumulated sufficient research data now to enable us to construct individualized programmed remedial systems using single concept films and controlled speed exposures and responses. At the Detroit Day School for the Deaf we have constructed visual materials for tachistoscopic projection as integral parts of the language and reading curriculums.

These materials are designed to develop perceptual skills, to improve the speed and accuracy of interpreting and patterning of sensory stimuli and to develop such cognitive skills and abilities as use of contextual clues, rapid organization of information, rapid classification of concepts and regrouping of concepts (Kopp, 1966).

The recent acceptance of the overhead projector as a basic teaching tool and the provision of these projectors to schools for the deaf by Media Services and Captioned Films, U.S. Office of Education, have enabled teachers to develop a form of visual reinforcement heretofore impossible to achieve. The overhead projector, along with filmstrip projector, slide projector, motion picture projector (16 mm and 8 mm), and television set, now permits visual reinforcement nearly equal to the already established auditory program. Can we provide both auditory and visual saturation?

To follow this line of thinking, how can we provide an instructional system which will compensate the acoustically handicapped child for the incidental learning that he misses because of his hearing impairment? Dr. William J. McClure, President, Florida State School for the Deaf and Blind, clearly identified this problem when he said,

> Some time ago several of us were discussing educational problems in our teachers lounge. One of our deaf teachers thought deaf children are now even more retarded in comparison with hearing children than they were when she was growing up. She felt this was so because hearing children are now exposed to the radio and particularly to television during almost all of their waking hours. They pick up a great deal of language and incidental information from these sources which are not available to the deaf child. Some years ago hearing children had only the stimulation of actual conversation and communication with the adults who are around them. Their experiences have been broadened while those of the deaf child have remained static. It is possible that the deaf child receives even less stimulation at home than formerly because his parents and siblings may be so engrossed in TV or the radio they do not take the time to communicate with the one who is deaf (McClure, 1966).

Being unable to hear the incidental remarks of people, brief comments by parents and teachers, and the countless verbal reinforcements in play activities is a severe experience handicap to the hearing impaired child. How do you devise a plan which will structure incidental learning? Media can assist in achieving this objective through their capability of replicating reality and their formation into a planned systems approach.

The best known application of the systems approach to learning is the work of Dr. S. N. Postlethwait, Professor of Biological Science at Purdue University. Dr. Postlethwait has developed what he calls the "Audio Tutorial System" or "An Integrated Experience Approach to Learning." He writes,

If one asks oneself "what kind of course would I structure if I had only one student?," it seems unlikely that the answer would be: a lecture on Monday, Wednesday and Friday, a lab on Wednesday afternoon and a recitation on Friday afternoon. Much more likely the one student and the instructor would arrange a convenient time to meet, the instructor would assemble those items which he hoped would help the student understand the subject and the two would sit among those items while the instructor tutored the student through a sequence of learning activities. This truly would be individualized instruction. Immediately one recognizes that this idealized arrangement is impractical in today's school for several reasons including the availability of capable instructors. However, one also recognizes that, even though one has a thousand students, each student is an individual and that if "one tutor one student" is best then we should try to provide this idealized situation for all students. While it is impractical on a literal basis, it is possible to simulate this arrangement through the use of appropriate media (Postlethwait, 1969).

Dr. Postlethwait mediated his lecture sessions and all laboratory sessions. The student was free to proceed at his own learning rate and pace. This system has been very successful; students are enthusiastic; grades have improved; and the costs are somewhat less than conventional methods. He makes a very interesting point about the instructional materials in such a plan.

> Probably the most critical point for utilization of media in individualizing instruction is the use of imagnation. For many years the image of the teacher has been "a means for the transfer of information." In many cases, media have been used as just another vehicle to accomplish this end. This is an unfortunate approach for media to provide us an opportunity to introduce students to new ideas in a new and exciting way (Postlethwait, 1969).

In closing his paper he stresses one of the advantages of the systems approach which has not been mentioned. When a true system of instruction has been evolved, it can be assessed, its weaknesses documented, and alterations made.

> In the final analysis, the success of any system is determined by whether students achieve through its use. Media enable us to structure a program which can be carefully evaluated and revised. The components of a sequence can be reorganized or replaced and the effect on learning determined. This is in contrast with the conventional presentation of lectures which are so highly variable that no determination can be made of the effectiveness of the individual ingredients. Media provides a potential for flexibility and individualization well beyond the wisdom of many of us. The challenge is to approach the use of these tools creatively and with real imagination (Postlethwait, 1969).

Although Dr. Postlethwait's system is based on an auditorial approach, it is a model that can work just as effectively for the acoustically handicapped when the appropriate media are selected to compensate for the student's hearing disability.

For the hearing impaired possibly television and the computer offer the greatest adaptation to the systems approach for the handicapped group. Dr. Harriet Kopp (1966) wrote:

> It is reasonable to picture our students each in his own cubicle with his own TV screen. The teacher seated at her control console can evaluate his responses

and thus his learning status continually throughout the lesson. He receives instant feedback to correct his mistakes. As his learning problems are diagnosed during the lesson, appropriate sequences are selected to provide needed reinforcement and to supplement the initial presentation.

She goes on to warn:

There is only one small cloud in the crystal ball. Who has prepared the sequences? Who has programmed the computer? We are being forced to overcome our historic reluctance to examine the human data processing system on which learning depends. Each new information input requires that the human memory bank be scanned. If the new signal is different from previous information, a new pattern is processed. Increase in learning reflects the ability of the human computer system to pattern information and to integrate the patterns. The task for the student becomes much simpler if he is not forced to deal with unrelated fragments of information. His processing is more efficient if he receives information in well planned, sequentially related units.

In an ideal classroom, the student would never fail, because the quantity and quality of information in the sequences would be tailored to his needs. To do this, we must view a curriculum as a continuum with horizontal enrichment and remedial and supportive teaching available at each level as required by the student. The student progresses along this continuum as rapidly as is commensurate with his learning ability. For any particular student, this rate may be different for different subjects at different times. Under such circumstances we may be able to generate active learning with strong internal motivation.

We are forced by the practicalities of existence to recognize that such curricula are not now available. How then, may we use machine-teaching now while we struggle towards development of curriculum? We must select those areas in which information can be presented better on an individualized basis, those in which immediate feedback is essential and can be given through programming and those where illustration can serve as reinforcement or where information must be repeated in varying forms to assure retention.

At the National Technical Institute for the Deaf, Rochester, New York, they foresee the computer as serving a mediated function by coordinating the application of educational media in their system. Dr. E. Ross Stuckless, Director of Instruction, reflects the absence of the programs and materials to fulfill this goal when he states:

We see CAI, as we conceptualize it, computerized multi-media instruction, playing a major role in the instruction of deaf students, particularly within the Vestibule Program. Our major efforts to date lie in the area of secondary level mathematics. However, again we find an absence of software, instructional programs which lend themselves to our specific needs. Accordingly, it remains for us to develop most of our instructional materials (Stuckless, 1969).

He also describes the dial access systems for retrieval of information that they are perfecting and the many uses being made of the various types of educational media in their program.

Obviously, the equipment is available; the technology is at hand; the systems approach for the acoustically handicapped student is feasible. Education of the hearing impaired needs the analytical study that the systems approach suggests.

Summary

The teacher of the future will be a learning mentor, an educator who functions as a guide, counselor, director, and one who is capable of prescribing instruction for each child in her academic custody (Yeager, 1969). The learning mentor will be equally as knowledgeable about educational media and the various learning resources as she is about diagnosis of hearing disorders and problems of language development. The identification of the learning problem is only the beginning of a series of analytical questions that the learning mentor must resolve if the student is to learn. We have been appalled by the slow rate at which the hearing impaired student learns, yet we have been unwilling to depart from the present laborious methods of teaching.

Dr. Harriet Kopp (1966) asks,

> Can we shake free from the shackles of didactic group teaching? Are teacher education programs oriented toward the professional education of individuals to perform these tasks effectively? Educators of the deaf and of the hearing, must re-examine their objectives and must master the new media of teaching if they are not to be overwhelmed by technological advances. Instrumentation must remain the willing servant of the skilled master.

Dr. Gabriel Ofiesh (1969), Director, Center for Educational Technology, Catholic University, Washington, D.C., spoke similarly when he said,

> The commitment of tomorrow's educational engineer should be to assist in the design of an educational system or systems which will provide the highest quality education to every individual within an ever-expanding mass educational system which is to be geared to individually prescribed learning. Educational engineers should be able to bring together and to integrate the numerous techniques, procedures and concepts of self-instructional learning systems. This will also allow us to make more effective use of those whom we now call master teachers and thereby eliminate many of the remedial problems facing education today.
>
> I think we must remember that educational technology is still very primitive. It is likely to take some very unusual forms in the next decade or two. We must be sensitive to the scientific developments in this field. We must then be able to readily translate these developments into technologies to fit our educational systems, especially those of us in special education. We should begin to prepare ourselves to use every possible tool and every possible bit of new knowledege which will assist us in helping every child . . . blind, deaf, defective by retardation and even those with illness . . . to become healthy. As human beings we must be willing to put into our armory any development to help us do our job.

Dr. Ofiesh defines the word technology as coming to us from the Greek derivative of "techne," meaning "art" or "craft" and the word "logos" indicating "a study of." In his words,

> It is the systematic application of scientific knowledge toward solutions of practical problems. Thus, educational technology is the systematic application of scientific knowledge toward the solution of problems in education. . . .
>
> Educational technology is, among many other things, the design and development of empirically valid learning systems which we then mediate and

package in order to mass-produce them and make them available to anyone, anytime, anywhere, when they want them and when they need them. Therefore, validated learning materials, which we are far from producing (although we do have a few viable learning materials) are those that have been engineered and tested to produce learning to a predetermined proficiency with representative groups of students. Programmed instruction is not a medium. Programmed instruction is a process bringing together all the necessary media to develop the most effective footlocker or kit of materials so we can have completely adaptive systems that can ultimately be sent through computers and remote access systems to human receivers. The media is the carrier. Too many of our teachers have been simply mediators and information dispensers. They haven't been managers of learning (Ofiesh, 1969).

The manager of learning, the learning mentor, must consider four components in the education process: man, media, message, and mode. To employ media skillfully teachers of the acoustically handicapped must be competent in message design. They must be able to recognize the appropriate channel or mode for the learner to receive ideas and for him to be able to retain a high level of understanding and comprehension. They must know the learner, not only his disabilities, but his capabilities. The learning mentor must be cognizant of the difference between the appropriate mode of reception for the learner and a selected mode of communication for the teacher. There is a difference.

Message design also implies creation and production of instructional materials in a form that can be easily decoded or understood by the learner. Message design suggests the need for order and structure to the lesson. Implicit in these thoughts is the belief that both teachers and students develop messages and create response media. Students should be encouraged to use and produce all types of instructional materials as part of their expressive language. Incidental, but essential, to message design is the need to know how to produce materials, operate equipment, select resources, and evaluate all forms of media.

The utilization of educational media and educational technology to prescribe individualized instruction or develop a systems approach cannot occur in a school without the proper administrative approval, classroom facilities, instructional media centers, and financial support. Special symposia on Research and Utilization of Educational Media for administrators and supervisors have been held as annual conferences at the University of Nebraska (Lincoln).

Plans have been drawn and discussed for the improvement of the classroom, or learning module as we sometimes refer to the space in which the study will take place, in order that better utilization may be made of available educational media. Is learning space for the acoustically handicapped special? Does it require architectural features not usually found in regular classrooms designed for hearing children? (Ray, 1968; Berenson, 1968). Conferences have been held and standards derived for the establishment and operation of school media centers (Darling, 1967). One of the key areas within the media center is the production equipment and facilities which permit both teachers and students to create their own instructional materials (Jackson, 1967). Financial support for the utilization of and experimentation with educational technology have been given considerable impetus by the Division of Training (Lucito, 1968), Division of Research (Moss, 1968), and Division of Educational Services (Withrow, 1968), Bureau of Education for the Handicapped. Four Regional Media Centers for the Deaf have been established by Media Services and Captioned Films Division of Educational Services to serve the many schools for the deaf (Gough, 1968). The Division of Research has established 14 Special Instructional Materials Centers which serve all areas and schools of special education (Olshin, 1968). Both the Division of Training and Media Services and Captioned Films have conducted workshops and media institutes for teachers and educators who prepare teachers. The workshops and institutes are particularly important to the process of re-educating the professional educator to the purposes and applications of the new technology (Hester, 1967). The groundwork has been done. It is up to the professional educator to implement the application of the emerging educational technology to the unique problems of educating the acoustically handicapped.

As educators of the hearing impaired, we must become learning mentors in the truest meaning of this title. First, we must realize that hearing impaired children have all the learning problems that normal children possess in addition to their auditory disorder. They may be slow readers, transpose letters in reading, be troubled by lateral dominance, have emotional disturbances, be bothered by social adjustments, and a multitude of problems related to being multiply handicapped. The whole child must be taught. Secondly, we must plan a strategy which capitalizes on the child's abilities rather than his disabilities. Too often, we teach solely to compensate for the hearing impairment and disregard avenues that would allow the child to accelerate and develop at a much more normal rate.

Thirdly, as a learning mentor, if you believe that a separate and distinct instructional strategy is required to be developed for each child, and if you believe in individual difference, then your strategy for teaching the hard of hearing will be different from your strategy for teaching the deaf. If your plan involves the child in learning activities, if you base your program on his capabilities, if you analyze his total educational problems, you vary your instruction to his needs. The one greatest asset in education today which makes such variations feasible is the vast variety and array of educational media available to the learner, as prescribed by his learning mentor.

The secret weapon in the education of the acoustically handicapped is the student himself. We have not developed the instructional strategies to challenge his whole potential. We must help him become an independent learner. We must help him to become socially interactive. We must help him to become vocationally self-sufficient. The hearing impaired student is delayed in his educational programs only because we (as educators) have not found the means to tap his intellectual resources. Media can play a vital role in assisting the hearing impaired student to develop his ability to conceptualize, to exercise his power of reasoning, to stimulate his interest in inquiry and discovery, to gain an appreciation of the world in which he lives, and to communicate with his associates.

He should be allowed to succeed or fail on the basis of his mental capacity and not because of his hearing deficiency (Stepp, 1967).

References

Behrens, Thomas, Linda Alprin, and Leland Clack. 1969. Mathematics curriculum supported by computer assisted instruction. American Annals of the Deaf 114(5): 889–892.

Berenson, Bertram. 1968. The educational implications of architecture for the deaf. American Annals of the Deaf 113(5):1030–1039.

Darling, Richard L. 1967. Implementating the media program in schools for the deaf. American Annals of the Deaf 112(5):712–718.

Delgado, Gilbert and John Gough. 1965. Some problems in audiovisual education of the deaf. American Annals of the Deaf 110(5):579–580.

Forsdale, Joan Rosengren. 1966. 8 mm films and the education of handicapped children. American Annals of the Deaf 111(5):625.

Frisina, Robert. 1966. The auditory channel in education of deaf children. American Annals of the Deaf 111(5):646.

Gough, John A. 1968. Educational media and the handicapped child. Exceptional Children, March:561–564.

Heinrich, Robert. 1966. Application of systems concept to instruction. American Annals of the Deaf 111(5):604–605.

Hester, Marshall S. 1967. In-Service education program for teachers of the deaf. American Annals of the Deaf 112(5):724–727.

Jackson, William D. 1967. Media production facilities in schools for the deaf. American Annals of the Deaf 112(5):680–687.

Kent, Alice A. 1966. Synthesizing language arts skills with the overhead projector. American Annals of the Deaf 111(5):617–618.

Kopp, Harriet Green. 1966. Application of systems concept to teaching the deaf. American Annals of the Deaf 111(5):670, 672, 673.

Laird, Rod. 1969. Educational media program at the Wyoming School for the Deaf presented at the 1969 Summer Educational Media Institute, University of Nebraska, Lincoln, Nebraska.

Leitman, Allan. 1968. The workshop classroom: furnishings in the learning module. American Annals of the Deaf 113(5):1–58.

Lennan, Robert. 1969. Use of programmed instruction with emotionally disturbed deaf boys. American Annals of the Deaf 114(5):906–911.

Lincoln Symposium Conferences on Research and Utilization of Educational Media in Teaching the Deaf, University of Nebraska, Lincoln, Nebraska.

Lucito, Leonard J. 1968. Division of Training programs—its mission. Exceptional Children, March:531–536.

McClure, William J. 1966. Current problems and trends in education of the deaf. Address presented at Combined Convention, California Association of Parents of Deaf and Hard of Hearing Children, California Association of Teachers of Deaf and Hard of Hearing Children, and California Association of Deaf in Los Angeles, California, November 6, 1965. The Record: Missouri School for the Deaf. October, 1966, pp. 4–5, 16–20; November, 1966, pp. 16–18.

Moore, O. K. 1965. The responsive environments project and the deaf. American Annals of the Deaf 110(5):604–614.

Moss, James W. 1968. Research and demonstration. Exceptional Children, March: 509–514.

Ofiesh, Gabriel. 1969. Educational technology and the necessary revolution in education. American Annals of the Deaf 114(5):893–905.

Olshin, George M. 1968. Special education instructional materials center program. Exceptional Children, March:515–522.

Pfau, Glenn. 1969. Project LIFE: p.i. analysis. American Annals of the Deaf 114(5): 829–837.

Postlethwait, Samuel. 1969. Mediated self-instruction. American Annals of the Deaf 114(5):874–879.

Rathe, Gustave H. 1969. Computer-assisted instruction and its potential for teaching deaf students. American Annals of the Deaf 114(5):880–883.

Ray, Henry W. 1968. Creating environments for learning. American Annals of the Deaf 113(5):1075–1085.

Sanford, Adrian B. 1966. The learner and the printed page—the place of graphics in a learning system. American Annals of the Deaf 111(5):631.

Schmitt, Robert J. 1966. A multi-media approach in the classroom of the deaf. American Annals of the Deaf 111(5):662–663.

Stepp, Robert E. 1965. A feasibility study to investigate the instrumentation, establishment and operation of a learning laboratory for hard-of-hearing children. Lincoln, Nebraska: University of Nebraska.

Stepp, Robert E. 1966. Introduction to final symposium report. American Annals of the Deaf 111(5):599–602.

Stepp, Robert E. 1967. Portions of this chapter are based on a presentation given at the dedication ceremonies of the new Primary Classroom Building at the Illinois School for the Deaf, Jacksonville, Illinois, March 15–17, 1967.

Stuckless, Ross. 1969. Planning for individualized instruction of deaf students at NTID. American Annals of the Deaf 114(5):868–873.

Withrow, Frank B. 1966–67. Speechreading 8 mm films. Lincoln, Nebraska: Midwest Regional Media Center for the Deaf, produced by University Photographic Productions, University of Nebraska.

Withrow, Frank B. 1968. Enlarged responsibilities for educational services to handicapped children. Exceptional Children, March:551–554.

Wyman, Raymond. 1968. A visual response system for small-group interaction. Audiovisual Instruction, September:714–717.

Wyman, Raymond. 1969. Mediaware: Selection, Operation and Maintenance. Dubuque: Wm. C. Brown Publishing Co.

Yeager, John L. 1969. A system for individualizing education: individually prescribed instruction. American Annals of the Deaf 114(5):861–867.

Recommended Readings

Books:

Bloom, Benjamin S. (Ed.). 1956. Taxonomy of Educational Objectives: Cognitive Domain. New York: David McKay Co.

Kemp, Jerrold E. 1968. Planning and Producing Audiovisual Materials, Second Edition. San Francisco: Chandler Publishing Co.

Krathwohl, David R. et al. 1964. Taxonomy of Educational Objectives: Affective Domain. New York: David McKay Co.

Mager, Robert F. 1962. Preparing Instructional Objectives. Palo Alto: Fearon Publishers.

Postlethwait, S. N., J. Novak, and H. Murray. 1964. An Integrated Experience Approach to Learning: With Emphasis on Independent Study. Minneapolis: Burgess Publishing Co.

Torkelson, G. M. 1968. What Research Says to the Teacher: Educational Media. Washington, D.C.: National Education Association, Bulletin 14.

Weisgarber, R. A. (Ed.). 1968. Instructional Process and Media Innovation. Chicago: Rand McNally and Co.

Wiman, R. V. and W. C. Meierhenry. 1969. Educational Media: Theory and Practice. Columbus: Charles E. Merrill Publishing Co.

Wittich, W. A. and C. F. Schuller. 1967. Audiovisual Materials: Their Nature and Use. New York: Harper & Row, Publishers.

Periodicals:

American Annals of the Deaf. 1965. Audiovisual research and the education of the deaf, complete issue, November.

American Annals of the Deaf. 1966. Systems approach in deaf education, complete issue, November.

American Annals of the Deaf. 1967. The educational media complex, complete issue, November.

American Annals of the Deaf. 1968. Designing instructional facilities for teaching the deaf: the learning module, complete issue, November.

American Annals of the Deaf. 1969. Individualizing instruction for the deaf student, complete issue, November.

Audiovisual Instruction. 1965. The systems approach, complete issue, May.

Audiovisual Instruction. 1966. Special education, complete issue, November.

Audiovisual Instruction. 1969. Special education, complete issue, November.

Exceptional Children. 1968. A richer future for handicapped children, complete issue, March.

Simpson, Elizabeth Jane. 1966–1967. The classification of educational objectives, psychomotor domain. Illinois Teacher of Home Economics 10(4).

Teaching Exceptional Children. 1968. All issues beginning with Vol. 1, No. 1

Volta Review. Curriculum; cognition and content, complete issue, September 1968.

Chapter 17

Educational Audiology

FREDERICK S. BERG, Ph.D.

The Problem

As many as 500,000 children in the United States are *educationally hard of hearing.* Some 15,000 of these children, especially those with severe hearing impairment, are enrolled in schools and classes where they are educated alongside of 25,000 deaf children. The other 485,000, particularly those with moderate hearing impairment, are mingled among hearing children (Eagles et al., 1963). Unfortunately, the special needs of hard of hearing children are inadequately met in both schools and classes for the deaf and in classes for normal hearing children because appropriate educational adjustments are often not made.

An individual normally accumulates and organizes a vast repertoire of information during the maturational process. This repertoire is ordinarily so extensive and well organized that it can be compared to a well-stacked library organized by floor, area, shelf, book, page, and line. DiCarlo (1968) indicates that hard of hearing children can discover, process, code, retrieve, and utilize information effectively. Typically, however, hard of hearing children do not meet this potential because of neglect to their unique needs.

New Specialization

A new specialization has emerged recently to contribute to the alleviation of the unmet needs of educationally hard of hearing children. Called *educational audiology,* it seeks for each hard of hearing child to identify the educational and audiological parameters of hearing impairment, to isolate the psychological and educational deficiencies arising from hearing loss, and to develop educational programs that will permit optimal adjustment in a hearing world (Berg and Fletcher, 1967).

The parameters that affect the educational programming of particular hard of hearing children are numerous. They include time of onset of hearing loss, hearing acuity, auditory discrimination, nature of auditory experience; linguistic exposure, academic opportunity, social stimuli; and perceptive, cognitive, and orectic potential. All of these variables and others are important

275

in and of themselves. But perhaps more important are their interactive effects upon the hard of hearing child.

A 70 db hearing loss, for example, precludes the hearing of conversational speech to a greater extent than does a 50 db hearing impairment. However, the child with the 70 db loss who has been properly fitted with a hearing aid and provided auditory training may hear speech better than the child with the 50 db hearing impairment who has not been provided the benefit of adequate amplification and training. Likewise, a severely hard of hearing child who receives special assistance in learning English may be less educationally retarded than a moderately hard of hearing child who receives little or no special help in acquiring the linguistic code.

The deficiencies rising from hearing disability among educationally hard of hearing children may be manifest in many ways: subnormal development of phonemes, morphemes, and vocabulary; inferior listening, speaking, pronunciation, reading, written compositional, and spelling skills; academic retardation in social studies, science, mathematics, and other substantive areas; uncertain self image, emotional instability, inattentiveness, introversion or aggression, and misbehavior.

Rationale for the New Label

The specialist of the new specialization is called an educational audiologist. The rationale for the use of the term *educational audiologist* to describe such a specialist is as follows:

1. Audiology may be defined as the science of hearing and the evaluation and habilitation of individuals with hearing disorders. As the profession has grown since World War II, it has fragmented into subspecialties such as clinical, experimental, and rehabilitative audiology.

2. Initially the term *rehabilitative audiology* may seem to encompass the habilitative needs of hard of hearing children because of emphasis upon such aural rehabilitative measures as utilization of speech remediation, speech-reading instruction, and auditory training.

3. With further analysis, the term *educational audiology* seems more appropriate than the label *rehabilitative audiology* for a specialization that encompasses the habilitative needs of educationally hard of hearing children rather than the rehabilitative needs of hearing impaired adults.

4. The term *teacher of the hearing impaired* seems to be too limiting to describe a specialist who has unique diagnostic and coordinating capabilities as well as educational competencies.

The Educational Audiological Evaluation

Whether working with an individual hard of hearing child or with a class of such children, the educational audiologist utilizes an integrated and comprehensive evaluational strategy to direct optimally learning and teaching activities. His evaluation provides a growing baseline from which more and more advanced concepts and skills can be taught to hard of hearing children. It also indicates gaps in learning experiences which can be closed through use of individualized learning programs.

The following diagram depicts a suggested chronological outline of areas of testing designed to facilitate the final educational attainment of the hard of hearing child.

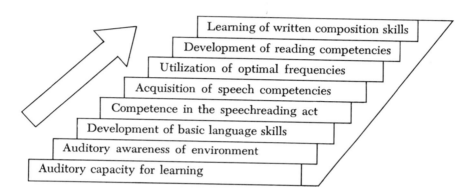

Learning of written composition skills
Development of reading competencies
Utilization of optimal frequencies
Acquisition of speech competencies
Competence in the speechreading act
Development of basic language skills
Auditory awareness of environment
Auditory capacity for learning

The Child's Capacity for Use of Audition

As a specialist with unique competencies, the educational audiologist recognizes the crucial importance of the infant and the preschool years to the final habilitative attainment of a hard of hearing child. He is aware that some profoundly hearing impaired children may learn the native language optimally and adjust to the environment best through the use of the auditory sensory modality. And he can accept responsibility in the locality in which he works for determining whether or not a hearing impaired child is hard of hearing or deaf. In the determination of such critical information for program planning, the educational audiologist works side by side with the otologist and with the clinical audiologist.

One strategy that may reveal that a hearing impaired infant is hard of hearing is described as follows:

1. A parent suspects that the infant does not respond normally to the auditory stimuli of the environment. An otologist supports this suspicion, and the child is referred to a clinical audiologist for audiometric evaluation.

2. The clinical audiologist may hypothesize through use of one or more audiometric techniques that the infant (a) does have a substantial hearing loss, but (b) can hear at least some auditory stimuli if presented at intense enough db levels. He may find, for example, that the infant responds binaurally to 250 Hz tones at 70+ db, 500 Hz tones at 80+ db, and 1000 Hz tones at 90+ db.

3.   A suitable wearable hearing aid is selected by the clinical audiologist for this infant. This device provides a sufficient undistorted output to package amplified sound into the hypothetical auditory area of the infant. For the infant with hearing thresholds as indicated above, the aid selected may be a body model binaural device. However, the aid might well be worn by the infant on a trial basis until further testing and experience substantiates the correctness of the fitting.

4.   The clinical or educational audiologist then fits the aid on the infant as the parents observe. He instructs the parents in the procedures used for day-by-day hearing aid use. And he monitors this continuing activity to ensure that the aid is comfortably fitted and that the parents are providing appropriate auditory stimulation. The initiation of infant vocalization within a month or so provides evidence that the fitting and characteristics of the hearing aid are at least partially suitable.

5.   As soon as the young child is 6 to 8 months of age, the educational audiologist then may conduct a precision teaching evaluation to evaluate use of hearing for the facilitation of prelinguistic vocalizations. He designs this evaluation to elicit a change of response rate with auditory-visual stimulation as compared to visual stimulation. For this purpose he may present a series of meaningful objects for the visual condition under which he obtains baseline data on vocalization rate. At this time, the hearing aid would be worn but be off and each object would be described verbally as presented. Then the educational audiologist presents the auditory-visual condition by orally describing each object he shows to the child with the aid on and the volume control turned up. As this procedure is carried out period by period, the specialist keeps a cumulative record of response rate under alternating visual and auditory-visual conditions. If the child perceives auditorially, his vocalization rate should be different under one condition as opposed to the other.

6.   The precision teaching experiment may next be modified in design to evaluate the prosodic and phonetic discrimination of the infant. Pairs of identical and different auditory stimuli, programmed and tape recorded, can be presented to the infant along with visual stimuli such as the objects mentioned above. Reinforcing events can then be presented or withheld from the infant dependent upon response and schedule of reinforcement. They might be a series of slides of interest to infants. Initially, reinforcement is given for response to the object only. Secondly, it is withheld for a response unless an auditory stimulus accompanies the presentation of the object. Thirdly, it is given for response to pairs of auditory stimuli, not to only one auditory stimulus. Fourthly, reinforcement is withheld unless the members of a given pair of auditory stimuli are different. At this stage of the evaluation of auditory discrimination, the infant may be responding differentially dependent upon perception of sameness or difference in sound stimuli. As recording of responses continues, the pairs of auditory stimuli are programmed to test from gross to refined prosodic and phonetic discrimination. All responses are recorded and graphed so as to document the results.

The Child's Auditory Awareness

The second major step in the educational audiological evaluation is a determination of whether or not the young hearing impaired child is auditorily aware of environmental stimuli. Ordinarily audition enables the infant to associate spoken stimuli uttered by family members with other auditory signals emanating from environmental events and activities. It also enables the infant to relate his own vocal utterances with those of another person's and with auditory stimuli from other events. The continual association of speech stimuli from self and others together with auditory stimuli from countless non-speech activities and events results in language development and environmental homeostasis.

We have designed a test to evaluate auditory awareness of environmental stimuli by infants and young children. It consists of 25 to 50 auditory tasks. Each task is made up of the following sequence of stimuli and responses.

1. A nonspeech environmental event such as a glass falling to the floor and breaking is presented.
2. The infant responds initially by turning toward the location of the environmental event.
3. A related speech event such as a woman's saying, "Oh, oh, a glass fell and broke," is presented.
4. The infant responds again by turning toward the location of this speech environmental event.

The test is administered to the infant in a room containing special projection devices. Each of three locations in the room contains a motion picture projector with a sound track and a daylight screen. The auditory tasks are programmed so that the infant cannot predict the location in which the auditory-visual nonspeech or speech stimulus will occur. The db and foot candle levels of each stimulus are sufficiently intense so as to be heard and seen respectively by the infant. The tester observes, records responses, and arrives at two scores. One score is a measure of auditory awareness of nonspeech environmental stimuli. The other score is a measure of auditory awareness of the contiguous speech stimuli.

The Child's Language Development

The third step in the educational audiological evaluation is the assessment of oral language development and related phenomena. One simple procedure to follow is to obtain a longitudinal sample of the child's verbalizations. The parents can assist by writing down several of the child's meaningful utterances each day. Table 34 illustrates the type of record which can be kept. Such responses can be analyzed syntactically, morphologically, and semantically. During this procedure use of tape recording permits phonological analysis as well as other types of linguistic study.

Table 34. Sample of Recorded Utterances of a Normal Hearing Child

Month	Selected Utterance
30	I want some medicine.
31	I'm going to put these together.
32	This is the best program I ever seen.
33	What Daddy turn light on in the kitchen for?
34	When I get big, my little teeth fall out and big teeth come in.
35	I'm not going home because I'm going to New York City with Louis Nils Berg.

Simmons (1967) suggests that longitudinal comparisons of oral language samples of a given child should make repeated use of the same stimulus. She utilizes a single picture to elicit these responses from hearing impaired children approximately every six months apart. An analysis of her tape recordings reveals that substantial increments of language growth typically occur from the first to each subsequent testing session. The use of one stimulus as described, however, is not sufficient to adequately sample language performance. Perhaps the solution to this problem would be the repeated use of the same series of stimuli for comparative analysis of language.

Berry (1969) describes materials and procedures for a more controlled elicitation and evaluation of oral language samples among children 11–36 months of age. She utilizes objects and pictures to stimulate a very young child to play imaginatively and vocally with the parent and specialist. A tape recording is made of the vocal interchange. Berry states that six to eight play sessions are probably necessary before an adequate language sample can be obtained. Perhaps fewer sessions would be necessary with the addition of a definite reinforcement strategy.

The Houston Test for Language Development (Crabtree, 1958) provides normative data on a comprehensive array of language related items from 6 months to 6 years of age. The items from the 6–36 month age span are a checklist of behaviors for categories of intonation, accent, gesture, articulation, vocabulary, grammatical usage, and dynamic content. The items for the next three years are aspects of spontaneous speech utterances including measures of self-identification, vocabulary, gesture, auditory judgments, communicative behavior, temporal content, syntactical complexity, and melody patterns.

Normative data on early language development is also available from use of the Utah Test of Language Development (Mecham, Jex, Jones, 1967). Fifty-one items from other standardized sources reveal many general features of receptive and expressive verbal language skills for the 1–15 year age range. Items at the 1–2 year level include, for example, *follows simple instructions* and *uses word combinations of two or more*, and six others.

The Oregon Language Development Profile (OLDP) provides a comprehensive test for the assessment of language and communication performance (Lillywhite, 1968). It is being standardized on 750 children from 3 months to 8 years of age. The areas of the test include verbal comprehension, verbal communication, articulation ability and speech intelligibility. Only certain items of the entire battery are utilized for a child of a given age. The infant test lasts 20 to 30 minutes and the others from 1½ to 2 hours. Every effort is made to observe the response of a child to each item and to supplement it with "reported" information.

The items of the OLDP are impressive. Most of them have been used in other language tests previously. All of them are placed on a progressive difficulty continuum rather than at specific age levels. Items test comprehension of function, actions, commands, categorization, tense, colors, and prepositions. They similarly test expression by ability to name objects, pictures, and actions; categorize objects; express wants, needs, and limitations; answer various questions; and determine inaccuracies in previously read stories.

One of the most widely used tests of language ability is the Illinois Test of Psycholinguistic Abilities (ITPA) (McCarthy and Kirk, 1961). It is standardized on children between the ages of 2.6 and 9.0 years of age and has been applied extensively to the evaluation of individuals with learning difficulties. The ITPA is made up of nine subtests: auditory decoding, visual decoding, auditory-visual association, visual motor association, vocal encoding, motor encoding, auditory-vocal automatic ability, and auditory-vocal sequential ability.

Another evaluative tool used with exceptional children is the Peabody Picture Vocabulary Test (PPVT) (Dunn, 1965). It provides a measure of the acquisition of content and has been standardized on children 2.3 to 18 years of age. The PPVT contains two equivalent forms, making it serviceable for pre-post training evaluation. The administration of the test includes presentation of verbal stimuli for a considerable number of items of varying difficulty. According to the test instructions, each verbal stimulus should be a spoken word. However, the test stimuli can be printed words as is often preferable for use with certain hard of hearing children who can read better than they can understand speech. When the verbal stimulus is presented, the child points to one of four pictures which appear on each page. The test can be administered in as little as 15 minutes. A verbal age can be derived from the number of items responded to correctly.

A measure of the acquisition of selected morphemes has been designed by Berry and Talbott (1966) after a test developed by Berko (1961). The stimuli are pictures of invented organisms called by coined names, such as *spuz* and *tass*. The child is asked to supply an appropriate grammatical inflection. Ordinarily the test is appropriate for children aged 5–8 years. Norms, not available on this type of a test as yet, would be useful comparative data by which to judge the performance of a hard of hearing child.

The Child's Speechreading Competence

The fourth step in the educational audiological evaluation is the testing of competence in the utilization of speechreading for speech reception. Speechreading, or lipreading to many people, has been referred to by Mason as visual hearing (Mason, 1942b). It provides visual correlates of certain distinguishing features of the speech act. The hearing impaired child should be encouraged to speechread after having learned to listen.

Faced with the task of filling in auditory gaps with visual signals, the child may acquire unusual competence in speechreading. Staffan Wedenberg, for example, was able to supply a movie producer with the entire script of a sound track after viewing a motion picture three times. The speechreading skill may be learned incidentally or through structured lessons.

Tests of speechreading performance currently are administered to a young hard of hearing child beginning at 3 years of age. By this time the listening skill has been basically established and speechreading can be aiding the speech reception process. If at this time, a speechreading test is administered and the hard of hearing child achieves a low score, training in visual speech comprehension is advisable. However, the listening act should continue to receive primary training support because of its superior capabilities for language learning, speech communication, and maintenance of environmental homeostasis.

Two current tests of speechreading competence for young children might be applied at this stage of the educational program. One of these tests was developed by Mason (1942a,b) and the other by Butt and Chreist (1968). Both are individually administered without use of audible voice. However, they can be adapted for employment under varying auditory-visual conditions.

The Mason test utilizes a silent film for the presentation of 15 words by a speaker. It requires that the young child point to one of four pictures after presentation of each word. A maximum score of 15 may be obtained. The test perhaps needs to be extended in length so as to increase its reliability.

The Butt and Chreist test may be a more valid measure of speechreading ability. It employed 70 items, each of which is a 3–5 word command or question. For example, items 53 and 55 are *Show me your teeth* and *Where are your feet?*, respectively. The test stimuli are presented by use of "live voice."

Butt has administered this test to 65 children from 3 to 9 years of age. The range of the mean scores varied from 19 for the 3 year olds to 44 for the 8 year olds. A .79 correlation existed between test scores and teacher rankings.

The Butt and Chreist test has a split-half reliability of .95 which makes it particularly applicable to a comparison of visual and auditory-visual speech comprehension. Half of the items can be presented by vision only and the other half by auditory-visual presentation. Thus, the specialist can determine the efficiency with which the hard of hearing child can supplement audition with visual clues in the speech perception process.

Additional speechreading tests can be administered as soon as the hard of hearing child develops intelligible speech and more advanced syntactical structure and vocabulary. The advanced tests are group instruments requiring written responses, but they can be administered individually and oral responses accepted (Utley, 1946; Taaffe, 1957). A test we are preparing may be especially suitable in that it includes three rather than the conventional two equivalent forms. One form can be administered auditorily, the second visually, and the third auditorily-visually. The stimuli are sentences borrowed from speech material described by Davis and Silverman (1960). These sentences were designed to be representative of everyday speech by meeting such criteria as sentence length, grammatical structure, and vocabulary.

The Child's Speech Skills

The fifth step in the educational audiological evaluation is obtaining measures of the speech skills of the hard of hearing child. This evaluative step may commence as soon as the child can speak reflexively and utilize syntax through a process of induction of the latent structure. Such proficiency emerges in the normal child at 33–36 months but may be delayed in the instance of a hard of hearing child.

Hard of hearing children and adults typically have defective speech. All usually employ distortions and omissions in the articulatory process. Many hard of hearing individuals have nasal voice quality. And some exhibit limited prosodic and rhythmic speech. In short, they often seem to speak as they may auditorily perceive.

The speech evaluation should measure performance in the use of articulation, voice, prosody, rhythm, and intelligibility. It should also test the oral communicative effectiveness of the hard of hearing child. Four currently used *speech tests* are particularly applicable: The Templin-Darley Tests of Articulation (1960), A Deep Test of Articulation by McDonald (1964), the Sherman Index of Nasality (1954), and the Hudgins and Numbers procedure (1942). Three additional evaluative techniques are also worthy of mention.

1. *The Templin-Darley Tests of Articulation* include a 50-item screening scale and a 176-item diagnostic scale. The sound elements tested include 43 segmental phonemes distributed in eight categories as follows: 12 vowels; 5 diphthongs; 9 single consonants in the initial medial, and final positions; 71 double-consonant blends; 19 triple-consonant blends; 12 vowels; and 5 diphthongs.

The task of the child is to say 50 or 176 words, depending upon the scale, in response to a series of pictures or in imitation of the tester. Each word contains one of the sound elements being tested, for example, *swing* includes /sw/. For each test item misarticulated in response to a picture or in imitation of the signal, the child is asked to imitate the sound in isolation, in a syllable and in a word.

The Templin-Darley Test has been standardized on 3–8 year old children (Templin, 1957). The articulation score achieved by a hard of hearing child may be equated with a particular articulation age norm. More importantly, a detailed recording of the child's responses to the test stimuli assists in the planning of a speech remedial program.

2. An even more detailed analysis of speech articulation may be obtained by use of *A Deep Test of Articulation* by McDonald. This test goes *deeper* than the Templin-Darley procedure in that phonemes which are typically misarticulated, such as /κ/, /z/, and /ʃ/, are tested in many more phonemic con-

texts than just initial, medial, and final positions of words. Pictures tend to serve as stimuli for the elicitation for these articulatory responses. The rationale of the depth procedure is that articulation in three positions does not adequately sample the entire population of phonemic contexts for a given speech sound. Both long (1964) and short (1968) forms of the test are available.

3. The task of identifying and judging the amount of hypernasality, where it exists, is managed by use of the *Sherman Index of Nasality* (1954). The procedure is to play back a sample of the connected speech of a child in a backward direction. This sample of reversed speech is then judged by several auditors on a point scale of hypernasality. Since the auditors cannot understand the message, they apparently make a more valid judgment of presence and degree of nasality.

4. Auditors are also employed in the *Hudgins and Numbers* speech evaluational procedure. They score a set of ten sentences for each hearing impaired child on the basis of intelligibility, articulation, and rhythm. The use of this procedure reveals that a positive correlation exists, as would be expected, between these three measures. In other words, both articulation and rhythm contribute to the intelligibility of the speech.

5. The obtaining of a sample of *connected utterance* is of particular importance to an analysis of the functional speech skills of a hard of hearing child. De Hirsh et al. (1964) note that comparison between a child's articulation of single words and of connected speech provides an appraisal of his resistance to articulatory disintegration in real life situations. They suggest the use of a tape recording of a story told by the child. The story can be elicited by use of a series of pictures.

6. Another technique for obtaining a connected speech sample from a child is the use of *spontaneous utterances* in an informal play situation. A miniaturized microphone-transmitter can be positioned on the child prior to the play session (Hoshiko and Holloway, 1968). The child's speech responses are transmitted via radio carrier wave, recorded on audio tape and played back for analysis of articulatory, vocal, prosodic, and rhythmic characteristics. A linguistic analysis can also be made.

7. The utilization of *video* recording and playback equipment is also valuable for speech testing. An audio-visual recording of a child's speech responses can be obtained through the combined use of a one-way window and an audio intercommunication system. The child need not realize that such a recording is being made. When the tape is played back for analysis, visual as well as audio correlates of the speech act are present. The inclusion of visual clues, according to Stewart (1968), assists the phonetician in evaluating the types of speech errors being used by the hearing impaired child.

The Audio Frequencies Used by the Child

The sixth step in the educational audiological evaluation is a determination of the audio frequencies being utilized by the hard of hearing child during the speech perception process. Boothroyd (1967) has developed a testing procedure that can provide this valuable information. He presents speech perception word lists to a hard of hearing child under varying high-pass and low-pass filter conditions. The speech stimuli for each list are 10 CVC words or 30 phonemes. The child repeats back each word as soon as it is orally presented. Rather than giving credit for each word repeated back correctly, 3.33 points are allowed for each phoneme reproduced.

Boothroyd plots "articulation" curves for the high-pass and low-pass conditions. The intersection of the two curves divides the audio frequencies used for speech reception into two equal parts. The frequency at which the intersection occurs may be very different for normal hearing individuals as compared with that for a hard of hearing child who is relying on an array of acoustic features quite unlike the pattern usually utilized for speech perception. Furthermore, a comparison of the child's auditory area, as determined from thresholds of acuity and discomfort for pure tones, and the audio frequencies being used for speech perception may reveal that a certain area of the frequency spectrum is not being utilized as it should be. Such a finding might indicate that a hearing aid with a different frequency response should be used instead of the child's present amplifying device. Also, it might suggest that auditory training should make use of new formant patterns so that substantial improvement in speech perception can occur.

The Child's Reading Competencies

The seventh step in the educational audiological evaluation is the utilization of tests designed to identify reading abilities and difficulties. This step is really a series of evaluations conducted on a periodic basis once the child has begun school. A description of the evaluative procedures covered by this step is included in an accompanying chapter by Clark.

The Child's Written Composition

The eighth and last step in the educational audiological evaluation is the employment of procedures used to measure the written compositional competencies of the hard of hearing child. Myklebust (1964) describes one of several tests being developed to evaluate written language competency. His test, called the Picture Story Language Test, may be of particular relevance to this discussion because compositional norms for hearing children 7 to 15 years of age have been established by use of it.

The stimuli for the Myklebust test consists of a single picture about which a child writes a story. Among the criteria used in the selection of the picture were: (1) it was of a school-aged child, (2) it showed action, (3) it had a definite figure and ground, (4) it provided an opportunity for imagination, and (5) it had not been used for teaching purposes. The Picture Story Language Test is scored in three primary ways: (1) productivity, (2) correctness, and

(3) use of abstraction. Productivity refers to the amount of language which is written; correctness to the grammar, punctuation, and types of errors; and abstraction to use of nonconcrete verbalization. The measure of productivity is primarily the number of words used per sentence; it often reveals the complexity of language usage. Another means of indicating linguistic structure from this test is an analysis of parts of speech, substitutions, omissions, additions, and word order. Criteria used for judging abstract-concrete behavior, with each age level having a continuum, include: (1) inappropriate, (2) concrete-descriptive, (3) concrete-imaginative, (4) abstract-descriptive, and (5) abstract-imaginative.

Further important data about the writing skills of the hard of hearing child can be derived by application of additional procedures. One such procedure is to present a sample of idioms, have the child write down the meaning of each, and in turn obtain a percentage score. A need exists to standardize such a test, using such items as those given below.

> Don't shoot off your mouth.
> Go jump in the lake.
> That's against my grain.
> She's the apple of his eye.
> He's always asking for the moon.
> You're barking up the wrong tree.
> It's an ace in the hole.
> You're adding fuel to the fire.
> Do you have an axe to grind?
> He's a ball of fire.

Results on such a test could give a measure of figurative language competency. Many similar such tests need to be developed, including a measure of morphemic competency. An adaptation of the Berko (1961) evaluation described elsewhere in this chapter offers an excellent start for morphemic evaluation.

As valuable as the above tests may be, of even more importance to the teacher is the task of day-by-day evaluation of change in language competency. The precision teaching procedures of Lindsley (1966) offer great promise to the teacher in this task. A behavior which should be modified is identified, teaching variables are systematically introduced, desired and undesired responses are counted, and the data is graphed to reveal the direction and results of the teaching process. It then becomes the specialist's responsibility to determine the contingencies that will result in optimal change.

Hearing and Speech Management

Another aspect of educational audiology is the focus placed upon hearing and speech management in the habilitation of the hard of hearing child. The nature of such management, the ages at which it may be appropriately applied and the goals of each component part are depicted in Table 35.

Table 35. Stages and Goals of Hearing and Speech Remediation

	Activity	Age in Years	Remedial Goal
1.	Initial auditory training	0–5	Development of basic listening competencies; emergence of imitative and generative sentences.
2.	Advanced auditory training	5–18+	Identification and utilization of key environmental sound clues; development of language and communication competencies.
3.	Speechreading instruction	3–18+	Identification and utilization of visual clues to facilitate language and speech acquisition, oral communication and acquisition of substantive concepts.
4.	Initial speech instruction	5–8	Optimal articulation, prosody, voice quality and pitch and loudness levels within the child's capabilities in selected speech signals.
5.	Advanced speech instruction	8–18+	Transfer of above speech competencies into all phonetic contexts within developing language competencies.
6.	Application of listening and speaking skills	5– Adult	Competency in conversation, explanation, classroom participation, interviewing, and other critical activities of oral communication.

A rationale for speech and hearing management for hard of hearing children is presented in the following pages of this chapter.

Man's Environment

The environment in which man learns and develops is multifaceted. Complex phenomena of space and time, position and motion and living as well as inanimate forms abound. The presence and characteristics of distinctive features of these phenomena are perceived by the normal human organism through the availability of the several sensory modalities. Visual, auditory and certain tactile aspects of phenomena are transmitted from their sources as vibratory energy. Olfactory, gustatory, proprioceptive and other tactile features are perceived more directly.

In contrast with other animate forms, man acquires information from the environment through both symbolic and nonsymbolic stimuli. He processes these two forms of data cognitively, and utilizes the resulting information to generate hypotheses and to evoke responses of a highly complex nature. In company with other humans, he functions in a highly differentiated and integrated manner.

Much of the symbolic and nonsymbolic stimuli utilized by man in learning about and adjusting to environmental influences is auditory in nature. The world in which we live is never silent. Countless sounds emanate from environmental activities, are transmitted distances as vibratory energy, and perceived by the human organism by use of the auditory sensory modality.

The human being can differentiate auditorily a tremendous range of non-speech and speech stimuli. He can recognize sounds that might vary greatly in intensity as indicated below.

Sound	Intensity in db
Watch tick	0–20
Pencil writing	20–30
Distant speech	30–40
Sink water	40–60
Nearby speech	60–80
Door slamming	80–100
Jet aircraft	100–160

He can distinguish among perhaps 340,000 tones (Stevens and Davis, 1938), including the linguistic elements of our spoken language. In many instances man can identify through audition the material of which an object is made, its thickness or shape, and its distance away and location. He can judge how fast an engine is rotating or how quickly a person is talking. And he can make many additional and equally remarkable perceptions by use of audition.

As compared with vision, audition is uniquely designed to permit man to learn the spoken language system (Liberman et al., 1968). It combines a refined versatility for processing physical speech variations with an uncanny competence for receiving stimuli simultaneously from any location within talking distance. It enables a person, for example, to meaningfully associate a glass dropping in one location and a comment, "a glass dropped," from another location. It also permits an individual to relate his vocal utterance with another person's and with the event. As this association procedure is applied in numerous situational instances, behavior becomes not only internalized but symbolized. And man develops a verbal language system.

The utilization of vision in the language learning process is important but not critical to a normal hearing individual. The environmental stimuli which vision encompasses are typically nonspeech in nature featuring such characteristics as size, shape, and movement. When these stimuli have utterance referents, only fragments of the vocalization act can be visualized. And when the acoustic detail corresponding to the complex manuevers of the speech act is translated electronically into a visual display, the eye is unable to process the significant features of this detail into meaningful linguistic correlates at anywhere near normal rate of speech.

Audition functions also as the dominant background and alerting sense (Myklebust, 1964). It enables a person to be aware of such phenomena as people talking, crickets chirping, water running, and a tornado coming. One person, for example, may overhear relatives talking in an adjacent room, and change his will as a consequence. Another person may open the front door of his house after hearing the doorbell ring. A third person may not bother to look up from a book he is studying after he becomes auditorily aware that it is a familiar person who is walking toward him.

Auditory Deprivation

Hard of hearing children, unfortunately, have communication problems that extend into adulthood. Table 36 depicts some of the audiologic parameters and resulting deficiencies characteristic of individuals with marginal to severe but not profound hearing impairment.

Table 36. *Selected Auditory Parameters and Arising Deficiencies of 10 Hard of Hearing Students at Gallaudet College*

Subject	Age (yrs)	db loss	PB (%)	Vocab. (yrs)	Characteristic Oral Sentence	Selected Articulation									
						r	v	θ_I	θ_m	$\eth_I$	$\eth_F$	z	tʃ	pr	st
1	22	73	28	11	I wear my hearing aid while I'm talk to hearing person.	*	f	θ	−	θ	v	s	ʃ	pw	-t
2	20	87	54	11	Then I went to the deaf school and graduated. . . .	r	v	θ	θ	ð	ð	*	tʃ	pr	st
3	20	58	74	10	I feel I can do better because of my education	r	v	θ	θ	ð	ð	dʒ	ʃ	p*	-t
4	19	77	88	16	When I take it off, little trouble.	*	v	θ	θ	ð	ð	θ	tʃ	pw	st
5	20	77	76	13	I decided not to take college prep courses because . . .	r	v	θ	θ	ð	ð	s	tʃ	pr	s-
6	19	77	84	17	From the 7th grade on to my senior year, I had a tutor.	r	v	θ	θ	ð	ð	z	tʃ	pw	st
7	20	63	74	13	In my school they don't have high school, . . .	r	f	θ	θ	θ	θ	s	*	pr	s-
8	19	67	34	11	I like very much.	*	f	θ	θ	θ	θ	d	ʃ	pw	-t
9	21	42	70	9	All my teachers deaf, so I have to go to sign language.	*	v	t	−	d	t	*	*	p*	s-
10	20	80	32	10	I attended two kinds of school. The first one . . .	r	v	θ	θ	d	θ	d	*	pr	-t
Mean	20	70	61	11	Correct responses-5	5	7	9	8	5	5	1	4	4	3

* indicates distortions

− indicates omission.

It may be noted that generally syntax and morphology are near normal but not vocabulary and speech articulation. Subject 8, however, functioned like a much younger hard of hearing person. Her utterance "I like very much" was the longest speech response she used in a lengthy interview. In general, these hard of hearing individuals understood and used speech effectively in quiet two-person conversation, especially when speechreading supplemented hearing aid use. However, they typically misunderstood oral communication in group discussion and in noisy environments. For all these subjects as well as hard of hearing persons in general, deficiencies such as those illustrated above are alleviated considerably by use of auditory training, speech reading instruction, and speech training.

Auditory Training

One of the highly promising aspects of hearing and speech management for hard of hearing children is that of auditory training. In the United States, systematic training of residual hearing stems from Max Goldstein, an otologist who founded the Central Institute for the Deaf in 1914. Goldstein (1939) noted that certain severely hearing impaired children at the Central Institute for the Deaf improved in ability to understand speech after systematic acoustic training. His educational approach was analytical in that isolated tones and phonemes made up the initial training stimuli. A focus was placed upon the production as well as upon the perception of phonemes and then syllables, words and sentences. His methodology was introduced from the Vienna-Doblin School for the Deaf where he had studied with Urbantschitsch in 1893. During an initial 6-month period, Urbantschitsch had reported the results below (Wedenberg, 1951):

	Before training	After training
Trace of hearing	32 children	11 children
Vowel perception	22 children	21 children
Word perception	6 children	16 children
Sentence perception	0 children	12 children
	60 children	60 children *

McGinnis (1963) a student of Goldstein, introduced a modification of this analytical approach in programming she developed for "aphasic" children at the Central Institute for the Deaf. She called her remedial approach the *Association Method* because of a constant training interplay among processes of attention, retention, and recall. She utilized the auditory modality as well as other modalities to improve the perception and production of phonemes, words, and sentences. Her students who were typically hard of hearing were required to say words and sentences before they learned the meaning of these

* From Acta Otolaryngologica, Supplementum 94, 1951, p. 18.

stimuli. After learning a considerable number of words and sentences through this analytic, expressive strategy, many of these children began to generate original utterances.

A contemporary, Hudgins (1953) of the noted Clarke School for the Deaf, conducted auditory training using profoundly hearing impaired children as subjects. He noted that these children, who were 8–12 years of age, improved in speech perception following two-year periods of academic instruction in which high quality group amplification equipment was employed. The speech perception gains were revealed through look and listen test scores of word recognition.

Another contemporary, Erik Wedenberg of Sweden, noted, also, that even profoundly hearing impaired children could benefit from auditory training (1954). He taught three such children, beginning at $1\frac{1}{2}$ to $2\frac{1}{2}$ years of age, to perceive auditorily dynamic, temporal, and certain phonetic features of speech. Daily stimulation, an auditory unisensory approach, and carefully selected speech signals were employed. The training stimuli were sound elements which spectrographic and audiometric analyses revealed might be perceived by these children. All of the children developed spontaneous speech and a *listening attitude* after many months of training. Wedenberg had literally assisted deaf children to become hard of hearing children, one of whom was his own son Staffan.

Extensive research by Gaeth (1960, 1963, 1966) indicated that special attention must be given to the utilization of the auditory sensory modality or the hearing impaired child will tend to rely on visual stimuli only. Gaeth designed equivalent tasks which were presented auditorily (A), visually (V), and auditorily-visually (AV) to thousands of children including hundreds with hearing impairment. The stimuli included verbal, nonverbal, meaningful, and nonmeaningful auditory and visual signals. The subjects were grouped in selected experiments according to age and degree of deficit of auditory acuity. Gaeth found that a unisensory presentation of any type of stimuli is as effective for learning as a bisensory (AV) presentation. In a bimodal presentation, attention is directed to the sensory modality which is most meaningful. For hearing children this is determined by the nature of the stimuli; for hearing impaired children, the visual modality is more meaningful regardless of content.

Kelly (1953, 1954) utilized listening drills in communication training for hard of hearing children from the public schools. He noted that speech perception scores typically improved about 20 percent following a six-week remedial program which included daily auditory training. The gains were revealed unisensorily (A) using alphabet letter sequences, words and sentences similar to the training stimuli. The children also improved in speech intelligibility. The latter gains might be attributed to a combination of transfer effect from perception to production and/or to practice in speaking during remedial periods.

Griffith (1967), Pollack (1964, 1967), and Whetnall and Fry (1964) also emphasized the importance of learning to listen. In separate locations they noted the development of speech perception and of language skills among the severely hearing impaired as a result of auditory training. Instructional activities were designed to improve listening competencies rather than lipreading skills. Griffin noted that the children with the greater hearing problems took longer to learn the auditory cues. However, Whetnall stated that if a child was old enough to have an audiogram, improvement in auditory competencies invariably occurred.

Pollack (1967) also has conducted auditory training with large numbers of hearing impaired infants. Her training guidelines stem from Huizing of the Netherlands (Huizing, 1952). This approach, called Acoupedics, gives special attention to the function of hearing in keeping the individual in constant contact with the environment. Whereas Griffith accepts lipreading as a facilitative avenue for language development, Pollack advocates the avoidance of use of the visual communicative avenue. Neither of these two specialists, however, plan lipreading activities as a part of training sessions.

Whetnall and Fry (1964) and Jeffers (1966) describe a rationale for the development of speech comprehension among severely hearing impaired children based upon spectrographic analysis. They clarify the nature of the auditory clues available to the individual for differentiating among English phonemes. Their explanations reveal that specialists can definitely assist a great many severely hearing impaired children to learn language by use of auditory training.

In a recent case study, Larson (1970) conducted auditory training with one 9-year-old male having a relatively flat binaural hearing impairment of 92 db. The instruction was conducted during a short period on a daily basis for ten weeks. During the first four weeks the subject demonstrated varying improvement in discrimination between members of many pairs of isolated consonants and vowels. During six additional weeks, he similarly improved in the auditory recognition of selected words. Larson's investigation also revealed that a higher percentage of correct responses occurred with the use of contingency management. In addition, pre-post spectrographic comparisons of training words uttered by the subject showed corresponding improvements in accuracy of speech production.

The faculty of the St. Joseph Institute for the Deaf in St. Louis have systematically incorporated the use of audition into language, speech, and academic instruction for many years (Fanchea, 1955). Persons who have visited this special school for hearing impaired children have been exceptionally impressed with the speech perception skills and speech competencies exhibited by the students. Hogan (1961) and Lorenz (1961) have developed materials and procedures that illustrate the work which is so enthusiastically conducted there.

Notwithstanding the positive results of the studies above, caution must be exercised in overgeneralizing the beneficial effects of auditory training to all hearing impaired children. Wedenberg (1954), for example, noted that severely hard of hearing children having recruitment were poor subjects for auditory training. He also found that children who had hearing impairment beyond 90 db generally did not benefit much from auditory training, particularly if instruction was delayed until school age. A critical variable in success or lack of success from auditory training is often the hearing aid which should *package* the acoustic signal into the *auditory area* of the child.

Hearing aids in auditory training. The hearing aid is a device that changes the characteristics of sound signals reaching the ears of a listener. Principally, it amplifies sound so that a hearing impaired person can perceive auditory phenomena of the environment.

The initial hearing aid used at the Central Institute for the Deaf was called the Simplex Tube. It consisted of a mouthpiece into which the instructor spoke, multiple tubes through which the speech signal was conducted, and multiple earpieces for each student. The instructor could auditorily stimulate many of the children, particularly those with moderate to severe rather than profound hearing impairment, by speaking through the system. The procedure was essentially unisensory inasmuch as the mouthpiece hid from view the lip movements of the instructor.

Shortly after World War I, Fletcher of the Bell Telephone Laboratories developed the first electro-acoustic hearing aid. The first models of this aid, called the Audiophone, were not portable, but later ones were (McConnell, 1968). By 1938 portable "audiophones" were being worn by many children at the Central Institute for the Deaf (Goldstein, 1939). The audiophone provided greater amplification and, therefore, had wider applicability than the simplex tube did. Also, it did not preclude the lipreading process. In the audiophone and wearable hearing aids that followed, the mouthpiece and tubes were replaced by a microphone.

The initial audiophone developed by Fletcher was a binaural hearing aid in that it incorporated two completely separate amplification systems, one for each ear. The rationale for binaural rather than monaural amplification is modern. The stereophonic feature may enable a child with equivalent bilateral hearing perception to localize the source of sound, to identify signal from noise, and to distinguish foreground stimuli from background sound. Today, binaural amplification is often represented in two miniaturized ear level hearing aids that are beneficially used by even profoundly hearing impaired persons.

After World War II, Silverman and Harrison of the Central Institute for the Deaf and Hudgins of the Clarke School for the Deaf collaborated on building and testing the effectiveness of high quality group hearing aids featuring compression amplification. These aids, built at the Central Institute for the Deaf, were capable of delivering undistorted speech signals through earphones so as to be heard by even profoundly hearing impaired children (Hudgins, 1953). The experiment was conducted with comparable classes of severely hearing impaired children, comprising experimental and control groups who used experimental aids and commercially available conventional aids. Both the experimental and control classes improved in look-listen word scores during two-year periods. However, greater gains in combined auditory visual speech perception resulted from use of better quality equipment.

During the postwar era, the auditory training investigations of Wedenberg (1951) were extended to include use of school-age children. Whereas preschool children had been subjected to nonamplified speech signals uttered from close range, the school-age children were trained by use of a speech audiometer equipped with low- and high-pass filters. Instructional focus was placed upon the perception of the formants of speech sounds or frequency regions where maximum energies occurred. At first, the children were trained to attend to the higher formants and then to all formants simultaneously. Finally, they were instructed in the identification of the vowels and voiced consonants through increased perception of the lower formants.

Wedenberg's results of auditory training with 14 severely hard of hearing children of school age were generally encouraging. The children who did not have recruitment and who generally had bilaterally symmetric pure tone audiograms improved in auditory perception of words and sentences. Wedenberg hypothesized that the cochleas of the children without recruitment were in better physiological condition than those with recruitment.

More recently Wedenberg conducted an auditory training experiment with the use of a coding amplifier or frequency transposer designed by Johansson. The subjects had a perceptive high tone loss type with no hearing above 1500 Hz. The coding amplifier transposed the 3000–6000 Hz frequency range into the range below 1500 Hz where the subjects had residual hearing. It also featured amplitude compression to prevent overloading with consequent distortion.

The coding amplifier enabled the subjects to perceive many unvoiced fricatives they had not heard before. The subjects described the transcribed fricatives as different scratch sounds. The total received speech signal now sounded different but became familiar again after up to 16 hours of training. Johansson noted that the systematic tests with this transposer revealed dramatic improvements in discrimination of fricative and stop consonants.

The coding features, however, also tended to introduce distortion into the speech sounds requiring transposition and those adjacent to it. The effect of transposed amplification needs to be clarified further. Wedenberg himself noted that great individual differences occur in the acquisition of the new auditory pattern. Ling (1968) replicated the Wedenberg experiment but was unable to demonstrate improvements in speech perception by use of frequency transposition. However, Wedenberg's own hearing impaired son wears binaural hearing aids featuring coding amplification and is convinced that he understands speech better because of it.

Another promising modification of the hearing aid is the inclusion of a very low audio frequency response. Ling (1964), for example, designed a wearable hearing aid having a frequency response beginning at 90 Hz. He compared the effectiveness of this hearing aid with that of a typical hearing aid having a response beginning at 800 Hz. Severely hearing impaired children he studied made significantly greater speech improvement using the experimental aid than those using the control aid.

The rationale for inclusion of the very low audio frequencies may be due to two factors. One is that the lowest formant (F_1) for most of the voiced phonemes occurs below 800 Hz. The second is that most severely hearing impaired children typically have better auditory acuity in this region than in any other frequency band of similar width.

DiCarlo (1962) reports that hearing impaired children whose frequency discrimination is adequate at 500 Hz employ amplification quite satisfactorily. He notes that 250 and 500 Hz do not include much of the information-bearing components for speech reception. However, the very low audio frequencies do contribute considerably to speech development through prosodic features of stress and accent that permit establishment of natural rhythm.

It is highly relevant that Lewis (1951) stated that during the first year of life the normal child progressively identified gross pitch patterning, then finer intonational features of speech as well as some articulatory correlates, and finally the remainder of the perceptual referents to articulation. The transition from perception of intonation to that of articulatory correlates was also noted in the early speech development of Staffan Wedenberg who received extensive auditory stimulation. The young Wedenberg developed melodic speech patterning initially and then articulatory competence.

We are increasingly becoming aware of the primacy of intonation to the speech act. Lieberman (1967) notes that the intonation contour is the primary feature of the constituent phrase or sentence which is the basic unit of speech. Without perception of the melodic or intonational aspects of speech, the hearing impaired child does not repeat his own vocalizations during early speech development as is normally done. He does not repeat the utterances of others. His vocalizations consist of only grunts and similar noises unless given special training. Even with special assistance his vocalizations typically are nonfluent and largely unintelligible (Morley, 1949; Angeloci, 1962; Calvert, 1962) unless systematic low frequency auditory stimulation is provided.

A combination of low audio frequency amplification and many frequency filters is incorporated in the SAVAG II hearing aid of Guberina of Yugoslavia (1969). Results from use of this aid, having a frequency response from 0.6 Hz to 15,000 Hz, are highly encouraging. Bellefleur (1967) reports that the speech of Guberina's most severely hearing impaired children, even those with profound losses, is superior to that of the children in any school for the deaf in the United States. He also mentions, however, that evidence seems to exist that at least part of the speech competence of these children may be attributed to a special rhythm program separate from use of SAVAG II.

Martin and Pickett (1968), however, have presented evidence that some severely hearing impaired persons using a hearing aid with an extended low frequency response may have poorer aided discrimination than would be obtained with amplification having a conventional low frequency roll off. Their reasoning is twofold: (1) masking of high frequencies by low frequencies, if such occurs, may be accentuated by use of low frequency amplification; and (2) such masking may be increased in noisy listening situations where low frequency energies commonly abound.

Another unique approach to electro-acoustic amplification is compression of the energies of the auditory signal into a narrower frequency range than normally exists. Haspiel (1969) is investigating the possible benefit of a laboratory hearing aid featuring *frequency compression,* differential frequency amplification, and continuously variable amplification from 0 to 130 db SPL. He plans to determine how hearing impaired persons react to various acoustic factors of the processed signal as a function of audiometric configuration and degree of hearing loss. One of the compression ratios he will use, for example, will contract the 0 to 4000 Hz energy band to 0 to 1600 Hz. Such compression may enable an individual who only hears the 0 to 1600 Hz energies to perceive all the distinguishing features of speech. Haspiel also plans to use both flat and 6 db rise/octave amplification responses. He anticipates that the device will become miniaturized and permit the severely hearing impaired individual to perceive and produce speech better than is presently possible.

Still another development in amplification devices is the feature of electromagnetic induction or loop amplification with a wearable hearing aid. Bellefleur (1968) proposes that electromagnetic induction offers not only an electronic device but a philosophy of education. Consistency of auditory input is assured, in contrast to use of individual or group hearing aids, because the child can hear a teacher's or parent's voice at considerable distance by means of induction, and his own voice and that of other children nearby via his microphone. He can use the same hearing aid in all circumstances rather than having to shift from one to another.

An extension beyond electromagnetic induction in the hearing aid development is the utilization of the *walkie-talkie* concept. A speaker talks into a wireless microphone, his speech is superimposed on a radio frequency carrier wave, the signal is transmitted through the air and received by a radio receiver device, the signal is then reamplified and delivered to the ear through earphones or through a wearable hearing aid type receiver.

The full possibilities of hearing aid use and auditory training for a hard of hearing child may best be realized in a laboratory setting. Training programs need to be developed to simulate the auditory tasks of numerous life situations. Such a facility can be equipped with capabilities for storage, retrieval, and delivery of both speech and nonspeech stimuli. Transfer effects can be studied by following children from contrived situations into a variety of real-life situations. These might include localization, discrimination of foreground from background and signal from "noise," and identification of the signal itself.

In or outside of the laboratory, criteria should be formulated to evaluate the preparation and presentation of an auditory training lesson. An example of criteria for older students is presented in Figure 10.
In this lesson, connected speech makes up the auditory signal. The main activity is imitation of the stimulus by the hard of hearing child. The strategy is synthetic rather than analytic in that the sentence is the primary stimulus unit. The perception of the intonational contour of the sentence is basic. Discrimination tasks employing parts of the sentence and then the complete stimulus unit again are utilized afterwards.

Clarke (1957) noted that a synthetic approach to auditory training was successful when an analytical strategy had not worked. He administered

Preparation Prior to Lesson	*Lesson Presentation*
1. Knowledge of auditory capacity	1. Stage manage the instructional session
2. Knowledge of speech acoustics	2. Use hearing aid properly
3. Use of optimal hearing aid	3. Check for and explain meaning of key words
4. Availability of lesson script	4. Follow a logical plan of presentation
5. Knowledge of lesson content	5. Be vocal, prosodic, articulate, fluent
6. Identification of key words	6. Compare stimuli with responses
7. Phonemic analysis of sentences	7. Paraphrase material as necessary
8. Detailed instructional plan	8. Reinforce and evaluate during and after lesson.

FIG. 10.   Criteria for teaching a concept through auditory training.

auditory training effectively to severely hard of hearing children in an English school for the deaf. The children revealed more improvement than a control group in speech perception, academic achievement and the like.

Speechreading Instruction

Another sensory mode which has been employed successfully for the understanding of speech by hard of hearing children is that of vision. The correct identification of thoughts transmitted via the visual components of utterance has been called speechreading or lipreading (O'Neill and Oyer, 1961). Lipreading may also be considered a learned form of linguistic behavior.

According to O'Neill (1968) the teaching of speechreading operationally encompasses facilitation of the following four areas: (1) the development of communication efficiency, (2) the acquisition of speech, (3) the development of language, and (4) educational, social, and vocational management.

O'Neill (1968) noted that training in visual communication involves the improvement of existing input systems, the expansion of the unused visual input systems, and finally the combination or integration of all input systems. Morkovin (1960) approximated this training model in his design for instruction called the *Contexual Synthetic Method of Teaching Speech Reading With Life Situation Motion Pictures*. His concept was that the visual sensory modality and channel is only one of several input systems that contribute to speech reception. Initial training should encompass separate activities for the perceptual improvement of each contributing sensory system. And final training activities should make use of all systems simultaneously.

Five prominent speechreading strategies have been utilized extensively in the United States since the beginning of the century. These are those of Nitchie (1950), Mueller-Walle (Bruhn, 1949), Brauckmann (Bunger, 1961), Mason (1942a, 1942b), and Morkovin (1960). Many of the features of these methodologists are similar but others are very different. Current hearing and speech remediation often encompasses an eclectic selection of components from various training sources.

The Nitchie approach is characterized by visual training and by aptitude instruction. According to this strategy, effective lipreading is partially based upon the ability of the eyes to recognize quickly the visible speech formations. However, it is more fully dependent on the training of certain qualities of the mind such as alertness, synthesis, and intuition. Materials are selected for instruction that reflect a synthetic rather than an analytical strategy. The approach is geared for adults but can be adapted to use with school age children.

During the past 20 years research investigations have substantiated and clarified the hypothesis of Nitchie. Seven of these studies with findings will be described briefly below.

1. O'Neill (1951) noted that a positive correlation existed between competence in visualizing designs, associating digit symbols, and speechreading performance.

2. He (1954) reported that normal individuals perceived visually only 45 percent of vowels, 72 percent of consonants, 64 percent of words, and 26 percent of phrases.

3. Stone (1957) noted that speaker differences and situational differences affected the speechreading process. He discovered, for example, that a grim expression was easier to speechread than a smiling face.

4. Wong and Taaffe (1958) determined through a multiple correlation technique that reasoning, ideational fluency, spontaneous flexibility, and association fluency were abilities important to speechreading.

5. Costello (1958a, 1958b) reported that among hard of hearing children a positive correlation existed between speechreading competence, thinking processes in Progressive Matrices tasks, and arranging picture sequences to depict social situations.

6. Simmons (1959) discovered that among hard of hearing individuals a positive relationship existed between speechreading competence and synthesizing ability.

7. Woodward (1957) found that individuals consistently identified only the lip movements associated with speech articulation. She hypothesized that speechreading was possible only because of the redundancy of phonemic, morphemic, and grammatical aspects of language. She discovered that listeners categorized the consonant phonemes into the following homophenous clusters: p b m; f v; wh w r; ch dz sh zh y; t d n l s z θ δ; k g h.

O'Neill and Oyer (1961) have designed tasks for the improvement of visual perception and intellectual aptitudes. The tasks may be presented by use of a tachistoscope so that stimuli can be presented at slow and rapid rates. The stimuli include incomplete single symbols, peripherally positioned symbol arrangements, and randomly positioned words from sentences. These tasks simulate the problem a speechreader faces in the correct identification of the thoughts of the speaker without the utilization of residual hearing.

The Mueller-Walle approach to speechreading instruction varies dramatically from that of the Nitchie strategy (Bruhn, 1949). It focuses attention upon the use of nonsense syllable and rhythm activities in typical lessons. The

The hard of hearing child typically has a more difficult time speechreading regular teachers than his special communication trainer. The nature of this problem may be exemplified in a modified version of the following table prepared by Dyer and Berg (1968).

The ratings of factors contributing to speechreadability varied from 1, which was highly desirable, to 5, which was highly undesirable. The teacher rated the highest was instructor 6 who was, incidentally, a communication training specialist. However, she herself used unnatural facial contortions.

It is of interest that instructors 2, 3, 4 and 6 received 4 or 5 ratings on one or more contributory factors. This finding suggests that guidance in the presentation of speech stimuli should be given to regular teachers of hard of hearing children. An initial step in the guidance process might be to share with the teacher a special videotape exemplifying both desirable and undesirable speech behaviorisms. After a discussion of this tape, the teacher might be guided in confronting a videotape showing her own lesson presentation. A check list including such factors as those in Table 37 might be made available to the teacher thereafter so that a continuing self-evaluation would take place.

The task the hard of hearing child faces in understanding classroom lectures and discussion might also be facilitated by use of tactual aids. Two recent experiments, the former by Pickett and Pickett (1963) and the latter by Kringleboton (1968), serve to illustrate the application with severely hearing impaired children. The devices employed in both experiments converted frequency phenomena of incoming speech to spatial patterns of vibrations on the fingertips.

Pickett applied ten 300 Hz bands of vibration to the 10 fingertips. He tested identification of all major phonemes with speechreading alone and with the addition of tactual reception. The utilization of the tactual device helped somewhat on speech distinctions that are extremely difficult to speechread such as voicing, nasality, and affrication.

Kringleboton designed and tested a simplified tactual vocoder employing only five vibrators applied to one hand. Five frequency ranges of the speech signal vibrated the fingers individually. The speechreading scores of the

Table 37. Ratings of Factors Contributing to the Speechreadability of Instructors

Contribution	1	2	3	4	5	6	Median
1. Lip movements	3	2	3	3	3	1	3
2. Mouth openings	3	2	4	4	3	1	3
3. Facing students	1	3	2	5	1	2	2
4. Eye contact	1	5	4	4	1	1	2.5
5. Expressive face	2	3	3	4	2	1	2.5
6. Makes "faces"	1	1	1	1	1	5	1
7. Hand gestures	2	2	3	2	2	1	2
8. Beard or moustache	1	4	1	5	1	1	1
Median	1	2	3	4	1	1	—

severely hearing impaired children used as subjects improved with the employment of this vocoder.

The Kringleboton vocoder may have particular application for some hard of hearing children. Speech distinctions that cannot be identified auditorily or visually might be recognized tactually. The hard of hearing child could receive tactual impressions with one hand, write some notes with the other hand, while visually attending to the face of the instructor as well.

Still another device designed to facilitate speechreading is a sound analyzer designed and used by Upton (1968) who is hard of hearing himself. Five display lamps, mounted on an eyeglass lens which also frames the speaker's face, light in response to voiced sounds, unvoiced fricatives, unvoiced stops, voiced fricatives, and voiced stops. The Upton analyzing device, which employs integrated circuitry, is concealed beneath his clothing. Upton reports that he is a poor speechreader unless he uses his speech analyzer.

Speech Instruction

Another characteristic problem of the hard of hearing child alluded to earlier is difficulty in oral transmission of thought. The problem is one of difficulty in speech articulation, voice production, and sometimes prosodic patterning. It is a problem that has resisted typically conducted speech remediation. Table 38 summarizes the percentages of 15 types of speech errors exhibited by young hard of hearing adults with normal language facility (DiCarlo, 1968). Misarticulations of consonant blends and arresting consonants as well as nasalization of vowels were particularly characteristic of the speech of these hard of hearing teenagers. However, the sentences in which the errors occurred were consistently intelligible.

The severity of defective speech seems to be closely correlated with degree of hearing impairment. Near the lower end of a continuum of defective

*Table 38. Types of and Percentage of Occurrence of Speech Errors Used by 15 Hard of Hearing Teenagers While Uttering Selected Sentences**

Error Type	Percentage of Occurrence
1. Consonant omission	2.5
2. Regular consonant substitution	8.3
3. Consonant substitution	7.9
4. Consonant blend	20.8
5. Abutting consonant	3.1
6. Releasing consonant	3.0
7. Arresting consonant	24.1
8. Nasalization of consonant	1.6
9. Substitution of vowel	9.0
10. Diphthong fractionization	8.3
11. Diphthongization of vowel	2.2
12. Neutralization of vowel	0.4
13. Nasalization of vowel	34.4
14. Abnormal rhythm in sentence	8.0
15. Arythmic sentence	1.3

*Data summarized from DiCarlo, 1968.

speech might be children with auditory thresholds between 30 and 45 db and with small perceptive hearing losses. At the upper end of this continuum might be children with auditory thresholds beyond 90 db and with little or no speech perception. The number of speech errors uttered by a child with minimal hearing loss might be very few as compared to the number typically employed by an individual with profound acoustic impairment. A review of some important findings from speech investigations of profoundly hearing impaired children might serve to clarify this situation.

Hudgins and Numbers (1942) conducted a classical investigation of the speech of 8–20 year old children in two oral schools for the deaf. They analyzed ten sentences orally read by each student to determine the frequency and types of errors made and their relationship to speech intelligibility. These children made a great many more errors of the types referred to in Table 38 than did hard of hearing children. They consistently misarticulated consonants and vowels as well as distorted stress and melodic patterns. Correspondingly, many of the sentences uttered were unintelligible to listeners. In addition, the voice quality used by the deaf was generally breathy and harsh in addition to often being nasal.

More recent investigations of the speech of deaf children substantiate and clarify the findings of Hudgins and Numbers. Angelloci (1962) noted that 8–12 year old deaf boys generally were unable to reach their targets on selected vowel production. Hood and Dixon (1969) found that the deaf were extremely limited in making full use of prosody to convey speech intelligibility.

In contrast to the deaf, hard of hearing children characteristically speak intelligibly within the framework of their grammar, vocabulary, and conceptualization. Their speech competencies typically include the following: correct production of most vowels, variation of syllable duration as a function of voicing, natural prosody and rhythm, normal level and control of pitch, and fluent utterance. However, the speech of the hard of hearing is usually noticeably defective because the articulatory and vocal manuevering for certain sounds is often incorrect.

We continue to await the day when hard of hearing children will speak as they are spoken to rather than as they perceive speech. Amazingly, some congenitally deaf persons have approximated this feat. They are evidence that a remedial speech program is plausible within the total habilitation program for hard of hearing children. At least seven variables might be critical in the development of an optimal remedial speech program for the hearing impaired as may be noted below.

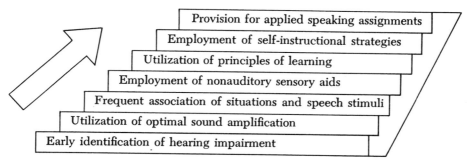

Provision for applied speaking assignments
Employment of self-instructional strategies
Utilization of principles of learning
Employment of nonauditory sensory aids
Frequent association of situations and speech stimuli
Utilization of optimal sound amplification
Early identification of hearing impairment

Identification of Hearing Problem

The presence and nature of the impairment should be ascertaained early in the life of a child with a hearing loss. It is during the first three years of life that speech intelligibility and fluency are basically attained. A remedial bypass of these years may result in a child who could be just hard of hearing being educationally deaf. A case in point is that of Staffan Wedenberg, the son of Erik Wedenberg, who despite a profound hearing loss virtually became a hard of hearing person because remediation was initiated early in his life. The elder Wedenberg (1967b) estimates that 80 percent of the children in schools for the deaf could have been educated in regular schools provided early identification and follow-up instruction existed.

Utilization of Hearing Aids

Optimal sound amplification should be utilized carefully from the beginning months of the life of a hard of hearing child. A hearing aid, if one is beneficial, should exhibit physical characteristics that facilitate perception of speech and nonspeech environmental sounds. Binaural amplification is preferable to monaural fitting provided the auditory channel capacities of the two ears are highly similar. The concern is to deliver as much undistorted sound to the auditory system of the hard of hearing child as possible.

Association of Situations and Speech Stimuli

Natural and contrived situations together with planned speech stimulation should be conducted on a daily basis by one or more parents of the hard of hearing child. Wedenberg (1967b) advocated daily play-talk situations between parent and child. Simmons (1967) recommended a minimum of 1200 hours of parent-child interaction for speech stimulation.

Simmons and her assistant at the Central Institute for the Deaf train parents to appropriately stimulate their hard of hearing children. They find that the preparation, eating, and cleanup surrounding meals and snacks provide a large number and extensive variety of significant situations for occasioning language development through audition. They focus particular attention on the utilization of clear articulation, intonational contrasts, and repetition of selected function words in various phrase and sentence utterances. Periodic tape recordings of the vocal utterances of young hard of hearing children reveal progressive gains in the employment of phonological, morphological, and syntactic forms.

Wedenberg (1951, 1954, 1967a) also recognize that the spoken stimulus was an important variable in speech remediation. During initial auditory training he limited the phonemic content of the speech stimuli to voiced sounds. He had noted that spectrographic and audiometric analyses revealed that voiced formants could be perceived by even severely hearing impaired children. In contrast, he discovered that the energies of the voiceless phonemes such as /s/ and /ʃ/ were distributed particularly in high audio frequency regions, an area typically not encompassed in the residuum of defective hearing. Wedenberg, it may be noted, recommended to one pair of parents that they call their son by his middle name "Valter" rather than his first name "Krister." He felt that it was important that the child be able to hear his own name.

Employment of Nonauditory Aids

Sometime between the hard of hearing child's third and fifth birthdays, speech remediation can be extended from sole use of auditory stimulation to employment of visual and tactual aids. The wise utilization of vision and taction encompasses employment of conventional media such as a mirror, a chalkboard, written notations, static illustrations, and clues of head vibration and airflow during speech. It also includes use of several promising electrosensory devices.

1. Utilization of the mirror enables the hard of hearing child to mimic labial, mandibular, and frontal aspects of lingual movements associated with speech production. Although limited to a small part of the intricate manuevering of articulate speech, mirror view can provide sensory clues not easily obtainable (if at all) through the use of the auditory sensory modality alone. For example, /p/, /t/, and /k/ may be differentiated more readily visually than auditorily.

2. Employment of a chalkboard and written and drawn notations of phonemes further enables the instructor and student to compare the speech of each other. These notations, such as /o/, and /f/ for sound elements and /'/ for stress, are helpful in speech remediation to the extent that the student can correlate them with motor speech characteristics. Although it is difficult to portray the physiological correlates of speech by notations, the corrective value of such symbols is considerable.

3. Utilization of illustrations of motor speech positions enables the instructor to convey to the student certain utterance activities hidden from mirror viewing. For example, the student can perceive that the /g/ is produced by laryngeal vibration, nasal port closure, and lingua-velar tongue positioning. As valuable as it is, static illustrations portray only fixed articulatory positions and some indications of the dynamics or movements of speech.

4. The tactual sensory avenue may be better designed for assisting with the teaching of the dynamic characteristics of speech. Typically, one hand of the child manuevers on the instructor's face and his other hand on his own face. A variety of tactual clues become perceptible including mandibular excursion and rate; voicing; nasality; and amount, speed, location, and direction of oral emission of air; and presence and amount of nasal escape of air during speech.

The child compares his productions with those of the instructor through tactual feedback and makes corrections within the limitations of the distinctive features of speech perceived through this sensory modality and the resistance of the organism to change. The hard of hearing child might differentiate the /s/ from the /ʃ/ or the /p/ from the /t/, sound pairs that may be difficult to discriminate by use of audition alone. It should be remembered that the deaf-blind Helen Keller developed rudimentary speech skills by use of the tactual sensory modality. Without such assistance, her vocalizations would have remained as grunts and similar noises.

The electro-sensory devices that are suggested offer promise for further refinement in the speaking competencies of the hard of hearing child. One of these devices, a broad band hearing aid, has been described earlier in this chapter. Additional aids are detailed below.

1. A Lissajou display, described originally by Pronovost et al. (1968) and called the voice visualizer, provides visual feedback of intensity, pitch, phonetic occurrence in simple syllables, speed of utterance, and voicing. Intensity can be perceived, for example, by the size of Lissajou pattern produced by a sustained vowel or by a consonant. Such information alerts the hard of hearing student to the need to increase vocal intensity which typically is weak in his utterances. It also enables him to recognize when he emits a particular phoneme with insufficient intensity, such as a final or arresting consonant.

The voice visualizer display reveals pitch change by Lissajou-pattern change. For example, a double circle turns into a single circle as the pitch level of a sustained /o/ is increased considerably. Conversely, it changes noticeably as pitch is lowered. Ordinarily, the hard of hearing child has a normal pitch level but may not produce normal intersyllable pitch change. Practice in continually varying a given Lissajou pattern during speech remediation may provide a beneficial transfer effect into actual speaking situations.

The Lissajou display also enables the instructor to focus the attention of the child on phonetic completeness in short syllables. A sequence of patterns corresponding to three phonemes can be retained. The child can perceive, therefore, whether he is omitting or otherwise changing the production of one of the phonemes.

In addition, the voice visualizer provides a useful feedback on rate of speech. Each time a syllable is uttered, a noticeable visual indication is provided. Also, sufficient detail appears on the screen to enable the instructor and the student to compare utterances at varying rates. Such practice is valuable, for example, when a child can only articulate a word like *kiss* if produced slowly.

One more advantage of the Lissajou display is the particularly good presentation of the voicing characteristic. The distinction, for example, between the /s/ and /z/ is readily seen in Figure 12. In addition, physical distinctions corresponding to allophonic variations of either phoneme can be recognized. Such detailed information is not available to the hard of hearing child by use of a defective auditory modality.

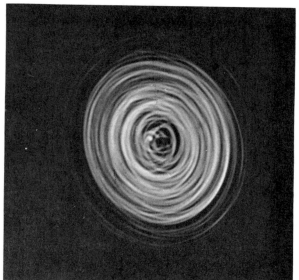

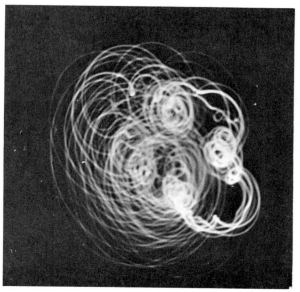

Fig. 12. Physical distinction between the /s/ and /z/. (Pronovost et al., 1968.)

2. A second type of oscilloscopic device presents a single spot of light that moves from position to position dependent on the vowel employed and independent of intensity (Pickett and Constam, 1968). The front vowels, characterized by high F_2 and F_1, deflect the spot from left to right as the back articulation becomes closer.

Figure 13 reveals the effect of the utterance of both sustained vowels and selected words upon the spot of the Pickett display. It may be hypothesized that the visual detail of this ceptrum display would assist the hard of hearing child to differentiate between two vowels, such as /i/ and /e/, which have similar formant patterns. Some hard of hearing children may misperceive such differences auditorily and correspondingly not distinguish between them in their utterances.

3. A third type of oscilloscopic device of benefit to a speech remediation program is a time swept contour indicator. Such a device depicts pitch or amplitude contours and provides durational information on connected speech as well. With a contour indicator, a hard of hearing child can compare intricate pitch and intensity patterns of his utterances with those of a target pattern made by an instructor.

The visual information on pitch and timing, or intensity and timing, vivifies the auditory perception of the hard of hearing child. It serves with audition as a firm base from which to improve prosodic and rhythmic speech features which may be lacking in the utterances of some hard of hearing children, particularly those with more severe hearing impairment. Phillips et al. (1968) state that severely hearing impaired children using a contour indicator may become aware that they possess a normal pitch range, that they can change their pitch and that pitch range need not be dependent on vocal intensity.

4. An alternative device for the control of pitch has been developed by Holbrook (1968a). The system called FLORIDA consists of a microphone, an amplifier, a 72 db octave bandpass filter, an overload circuit, a target unit that signals appropriate frequency range, a monitor oscilloscope, and an oscillator.

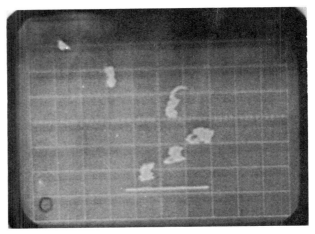

Fɪɢ. 13.   Speech patterns of the Gallaudet visual speech trainer. *Left,* sustained vowel sounds, from above down, /i/, /e/, as in bait, /ɛ/ as in bet, /a/, /ɔ/ as in awe, /o/ as in rode, /u/ (appears as horizontal line). (Pickett, 1968.)

Normal fluctuations in vocal frequency activate a green light viewed by the subject and an electric timer seen by the instructor. Consequently, the student knows immediately that he is on target, and the instructor has a record of duration of this behavior. Also, a reward contingency such as number of tokens is prearranged based on the time the green light is on. When the student speaks too loudly, the overload circuit is activated, the green light and timer go off, and a red light is viewed by the student.

5. Another electro-sensory device of value in a speech remedial program for the hard of hearing child is a nasality indicator. Of several such devices becoming available to the specialist, the nasality indicator designed by Holbrook (1968b) is particularly worthy of description. It consists of a capsulated phonograph cartridge, an amplifier-rectifier-relay and a signaling device such as a light. A small drop of solder is placed on the cartridge to provide mass. The small capsule is then taped to the nose of the child. As the child speaks or vocalizes, the movement of a nare signals hypernasality.

Hypernasality is characteristic of the speech of many hard of hearing children. Some hard of hearing children have not learned to port off their nasal cavities. Others can do so voluntarily but do not transfer this velopharyngeal competence into speech production. Because only three of the English phonemes are articulated with an open nasal port, our speech normally has an oral rather than a nasal quality. For the child who cannot voluntarily close the nasal port, rapid control of sphinctering is learned by tetanizing the lateral and posterior pharyngeal walls with electrical muscle stimulation (Yules, 1968).

6. A combination of cinefluorographic and photographic equipment provides still another advantageous electro-visual display for speech remediation (Grey et al., 1961). It enables speech manuevers hidden from normal view to be radiographed, photographed, and played back as pairs of correctly and incorrectly articulated syllables.

Film loop projectors, which feature forward and reverse motion, variable speed, and remote control, are commercially available. They permit repetitive analysis of the radiographed manuevering of the tongue, palate, and vocal folds. Target manuevering by the instructor and incorrect manuevering by the child, corresponding to articulate and inarticulate speech, are radiographed in advance of the remedial sessions. Comparisons of words, phrases, and sentences can also be made. A limited amount of remedial stimuli can be prepared at any one time, however, because of the danger of overexposure to x-rays.

The above array of devices provide a firm cybernetic basis for dramatic improvement of the speech competencies of hard of hearing children. Feedback far beyond that which has been utilized in the past is available today. Particularly if speech remediation can begin early in life and under skilled hands, the hard of hearing child may acquire intelligible and even near-normal vocal competencies.

Utilization of Learning Principles

The application of principles of learning will further facilitate the effectiveness of a speech remedial program for hard of hearing children. Provision should be made for evoking, shaping, and stabilizing responses by use of careful reinforcement (Keller and Shoenfeld, 1950) and sufficient trials (Berg, 1960, 1963). Discriminative stimuli should be incorporated into remedial schedules from the beginning so that articulations and vocalizations are not only correct but linguistically appropriate. The chaining of correct responses into the sequences of contextual speech should be carefully programmed. And transfer of learning of skills from one phonetic context to many others should be planned.

The tried and proved procedures of the past might well be incorporated into the promising strategies of the present and the future. The successful procedures of the past include Avondino's (1929) vocal play activities, Connery and Young's (1935) techniques of vocal improvement, Haycock's (1941) cerrections for articulatory errors and drills for production of the rhythmic aspects of speech, Hudgins' and Numbers' (1942) prosodic and rhythmic activities, New's (1942) use of color for indicating voicing and nasality, Alcorn's (1949) employment of vibration, Silverman's (1954, 1957) differential selection of sensory aids, Zaliouk's (1954) employment of tactual and visual clues of speech dynamics, Van Riper and Irwin's (1958) feedback techniques, Van Riper's (1963) stimulation activities, Mowrer's (1969) use of prosthetic aids for the elicitation of difficult phonemes, and Winitz's (1969) psycholingustic approach to speech remediation.

One of the most promising instructional strategies for speech remediation is that of precision teaching (Lindsley, 1966). It requires pinpointing the behavior to be taught, systematic introduction of teaching variables one by one, counting all desired and undesired responses, and graphing all data on logarithmic paper. This approach introduces an experimental rigor into speech remediation such as has not existed before. Also, the counting and graphing of responses has beneficial reinforcing and motivational effects upon learning.

A frequently employed component of newer strategies of teaching is the establishment of criteria of learning. Mowrer (1969b), for example, includes two criteria in time delay and distraction activities designed to stabilize the production of a target phoneme. The criterion during time delay simulation is 85 percent correct in 330 responses; during distraction simulation it is 90 percent accurate in 45 responses. Mowrer utilizes these activities because he finds that a child who has received minimal training in producing a target phoneme does not continue to elicit it when an interruption or time delay occurs between responses. As soon as a response pattern is interrupted, or a distraction occurs (for example, by a phone call or a book dropping to the floor), errors in production which were not occurring begin to exist.

A second example of use of criteria in learning appeared in a study of stimulus control conducted by White (1970). Using procedures developed by McLean (1967), White taught a severely hearing impaired child to articulate the /tʃ/ phoneme under echoic, picture, graphemic, and intraverbal conditions. He found that once the /tʃ/ came under good control and was emitted at high stable levels under one stimulus type, it tended to be shifted readily to other stimuli which had not previously evoked the response. McLean had hypothesized that if the response became functional in a wide range of stimulus conditions, it tended to become functional under all similar conditions. The criterion of learning used for moving from the picture to the graphemic condition was 20 consecutive correct responses. Similar criteria were set up for the other two stimulus conditions.

Another characteristic component of the newer strategies of teaching is the utilization of subspecialists in speech management. In a description of programming and behavioral modification for speech defective children, Mowrer (1969b), outlines three distinct but overlapping tasks: (1) evoking and stabilizing the target phoneme, (2) incorporating it into morphemes, and (3) utilizing it in contextual units. He noted that the first two tasks could best be performed by a specialist or a trained aid. The third task could well be done by parents and siblings, peer members, and classroom teachers, all of whom would employ precision teaching procedures.

Mowrer's (1969b) inclusion of the phoneme into morphemic and syntactical forms is exemplary, also, of the latest strategies of speech remediation. The linguistic approach recognizes that the phonological, morphological, and syntactic forms are subsystems of language itself. The impact of the application of this approach should facilitate speech mastery among hard of hearing children.

Employment of Self-Instruction

Another modern strategy with considerable promise for speech management is the utilization of self-instructional devices. An example of one of these devices is the Electronic Futures Incorporated audio tutor system. This device consists of a modified 2-channel tape recorder, an amplifier, and individual earphones as desirable. Utilization of four pushbuttons, audio flashcards, and recorded speech signals control the learning activity. Up to a 6-second speech signal can be recorded on each channel. A hard of hearing child can hear the auditory stimuli, see facilitative notations inscribed on the flashcards, respond verbally to the stimuli and playback responses for comparison and correction.

An EFI audio tutor or similar device can provide a medium through which a hard of hearing child may increase the intelligibility with which he says literally thousands of speech signals. A flashcard library can be prepared, criteria for completion of tasks can be established, specific rewards can be arranged, and a cumulative record of achievement on each hard of hearing child can be kept. Such a self-instructional system might be employed in a special learning laboratory containing cubicles, storage facilities, and facilities for programming, monitoring, and evaluating responses.

Provision for Social Speaking

The final stage of a remedial program for a hard of hearing child is the application of oral communication skills into everyday speaking situations.

Henning (1966) describes oral communication as "the integrated use of words, voice, and action by the speaker for the purpose of accurate and skillful communication of his ideas and feelings to a listener." Each child should be helped to establish and meet individualized goals in oral communication.

Oliver, Zelko, and Holtzman (1968) suggest that oral communication is mutual induction more than message transmission. Mutual induction occurs by initial preparation of oneself for interaction with others in varying communication situations and then by speaking. Part of this preparation requires that the hard of hearing child become sensitive to communication bonds and barriers, develop a sense of communicative purpose, and become increasingly aware of communication feedback systems.

The development of oral communication competencies by the hard of hearing child will be assisted by as well as feed a growing awareness of the various environmental sensory stimuli. It will also be reciprocally related to language learning and levels of substantive learning. An emphasis given to the acquisition of oral communication skills in remediation will correspondingly enhance feelings of personal worth as well as result in highly desirable social and career opportunities.

Professional Preparation

One last requirement in educational audiology is the availability of well-prepared clinical and educational specialists. The competencies required are rigorous, encompassing various substantive, practical, and professional talents. A critical need exists for the professional preparation of such talented individuals to assist hard of hearing children.

Mowrer (1969b), for example, describes needed skills for his precision clinical training program. These skills cover competencies required before, during, and following remediation. The pre-remedial competencies include design and operation of audiovisual media, auditory discrimination of allophones, judgment of correctness of speech responses, design of behavioral objectives, and of instructional sequences. The remedial competencies encompass presentation of general and branching programs; visual, auditory, kinesthetic, and prosthetic cueing techniques; training peer members to monitor speech; and management of consequent events. The post-remedial skills include graphical analysis of response rates, design of daily parent and teacher programs, and arrangement of pay-off contingencies for peer monitors.

Another approach to professional preparation is employed by Boone (1969). Audiotape and videotape self-confrontation are used to assist prospective specialists to develop clinical skills in speech remediation. Self-confrontation refers to a feedback procedure in which an individual hears and/or sees an audiotape, videotape, or film of his own behavior in a particular situation. Boone and Goldberg require the prospective clinician who is being confronted with his own remedial interplay with a client to categorize observed behaviors and discuss them with a supervisor. Behavioral principles are applied to reinforce desired clinical behavior with particular emphasis on self-reinforcement.

The advantages of self-confrontation are at least twofold. First, the prospective clinician can note how his particular behaviors affect client behavior and influence the remedial session. Secondly, the supervisor can provide reinforcement to the trainee as he is reviewing his behaviors.

Summary

In resumé, educational audiology is a new strategy being developed to contribute substantially to the alleviation of the unmet habilitative needs of hard of hearing children, particularly those with marginal to severe acoustic impairment. This strategy integrates promising evaluational and management procedures to optimize educational advancement. Special emphasis in this endeavor is given to the wise utilization of various sensory modalities, especially that of audition because of its unique capabilities for language learning and for oral communication.

References

Alcorn, K. 1949. Speech developed through vibration. Volta Review 1949:633–638.

Angelocci, A. A. 1962. A comparative study of vowel formants of deaf and normal-hearing eleven- to fourteen-year-old boys. Ph.D. Dissertation, Wayne State University.

Avondino, J. 1929. The babbling method. A System of Syllable Drills for the Natural Development of Speech. Washington, D.C.: The Volta Bureau.

Bellefleur, P. 1967. Comments on European programs for the hearing impaired. Institute on Characteristics and Needs of the Hard of Hearing Child. Unpublished material, Utah State University.

Bellefleur, P. 1968. Uses of Electromagnetic Induction (Loop) for the Hearing Handicapped. Philadelphia, Pa.: Pennsylvania School for the Deaf.

Berg, F. 1960. Serial learning: an approach to auditory training. Unpublished Ph.D. Dissertation, Southern Illinois University.

Berg, F. 1963. Serial learning—an approach to a rationale for auditory training. Report of the Proceedings of the International Congress on Education of the Deaf and of the 41st Meeting of the Convention of American Instructors of the Deaf. Washington, D.C.: Gallaudet College.

Berg, F. and S. Fletcher. 1967. The hard of hearing child and educational audiology. Proceedings of International Conference on Oral Education of the Deaf 1. Washington, D. C.: The Volta Bureau. Pp. 874–885.

Berko, J. 1961. The child's learning of English morphology. In S. Saporta (Ed.) Psycholinguistics. New York: Holt, Rinehart and Winston. Pp. 359–376.

Berry, M. 1969. Language Disorders of Children. New York: Appleton-Century-Crofts.

Berry, M. and R. Talbott. 1966. Exploratory Test of Grammar. 4332 Pince Crest Rd., Rockford, Ill., 61107.

Boone, D. and A. Goldberg. 1969. An experimental study of the clinical acquisition of behavioral principles by video-tape self-confrontation. Final Report. Project 4071. Washington, D.C.: Office of Education.

Boothroyd, A. 1967. Theoretical aspects of auditory training. Proceedings of International Conference on Oral Education of the Deaf 1. Washington, D.C.: The Alexander Graham Bell Association for the Deaf. Pp. 705–729.

Bruhn, M. 1949. The Mueller-Walle Method of Lipreading for the Hard of Hearing. Washington, D.C.: The Volta Bureau.

Bunger, A. 1961. Speech Reading: Jena Method. Danville, Ill.: The Interstate.

Butt, D. and F. Chreist. 1968. A speechreading test for young children. The Volta Review 70:225–239.

Calvert, D. 1962. Speech sound duration and the surd-sonant error. The Volta Review 64:401–402.

Clarke, B. 1957. Use of a group hearing aid by profoundly deaf children. In A. Ewing (Ed.) Educational Guidance of the Deaf Child. Washington, D.C.: The Volta Bureau. Pp. 128–159.

Connery, J. M. and I. B. Young. 1935. Voice building. Beginning the Technique of Developing the Voice of the Deaf Child and Conserving Natural Quality in the Voice of the Hard-of-Hearing. St. Louis: Central Institute for the Deaf.

Costello, M. R. 1958a. A study of speechreading as a developing language process in deaf and hard of hearing children. Ph.D. Dissertation, Northwestern University.

Costello, M. R. 1958b. Language Development Through Speechreading. Reprint No. 705. Washington, D.C.: Volta Bureau.

Crabtree, M. 1958. The Houston Test for Language Development. Houston: The Houston Test Company.

Davis, H. and S. R. Silverman (Eds.). 1960. Everyday speech (CID), Appendix 9. Hearing and Deafness. New York: Holt, Rinehart and Winston.

De Hirsh, K., J. Jansky, and W. Langford. 1964. Oral language performance of two groups of immature children. Folia Phoniatrica 16:109–122.

DiCarlo, L. 1962. Some relationships between frequency discrimination and speech reception performance. Journal of Auditory Research II:47–59.

DiCarlo, L. 1968. Speech, language, and cognitive abilities of the hard-of-hearing. Proceedings of the Institute on Aural Rehabilitation. Supported by SRS 212-T-68. University of Denver. Pp. 45–66.

Dunn, L. 1965. Peabody Picture Vocabulary Test. Minneapolis: American Guidance Service.

Dyer, D. and F. Berg. 1968. Ratings of factors contributing to the speech-readability of instructors. Unpublished paper read at Summer Meeting of Alexander Graham Bell Association for the Deaf.

Eagles, E. L., S. M. Wishik, and L. G. Doerfler. 1963. Hearing sensitivity and related factors in children. Monograph. St. Louis: The Laryngoscope.

Fanchea, M. 1955. Auditory training at St. Joseph's Institute. The Volta Review 57:260–262.

Fisher, C. 1968. Present and future use of closed circuit and commercial television in training the hard of hearing. Proceedings of the Institute on Aural Rehabilitation. Supported by SRS 212-T-68. University of Denver. Pp. 103–108.

Gaeth, J. 1960. Verbal learning among children with reduced hearing acuity. Office of Education Project 289. Final Report. Washington, D.C.: Office of Education.

Gaeth, J. 1963. Verbal and non-verbal learning in children including those with hearing losses. Office of Education Cooperative Research Project No. 1001. Washington, D.C.: Office of Education.

Gaeth, J. 1966. Verbal and non-verbal learning in children including those with hearing losses. Part II. Office of Education Project No. 2207. Washington, D.C.: Office of Education.

Goldstein, M. 1939. The Acoustic Method For the Training of the Deaf and Hard of Hearing Child. St. Louis: The Laryngoscope Press.

Grey, H., F. Sloan, F. Ashley, E. Hahn, and W. Hanafee. 1961. Cinefluorography as an aid to more intelligible speech. Volta Review 63:323–327, 356.

Griffith, C. 1967. Auditory training in the first year of life. Proceedings of International Conference on Oral Education of the Deaf 1. Washington, D.C.: The Alexander Graham Bell Association for the Deaf. Pp. 758–772.

Guberina, P. 1969. The verbotonal method. Questions and answers. The Volta Review 71(4): 213–224.

Haspiel, G. S. 1969. Measurement of acoustic parameters for speech compression-transposition. Project No. RD-2575-S. Progress Report, Social Rehabilitation Service.

Haycock, S. 1941. The Teaching of Speech. Washington, D.C.: The Volta Bureau.

Heider, G. 1934. Psychological research in lipreading and language. The Volta Review 36:517–520.

Henning, J. 1966. Improving Oral Communication. New York: McGraw-Hill.

Hogan, J. 1961. The ABC of Auditory Training: A Manual for Classroom Use with Young Deaf Children. St. Louis: St. Joseph Institute for the Deaf.

Holbrook, A. 1968a. A device for automatic modification of vocal frequency and intensity. Unpublished paper, Florida State University, Tallahassee.

Holbrook, A. 1968b. Nasality indicator. Working papers, Florida State University, Tallahassee.

Hood, R. and R. Dixon. 1969. Physical characteristics of speech rhythm of deaf and normal-hearing speakers. Journal of Communication Disorders 2:20–28.

Hoshiko, M. and G. Holloway. 1968. Radio telemetry for the monitoring of verbal behavior. Journal of Speech and Hearing Disorders 33:48–50.

Hudgins, C. 1953. The response of profoundly deaf children to auditory training. Journal of Speech and Hearing Disorders 18:273–288.

Hudgins, C. V. and R. C. Numbers. 1942. An investigation of the intelligibility of the speech of the deaf. Genetic Psychological Monograph 1942:337–360.

Huizing, H. 1952. Auditory training. Acta Oto-Laryngologica, Supplementum 110: 158–163. Stockholm.

Jeffers, J. 1966. Formants and the auditory training of deaf children. The Volta Review 68:418–423, 449.

Johansson, B. A new coding amplifier system for the severely hard of hearing. Reprinted from Proceedings 3rd International Congress on Acoustics. Amsterdam: Elsevier Publishing Company. Pp. 655–657.

Keller, F. and W. Schoenfeld. 1950. Principles of Psychology. New York: Appleton-Century-Crofts.

Kelly, J. 1953. Clinician's Handbook for Auditory Training. Dubuque, Iowa: William C. Brown Co.

Kelly, J. 1954. A summer residential program in hearing education. Journal of Speech and Hearing Disorders 19:17–27.

Kringleboton, M. 1968. Experiments with some vibrotactile and visual aids for the deaf. Proceedings of the Conference on Speech Analyzing Aids. American Annals of the Deaf 113:311–317.

Larson, D. 1970. Operant and nonoperant tasks in auditory training. Unpublished master's thesis, Utah State University, Logan.

Lewis, M. M. 1951. Infant Speech: A Study of the Beginnings of Language. New York: Humanities Press. London: Routledge and Kegan Paul.

Liberman, A., F. Cooper, D. Shankweiler, and M. Studdert-Kennedy. 1968. Why are speech spectrograms hard to read? American Annals of the Deaf 113:127–133.

Lieberman, P. 1967. Intonation, Perception, and Language. Cambridge, Mass.: The MIT Press.

Lillywhite, H. 1968. Working papers. The Oregon language development profile. Portland, Oregon: University of Oregon Medical School.

Lindsley, O. 1966. An experiment with parents handling behavior at home. Johnstone Bulletin 9:27–36.

Ling, D. 1964. Implications of hearing aid amplification below 300 cps. The Volta Review 66:723–729.

Ling, D. 1968. Three experiments on frequency transposition. American Annals of the Deaf 113:283–294.

Lorenz, M. 1961. Speech and Auditory Training: Manual for the Deaf Child in the Intermediate Grades. St. Louis: St. Joseph Institute for the Deaf.

Martin, E. and J. Pickett. 1968. Sensorineural hearing loss and upward spread of masking. Unpublished paper, Gallaudet College, Washington, D.C.

Mason, M. 1942a. A cinematographic technique for testing more objectively the visual speech comprehension of young deaf and hard of hearing children. Doctoral Dissertation, The Ohio State University.

Mason, M. 1942b. Teaching and testing visual hearing by the cinematographic method. The Volta Review 44:703–705.

McCarthy, J. and S. Kirk. 1961. Examiners' Manual. Illinois Test of Psycholinguistic Abilities (Experimental Education). Urbana, Ill.: University of Illinois Press.

McConnel, F. 1968. Philosophical framework for rehabilitation and habilitation of the hard of hearing. Proceedings of the Institute on Aural Rehabilitation. Supported by SRS 212-T-68. University of Denver. Pp. 2–13.

McDonald, E. 1964. Articulation Testing and Treatment: A Sensory-Motor Approach. Pittsburgh: Stanwix House.

McDonald, E. 1964. A Deep Test of Articulation. (Picture and Sentence Forms) Pittsburgh: Stanwix House.

McDonald, E. 1968. Screening Deep Test of Articulation. Pittsburgh: Stanwix House.

McGinnis, M. 1963. Aphasic Children. Identification and Education by the Association Method. Washington, D.C.: Alexander Graham Bell Association for the Deaf.

McLean, J. 1967. Shifting stimulus control of articulation responses by operant techniques. Parson's Demonstration Project. Report 82. Lawrence, Kansas: Parsons Research Center.

Mecham, M., J. Jex, and J. Jones. 1967. Manual of Instructions: Utah Test of Language Development (Revised Edition). Salt Lake City: Communication Research Associates.

Morkovin, B. 1960. Through the Barriers of Deafness and Isolation. New York: Macmillan.

Morley, D. 1949. An analysis by sound spectrograph of intelligibility variations of consonant sounds spoken by deaf persons. Ph.D. Dissertation, University of Michigan.

Mowrer, D. 1969a. Evaluation speech therapy through precision recording. Journal of Speech and Hearing Disorders 34:239–244.

Mowrer, D. 1969b. Working papers on the management of articulation. Arizona State University, Tempe.

Myklebust, H. 1964. The Psychology of Deafness. New York: Grune & Stratton.

New, M. 1942. Color in speech teaching. The Volta Review 44:133–138.

Nitchie, E. H. 1950. New Lessons in Lipreading. Philadelphia: Lippincott.

Oliver, R., H. Zelko, and P. Holtzman. 1968. Communicative Speaking and Listening. New York: Holt, Rinehart and Winston.

O'Neill, J. 1951. An exploratory investigation of lipreading ability among normal hearing students. Speech Monographs 18: 309–311.

O'Neill, J. 1954. Contribution of the visual components of oral symbols to speech comprehension. Journal of Speech and Hearing Disorders 19:429–439.

O'Neill, J. 1968. Lipreading–significance and usage for children and adults. Proceedings of the Institute on Aural Rehabilitation. Supported by SRS 212-T-68. University of Denver. Pp. 45–66.

O'Neill, J. and H. Oyer. 1961. Visual Communication for the Hard of Hearing. Englewood Cliffs, N.J.: Prentice-Hall.

Phillips, N., W. Remillard, W. Pronovost, and S. Bass. 1968. Teaching of intonation to the deaf by visual pattern matching. Proceedings of the Conference on Speech-Analyzing Aids for the Deaf. American Annals of the Deaf 113 pp. 239–246.

Pickett, J. 1963. Tactual communication of speech sounds to the deaf: comparison with lipreading. Journal of Speech and Hearing Disorders 28:315–330.

Pickett, J. 1968. Recent research on speech-analyzing aids for the deaf. IEEE Transactions on Audio and Electroacoustics 16:227–234.

Pickett, J. and B. Pickett. 1963. Communication of speech sounds by a tactual vocoder. Journal of Speech and Hearing Research 6:207–222.

Pickett, J. and A. Constam. 1968. A visual speech trainer with simplified indication of vowel spectrum. Proceedings of the Conference on Speech-Analyzing Aids for the Deaf. American Annals of the Deaf 113:253–258.

Pollack, D. 1964. Acoupedics: a uni-sensory approach. The Volta Review 66(7).

Pollack, D. 1967. Acoupedics. Proceedings of International Conference on Oral Education of the Deaf 1. Washington, D.C.: The Alexander Graham Bell Association for the Deaf. Pp. 821–833.

Pronovost, W., L. Yenkin, D. C. Anderson, and R. Lerner. 1968. The voice visualizer. American Annals of the Deaf 113(2):230–238.

Sherman, D. 1954. The merits of backward playing of connected speech in the scaling of voice quality disorders. Journal of Speech and Hearing Disorders 19:312–321.

Silverman, S. R. 1948. Educational therapy for the hard of hearing: speech reading. In E. Froeschels (Ed.) Twentieth Century Speech and Voice Correction. New York: Philosophical Library. Pp. 142–151.

Silverman, S. R. 1954. Teaching speech to the deaf—the issues. The Volta Review 56:385–389, 417.

Silverman, S. R. 1957. Clinical and educational procedures for the deaf. In L. E. Travis (Ed.) Handbook of Speech Pathology. New York: Appleton-Century-Crofts. Pp. 389–425.

Simmons, A. 1959. Factors related to lipreading. Journal of Speech and Hearing Research 2:340–352.

Simmons, A. 1967. Unpublished material. Institute on Characteristics and Needs of the Hard of Hearing Child. Utah State University, Logan.

Stepp, R. E. 1966. A speechreading laboratory for deaf children. The Volta Review 68(6):408–415.

Stevens, S. and H. Davis. 1938. Hearing—Its Psychology and Physiology. New York: John Wiley.

Stewart, R. 1968. By ear alone. American Annals of the Deaf 115:147–155.

Stone, L. 1957. Facial clues of context in lipreading. John Tracy Clinic Research Papers V.

Taaffe, G. 1957. A film test of lip reading. John Tracy Research Papers II. Los Angeles: John Tracy Clinic.

Templin, M. 1957. Certain language skills in children. Institute of Child Welfare Monograph No. 26. Minneapolis, Minn.: The University of Minnesota Press.

Templin, M. and F. Darley. 1960. The Templin-Darley Tests of Articulation. Iowa City: Bureau of Educational Research, State University of Iowa.

Upton, H. 1968. Wearable eyeglass speechreading aid. Proceedings of the Conference on Speech-Analyzing Aids for the Deaf. American Annals of the Deaf 113:222–229.

Utley, J. 1946. Factors involved in the teaching and testing of lipreading ability through the use of motion pictures. The Volta Review:657–659.

Van Riper, C. 1963. Speech Correction: Principles and Methods. Englewood Cliffs, N.J.: Prentice-Hall.

Van Riper, C. and J. Irwin. 1958. Voice and Articulation. Englewood Cliffs, N.J.: Prentice-Hall.

Wedenberg, E. 1951. Auditory training of deaf and hard of hearing children. Acta Otolaryngologica, Supplementum 94:1–129.

Wedenberg, E. 1954. Auditory training of severely hard of hearing preschool children. Acta Otolaryngologica, Supplementum 110. Stockholm.

Wedenberg, E. 1967a. Experience from 30 years, auditory training. The Volta Review 69:588–594.

Wedenberg, E. 1967b. Institute on Characteristics and Needs of the Hard of Hearing Child. Utah State University, Logan.

Whetnall, E. and D. Fry. 1964. The Deaf Child. Springfield, Ill.: Charles C Thomas.

White, W. 1970. Stimulus manipulation in articulation therapy with a hearing impaired child. Unpublished master's thesis, Utah State University, Logan.

Winitz, H. 1969. Articulatory Acquisition and Behavior. New York: Appleton-Century-Crofts.

Withrow, F. 1965. The use of audiovisual techniques to expand lipreading and auditory experiences of young deaf children. American Annals of the Deaf 110:523–527.

Wong, W. and G. Taaffe. 1958. Relationships between selected aptitude and personality tests of lipreading ability. John Tracy Clinic Research Papers VII.

Woodward, M. 1957. Linguistic methodology in lipreading research. John Tracy Clinic Research Papers IV.

Yules, F., J. Welch, J. Urbani, and R. Elliot. 1968. Untraining hypernasality. Presented at American Cleft Palate Association Convention.

Zaliouk, A. 1954. A visual-tactile system of phonetical symbolization. Journal of Speech and Hearing Disorders:190–207.

Chapter 18

The Advantage of Auditory Training:
A Case Report

ERIK and MARTA WEDENBERG

The eye is the mirror of the soul, but the ear is the gateway to the soul. The old Greek philosophers were of that opinion as early as 3–400 B.C. They had noticed how very much easier it was to communicate with a blind child than with a deaf child, and so the quoted sentence became an eloquent expression for their opinion.

The majority of the deaf, or rather hearing impaired, are not totally deaf. Very often they have remnants of hearing—as if the gate were slightly open, and through this narrow opening we try to reach the child either through speaking directly into the ear of the child or by using speech amplified in a hearing aid. This is auditory training.

Speech is our most important medium for communication and also the natural therapeutic measure for the treatment of hard of hearing persons. Voiced speech sounds are formed by the vibration of the vocal chords. A spectrum is formed consisting of a voice fundamental plus harmonically related overtones (Fig. 14, 15). The pitch level in the male voice is about 125 Hz and in the female voice about 250 Hz. Characteristic intensity maxima, so-called formants, appear as a result of cavity modulation in the spectra of all speech sounds. Spectra of vowels for the male voice have four obvious formants. The two lowest and the most important lie within the frequency range from 200–850 and 600–2500 Hz, respectively. The third formant lies within the frequency range 1900–3300 Hz and the fourth within the range 3000–4000 Hz. The two lowest are said to be variable, since their positions for the various vowel sounds change appreciably. The third and the fourth we call *fixed* formants, due to their relatively small variations in speech. Voiced consonants have formants similar to those of the vowels. Toneless consonants have formants of greater bandwidth over a great part of the spectrum.

Here we have the tools—now we shall speak about how we have used them.

In 1939 we began with our first case. It was a 2½-year-old boy—our own son Staffan. We knew that he was very severely hard of hearing, perhaps totally deaf; but we hoped that he had some remnants of hearing. We could not then obtain good audiograms as we can today, but the auditory testing showed that his audiogram possibly had this appearance (Fig. 16), which

319

Formants of Swedish speech sounds. Male data. Level above ASA free-field threshold at 2 cm from the lips of the speaker. Data from Fant (LME). The following vowel symbols are used (IPA equivalents within brackets).

Symbol	Key word	IPA	Symbol	Key word	IPA
o_1	rot	u:	i_1	dit	i:
o_2	rott	U	i_2	ditt	I
$å_1$	våt	o:	y_1	byt	y:
$å_2$	vått	ɔ	y_2	bytt	Y
a_1	fat	ɑ:	u_1	Rut	ʉ
a_2	fatt	a	u_2	rutt	ɵ
$ä_1$	rät	ɛ:	$ö_1$	röt	ø:
$ä_2$	rätt	ɛ̞	$ö_2$	rött	œ
$ä_3$	är	æ:	$ö_3$	för	œ̞:
e_1	ek	e:			

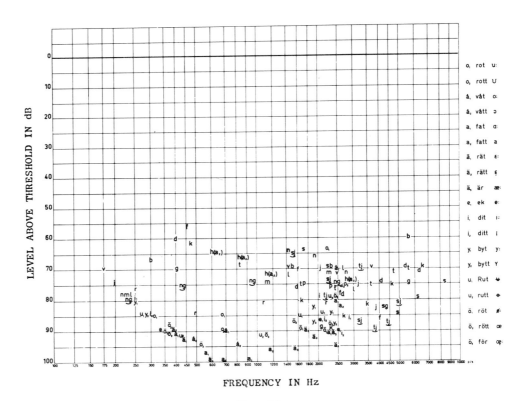

FREQUENCY IN Hz

FIG. 14.

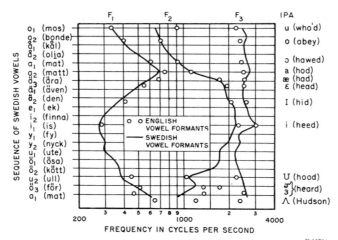

FIG. 15.   Sequential diagram of Swedish and American English vowels.

afterward was confirmed. According to the American Committee on Nomenclature of 1937 he was deaf in that he belonged to "those in whom the sense of hearing was non-functional for the ordinary purposes of life" (American Annals of the Deaf 83:1, 1938). According to another terminology, suggested by Urbantschitsch of Vienna in 1895, Staffan should have been able to hear sounds. Urbantschitsch divided the deaf into five groups: (1) the totally deaf, (2) the sound-hearing, (3) the vowel-hearing, (4) the word-hearing, and (5) the sentence-hearing. The little boy was not totally deaf, but he heard sounds. But which sounds? It must have been the first vowel and consonant formants of the lower frequency range where he had his hearing remnants (below his audiogram, Fig. 17). Instead of hearing four formants he was only able to hear the first one. Was it possible to teach him to discriminate between the *vowels* although, when speaking into his ear, he only heard the first *formants*? If this were the case, he could be moved up to the next group: the vowel-hearing.

To a normal hearing child the vowel *a* is perceived as a whole chord composed of the fundamental tone and a series of overtones which the brain interprets as *a*. A chord of the piano is like sounding several keys simultaneously. But when this hard of hearing child heard the vowel *a* spoken into his ear, he perceived only a very weak fragment of the vowel. It was like striking only *one* key on the piano.

We thought we should in the beginning speak into the ear without any amplifier so as not to give the child any chance of lipreading. One must diminish the visual impression in order that the auditory stimuli might exercise a first claim upon the consciousness. We did not give the method any name. Today it is called the *unisensory approach,* and it is accepted as superior to the multisensory approach. Which vowels should we begin to speak into the ear? We chose *o* and *a* because these vowels had first formants which lay furthest apart, 300 and 550 Hz respectively, corresponding to the English sounds underlined in wh*o*'d and h*a*wed (Fig. 14, 15, and 17).

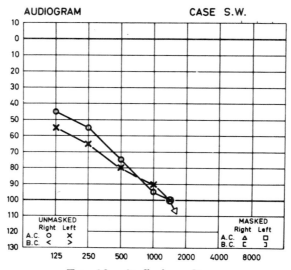

FIG. 16.   Staffan's audiogram.

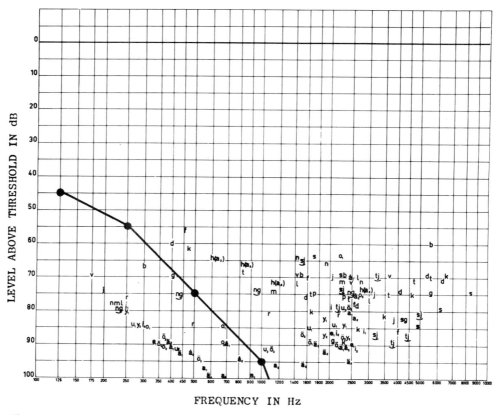

FREQUENCY IN Hz

FIG. 17.   Formants of Swedish speech sounds with Staffan's audiogram inserted.

These vowels were, also, we felt, from the psychological standpoint, well chosen, since in the Swedish language they ejaculate surprise.

The training began with our crawling on the floor saying these vowels into the boy's ear. That was fun for a 2-year-old. An important principle in all training is that it should be fun. Hearing and speaking should develop in play. My wife temporarily gave up her profession and devoted all her time to our son. In this manner we succeeded in teaching him to recognize these two vowels, and later to repeat them. That was proof that there was a remnant of hearing.

We continued with other vowels: *a - e, a - ö, a - ä*. The closer together in the spectrum the first formants of the vowels were located, the more frequent were the mistakes. Nevertheless, the boy had *advanced from sound perception to vowel perception*. Through combining into words the vowels he had already learned and voiced consonants with low first formants (v, j, b, d, g, m, n, ng, r, l) he was taught to perceive and differentiate such as *ja, aj, adjö, mamma*, etc. (Fig. 17). Thus, he had *advanced to the word hearing group*. We made up a list comprised of meaningful words of this kind, but it included a very limited vocabulary in that many words important for a little child were lacking because they contained unvoiced consonants inaudible for the boy (sova, komma, pappa, höra, etc.). However, after some time we also spoke such words into the ear and to our astonishment he was able to perceive them. How was it possible? He understood them through the tactile impression they made in the auditory canal. In this way the boy was taught to discriminate between different voiceless consonants. Through combination of hearing the first formants of the vowels and voiced consonants in the lower frequency range and the use of the tactile sense in the perception of the voiceless consonants in the high frequency range inaudible for him, he little by little perceived all words spoken into the ear.

After 14 months of training he had a vocabulary of only 25 words. This seemed like a very modest result, but it should be compared with the 12 months of listening it usually takes before a normal child starts saying the first few words. At this stage we combined the learned words into two-word sentences: *ja mamma, adjö mamma*, etc. He perceived the sentences and had *advanced to the sentence hearing group* (Fig. 18).

Speech reading was practiced very little at this early stage. In our opinion the natural synergism between hearing and the visual sense, which exists in normal persons, is highly disturbed in these cases of impaired hearing. Approximately 90 percent of the conceptions of a person with completely normal senses are based upon the visual sense. The complete or partial loss of the auditory sense results in an even greater concentration on the other senses and an intensification of their use. The unimpaired visual sense appropriates the greater part of attention to the detriment of the impaired auditory sense. The residual hearing that exists is not rationally utilized. On the contrary, the peripheral damage is augmented by an inability to use the hearing which, especially for a child building up his speech, is fatal. The task is to restore the synergy as far as possible by giving the child an auditory pattern through the normal channel. The hearing sense, although defective, should be used at

WORDS AND SENTENCES USED IN THE TRAINING OF PRE-SCHOOL CHILDREN

Interjections

aj ['aɪ:]	ouch
ja ['ɪaˑ]	yes
nej ['nɛɪ:]	no
oh ['u:]	Oh!
åh ['o:]	aha
äh ['ɛ:]	pooh

Greetings

adjö [a'ɪø:]	good bye
god dag [guˈda:]	hello
god morgon [guˇmɔr:ɔn]	good morning

Animal sounds

bä ['bɛ:]	ba
miau ['mɪa:u]	miaw
vovvov [ˇvɔʋ:ɔʋ]	bow-wow

Adverbs

opp ['ɔp:]	up
var? ['va:r]	where?
hur? ['hϴ:r]	how?

Verbs

bada [ˇba:da]	bathe
bo ['bu:]	reside
bolla [ˇbɔl:a]	play ball
bära [ˇbæ:ra]	carry
gå ['go:]	go, walk
har ['ha:r]	have
hjälpa [ˇɪɛl:pa]	help
hoppa [ˇhɔp:a]	jump
höra [ˇhœ:ra]	hear
jama [ˇɪa:ma]	mind
klappa [ˇklap:a]	pet
komma [ˇkɔm:a]	come
låna [ˇlo:na]	borrow
låt bli [lot 'bli:]	let alone
må ['mo:]	must, may
måla [ˇmo:la]	paint
ramla [ˇram:la]	fall
råma [ˇro:ma]	roar
sova [ˇso:va]	sleep
vakna [ˇva:kna]	wake up
vara [ˇva:ra]	be
vill ha [vil 'ha:]	want
är ['æ:r]	am, is, are

Nouns

baby ['bɛɪbi]	baby
bär ['bæ:r]	berry
bio ['bi:u]	movie
lamm ['lam:]	lamb
lampa [ˇlam:pa]	lamp
mamma [ˇmam:a]	mama
mun ['mun:]	mouth
nam-nam [ˇnam:nam]	yum-yum
orm ['ur:m]	snake
pappa [ˇpap:a]	papa
penna [ˇpɛn:a]	pencil
radio ['ra:diu]	radio
vovve [ˇvuʋ:ə]	doggie
år ['o:r]	year
åra [ˇo:ra]	oar
öga [ˇø:ga]	eye
öra [ˇœ:ra]	ear

Numbers

Easiest to perceive:

åtta [ˇɔt:a]	8
elva [ˇɛl:va]	11
femton [ˇfɛm:tɔn]	15

Adjectives

bra ['bra:]	good
gammal [ˇgam:al]	old
hungrig [ˇhϴngːrig]	hungry
lång ['lɔng:]	tall
rar ['ra:r]	nice, dear
rolig [ˇru:lig]	funny
rädd ['rɛ:d]	afraid, careful
varm ['va:rm]	warm

Colors

Easiest to perceive:

blå ['blo:]	blue
brun [br∅:n]	brown
röd ['rø:d]	red

Pronouns

jag ['ɪa:(g)]	I
du ['dϴ:]	you (sing.)
v ['vi:]	we

Sentences

Short sentences were made up using these words. For example: Var har du varit? [var ha· dϴ ˇva:rit] Where have you been? - Var bor du? [var 'bu:d ϴ] Where do you live? - Mår du bra? [ˌmo· dϴ 'bra:] Do you feel well? - Opp och hoppa! ['ɔp:ɔ ˇhɔ:pa] Let's go! - Gå å bada. [go· ɔ ˇba:da] Go take a bath. - Gå på bio. [ˌgo po 'bi:u] Go to the movies. Et cetera.

FIG. 18.

every opportunity. Speech reading should not be extensively introduced until after the child has acquired this auditory pattern, which he demonstrated by approaching and wanting to have words spoken into his ear; in other words, not until he has the *listening attitude.* The child's vocabulary may then be rapidly increased. *Lip reading* had already begun to play an important role for this boy. It was, therefore, necessary to discourage it because, in our opinion, if he grew too dependent upon speech reading, he would never learn to listen.

The initial progress is slow with this procedure in comparison to that in the cases in which the patients, having learned to depend upon speech reading from the beginning, achieve relatively rapid results. The handicap is gradually overtaken, however, by the *auditory trained* who is considerably more auditorially focused and, therefore, more normal. When the child has been successfully brought to the listening attitude, his restless, uneasy roaming from one occupation to another is replaced by a quieter and more harmonious manner. He can sit still, busy with the same thing for long periods. It might be said that he becomes normalized in this respect.

At first Staffan's pronunciation was very poor. He was not discouraged by corrections. However, we considered it more desirable that he develop a defective but spontaneous and word-rich speech than a speech with better pronunciation which showed no real yearning to speak but instead served more as an artificial product to be used during the lessons. A phenomenon observed shortly after the boy acquired the listening attitude was his talking in his sleep, an occurrence which was interpreted as a sign that the child's speech development had reached the stage where a certain form of automatism existed.

Objects that made sounds were also important in his education. The boy was "bathed in sound" by many audible playthings. He was trained to recognize musical instruments which were played. A chime played with a little rubber hammer proved to be a convenient instrument. When the chime was played behind him he showed that he heard by quickly turning around and, after a period of training, attempting to strike the same tone. This was repeated at increasing distance from the chime until it was apparent that he could no longer perceive the tones. Striking the keys of the piano was another musical game. How much he heard was soon apparent. When he had acquired a small vocabulary, he said that the upper octaves of the piano were broken and silent. Everything in his environment that had a sound was explained to him. For example, he was told what the animals said; the cow's "moo, moo" and the dog's "woof, woof" were spoken into his ears.

He said his first sentence at 4 years of age, under the great stress of fear that the dog Tutta would be trampled by a horse. "Toto, Utta, aj-aj!" (Horsie, Tutta, be careful!) By the time he reached 5½ his vocabulary had increased to 400 words. He formed many sentences and began to use verbs in the perfect and future tenses. His pronunciation was very poor. However, he was unafraid and started conversations willingly with strangers. When they failed to understand him, he said *they* could not hear. There was nothing the matter with *him!* He had the spontaneous desire to speak, used no signs, was completely uninhibited and found friends among normal hearing children of his own age.

At 6½ years of age his vocabulary included 600 words. He entered ordinary school at the age of 7 (the normal starting age in Sweden) and transferred later to a class for hard of hearing children. From there he entered junior high school on trial. He then attended the first class in upper or high school, and he received better than passing grades in the majority of his subjects. Swedish composition was the most difficult for him, but he received better than passing grades in German and French and passing in Swedish and English. After graduating from college in 1960, he entered the University and became an officer of forestry in 1966. He is now running a forest farm in Sweden. After studying English for 9 years, he speaks English fluently. He reads and understands German and French, but has no training in speaking these languages. The melody in his speech is not perfect, but the accents are good.

His vocabulary, according to a test (in November 1953) at the University of Stockholm, was rather extensive, corresponding to the requirements for adults of above normal intelligence. His sentence structure was normal. His spoken sentences contained eight words on the average; the written contained ten. His speech, according to an improvised intelligibility test, was almost entirely comprehensible.

As soon as his auditory training started at 2½ years of age, Staffan received speech exercises from a lady teacher of the deaf. She worked with him before a mirror half an hour twice a day. To help explain the anatomical background for pronunciation we arranged plaster models of the upper and lower jaw in a dentist's articulator (an artificial joint). With a tongue made of soft rubber we could show the movements of the tongue against the teeth for making different sounds. The teacher, however, felt dubious as to our auditory training and, therefore, left us after two months. At that time we lived in the little town of Skellefteå, 600 miles north of Stockholm; therefore, we had difficulties in giving him phoniatric help. We then had to travel to Stockholm and stay there for a week at a time several times a year. We did not, however, consider that his phoniatric training was sufficient, and for that reason we moved to Stockholm where he received regular phoniatric lessons by teachers of the deaf and by speech therapists.

The hearing aid was not used from the beginning. Only speech into the ear was employed. The reasons for this procedure are both psychological and technical. A mother is close to her child during the first year, when the child needs her more than during any later period. For this reason it is entirely natural that she speaks close to the child, close to its ears. She carries the baby in her arms and talks to it then, also. The child feels its mother's nearness; it feels and hears her speech. This creates a sense of security. Auditory training comprises nothing that deviates from the normal. This is especially true since the words spoken to a child with normal hearing and which it, therefore, first learns to say itself are composed of sounds with low frequency and high intensity. These are practically the same as the words used in the auditory training of "deaf children."

The technical disadvantages in the use of hearing aids are: (1) possible excessive amplification in hearing aids not equipped with automatic volume control or peak clipping. Most hearing aids belong to this category; (2) amplitude and frequency distortion; for instance, intermodulation; (3) overloading due to a flat response of a hearing aid causing masking in the cases of perceptive hearing loss; and (4) amplification of background noise; e.g., clothes.

There is a great difference in quality between the sound amplified by speaking into the ear and by using hearing aids. When speaking into the ear all sounds are amplified in a linear way and without any distortion. With hearing aids, of the vowels only *a* and *o* are well reproduced while distortion makes *ä, ö, e,* and *i* very difficult to discriminate.

Staffan has poor discrimination of pure tones. He can perceive the difference between two pure tones only when in the range 0 to 400 Hz the difference in frequency is at least 50 Hz. This explains why Staffan originally obtained very little advantage from hearing aids, which in the 1940s and 1950s amplified nothing lower than 400 Hz. However, they were of importance to him in order to get in touch with what is spatially remote, even if the discrimination was not great. He thereby perceived an acoustic phenomenon that perhaps had significance for him and he was able to interpret with a combination of hearing and sight, thus understanding what went on around him.

Social Behavior and Adaptation

The family is the primary group in our community. Therefore, it is of the greatest importance that each member fully understands the extraordinary demands on the family where one of them has hearing difficulties. Staffan's sister and brother had the right attitude and were tireless when it came to explaining things, introducing him to different situations, and training his hearing. The whole family took part.

Skellefteå is a small town. For a child wtih hearing difficulties it is a great advantage to live in a small community where everyone knows one another and everybody takes a personal interest in his neighbor. Very early Staffan made good friends who were kind and tolerant and did not show impatience when conversation proceeded slowly. These were happy years for him. The situation changed considerably when we moved to the big city of Stockholm. It took several years there before he made lasting friends.

High intelligence can to a certain degree compensate hearing difficulties. Staffan's IQ is above 130. Hence, he has been able to explain his situation to us and give suggestions as to how we could improve conditions. He has told us how he felt and thought when at the age of 26 months he was at a children's hospital in Stockholm for observation. His story has been verified by details he described from this hospital which he has never visited since. He tells how he experienced his situation. He thought that he was still in his home town Skellefteå, was grieved that his mother and father had left him and could not understand why. We find it surprising that at this stage he could think—without having learned one single word.

It was difficult to teach him abstract expressions, but even here he gave us intelligent solutions, i.e., in explaining *tomorrow:* sleep—wake up; *day after tomorrow:* sleep—wake up, sleep—wake up.

One day when he was about 7 years old, Staffan came to us and said: "I don't want my name Staffan." We asked him why he did not want it. "No," he said, "I do not hear the name when I say it myself."

"What do you hear when you say it?" we asked.

"I hear only *a - a.*"

A glance at his audiogram proved he was right. He heard only *a -a* (Fig. 17). Then he asked, "What do you want to be called? Can you suggest a name?" "Yes," he said, "I want to be called Douglas, because I can hear that." Another check of his audiogram showed that he was quite right. "Yes, you can have that name." The decision was made, and the name Douglas is now on his visiting cards.

The hearing aids have been a constant source of trouble for Staffan. Because of his own poor discrimination he was never satisfied with their performance and was always thinking of possible improvements. One day he came and said: "I hear the strong sounds very loud in the hearing aid, but the weak sounds I do not hear at all. I want a hearing aid that increases the weak sounds and decreases the loud sounds."

We went to our good friend Bertil Johansson, the engineer who constructed hearing aids, and asked: "Can you make such an apparatus?"

"Yes," he said. "That is called compression." This resulted in the building of such an apparatus. However, Staffan obtained very little from this compression. He had been used to gaining a lot of information from the level variations which were now lost through this compression.

Many attempts were made to build a hearing aid with good reproduction of vowels, but Staffan complained about the apparatus and said: "What do I gain from hearing only vowels? I must hear the toneless consonants which mean so much to me. Without toneless consonants speech is not understandable."

Eventually Bertil Johansson constructed the so-called transposer; that is, the hearing aid which transposes for him the inaudible toneless consonants into Staffan's hearing range. By this means he could distinguish all sounds— even those which previously laid outside his small hearing range. But he has never been completely satisfied (Fig. 19).

As we have said before, we only worked with auditory training with the unisensory approach and never taught lipreading. In spite of this, Staffan became an excellent lipreader. Why? Because he acquired through the intensive auditory training a much larger vocabulary than normal, and this makes it possible for him to lipread better than those who have never had any auditory training, and, therefore, have a very limited vocabulary.

As an example, we can relate the following: Staffan was called by a film company who had made a movie about the wild youth in Sweden. The sound tape had been destroyed, and there they were with a silent film. They asked Staffan if he could lipread the film. They intended to have a première in a month, so time was short. He lipread the whole film and new film stars were

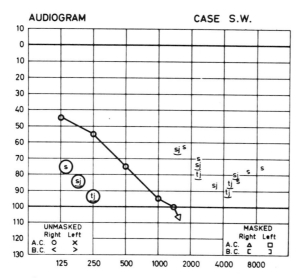

Fig. 19.   Results of frequency transposition of the Swedish toneless consonants "s," "sj," and "tj." The transposer hearing aid shifts the high frequency speech sounds into Staffan's auditory range as denoted by symbols within circles.

hired to speak it in. But he said to us: "The language the youngsters used was not the best."

We said, "That we can understand, but you had no difficulties?"

"No," he said, "I did not." He was normal even in this respect.

In order to increase his vocabulary quickly and to teach him sounds he could not hear, he was taught to read and write very early. He learned to read at 4½ years of age. We used cardboard letters about 4 inches high which could be set up in a reading frame. Taking these letters and setting them up in the frame became a sort of game for him. The vowels were taught first, followed by the low frequency consonants. The letters were then combined into words which were already familiar to him through his previous training. During these reading lessons all instructions were spoken into his ear. When he heard a definite sound, he set up the letter it represented in the frame; later he followed the same procedure with words. Finally, when he was very advanced, sentences were also handled in the same manner. In learning to read, Staffan enlarged his vocabulary very rapidly, making possible the explanation of high frequency sounds which he had no chance to hear and, thereby, the incorporation of many new words into his vocabulary. The words were more firmly fixed in his mind when he could hear them, see them on the speaker's lips, read them, and write them. However, ordinary textbooks with their word selection were not suitable for him; both because the word examples were unfamiliar to him and also because these contained many high frequency sounds.

We have already mentioned that Staffan's vocabulary the first few years was much smaller than for normal hearing children. At the age of 3½ he had 25 words, at 5½, 400, and 6½ years, 600 words. Not before he was 14, after 12 years of training, did his vocabulary approach the normal. At 17, according to a test in November, 1953, it was rather extensive compared with the requirements for intelligent adults. We have trained every word in the different languages by speaking into the ear. As we have already mentioned, speech through a hearing aid is a poor alternative, due to technical disadvantages. Therefore, he has first heard the new word spoken into the ear and then amplified in a hearing aid which he must use in his daily life.

Staffan's manner is easy with everybody. He has absolutely no difficulty in his social relationships. While he enjoys listening to popular music, he is not particularly interested in playing himself. He started to play the piano, however, and learned to read music at 7 years of age. After two years he voluntarily changed over to the cello, but stopped playing after one year.

He has had no privileges in school or at the university. The difficulties have been especially great at the university in forestry, where during excursions the lectures are often outdoors and, therefore, especially hard to follow. The classmates were most understanding and helped him as much as time would allow.

Staffan has gone to a hard school ever since he was $2\frac{1}{2}$ years old. He has felt many hard blows, but he is a stubborn optimist with speedy recovery. Looking back on his early days, he says he was always jealous of normal hearing children who were playing while he had to work with his vocabulary, even during summer holidays. Today, however, we fail to find any ill effects from the hard training routine. He is an extrovert, a good sportsman, and a sailor. The other day when we were discussing handicaps of different kinds, Staffan revealed his own view of his present situation: "I am not handicapped, am I?"

References

Fant, G. 1959. Acoustic analysis and synthesis of speech with applications to Swedish. Reprint from Ericsson Technics No. 1.

Fant, G. 1968. Analysis and synthesis of speech processes. Reprint from Manual of Phonetics, Bertil Malmberg (Ed.). North-Holland Publishing Company: Amsterdam.

Fletcher, H. 1929. Speech and Hearing. D. van Nostrand Co.: Princeton, N. J.

Johansson, B. 1959. A new coding amplifier system for the severely hard of hearing. Proceedings 3rd International Congress on Acoustics, Elsevier Publishing Company: Amsterdam.

Wedenberg, E. 1951. Auditory training of deaf and hard of hearing children. Acta Otolaryng., Suppl. 94, Thesis: Stockholm.

Wedenberg, E. 1954. Auditory training of severely hard of hearing pre-school children. Acta Otolarvng., Suppl. 110, Stockholm.

Wedenberg, E. 1959. Auditory training of the severely hard of hearing using a coding amplifier. Proceedings 3rd International Congress on Acoustics, Elsevier Publishing Company: Amsterdam.

Wedenberg, E. 1967. Experience from 30 years, auditory training. The Alexander Graham Bell Association for the Deaf, Reprint No. 891, Washington, D.C.

Chapter 19

Language and Reading in the Educational Process of the Hard of Hearing Child

THOMAS C. CLARK, M.A.

Language

"Dear Coach, I am sorry for you. I am not a football. I never was a football." This was the written response of a 17-year-old hearing impaired boy to a coach who had asked him to come to school early to play ball. As one works with hearing impaired, language deprived children, one cannot but strive, hope and perhaps even pray that through his efforts the communication ability of these students will be improved. This chapter is a meager attempt to help such hearing impaired children, especially those who are hard of hearing.

Language Problems of the Hard of Hearing

On many occasions the author has heard his fellow teachers say that hard of hearing children do not belong in the same educational environment as deaf children because the deaf children need a structured, systematic language program which is much too slow for hard of hearing children. Brill (1954) adequately expressed the feeling of most educators of the deaf: "The necessity of developing language, the methods of teaching content subjects, and the methods of teaching speech, all should differ as applied to the two groups" (deaf and hard of hearing). There are numerous plans for language development for the deaf. Most of the schools for the deaf have a language course of study or detailed curriculum guide for language development and instruction. Schools for the deaf are for the deaf; they generally have no separate curriculum or language-academic program for the hard of hearing children. In a recent survey of programs for hard of hearing children in schools for the deaf, 14 schools responded and none of these schools had a special curriculum for hard of hearing children. Only one school had separate classes for the hard of hearing.

The obvious question at this point then is: What type of language program should the hard of hearing child have? Brill (1954) feels that the hard of hearing child should be educated in a school for hearing children, with a special program for these children. But what program? For the deaf or for the normal child? There have been no language-reading programs published specifically for hard of hearing children. Therefore, the purpose of this chapter is to provide a philosophy and guide for language and reading instruction, development and remediation for hard of hearing children.

The definition of hard of hearing which will be used is the one described by Berg in an early chapter of this book. Webster's (1969) definition of language will be used, i.e., *any means, vocal or other, of expressing or communicating feeling or thought.* Language instruction will be used to mean that body of material and procedures used in instruction of the English language. The discussion will not consider the merits or weaknesses of individual language programs for the deaf. It will, however, examine the application of a structured language program to hard of hearing children. Children who are functioning educationally as deaf obviously need a visual approach to language; however, our concern here is the hard of hearing, not the deaf.

This chapter considers the child in the educational setting, not in a clinical setting. In this educational setting, a program for the individual child is the consideration.

Language and reading are discussed together in one chapter because of the inter-relationship of the two. Heilman (1966) feels that learning to read is related to, and built upon, past language experiences and that learning to read should be a natural outgrowth of past language experiences. He further states that reading is an extension of the communicative process which involves learning the printed equivalent for the known spoken symbols. Reading is another facet of the language-communicative skills a child has developed; it is not normally taught nor learned outside of language. Therefore, language and reading for the hearing impaired are considered together in this chapter.

As one struggles with language instruction for severely hearing impaired children one wonders what philosophies and theories of language, cognition, child development, and psychological development underlie the long-used structured methodologies for teaching language to these children. There seems to be no philosophical theory that can be substantiated by studies in language development, cognition, or other related fields. The main premise is that the special methodologies are visual and logical. They are all based on a grammatical background. One who works with traditional grammar finds cause to doubt that any system based on traditional grammar is logical. As this discussion on language for the hard of hearing unfolds, it seems of paramount importance to discuss philosophies and theories which are the basis of the program.

1. The "normal" means of acquiring a verbal language is through the sense of hearing. There *appears* to be no "natural" *substitute.* (There *is* a *complexity* of verbal stimuli received by the hearing mechanism which combine to make possible the understanding of the spoken word. Even partial sound stimuli are of definite value in acquiring language.)

2. Linguistic competence is acquired early in childhood.

3. Language probably cannot be taught. It is acquired. A structured grammatical language approach leads to structured grammatical "language" and not normal language.

4. Reading and writing are facets or extensions of verbal language ability but are not language in themselves. Language competence is not gained through reading and writing.

5. Hearing that is faulty is often sufficient for development of language, but because of inconsistent sound stimuli, that language is often faulty. It is often more complicated with errors than the language of a deaf child with a structured, limited language.

The results of a lack of the auditory sensory stimulation certainly demonstrate the relationship of that sensory avenue in the development of normal language. Tervoort states:

> If the deaf child is left by himself there is no adaptation to the world around of the speech sounds, and therefore, no extensive training of all possible phonemic combinations prior to their symbolic usage as words. Consequently, there is no single word phase, no morphological and syntactical refinement; in short: no language learning. And, therefore, and consequently there is no subtle and effective control of the environment, no highly sophisticated system of symbolic references, and no totally satisfactory interhuman emotional communication. (Simmons, undated, p. 3.)

Educators have for many years been trying to find a "natural" substitute for hearing in the learning of language. What they developed were actually visual methods which could be used in part to fill the communication void caused by deafness. These systems worked as communicative means for those deafened people who had language. It was presupposed that if the system would work in this way it would work in developing language where language was nonexistent. This is where the visual systems have failed. They cannot be used an natural substitutes for hearing in the development of natural language. Lipreading is the visual method which has been used as a substitute for auditory language learning. The lack of success of lipreading as a tool to develop language is certainly testimony enough of its inadequacies in filling this need.

> . . . In spite of the fact that we still do not know what makes a good lipreader schools contend with futile optimism that most of the children who now go to school will become lipreaders. And, mind you, these children have to learn language through lipreading, which is again another matter. It is one thing to be deaf and know language and then learn lipreading. This is the reason why oralism become so prevalent, because 50 years ago most of the children in schools for the deaf were children who became deaf. Acquired deafness is now very rare. The vast majority of the children are now children who do not know language. The main problem is no longer speech or lipreading. The main problem is linguistic competence. It is obvious that if lipreading were a viable method of learning language, all children would learn language, because, certainly the deaf child is as motivated as any other child to socialize. If the lipreading method could work you would find children picking up language just by living in a hearing environment, but they don't do this. (Good lipreaders) . . . are as rare as a Beethoven or a Michaelangelo (Furth in Kavanagh, 1968, p. 197).

Others besides Furth have been critical of the education of the hearing impaired. This criticism has mainly been aimed at the failure of lipreading as a natural substitute for hearing. With the hard of hearing child, the only logical approach to language development is through the auditory channel. Speech reading can be a valuable communicative skill when the hard of hearing child has language.

A hearing screening program, identification of hearing loss in the first few months of life, and an effective home language situation are necessities in an effective language program. Linguists are pointing out the area of early childhood as the natural time for language development. Moores (1967) states that children learn language rapidly and that they are superior to adults in learning a second language. He states that it is highly possible that a critical period, or at least an optimal period exists for language acquisition. The specific ability to develop language appears to hit a peak around the ages of 3 to 4 years and declines thereafter. "Perhaps any language development program that is initiated after the age of five, no matter what method is used is doomed to failure for the majority of deaf children."* Simmons (1967) uses a recently suggested possibility that early stimulation may be crucial in laying the psychological foundations for the capacity to process information. If this should be true, early stimulus deprivation may create a lifelong handicap in response capacity and in the assimilating and manipulating of facts and ideas. She states that an accumulation of evidence gives support to the concept that sensory deprivation early in life causes impairment in the child's later functioning which may be permanent. This discussion leads us back to point (2): linguistic competence is acquired in early childhood and thus any language program for the hearing impaired must include the first years of a child's life.

Structured methodology for teaching language to the hearing impaired through grammatical programs such as the Fitzgerald Key have taught these children an excellent command of grammar and yet the majority of them do not have normal usage of English. Their usage is structured, stereotyped, elementary in construction and completely lacking in the generative aspect of normal language. Deaf children know grammar but not language. Perhaps the lowest day of the writer's professional life was the day when the instructor in College Freshman Remedial English informed him that the hearing impaired students in her class were among the best grammarians she had ever had, but that they were unable to generate English forms comparable to remedial freshmen students with normal hearing. She said that the best hearing impaired students in the class were good enough to fail but that the others would have to drop the class because they did not even have the abilities for a remedial class. Yes, we teachers of the hearing impaired are good grammar teachers. The significance here is that a child's language has to develop normally; the value of grammar is not in development but in refining, remediating

* Moores, 1967, p. 5.

and describing that language which he already has. Moores (1967) gives emphasis to this point.

> The frightening possibility must be faced that language cannot be taught but must be learned by the child. If children in all cultures learn languages by progressing similarly through a number of stages, perhaps this sequential process is mandatory. If so, attempts to teach language by direct imposition of an adult grammatical model will never succeed. In the final analysis, the most efficient approach is to provide the child a language environment as close as possible to that enjoyed by the hearing child. If language cannot be taught, we should be able to structure the environment in such a way as to enable the deaf child to learn it. (Moores, 1967, p. 6.)

The fourth point mentioned as basic to a philosophy of language for the hearing impaired, i.e., reading and writing, are facets or extensions of verbal language ability but are not language in themselves, is discussed in the section on reading.

While faulty auditory mechanisms and thus unreliable auditory stimuli are often sufficient stimulus for the development of nouns, verbs, and adjectives, they leave deficiencies in a child's language. Often the hard of hearing children develop a more faulty pattern of language than deaf children. Although the deaf child's language is highly structured and stereotyped, he often operates well within the pattern he has been taught. This is not so with many hard of hearing children. Their language pattern often reflects their listening pattern. They leave off inflectional endings, omit phonetically obscure words, and misuse much vocabulary. The author found more errors per 100 words on original compositions of moderately to severely hard of hearing students than on the compositions of deaf children. The hard of hearing student's language was more elaborate, more sophisticated in vocabulary, more complex in construction, but contained a greater number of mechanical and structural errors.

The basic philosophy of language developed herein is:

1. The main approach to language development should be through the auditory channel.
2. Lipreading should be used as a supplement to the auditory system.
3. Partial sound stimuli can be of great value to the "well-trained ear."
4. The language development plan for a hard of hearing child should start in infancy. The hearing aid should be fitted before the child is 1 year old. Language development must happen in the home before the child begins school.
5. Natural language probably cannot be taught; it is acquired.
6. A structured language approach is not appropriate for hard of hearing children.
7. A child's reading ability depends on his language ability; he will only be able to read *up to* that language ability.
8. Hard of hearing children often have language that is very complicated with error patterns.

Early Amplification and Programming

The language program should start with the infant in the home. After the child's hearing loss has been diagnosed, he should be fitted with the proper hearing aid. Taylor and Clark have developed a hearing, screening, testing, fitting, and aid adjustment program for hearing impaired children. The children are located through hospital screening and doctor referrals. The hearing is evaluated with EEG audiometry and information testing techniques, then the aid is fitted. Parents come to the clinic weekly and the clinician goes to the home weekly for the first month. The first part of the program is the correct fitting of the aid followed by careful orientation of the parents to insure maximum efficiency and amplification from the aid.

An infant language program can be built around the private home-visiting teacher concept as described by Calvert and Baltzer (1967) or the home demonstration program as described by Simmons (1966).* The essential thing is that the parents are cognizant of their responsibility and completely aware that language learning takes place in the home. This home environment must be a place where meaningful language experiences are continuous. Craig's (1964) research gives emphasis to the theory that language must happen in the home. He found that children with preschool experience had no better language skills than those who had not had preschool. A good preschool program should be of value to a hearing impaired child but it can never replace the home for language development. A hearing aid properly fitted in early infancy, a good active home language program, and a supplemental preschool program seem to be the optimal combination for hard of hearing children.

A Language Program

Developing and describing a complete language education program for hard of hearing children would indeed be a monumental task. Word lists, curriculum guides, and material guides, are not a language program. A language curriculum would include a developmental language text program from first to twelfth grades, a developmental reading basal text program, supplemental and individualized language and reading material—all designed specifically for the hard of hearing child. A special language curriculum for the deaf or the hard of hearing does not exist today. All schools and classes for the hearing impaired use language curriculum material that has been developed and published for the normal school child. This material is usually inappropriate for most severely hard of hearing children and for many moderately hard of hearing children. There are various isolated programs for the deaf dealing specifically with some aspect of language but none of them are complete language curriculums and a good number of the mini-language programs are antiquated. Thus, we are faced with the rather awesome task of

* A comprehensive description of current practices and programs in infant hearing impaired education is described by McConnell (1968) in a workshop summary.

either writing a language-reading curriculum for the hearing impaired or attempting to alter the regular public school curriculum material. It seems that we will not have adequate material until we do so. For the present, this leaves the individual teacher the task of altering, modifying, and supplementing the language curriculum material that is available to him.

How appropriate the language-reading curriculum is and thus the amount of modifying and supplementing necessary depends on the child's hearing loss, his ability to use what hearing he has, his total language reception capacity, his expressive language ability, and whether he has language competence. Language competence is defined here as the ability to generate acceptable language patterns to express whatever a person wishes to the extent of his understanding. If the child has language competence, the material can generally be adjusted to his capacity and level. If he does not, the material for the regular public school child is inappropriate and the child will be unable to learn from this material. There are particular guides, methods, procedures, and special materials that can be of great assistance to the teacher in using the curriculum provided by his school. While this chapter cannot attempt to describe a complete developmental language curriculum, it can provide some of these special guides, methods, procedures, and materials.

Language series books usually are not used until the third or fourth grade. The design of the elementary curriculum is that of expanded language skills and experiences. Here the teacher of the hard of hearing can develop a language program to fit the needs, potentials, and problems of the child. An experience language environment is where the child will develop the language skills necessary to carry him through his academic experience. The teacher must be aware of the language principles which a child needs at the various stages in his education in order to structure the environment to enable the child to have meaningful language experiences. These invoke within him the desire and need for language. Repeated meaningful language experiences will develop and reinforce the desired language. Once the child discovers that he can manipulate his environment through language to obtain things he desires, his language will flourish.

The basic primary language program should be in a dynamic, child-oriented environment. The teacher should create, as nearly as possible, natural circumstances where the desired language can be gained through using it. Reinforcement can be built through specific language programs for the hearing impaired. These programs can give guidance for the teacher in sequential language development and provide some reinforcement for the student. A teacher should be aware that these programs can provide only guideline suggestions and that the language program is a natural language environment built around the needs of the child.

If a hard of hearing child has the ability to understand and use simple sentences by the time he is in the fourth grade, he can use a modified language textbook.

Special developmental work with vocabulary will be a necessary part of the language program for these children. If a child has an educationally significant hearing loss he will usually need supplemental vocabulary work. Vocabulary programs for the deaf have attempted to develop all types of vocabulary at the same time. This includes a receptive oral vocabulary, an expressive oral vocabulary, a reading (sight) vocabulary, and a written vocabulary. This vocabulary introduced in a structured method expects the child to learn the meaning of the word, how to say it, how to read it, and how to use it in written language simultaneously. This is not the way children normally learn vocabulary. In a natural situation, they learn to understand a word when they hear it, then they learn to speak that word. Following this they learn to read the word and only when they have read the word many times are they ready to write it in an original composition. The development of a receptive, expressive, and reading vocabulary is a natural outgrowth of these. The teacher can have a child write a word to help him become familiar with the form of the word as the child is learning this word as sight vocabulary (Farnald, 1943; Buswell, 1945). He should not expect the child to use this word in original compositions until that word has been mastered as a sight vocabulary word. Using words in a composition requires a more sophisticated understanding. It requires the child to know the meaning, the spelling, and the grammatical usage in that particular sentence. Having a hard of hearing child use a word in original composition before he has mastered its usage results in fiascoes such as "The pencil *descended* from the desk," "The letter was *transcript*," and Newspapers are an *antecedent* event." It would appear from these sentences that the writer has an elementary understanding of the italicized words, but did not have enough of an understanding to use them correctly in written composition. The child's educational environment should provide numerous meaningful experiences with the new vocabulary and then the teacher can guide him to use the words in his original composition when he is ready.

Reading

When considering a reading program for hearing impaired children, the author is reminded of an elderly deaf man who lost his hearing at 10 years of age but went on to become a very successful civil engineer. He made the statement that reading was the liberation of his mind and intellect. The state engineer of his home state had written a letter to this man stating that he believed him to be the best read civil engineer in the state. For this reason he did not consider the man's deafness a professional handicap. If we could guide all hearing impaired children to a full functional reading capacity they could largely overcome hearing impairment as an educational handicap and go on to an education commensurate with their intellect.

Reading Problems Associated with Hearing Loss

Before discussing a reading program for hard of hearing children, it seems of paramount importance to ask the question, why does a hearing impaired child with normal visual acuity and function and normal intelligence not learn to read like his hearing peer? Furth states in Kavanagh (1968) that 90 percent of deaf children don't learn to read above grade four. Wright, Stone, Aronow, and Moskowitz did a study on the reading achievement of deaf children (Furth, 1966). This study indicated that a study population of 654 deaf children of 10½ and 11½ years of age had a mean reading grade equivalent of 2.7 while 1075 deaf children of ages 15½ to 16½ had a mean grade equivalent of 3.5.

McClure (1966) found the following results on a study of 93 percent of deaf pupils in United States schools for the deaf. Thirty percent were functionally illiterate, 5 percent achieved at a tenth grade level or better, and 60 percent were at the 5.3 grade level or below. If a child has an educationally significant hearing loss, he is usually a "retarded" reader or a nonreader. Again the question, why? Liberman in Kavanagh (1968, p. 201) states: "But the obvious, simple fact that we have been hearing is that congenitally deaf children do not learn to read very well. And they don't learn to write very well. There is nothing obviously wrong with the eye as a channel, but for some reason, it doesn't work very well for language." The answer to the question lies in the realm of language. Reading is an extension of the communicative processes which involves learning the printed form for the known spoken word. Furth (1966) supports this theory:

> It should be noted that a 14 year old deaf youngster with a reading level of Grade 3 is not comparable to a hearing peer who may have difficulty reading. The hearing individual enjoys a comfortable mastery of the language even though he may be retarded in reading. For the deaf, on the other hand, the reading level is his ceiling of linguistic competence. It is quite inappropriate to designate this latter condition as retardation in reading. It is properly termed incompetence or deficiency in verbal language, a condition rare among the hearing but almost universal among the deaf. (Furth, 1966, p. 15.)

Foulke in Kavanagh (1968) states that blind children do have reading difficulty but from his experience, children in schools for the blind have no more difficulty in mastering the Braille reading system than sighted children have in mastering the printed word. Blind children have language competence, and reading Braille is merely a continued extension of this language ability.

In an unpublished research project with a large population of Navajo students, Viehweg and Clark found the same relationship between language deprivation and inability to read in this Indian population that exists in the hearing impaired population. They found that the written compositions of the Indian students were much like those of the deaf. They made the same type of grammatical errors, had the same type of sentence structure, and used nonabstract ideas. Even though some of these Indian students had been in school for years, their reading ability was extremely retarded; indeed, in many cases it was nonfunctional. The home environment of these Indian students reveals a language deprivation nearly as acute as that of a severely hearing impaired child. Here again, language deprivation appears to be the main cause of the reading inadequacies.

Furth's (Kavanagh, 1968, p. 195) comments seem noteworthy. "If you say the deaf have reading difficulties, this is the understatement of the century. They don't have reading difficulties; they have language difficulties. . . . I have not been able to come up with any specific reading difficulty" [of the deaf]. Most hearing impaired children are unable to find success in reading because their language inability prevents them from being in a state of reading readiness. When the child is introduced to reading in this nonreadiness state he soon becomes frustrated and his inability to read is further complicated by emotional and psychological factors which render him incapable of becoming a competent reader.

The task of any first grader who is in a reading readiness state is that of developing a sight vocabulary. He has to accomplish three tasks to develop this sight vocabulary: (1) He must know the meaning of the word. (2) He must know how to pronounce the word. (3) He must know the form of the word. The average hearing child comes to the task with the first two aspects accomplished; that is, he understands the meaning and knows how to pronounce all the words he will encounter in his first grade books. He has merely to learn the form of the word which is a simple matter of developing word attack skills. On the other hand, most hearing impaired children come to this task with none of the above skills. They are unable to develop an adequate sight vocabulary and, therefore, are unable to develop the word attack skills necessary to become a competent reader. A child who has developed the necessary reading skills has the tools to progress independently. Reading can then become an effective means of increasing language ability. Without sufficient language and reading readiness, however, he cannot even begin the task of reading.

In summary of the discussion on the relationship of language to reading, and hearing loss to language deprivation it seems clear that children without adequate skills will not master the reading process and hearing impaired children taught through visual methods will usually not be competent in language. The writer's experience leads him to believe that the hard of hearing child's opportunity to become a competent reader is through complete use of his auditory channels to develop and to build receptive language ability.

What, then, are the components of an effective reading program for the hard of hearing? A brief outline includes:

1. Identification and early fitting of a hearing aid
2. Development of an effective means of language development through the auditory channel
3. A parent-home program which makes the home an effective language environment for developing natural language
4. An effective preschool program to assist the parents and supplement the home environment
5. A realistic philosophy for developing reading skills
6. A reading measurement program to indicate the correct reading level of the child

7. An effective diagnostic program to locate specific individual reading difficulties

8. A realistic plan for selection of reading materials suited to the child's reading level (grade) and to his individual weaknesses and strengths

9. The reading program—a phonic approach and/or a word analysis approach and

10. Special methods, procedures, and materials applicable to the hard of hearing.

Topics (1), (2), and (3) have been discussed previously in this chapter. An effective preschool reading program would encompass two areas: language enrichment and a reading readiness program. The preschool class experience can give enrichment to the child's language. If the child is lacking in vocabulary the preschool can help him to incorporate into his vocabulary the words that will be used in the first grade readers. These readers can be the teacher's guide to vocabulary development and language enrichment. By the time the child leaves preschool, he should be familiar with most of the words in the first grade books and be able to use expressively the types of sentences found in these basal readers. The normal preschooler is not exposed to the printed word. A reading readiness program prepares the child for introduction to formal reading which he will receive in the first grade. There are an adequate number of reading readiness programs printed by the publishers of basal texts. Most of these programs can be used very effectively with hard of hearing children.

Phonics or Structure

The question arises, should a preschool hard of hearing child be expected to read the printed word? There seems to be no reason to do so when one considers that the hearing child who usually has a more sophisticated language system is not expected to read the printed word. For the prelingual deaf child who has no language at all, there may be benefit in introducing the printed word. Quigley's (1969) studies seem to indicate that fingerspelling can be of value to these children. A child who is gaining a usable verbal language through the auditory channel should not need the printed word in his preschool experiences.

The task of the preschool should be to supplement the home language program and provide a reading readiness program. As Heilman says,

> The child first develops oral language, acquiring the ability to make sounds in isolation and then in combinations as sounds are combined into words they become associated with meanings. The child beginning school has a speaking vocabulary of several thousand words. He can say, and has concepts for a great variety of speech sounds. The degree of the child's mastery of communication skills determines to a large extent his readiness to do school tasks and to profit from instruction. Although he cannot read, spell or write when he starts school he has had years of experience with language. (1963. pp. 33-34.)

When the hard of hearing child reaches the first grade and his career as a reader is ready to commence, it is incumbent upon the educator of the hard of hearing child to develop a philosophy which will be appropriate for these children. There are no graded basal reading programs for the hard of hearing. There are some supplemental materials, but nothing that can be used as the basis of a developmental reading program.

In choosing a basal reading program, the educator of the hard of hearing is faced with the problem of choosing a phonic or a word analysis approach. It is imperative that he is cognizant of the individual differences and needs of these children. They not only have the normal differences expected in hearing children, but also many differences associated with hearing loss. Two children with the same intelligence, ability, and age, but with different hearing losses could require a different approach to reading. With these differences in mind we can look at the question of phonics and/or structure.

Children who have good speech and who can discriminate individual sounds in their own oral speech could benefit from a phonic approach in reading. This auditory feedback can and will be of value in building a sight vocabulary. Work in phonics could also help the child's speech and listening ability. When the audiologist is unable to obtain any kind of satisfactory speech discrimination scores, however, it seems foolish to put this child into a reading program built on phonics. While a child who is capable of learning to read can usually be taught by either method, hearing impaired children whose hearing loss is so severe it precludes individual sound discriminations, can and should be taught mainly by a structural method. Buswell (1954) describes a nonoral method used in the Chicago City Schools which has been highly successful for thousands of hearing children. This method is used in the first grade to establish a sight vocabulary before the children go into a regular basal text.

Reading Material and Evaluation

The first three grades are the crucial area when the child's attitudes, skills, and likes or dislikes in reading are developed. When the basic program of phonics or structure is decided a basal reading program can be chosen. If the child is in a state of reading readiness, his exposures to reading are happy ones, and if the correct materials are used, the child should learn to read. There are no magic buttons to push. However, we will discuss some special methods which can be used by the teacher of the hearing impaired. It is neither the intent nor the purpose of this chapter to outline and describe the developmental sequence and program a child goes through.

Beyond the child's own physical, emotional, psychological, and intellectual makeup, the single most important component of a successful reading program is the material the child reads. Even though all of the other variables are in optimum existence, if the child is put in material that is too difficult for him he will become frustrated and not learn reading skills as he should. This is true of any child, hearing or hearing impaired. It is absolutely necessary that the educator of the hard of hearing be able to choose appropriate material for these children. The first step in this procedure is to obtain a valid grade level reading achievement of the child. Next, find the child's basal instructional and frustration level of reading. This can best be done by first using the reading achievement grades from standardized achievement tests. If this information is outdated or questionable, a reading survey test can be administered. This will give the maximum grade level reading ability. This tells us that the child cannot read any better than this. Using this score as a beginning point, one can then give the Informal Reading Inventory as first described by Betts (1946). There have been later modifications of this test such as Silvaroli's (1969) Classroom Reading Inventory.

Using this test one can ascertain the basal or free reading level, the instructional level and the frustrational level. The child's library reading material should be on the free reading level (99 percent correct oral reading and 90 percent comprehension). He is not learning to read at this level, but here is where he will gain a love for reading as he reads material that he completely understands. The child's reading text for his school work should be at the instructional level (95 percent correct oral reading and 75 percent comprehension). At this level, the child understands most of what he reads and thus is able to increase his reading capacity. A child should never be allowed to read at the frustration level (below 90 percent correct oral reading and below 50 percent comprehension).

The Informal Reading Inventory can be given to hard of hearing children with little alteration or difficulty. The only alterations necessary are not to count pronunciation errors that are inherent in the child's speech and to write out the comprehension questions in case the child has difficulty understanding the oral question. Other than these changes it can be given as described and can be an excellent tool in choosing the grade level of the basal text.

If some children have reading difficulties, none of these tests will isolate these difficulties to enable the teacher to choose appropriate material and to form a remedial plan to solve these specific reading problems. Perhaps the best indication of specific reading difficulties can be obtained by administering an individual reading analysis test. Since these tests are usually highly oral they must be revised to be effectively used with hard of hearing children. The author has used a modified procedure for administering the Durrell Analysis of Reading Difficulty (1955) so that it gives quite accurate information on specific areas of reading. The oral reading section can be given to hard of hearing children with some modification. Time should not be a factor and the oral reading level should not be established by time. Of course, articulation errors that are inherent in the child's speech should not be counted. All questions for all tests should be written out on a card in case the child does not understand the question asked orally. The silent reading test can be given according to the manual. The listening comprehension seems to be too traumatic for hard of hearing children and the results are invalid. This section of the test can be omitted. The word recognition and word analysis tests can be given exactly as directed and are excellent checks on the child's sight vocabulary and his word analysis skills. The only other sections of the test applicable to hard of hearing children are the visual memory of words and the spelling tests. The visual memory test can be given exactly as directed. Its results seem to be valid for hard of hearing children and will give a good measure of their ability to analyze and remember words. The spelling test may present problems for some severely hard of hearing children as it may be in essence a lipreading test. It is essential to remember that this test does not indicate grade level ability for reading material but will show areas of reading problems.

When the teacher knows the instructional reading level of the child and is aware of his individual reading problems he is ready to select the reading material. The first concern is the reading level of the child and the level of the material. Now that the teacher knows the true instructional level of the child he can select appropriate material on the correct level. Next is the question of a phonic approach, a structural approach, or a combination of the two. Basal reading series are available which meet any one of these criteria. The author's experience has been that a series that employs both approaches is best suited for hard of hearing children. The phonic program can be used with those children whose hearing makes this approach profitable while other children are appropriately placed in a reader that emphasizes a structural approach. If the audiologist is unable to get a speech reception threshold the child will not profit from a purely phonic approach. If completely inadequate speech discrimination scores are obtained, the child should be on a structural approach.

A basal reading series must be carefully evaluated to ascertain how appropriate it is for hard of hearing children. There should be a reasonable vocabulary load with a small number of new words, less than ten, introduced in each story. This vocabulary should be repeated as much as possible in the next few stories and throughout the book. If the children are using simple sentence structure, they will have difficulty reading a book which uses large numbers of complex sentences and sentences with long complicated phrases; therefore, the book should have a sentence and paragraph structure which the children are capable of understanding. The more prepositional phrases in the selections, the harder will be the reading. Those familiar with the problems of the hard of hearing know that idiomatic expressions present special difficulties. If there are only a few in a story, the child has a much better chance of understanding the story and of learning the new expressions. This same principle applies to colloquialisms, sayings, puns, and unusual sentences. There are other features of a basal reader which make it desirable—whether it is for hard of hearing or hearing children. These items include attractive and appropriate illustrations, interesting stories, workbooks for independent use by the students which are closely related to the reading selections, and a good teacher's manual which includes vocabulary lists, lesson plans for each story, unit lesson plans, and evaluation guides. It is appropriate to state again emphatically that the most important part of a reading program is to have the children reading in appropriate material. Children cannot learn to read in material that is at the frustration level.

A Reading Program

The confines of this chapter simply will not allow complete description of a developmental reading program from first to sixth grades. The intent herein is to discuss some of the special kinds of problems that will appear in a reading program for the hard of hearing and some special methods which can be used to teach reading to these children.

As stated in the language section, one of the greatest and most persistent problems will be that of vocabulary deficiency. In this discussion we are concerned with vocabulary as it is relevant to reading and a sight vocabulary.

What vocabulary should be developed and when? The Dolch Basic 220 words should be in the sight vocabulary of a child by the third grade. The vocabulary lists in the basal readers are probably the most needed vocabulary for the child. He should be familiar with most of these words receptively and expressively before he is expected to read them. The teacher should have the vocabulary lists for the reader that the child will use the following year. If the child is introduced to these words and learns to use them receptively and expressively in numerous natural meaningful experiences, he will be ready to learn the form of these words when he is introduced to them in reading. Listing new words on the chalkboard, giving a dictionary meaning for the word, using the word in a sentence, then expecting the child to use that word as part of his sight vocabulary while he reads the story is a futile way to develop a reading vocabulary. If the child already knows the meaning of the word, he will have little or no trouble learning the printed form.

The question of how to develop a sight vocabulary is, indeed, a challenging one. After one has determined what vocabulary is needed, the task is to reconstruct the situations in which children with normal hearing learn this vocabulary. Give the child numerous experiences with the vocabulary; once is not enough. Hearing impaired children should not be taught words in isolation for it causes a word and a meaning to become a fixed entity in the childs' mind on a one-to-one ratio; i.e., one word with one meaning. The child develops rigidity in meaning and tries to give all forms of the word the fixed meaning he has learned. But a word has no fixed meaning; it means only what the context surrounding it allows it to mean. When a child is taught one meaning for a word, he never learns to generalize; without this ability he will never become a competent reader. A teacher asked a severely hearing impaired boy what "Welcome" meant. He replied, "It is the green thing in front of the door that you wipe your feet on." He knew that was what it meant because it said so right on the mat. Another severely hearing impaired child was told "tie your shoe." He took off his shoe and put it up to his neck as if to make a tie out of it. Obviously, he was using the one meaning he had been taught for *tie* and failed to apply to it another meaning.

One of the most difficult situations in teaching reading to hearing impaired children is keeping contact with them while they are reading. With normal hearing children this contact is maintained through the auditory channel, but one loses contact with the hearing impaired the minute they put their heads down to read. The overhead projector is the best answer to this problem. The teacher can disassemble his reading book to make transparencies of all the pages. These can then be put together in a notebook binder and used for years. Transparencies allow the teacher to maintain eye contact with the students while discussing the reading material. Using marking pens, the teacher can explain or discuss any of the material without having to turn his back on the children to write it on the board.

In developing, teaching, and evaluating a reading lesson it is well to have a specific goal in mind for that lesson. It is often futile to try to work on word meaning, paragraph meaning, reading for facts, idiomatic expressions, and development of reading word attack skills all in one lesson. Each lesson or story will lend itself to a particular usage. One lesson may be excellent for developing sequence while another lesson may lend itself to teaching of idiomatic expressions. A reading lesson should not be made into a speech, speech reading, nor a writing exercise, for above all, every lesson should be exciting and fun for the child. If he is expected to lipread words and sentences, work on correct speech articulation, and have a written question exercise with each story, he hasn't a chance of learning to enjoy reading for its own sake.

The question of oral reading in a classroom situation arises. Should hearing impaired children read aloud in the classroom? It seems that the answer can be found in the purpose of the reading lesson itself. A child should read to improve his reading skills and to develop a genuine enjoyment in reading. Hearing children love to hear stories. Many of them enjoy reading orally. This, then, is the purpose of reading aloud. The same principle should apply in the class for hard of hearing children. If the students enjoy reading aloud and the other students enjoy listening then, by all means, have oral reading. However, if the child's hearing precludes listening to the reader and following the printed word and his speech is such that the other children cannot understand him, there is no place here for oral reading as a class activity. Oral reading in this situation is embarrassing to the child reading and meaningless to the children trying to follow. Oral reading can be a vital part of such a program, but is best done on an individual pupil-teacher basis. This gives the student the opportunity to develop oral reading skills without embarrassing him and confusing the other children.

Summary

The time has come to educate hard of hearing children as children with hearing rather than as deaf children without it. Hard of hearing children in classes for the deaf using structured, visual methods find themselves with the "school for the deaf syndrome." Language and reading programs must be designed specifically for these children. Most hard of hearing children will reach their true potential only in an auditory-sound environment.

Language and reading are as interrelated as walking and running, and you must have one before you acquire the other. Reading is built upon past language experiences, and learning to read is a natural outgrowth of these experiences.

The normal means of acquiring a verbal language is using the sense of hearing, and there appears to be no natural substitute. A child acquires linguistic competence early in childhood and builds all of his later academic skills on this competency. Linguistic competence is acquired through natural, environmental experiences, and these language competencies probably cannot be taught through structured academic methods.

Hearing that is faulty is often sufficient for development of language, but because of inconsistent sound stimuli, that language is often faulty. Lipreading can be a valuable supplement to hearing, but cannot be depended upon by itself as a receptive language development facility.

A language development program for hearing impaired children should start at birth with the early home environment as the most important part of that program. Fitting of the child in early infancy with a hearing aid will insure the maximum use of hearing in later life.

There are some specific methodologies and materials that can help hard of hearing children in the language and reading areas, but there is no basic curriculum for the hard of hearing child; therefore, the teacher will have to adapt materials written for normal children. Guides have been provided for the adaption for this material, but each child will need special consideration.

References

Alport, F. H. 1924. Social Psychology. Boston, Massachusetts: Riverside Press.

Baer, D. M., R. F. Peterson, and J. A. Sherman. 1967. The development of imitation by reinforcing similarity to a model. Journal of the Experimental Analysis of Behavior. (10):405–412.

Berko, J. 1961. The child's learning of English morphology. In S. Saporta (Ed.) Psycholinguistics. Holt, Rinehart, and Winston, New York, Pp. 359–376.

Betts, E. A. 1946. Foundations of Reading Instruction. New York: Cincinnati, Ohio: American Book Company.

Brill, R. G. 1954. Education of the deaf and the hard of hearing. Exceptional Children XXIII, p. 198.

Buswell, G. T. 1945. Non Oral Reading: A study of its use in the Chicago schools. Chicago, Illinois: The University of Chicago Press.

Calvert, D. R. and S. Baltzer. 1967. Home management in a comprehensive preschool program for hearing impaired children. Exceptional Children.

Craig, W. N. 1964. Effects of pre-school training on the development of reading and lipreading skills of deaf children. American Annals of the Deaf, 109:280–296.

Durrell, D. D. 1955. Durrell Analysis of Reading Difficulty. New York: Harcourt, Brace and World, Inc.

Farnald, G. 1943. Remedial techniques in basic school subjects. New York: McGraw Hill.

Furth, H. G. 1966. A comparison of reading tests norms of deaf and hearing children. American Annals of the Deaf, 111:461–462.

Furth, H. G. 1966. Thinking Without Language. Psychological Implications of Deafness. New York: Free Press.

Heilman, A. W. 1966. Teaching Reading. Columbus, Ohio: Charles E. Merrill.

Kavanagh, J. F. (Ed.). 1968. Proceedings of the conference on communicating by language—The reading process. Bethesda, Maryland: U.S. Department of Health, Education and Welfare.

McClure, W. J. 1966. Current problems and trends in the education of the deaf. Deaf American, 1966:8–14.

McConnell, F. 1968. Proceedings of the conference on current practices in the management of deaf infants (0-3 years). Nashville, Tennessee: Bill Wilkerson Hearing and Speech Center.

Moores, D. F. 1967. Projected trends in language development for the deaf. The Deaf American 20(4):5–7.

Quigley, Stephen P. 1969. The influence of fingerspelling on the development of language, communication and educational achievement in deaf children. Institute for Research on Exceptional Children, University of Illinois.

Silvaroli, N. J. 1969. Classroom Reading Inventory. Dubuque, Iowa: Wm. C. Brown.

Simmons, A. 1967. Factors contributing to language development. (Mimeographed handout material). Institute on Characteristics and Needs of the Hard of Hearing Child. Logan, Utah: Utah State University.

Simmons, A. A. 1966. Language growth for the Pre-nursery deaf child. The Volta Review 68(3):201–205.

Index of Authors

Index of Subjects